Communications in Computer and Information Science 2881

Rationale

The CCIS series is devoted to the publication of proceedings of computer science conferences. Its aim is to efficiently disseminate original research results in informatics in printed and electronic form. While the focus is on publication of peer-reviewed full papers presenting mature work, inclusion of reviewed short papers reporting on work in progress is welcome, too. Besides globally relevant meetings with internationally representative program committees guaranteeing a strict peer-reviewing and paper selection process, conferences run by societies or of high regional or national relevance are also considered for publication.

Topics

The topical scope of CCIS spans the entire spectrum of informatics ranging from foundational topics in the theory of computing to information and communications science and technology and a broad variety of interdisciplinary application fields.

Information for Volume Editors and Authors

Publication in CCIS is free of charge. No royalties are paid, however, we offer registered conference participants temporary free access to the online version of the conference proceedings on SpringerLink (http://link.springer.com) by means of an http referrer from the conference website and/or a number of complimentary printed copies, as specified in the official acceptance email of the event.

CCIS proceedings can be published in time for distribution at conferences or as post-proceedings, and delivered in the form of printed books and/or electronically as USBs and/or e-content licenses for accessing proceedings at SpringerLink. Furthermore, CCIS proceedings are included in the CCIS electronic book series hosted in the SpringerLink digital library at http://link.springer.com/bookseries/7899. Conferences publishing in CCIS are allowed to use our online conference service (Meteor) for managing the whole proceedings lifecycle (from submission and reviewing to preparing for publication) free of charge.

Publication process

The language of publication is exclusively English. Authors publishing in CCIS have to sign the Springer CCIS copyright transfer form, however, they are free to use their material published in CCIS for substantially changed, more elaborate subsequent publications elsewhere. For the preparation of the camera-ready papers/files, authors have to strictly adhere to the Springer CCIS Authors' Instructions and are strongly encouraged to use the CCIS LaTeX style files or templates.

Abstracting/Indexing

CCIS is abstracted/indexed in DBLP, Google Scholar, EI-Compendex, Mathematical Reviews, SCImago, Scopus. CCIS volumes are also submitted for the inclusion in ISI Proceedings.

How to start

To start the evaluation of your proposal for inclusion in the CCIS series, please send an e-mail to ccis@springer.com

Honghai Liu · Hui Huang · Hongxun Yao ·
Shengping Zhang · Weihong Ren · Zhiyong Wang
Editors

Emotional Intelligence

Third CSIG Conference, CEI 2025
Shenzhen, China, December 5–7, 2025
Proceedings

Editors
Honghai Liu
Harbin Institute of Technology
Shenzhen, China

Hui Huang
Shenzhen University
Shenzhen, China

Hongxun Yao
Harbin Institute of Technology
Harbin, China

Shengping Zhang
Harbin Institute of Technology
Weihai, China

Weihong Ren
Harbin Institute of Technology
Shenzhen, China

Zhiyong Wang
Harbin Institute of Technology
Shenzhen, China

ISSN 1865-0929 ISSN 1865-0937 (electronic)
Communications in Computer and Information Science
ISBN 978-981-95-9492-4 ISBN 978-981-95-9493-1 (eBook)
https://doi.org/10.1007/978-981-95-9493-1

This Springer imprint is published by the registered company Springer Nature Singapore Pte Ltd.
The registered company address is: 152 Beach Road, #21-01/04 Gateway East, Singapore 189721, Singapore

Preface

The 3rd CSIG Conference on Emotional Intelligence (CEI 2025) was successfully held from December 5 to December 7, 2025, at the International Conference Center of Shenzhen University Town, Shenzhen, Guangdong Province, China. The conference was organized by the China Society of Image and Graphics (CSIG), and hosted by Harbin Institute of Technology, Shenzhen together with the CSIG Technical Committee on Affective Computing and Understanding. The conference aimed to provide a high-level academic platform for in-depth exchange and collaboration in the field of emotional intelligence.

The conference was honored to invite several renowned scholars to deliver keynote speeches and academic invited talks, including Baoliang Lu from Shanghai Jiao Tong University, Shaoliang Peng from Hunan University, Yang Li from Beihang University, and Professor Xiu Xu from the Children's Hospital affiliated with Fudan University. These distinguished experts shared their latest research achievements and insights through keynote reports and thematic academic sessions, stimulating extensive discussion among participants. The conference program was rich and diverse, featuring special reports on theories and applications of emotional intelligence, tutorials, poster sessions, academic exchanges, industry presentations, and the annual meeting of the CSIG Technical Committee on Affective Computing and Understanding. The conference focused on frontier research topics and the latest technological advances in affective computing and artificial intelligence, highlighting the applications of emotional intelligence across multiple disciplines, domains, and real-world scenarios. Through these activities, the conference explored future development trends of emotional intelligence and promoted interdisciplinary integration between academia and industry.

The conference received a total of 79 submissions, including full papers and abstracts. After a rigorous peer-review process conducted by the Technical Program Committee and expert reviewers, 21 full papers were accepted for presentation and inclusion in the conference proceedings, resulting in an acceptance rate of 26.6%. Each submission received three single-blind reviews, on average. This selective review process ensured the academic quality, originality, and relevance of the accepted contributions. The proceedings of the CEI 2025 reflect the collective intellectual achievements of the participants and provide a valuable reference for future research and applications. The Organizing

Committee sincerely thanks all keynote speakers, authors, reviewers, committee members, and participants for their valuable contributions and strong support, which made the conference a great success.

December 2025

Honghai Liu
Hui Huang
Hongxun Yao
Shengping Zhang
Weihong Ren
Zhiyong Wang

Organization

Honorary Chair

Yaonan Wang	Hunan University, China

General Chairs

Honghai Liu	Harbin Institute of Technology, Shenzhen, China
Hui Huang	Shenzhen University, China
Hongxun Yao	Harbin Institute of Technology, China

Program Chairs

Zhiguo Zhang	Harbin Institute of Technology, Shenzhen, China
Kejun Zhang	Zhejiang University, China
Wenming Zheng	Southeast University, China
Shiguang Shan	University of Chinese Academy of Sciences, China
Xiaopeng Hong	Harbin Institute of Technology, China
Xiaohua Huang	Nanjing Institute of Technology, China

Organization Committee Chairs

Jia Jia	Tsinghua University, China
Sicheng Zhao	Tsinghua University, China

Publication Chairs

Shengping Zhang	Harbin Institute of Technology, Weihai, China
Weihong Ren	Harbin Institute of Technology, Shenzhen, China

Tutorial Chairs

Xiangyang Xue	Fudan University, China
Yue Gao	Tsinghua University, China

Poster Chairs

Jufeng Yang	Nankai University, China
Yixuan Sheng	Harbin Institute of Technology, Shenzhen, China

Sponsorship Chairs

Yuanyuan Liu	China University of Geosciences, Wuhan, China
Yuquan Leng	Harbin Institute of Technology, Shenzhen, China

Registration Chairs

Leida Li	Xidian University, China
Zhiyong Wang	Harbin Institute of Technology, Shenzhen, China

Special Session Chairs

Xiaoli Li	Beijing Normal University, China
Shiqing Zhang	Taizhou University, China
Qirong Mao	Jiangsu University, China
Kehai Chen	Harbin Institute of Technology, Shenzhen, China
Tong Chen	Southwest University, China
Sujing Wang	University of Chinese Academy of Sciences, China
Jingting Li	University of Chinese Academy of Sciences, China
Jing Huo	Nanjing University, China
Luntian Mou	Beijing University of Technology, China
Qian Yu	Beihang University, China
Shuai Yang	Peking University
Zheng Lian	University of Chinese Academy of Sciences, China
Rui Liu	Inner Mongolia University, China

Baixi Xing	Zhejiang Sci-Tech University, China
Ziqian Bai	Southern University of Science and Technology, China
Yong Li	Southeast University, China
Na Liu	Jiangsu University, China
Jianping Lu	Shenzhen Kangning Hospital, China
Shuzheng Chen	Li Shui Maternity and Child Health Care Hospital, China
Zhitian Xiao	Shenzhen Children's Hospital, China
Xiaolong Zhou	Quzhou University, China

Contents

Attention-Enhanced 3D ResNet for Facial Muscle Movement Assessment in Dysarthria

Mengjie Li[1,2], Yuxing Wang[1(✉)], Boyan Fang[3], Peijun Gong[1], and Zhaojie Ju[1]

[1] College of Biomedical Engineering and Instrument Science, Zhejiang University, Hangzhou, China
wangyuxing@zju.edu.cn

[2] Polytechnic Institute, Zhejiang University, Hangzhou, China

[3] Beijing Rehabilitate Hospital, Capital Medical University, Beijing, China

Abstract. Dysarthria is commonly associated with impairments in lip and tongue muscle movements, which substantially reduce speech intelligibility and complicate both early diagnosis and rehabilitation assessment. Conventional clinical evaluation methods rely heavily on subjective rating scales or specialized measurement equipment, making it difficult to achieve both accuracy and practicality in real-world settings. To address this issue, we propose a video-based, fully sensor-free automated framework for assessing facial motor function, providing a more feasible solution for both clinical and remote rehabilitation scenarios. Specifically, we develop an attention-enhanced three-dimensional residual network (AE-3DResNet), in which a three-dimensional multi-scale attention module (3D-Efficient Multi-Scale Attention,3D-EMA) is integrated into the 3D ResNet-18 backbone to selectively enhance fine-grained spatiotemporal motion cues that are highly relevant to dysarthria assessment. In addition, we construct the first patient video dataset covering multi-level lip and tongue movement tasks, and alleviate its inherent long-tail distribution using a combination of Focal Loss and data resampling strategies. Experimental results show that the proposed framework achieves accuracies of 77.14% and 77.19% for three-level severity classification of lip and tongue motor dysfunction, corresponding to relative performance improvements of 6.66% and 7.89% over baseline models, respectively. This study not only provides a feasible technical pathway for objective and quantitative dysarthria assessment, but also features a deployment-friendly design that requires no additional hardware, showing strong potential for future clinical application and tele-rehabilitation.

Keywords: Facial motor dysfunction assessment · Lip and tongue movement · Multi-scale attention mechanism · 3D ResNet · Dysarthria

1 Introduction

Dysarthria is a common complication in neurological disorders such as Parkinson's disease and amyotrophic lateral sclerosis (ALS), primarily caused by dam-

H. Liu et al. (Eds.): CEI 2025, CCIS 2881, pp. 1–17, 2026.
https://doi.org/10.1007/978-981-95-9493-1_1

age to the central or peripheral nervous system. Its core pathophysiological mechanism lies in impaired motor control of the articulatory musculature. Patients typically exhibit impaired coordination of speech organs–including the lips, tongue, and jaw–leading to the classic triad of symptoms: reduced speech intelligibility, disrupted prosodic structure, and decreased overall comprehensibility [1–3]. Clinical studies have demonstrated that the functional state of facial muscle groups, particularly the laryngeal muscles and the liptongue complex, is closely associated with speech production quality. The coordination and muscle tone of articulatory organs are critical determinants of dysarthria severity [4]. Therefore, establishing a deep learningbased assessment framework for facial motor function holds significant clinical value for precise diagnosis, therapeutic evaluation, and rehabilitation monitoring of dysarthria [5].

Currently, the clinical assessment of dysarthria primarily relies on perceptual rating scales such as the Frenchay Dysarthria Assessment (FDA) [6]. These evaluations are conducted by speech-language pathologists (SLPs) using standardized scales; however, the outcomes are highly dependent on the examiner's experience and exhibit limited reproducibility. To address this limitation, some studies have employed instrumental approaches such as surface electromyography [7–9] and three-dimensional electromagnetic articulography [10]. Nevertheless, the invasiveness, operational complexity, and poor patient tolerance of these methods hinder their large-scale clinical application. With the rapid advancement of computer vision, video-based, contact-free facial motion analysis has emerged as a promising alternative [11]. By tracking facial landmarks, this approach enables objective quantification of articulatory movement patterns. In particular, three-dimensional convolutional neural networks (3D-CNNs), with their spatiotemporal feature extraction capability, have shown considerable advantages in micro-motion recognition [12]. Their end-to-end learning paradigm effectively captures the dynamic characteristics of articulatory organs. However, most existing studies focus on general facial expression recognition, leaving the systematic application of deep learning to dysarthric facial motion assessment underexplored. Consequently, striking an effective balance between accuracy and clinical practicality remains a significant challenge.

To address this research gap, we propose an automated assessment method for facial muscle dysfunction based on an enhanced 3D ResNet architecture, focusing on the lip and tongue as primary articulatory organs most affected by dysarthria. The main contributions of this study are as follows:

1 **Architecture design:** We propose AE-3DResNet (attention-enhanced 3D ResNet), integrating a 3D multi-scale attention (3D-EMA) module with residual skip connections. This dual channel-spatial recalibration strengthens focus on dynamic, clinically relevant regions.
2. **Severity grading:** We design a kinematics-based 3-level framework to quantitatively distinguish dysfunction severity (no impairment → moderate impairment).
3. **Imbalanced data handling:** A hybrid strategy mitigates class imbalance: *ImbalancedDatasetSampler* balances healthy/patient mini-batches (data

level); Focal Loss with $(1 - p_t)^\gamma$ suppresses easy majority-class gradients and enhances sensitivity to underrepresented patient patterns (loss level).

2 Related Work

2.1 Medical Assessment Methods

For evaluating facial motor dysfunction in dysarthria, SLPs commonly rely on instruments such as the Frenchay Dysarthria Assessment (FDA) [6] and the Radboud Dysarthria Assessment (RDA) [13], which systematically examine articulatory coordination, muscle tone, and speech intelligibility across lip, tongue, and jaw movements. Notably, the RDA incorporates a video-based paradigm, providing five-level quantitative ratings of articulatory function in terms of amplitude, speed, and rhythm. Although these scales are clinically convenient, their heavy dependence on subjective expertise reduces sensitivity to subtle dysfunctions such as tongue tremor or lip fasciculations. To enhance objectivity, some studies have employed high-precision measurement techniques. Electromagnetic articulography (Ema) [14,15] tracks three-dimensional trajectories of articulators using sensors, and surface electromyography (sEMG) [16] quantifies facial muscle activity by extracting features such as root mean square (RMS) and mean frequency for classification. While effective, these invasive procedures can cause discomfort and are associated with high equipment costs, limiting their clinical applicability.

Recently, non-contact video-based approaches have gained traction [17–19]. By recording speech tasks with 3D cameras and extracting kinematic features, researchers demonstrated strong correlations with perceptual clinical ratings. These findings suggest that automatically derived motion features can capture clinically relevant patterns, providing theoretical support for video-based assessment of facial motor dysfunction.

2.2 Computer Vision Approaches

With the rapid development of computer vision, non-contact video-based facial motion analysis has emerged as a promising approach for assessing facial muscle dysfunction in dysarthria. Early studies applied the Lucas-Kanade algorithm [20] to extract motion vectors of facial keypoints, but this method is sensitive to illumination changes and background noise, and struggles to model coordinated movements of multiple muscle groups. The advent of deep learning has enabled the application of 2D convolutional neural networks (2D-CNNs) for pathological facial image analysis; for example, [21] proposed a fusion model using lip and tongue images for binary classification of oral cancer. However, 2D networks neglect temporal dynamics and cannot effectively capture continuous articulatory motion. To overcome this limitation, 3D neural networks introduce temporal convolution kernels (e.g., C3D [22], I3D [23] to directly extract spatiotemporal features from video sequences, demonstrating remarkable advantages in micro-movement recognition tasks [24]). Innovations in this domain can be categorized into three directions:

1. **Temporal feature enhancement:** A 3D-CNN-LSTM hybrid [25] models anxious subjects' micro-expression dynamics via LSTM;
2. **Feature representation optimization:** A label-distribution-aware model [26] maps temporal features to continuous pathological severity space using KL divergence for Parkinson's motor score prediction;
3. **Imbalanced data handling:** A 152-layer 3D ResNet [27] uses skip connections to mitigate gradient vanishing.

Building on prior advances, this study proposes AE-3DResNet to reduce non-keyframe interference in long videos. Integrating a 3D-EMA module into a ResNet-18 backbone, the model jointly optimizes temporal and spatial features. With multi-scale attention across channel and spatial dimensions, it effectively captures key lip and tongue movement characteristics, significantly improving experimental performance.

3 Method

This study proposes an automated facial motor assessment method based on AE-3DResNet for identifying the severity of dysarthria. As illustrated in Fig. 1, the overall framework focuses on evaluating both lip and tongue motor functions. First, the input raw liptongue motion videos are processed by the FPN-StackedHGNet model to detect facial landmarks and extract the regions of interest (ROI) corresponding to the lips and tongue, resulting in standardized temporal segments for each region. Subsequently, the temporal segments from different anatomical regions are fed into their corresponding AE-3DResNet submodels for feature learning and classification.

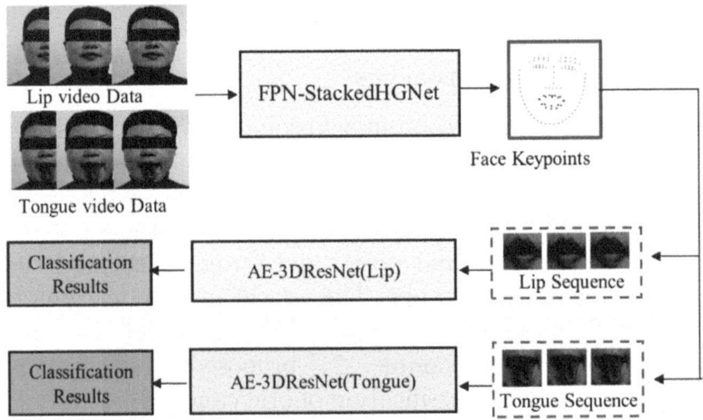

Fig. 1. Facial Motion Assessment Framework for Dysarthria.

In this framework, lip and tongue videos are modeled using two fully independent AE-3DResNet branches, each producing separate prediction results to accommodate the distinct motion characteristics of the two motor tasks. The proposed AE-3DResNet is built upon the traditional 3D ResNet architecture, with a hierarchical 3D-EMA module embedded at the output of selected residual stages to achieve multi-scale spatiotemporal feature fusion. At the end of the network, a global spatiotemporal pooling (GSTP) layer is employed to compress the learned features, followed by a fully connected layer that outputs the probability distribution across three severity levels: healthy control (HC), mild dysarthria (MD1), and moderate dysarthria (MD2).

3.1 Data Preprocessing and Augmentation

The system takes as input raw lip and tongue motion video sequences (resolution 1920×1080 pixels, frame rate 30 fps). In the data preprocessing stage, each frame of the original videos is first subjected to face detection, and the facial region of interest (ROI) is cropped, with the resolution standardized to 512×512 pixels. Subsequently, 98 facial landmarks are detected using the FPN-StackedHGNet model pretrained on the WFLW dataset, precisely localizing 20 key points within the lip and tongue regions. Based on these dynamic landmarks, a convex hull is constructed and expanded outward by 10 pixels to form an adaptive bounding box, ensuring full coverage of the motion trajectories.The structure of the FPN-StackedHGNet model is shown in Fig. 2. It is a targeted improvement based on the classical cascaded Hourglass network architecture. By introducing attention modules and multi-scale feature fusion strategies, the model places greater emphasis on the 20 key points closely associated with lip and tongue motion. Accurate extraction of these landmarks provides a reliable basis for adaptive segmentation of the lip and tongue regions.

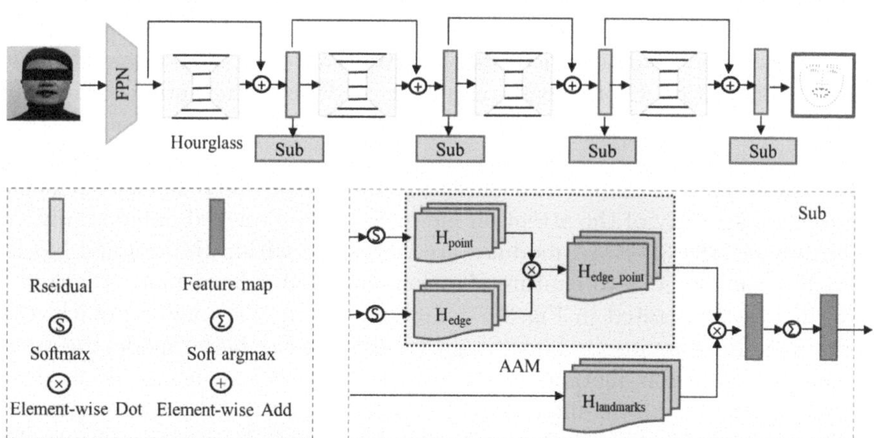

Fig. 2. FPN-StackedHGNet: A Feature Pyramid Network based Stacked Hourglass Architecture for Facial Landmark Detection.

After obtaining the motion regions, the cropped segments are normalized to 256×256 pixels and converted into frame-by-frame JPEG images. To enhance consistency across different subjects, all images are further scaled to 240 pixels. Prior to network input, the model extracts temporal clips of 64 frames from each video segment, with each frame resized to 112×112 pixels in 3-channel format. The resulting input tensor to the model is:

$$\mathbf{X} \in \mathbb{R}^{3\times T\times 112\times 112} \tag{1}$$

To address the limited size of the self-constructed dataset, a data augmentation strategy is designed: random cropping regions are generated to adapt the original 240-pixel images to the 112-pixel input size. Additionally, an innovative uniform interval sampling mechanism is introduced, where the sampling interval is dynamically calculated based on the input video length T. This ensures that the extracted three 64-frame clips both cover the complete motion cycle and avoid fragmentation of motion features, satisfying the input requirements of temporal modeling networks.

3.2 Construction of AE-3DResNet

In this study, the overall architecture of the AE-3DResNet model is illustrated in Fig. 3. It consists of a lip modeling branch and a tongue modeling branch, with network structures differentially designed and fine-tuned for the two facial regions to enable more targeted learning of pathological features and accurate classification. At the input stage, the preprocessed video sequences are fed separately into the two branches. The model first applies an initial 3D convolution layer to extract local spatiotemporal features from the input videos, combined with Batch Normalization and ReLU activation to achieve feature standardization and nonlinear mapping. The core of the model employs a 3D ResNet-18 backbone based on residual structures, effectively capturing cross-frame dynamic semantic information. On this basis, a multi-level 3D-EMA attention mechanism is introduced, significantly enhancing the network's ability to focus on dynamically critical regions.

For the distinct muscular motion characteristics of different facial regions, the insertion strategy of the attention modules is also designed differentially. In the lip branch, the 3D-EMA modules are embedded within the residual blocks of Stage 1 and Stage 2 to capture the slow and well-defined motion patterns of the lips (as illustrated in Fig. 3(a)). In contrast, in the tongue branch, the attention modules are inserted into Stage 3 and Stage 4 to better model the rapid and complex muscular motions of the tongue, thereby enhancing the model's ability to recognize subtle differences (Fig. 3(b)). The two branches output the Lip Feature and Tongue Feature, respectively. In the classification stage, the network employs a global spatiotemporal pooling (GSTP) layer to compress the features:

$$\mathbf{Z} = \mathrm{GSTP}(\hat{\mathbf{F}}) \in \mathbb{R}^{d} \tag{2}$$

The resulting feature vector is then mapped to the three-class probability space via a fully connected (FC) layer:

$$\mathbf{P}(y|\mathbf{X}) = Softmax(\mathbf{W}_f\mathbf{Z} + \mathbf{b}_f) \tag{3}$$

where $y \in \{\mathrm{HC}, \mathrm{MD1}, \mathrm{MD2}\}$ corresponds to the healthy control group, mild dysfunction group, and moderate dysfunction group, respectively.

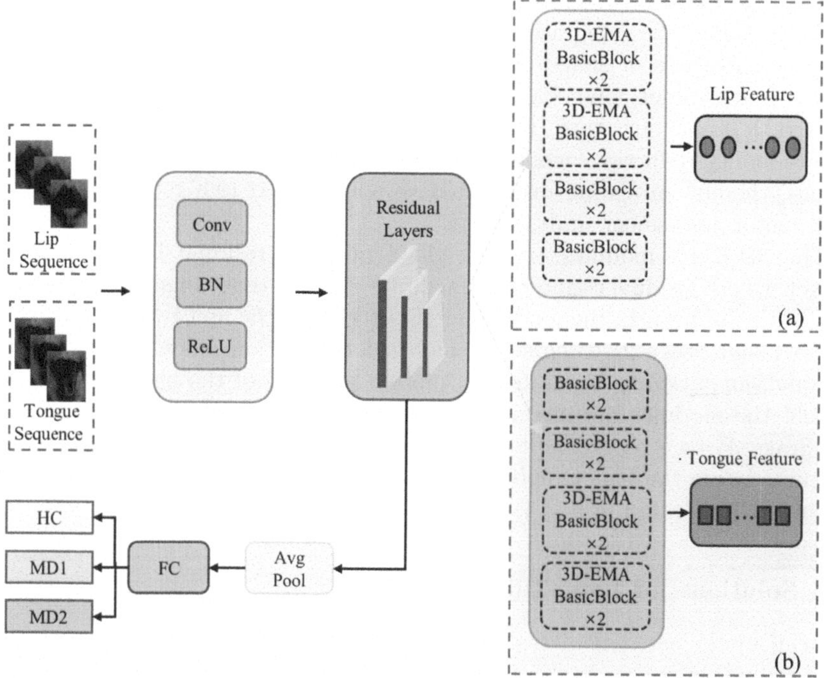

Fig. 3. AE-3DResNet: A Differentiated Dual-Branch Model for Lip and Tongue Regions (a) Placement strategy of the attention module for the lip branch, (b) Placement strategy of the attention module for the tongue branch.

3.3 3D-EMA Design

To strengthen spatiotemporal feature extraction, 3D-EMA attention modules are embedded into the 3D convolutional backbone, the specific structure of the 3D-EMA module is illustrated in Fig. 4(d). Built upon Efficient Multi-Scale Attention (EMA), the module recalibrates channel–spatial responses and enhances cross-scale feature representation, formulated as

$$\hat{\mathbf{F}} = \sigma(\mathbf{W}_s * \mathbf{F} + \mathbf{W}_c \cdot \mathrm{GAP}(\mathbf{F})) \odot \mathbf{F} \tag{4}$$

where $\mathbf{F} \in \mathbb{R}^{C\times T\times H\times W}$ denotes the input feature map, $\mathbf{W}_s$ and $\mathbf{W}_c$ represent spatial and channel attention weights, GAP$(\cdot)$ is global average pooling, $\sigma(\cdot)$ is the Sigmoid function, and $\odot$ indicates element-wise multiplication.

To capture complementary information, input channels are grouped, with subsets reshaped into the batch dimension for independent spatial feature extraction in parallel sub-networks. Global context is modeled via adaptive average pooling along horizontal and vertical directions, fused through 1×1 convolutions, while local structural details are extracted using 3×3 convolutions. Cross-space attention weights are computed by Softmax and matrix multiplication, enabling the integration of global and local representations. For video sequences, features of shape $[B, C, D, H, W]$ are reshaped by merging temporal and batch dimensions. EMA is then applied frame-wise, and the output is restored to its 3D structure. This design preserves channel information without dimensionality reduction, while establishing both short- and long-range dependencies, thereby providing discriminative and context-rich representations for facial motor assessment in dysarthria.

The 3D-EMA modules are embedded into the residual layers of the 3D ResNet, where residual connections facilitate stable cross-frame feature propagation. In the lip branch, the modules are inserted into the first two residual stages (Stage 1 and Stage 2) to enhance shallow local motion modeling and capture the *small-amplitude yet well-defined* motion patterns of the lips. In the tongue branch, the modules are integrated into the last two residual stages (Stage 3 and Stage 4) to strengthen the perception of deep abstract features, thereby accommodating the *large-amplitude and rhythmically complex* movements of the tongue (as illustrated in Fig. 4).

3.4 Solutions for Long Tail Data

In facial motor assessment tasks for dysarthria, datasets often exhibit a long-tail distribution, where healthy subjects are overrepresented while samples with higher severity are scarce. Directly training on such imbalanced data may bias the model toward majority classes, affecting classification performance. To mitigate this issue, we adopt the following strategies:

1. **Data re-sampling (ImbalancedDatasetSampler)**
We employ the `ImbalancedDatasetSampler` to perform data re-sampling, enabling the model to learn more balanced representations across different classes during training. Specifically, the inverse class weight w_i is defined as:

$$w_i = \frac{1}{n_{c(i)}} \tag{5}$$

where $c(i)$ denotes the class of the i-th sample, and $n_{c(i)}$ is the total number of samples in that class. Consequently, samples from minority classes are assigned higher weights, increasing their likelihood of being selected during sampling.

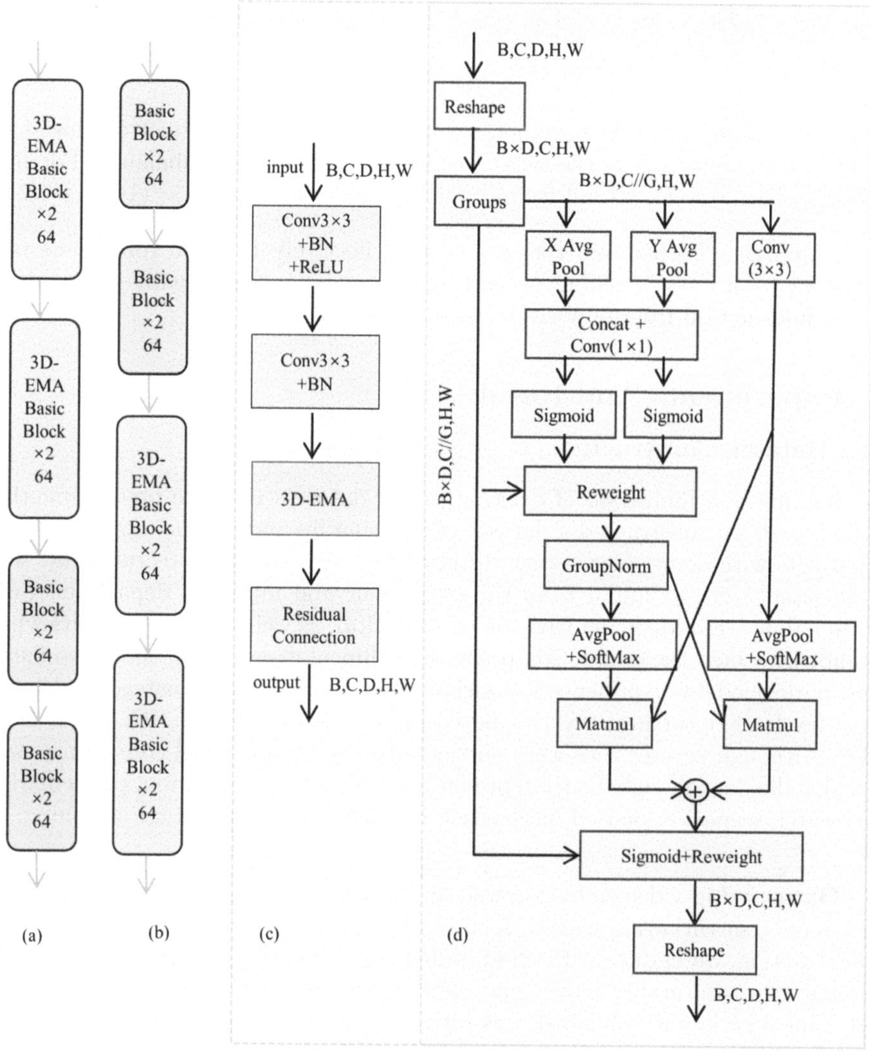

Fig. 4. Insertion Locations of the 3D-EMA Modules: (a) 3D-EMA module insertion positions for the lip assessment model (b) 3D-EMA module insertion positions for the tongue assessment model (c) 3D-EMA Basicblock (d) 3D-EMA Module module.

2. **Focal Loss**

Traditional cross-entropy loss may bias the model toward majority classes under class imbalance, ignoring minority samples. To address this, we adopt Focal Loss, which introduces a modulating factor $(1 - p_t)^\gamma$ on top of cross-entropy, reducing the loss contribution of easy samples while focusing on hard-to-classify examples. The Focal Loss is formulated as:

$$\mathrm{FL}(p_t) = -\alpha_t(1 - p_t)^{\gamma} \log(p_t) \tag{6}$$

where γ is the focusing parameter, typically set to 2, to adjust the loss for difficult samples; α_t is the class weight to handle class imbalance. For lip evaluation, $\alpha_t = (1.3, 1.5, 1.0)$, and for tongue evaluation, $\alpha_t = (1.8, 1.8, 1.2)$.

By applying Focal Loss, the model can effectively improve robustness on imbalanced datasets, avoiding overfitting to majority classes while preserving crucial information from minority classes.

4 Experiments And Result

4.1 Dataset Construction

To overcome the limitation of existing public datasets that are predominantly audio-based, we constructed a dataset comprising lip and tongue motion videos of patients with neurogenic speech disorders through volunteer recruitment. All participants were recruited from the outpatient and inpatient departments of the Rehabilitation Medicine Division of a hospital, as well as healthy adults who voluntarily joined the study. Comprehensive clinical diagnoses of the video data were performed by experienced clinicians, and subjects were categorized into three levels of dysarthria severity based on assessment scores: HC, MD1, and MD2. Although severe cases were not included due to practical constraints, we consider the dataset sufficiently representative for model validation, particularly in research scenarios focused on low-risk populations or early-stage screening.

Lip Dataset Lip video collection was conducted with reference to the modified Frenchay Dysarthria Assessment, focusing on three types of movements: lip corner retraction, lip closure with cheek puffing, and alternating movements. Considering that alternating movements better capture multi-muscle coordination and clinical variability, this task was ultimately selected as the core assessment. A total of 122 participant videos were collected (resolution: 1920×1080, duration: 3–8 s), including 67 healthy controls, 38 individuals with mild dysarthria, and 17 with moderate dysarthria. The dataset covers clinical manifestations ranging from slightly unstable rhythm to markedly restricted motion transitions.

Tongue Dataset Tongue movements included protrusion, elevation, and lateral motion. Preliminary experiments demonstrated that lateral motion more effectively reflected severity differentiation in dysarthria, and thus it was chosen as the core input. A total of 118 participant videos were collected (resolution: 1920×1080, duration: 3–8 s), comprising 68 healthy controls, 33 individuals with mild dysarthria, and 17 with moderate dysarthria. The data span clinical features from mildly reduced amplitude and unstable rhythm to significant loss of coordination and abnormal deviation.

4.2 Basic Settings

To comprehensively evaluate the performance of the model on multi-class classification tasks, accuracy and F1-score were employed as evaluation metrics. Both the lip and tongue datasets were divided into training and validation sets at a ratio of 7:3. After data augmentation, the lip dataset consisted of 249 training samples and 105 testing samples, while the tongue dataset consisted of 240 training samples and 114 testing samples. The specific experimental parameters for the lip and tongue tasks are summarized in the table below. A linear decay learning rate scheduler with a warm-up period of 10 epochs was adopted in all experiments (Table 1).

Table 1. Experimental Setup for Lip and Tongue Datasets.

Experiment	Batch size	Learning Rate	Epoch	Focal loss
Lip	10	5×10^{-4}	100	(1.3, 1.5, 1.0)
Tongue	10	1×10^{-3}	100	(1.8, 1.8, 1.2)

4.3 Comparative Experiment And Result Analysis

To validate the effectiveness of the proposed AE-3DResNet in facial motion recognition for dysarthria assessment, a series of systematic comparative experiments were conducted. Three representative three-dimensional convolutional networks were selected as baselines, including the standard 3D ResNet-18, the spatiotemporal factorized ResNet (2+1)D, and the feature-reuse-oriented 3D DenseNet.

- **3D ResNet-18**: A conventional 3D residual network with strong spatiotemporal joint modeling capability, widely applied in video action recognition tasks.
- **ResNet (2+1)D**: Decomposes 3D convolution into a sequential combination of 2D spatial convolution and 1D temporal convolution, which improves modeling efficiency while enhancing the disentanglement of temporal features.
- **3D DenseNet**: Incorporates dense connectivity to effectively alleviate the vanishing gradient problem in deep networks and enhance feature reuse.

Analysis of Lip Experiment Results The experimental results in Table 2 demonstrate notable differences in lip feature modeling across methods. The conventional 3D-ResNet suffers from limited temporal modeling, yielding an F1-score of only 67.92%. ResNet2p1d, despite its advantage in spatial feature extraction, fails to achieve sufficient spatiotemporal interaction due to separated

2D and 1D convolutions, leading to a further drop in F1-score (58.28%). The 3D-DenseNet improves feature propagation through dense connections and achieves 75.24% accuracy, though its precision–recall gap indicates suboptimal temporal alignment. In contrast, AE-3DResNet leverages channel grouping, bidirectional pooling, and attention weighting to capture fine-grained intra-frame deformations and enhance cross-frame dynamics, thus balancing precision and recall. As a result, it achieves the highest F1-score of 75.37%, surpassing the second-best model by 5.28%, confirming the effectiveness of the 3D-EMA module in subtle motion modeling.

Table 2. Comparison of Experimental Results of Different Models on lip features.(%)

Method	Accuracy	Precision	Recall	F1
3D-ResNet	70.54	68.96	69.86	67.92
ResNet2p1d	61.96	62.85	62.28	58.28
3D-DenseNet	75.25	70.45	71.71	70.09
AE-3DResNet	**77.14**	**76.22**	**76.22**	**75.37**

Table 3. Comparison of Class-wise Evaluation Accuracy of Different Models on Lip Features(%).

Method	Acc_MD1	Acc_MD2	Acc_HC	Acc
3D-ResNet	63.62	71.41	74.53	70.54
ResNet2p1d	40.73	50.02	84.14	61.96
3D-DenseNet	56.71	57.73	**95.93**	75.25
AE-3DResNet	**78.88**	**71.43**	78.43	**77.14**

The classification results in Table 3 further reveal that traditional models perform inconsistently across severity levels, with weaker accuracy on mild and moderate dysarthria. AE-3DResNet not only attains the highest overall accuracy (77.1%) but also maintains balanced performance across categories, achieving 78.8% accuracy on the most challenging MD1 class. Confusion matrix analysis (Fig. 5(a)) indicates that the proposed cross-frame attention calibration effectively amplifies subtle dynamic cues, thereby enhancing the discrimination of mild and moderate dysarthria.

Analysis of Tongue Experiment Results The results in Table 4 show that conventional 3D-ResNet and 3D-DenseNet, which rely on fixed convolution kernels for spatiotemporal modeling, fail to dynamically weight nonlinear tongue

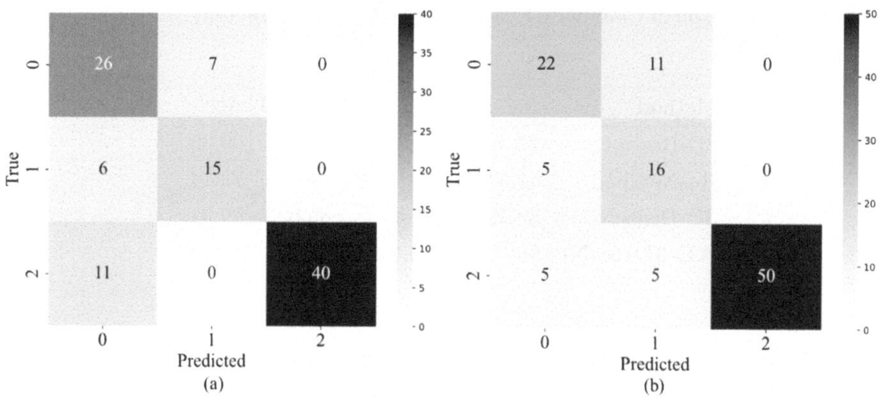

Fig. 5. Confusion Matrix. (a) Confusion matrix of the lip EMA-3DResNet model(b) Confusion matrix of the tongue EMA-3DResNet model.

deformations, yielding relatively low F1-scores of 65.64% and 62.63%. Their negative correlation between precision and recall further highlights limitations in feature coupling. Although ResNet2p1d improves overall accuracy (73.68%) through separated 2D spatial and 1D temporal convolutions, its F1-score drops to 63.61%, suggesting insufficient modeling of transient and irregular tongue motions. In contrast, AE-3DResNet achieves the best overall performance with 77.19% accuracy and a balanced F1-score of 72.99%, outperforming the second-best method by 7.35%.

Table 5 further details per-class accuracy across severity levels. Traditional models exhibit large discrepancies, e.g., 3D-ResNet achieves 75.8% on mild dysarthria but only 57.1% on moderate cases; ResNet2p1d shows a "normal-sample advantage" with 96.7% accuracy on HC but poor generalization to disordered classes; 3D-DenseNet performs well on HC (85.0%) but drops sharply on MD1 and MD2. In contrast, AE-3DResNet maintains balanced accuracy across categories, outperforming others by more than 4% on the most challenging MD2 class. This confirms its ability to capture low-contrast and fine-grained tongue movements (see Fig. 5(b)).

Table 4. Comparison of Experimental Results of Different Models on Tongue Features (%).

Method	Accuracy	Precision	Recall	F1
3D-ResNet	69.35	66.38	67.63	65.64
ResNet2p1d	73.74	63.77	63.68	63.61
3D-DenseNet	69.31	66.79	65.27	62.63
AE-3DResNet	**77.19**	**72.92**	**75.40**	**72.99**

Table 5. Comparison of Class-wise Evaluation Accuracy of Different Models on Tongue Features(%).

Method	Acc_MD1	Acc_MD2	Acc_HC	Acc
3D-ResNet	**75.82**	57.14	70.04	69.35
ResNet2p1d	51.53	42.97	**96.74**	73.74
3D-DenseNet	39.42	71.46	85.03	69.31
AE-3DResNet	66.70	**76.23**	83.30	**77.19**

4.4 Ablation Experiments and Result Analysis

To systematically evaluate the impact of the 3D-EMA module insertion position on model performance, we designed a series of ablation experiments. Specifically, the module was placed at shallow layers (the first two residual blocks), deep layers (the last two residual blocks), and all layers (all four residual blocks). The performance across lip and tongue motion assessment metrics was then compared. The results provide insights into optimizing the model architecture and improving the accuracy of facial motion evaluation in dysarthria assessment.

Table 6. Ablation Experiment Results on Lip Features (%).

Method	Acc_MD1	Acc_MD2	Acc_HC	Acc	F1
EMA (all)	66.72	61.94	**94.14**	**79.06**	73.08
EMA (front-2)	**78.88**	**71.43**	78.43	77.14	**75.37**
EMA (end-2)	75.82	61.91	80.43	75.22	71.80

Table 7. Ablation Experiment Results on Tongue Features (%).

Method	Acc_MD1	Acc_MD2	Acc_HC	Overall Acc	F1
EMA (all)	63.61	57.19	76.70	69.36	64.71
EMA (front-2)	**72.72**	42.92	75.04	68.47	62.85
EMA (end-2)	66.70	**76.23**	**83.30**	**77.19**	**72.99**

In lip assessment (Table 6), the EMA (all) scheme achieves 79.0% accuracy and an F1 score of 0.7308, verifying the effectiveness of fully embedding 3D-EMA modules. However, performance across classes is imbalanced. The EMA (front-2) scheme improves MD1 and MD2 accuracies to 78.8% and 78.4%, with the F1 score rising to 0.7537, indicating that shallow modules enhance basic feature extraction and mitigate class imbalance. By contrast, the EMA (end-2) scheme maintains high HC accuracy (80.4%) but yields lower overall performance, suggesting that deep modules alone are insufficient.

The tongue assessment results, shown in Table 7, indicate that the EMA (all) scheme achieves an Acc of 69.3% and an F1 score of 0.6471. Switching to the EMA (front-2) scheme increases the MD1 accuracy to 72.7%, but MD2 accuracy drops sharply to 42.9%, with a concurrent decrease in F1 score. This demonstrates that shallow 3D-EMA modules facilitate the extraction of basic tongue features, but also reveal limitations in feature processing. Notably, the EMA (end-2) scheme exhibits different characteristics: MD2 and HC accuracies increase to 76.2% and 83.3%, respectively, and the overall Acc and F1 scores surpass those of the other two schemes, indicating that deep 3D-EMA modules significantly enhance high-level semantic features of the tongue.

The embedding position of the 3D-EMA module has a significant impact on model performance. Shallow modules primarily enhance low-level feature extraction, making them more effective for lip assessment, which relies on intuitive visual cues such as edges and textures. In contrast, deep modules optimize cross-channel semantic associations and are better suited for modeling tongue features that require contextual and semantic complexity. Consequently, shallow 3D-EMA modules improve the discriminability of lip classification, while deep modules yield superior performance in tongue evaluation.

5 Conclusion

This study proposes an approach, AE-3DResNet, which integrates an efficient attention mechanism with a three-dimensional residual network for assessing facial muscle movements in patients with neurogenic speech disorders. Experimental results demonstrate that the method achieves classification accuracies of 77.14% and 77.19% for lip and tongue movement grading, respectively, representing significant improvements over baseline models. This validates the advantage of the 3D-EMA module in cross-dimensional feature interaction and dynamic semantic modeling. The proposed approach provides clinicians with an objective and quantitative tool for evaluating lip and tongue movement disorders, showing potential practical value. Despite these promising results, some limitations remain. The classification process tends to favor easily distinguishable samples, and the assessment is limited to lip and tongue movements, making it challenging to fully capture the complexity of facial muscle disorders. To address these limitations and improve model generalization, future work will focus on expanding the self-constructed dataset to cover more diverse subjects and motion patterns, alongside exploring few-shot learning and multi-action sequence modeling. With the advancement of multimodal fusion and real-time assessment systems, this approach is expected to move closer to clinical application, serving as an important support for facial movement evaluation and personalized intervention in neurogenic speech disorders.

References

1. Enderby, P.: Disorders of communication: dysarthria. In: Barnes, M.P., Good, D.C. (eds.) Handbook of Clinical Neurology, vol. 110, pp. 273–281. Elsevier, Amsterdam (2013)
2. Ball, M.J.: An Introduction to Speech Disorders. In: Manual of Clinical Phonetics, pp. 65–74. Routledge, London (2021)
3. Feng, X., Yue, W., Chen, Z., Wu, H., Qin, X.: Articulatory kinematic characteristics during speech production for individuals with dysarthria: A study based on electromagnetic articulography. Chin. J. Rehabil. Theory Pract. **25**, 7–16 (2019)
4. B., A.B., Kumar, S.A., T., K., Sasikala, S., V., K.P.C.: Towards improving the performance of dysarthric speech severity assessment system. In: 2022 International Conference on Computer Communication and Informatics (ICCCI), pp. 1–6. IEEE, Coimbatore (2022). 10.1109/ICCCI54379.2022.9740812
5. Allison, K.M., Yunusova, Y., Campbell, T.F., Wang, J., Berry, J.D., Green, J.R.: The diagnostic utility of patient report and speech-language pathologists' ratings for detecting the early onset of bulbar symptoms due to ALS. Amyotrophic Lateral Sclerosis and Frontotemporal Degeneration **18**(5–6), 358–366 (2017). https://doi.org/10.1080/21678421.2017.1303515
6. Enderby, P., Palmer, R.: Frenchay dysarthria assessment. Int. J. Lang. Commun. Disord. **43**(1), 99–115 (2008)
7. Zhang, Y., Long, Y., Shen, X., et al.: Articulatory movement features for short-duration text-dependent speaker verification. Int. J. Speech Technol. **20**(4), 753–759 (2017)
8. Harada, R., Hojyo, N., Fujimoto, K., Oyama, T.: Development of communication system from EMG of suprahyoid muscles using deep learning. In: 2022 IEEE 4th Global Conference on Life Sciences and Technologies (LifeTech), pp. 5–9. IEEE, Osaka (2022). https://doi.org/10.1109/LifeTech53646.2022.9754898
9. Rong, P., et al.: Predicting speech intelligibility decline in amyotrophic lateral sclerosis based on the deterioration of individual speech subsystems. PLoS ONE **11**(5), e0154971 (2016)
10. Duan, S., Zhang, X., Yan, M., Zhang, J.: Statistical distribution exploration of tongue movement for pathological articulation on word/sentence level. IEEE Access **8**, 91057–91069 (2020)
11. Fahmy, G.: Detection of micro movements of facial muscles in facial videos. In: 2021 9th Int. Japan-Africa Conf. on Electronics, Communications, and Computations (JAC-ECC), pp. 1–4. IEEE, Alexandria (2021). https://doi.org/10.1109/JAC-ECC54461.2021.9691309
12. Chanda, B., Nyeem, H.: Multilevel fusion with dual stream 3DCNN-LSTM for advancing dynamic hand gesture recognition. In: 2023 26th Int. Conf. on Computer and Information Technology (ICCIT), pp. 1–6. IEEE, Cox's Bazar (2023). https://doi.org/10.1109/ICCIT60459.2023.10441489
13. Knuijt, S., Kalf, J., van Engelen, B., et al.: The Radboud Dysarthria Assessment: Development and clinimetric evaluation. Folia Phoniatr. Logop. **69**, 143–153 (2017)
14. Lee, J., Bell, M., Simmons, Z.: Articulatory kinematic characteristics across the dysarthria severity spectrum in individuals with amyotrophic lateral sclerosis. Am. J. Speech-Lang. Pathol. **27**, 258–269 (2017)
15. Teplansky, K.J.: Tongue and lip acceleration as a measure of speech decline in amyotrophic lateral sclerosis. Folia Phoniatr. Logop. **75**, 23–34 (2023). https://doi.org/10.1159/000525514

16. Nair, R., et al.: Study of muscle activation during the articulation of phoneme using features extracted from electromyography signals. In: 2023 IEEE 20th India Council International Conference (INDICON), pp. 713–717. IEEE (2023). https://doi.org/10.1109/INDICON59947.2023.10440783
17. Rong, P., Yunusova, Y., Richburg, B., Green, J.R.: Automatic extraction of abnormal lip movement features from the alternating motion rate task in amyotrophic lateral sclerosis. Int. J. Speech-Lang. Pathol. **20**, 610–623 (2018). https://doi.org/10.1080/17549507.2018.1485739
18. Jafari, D., Simmatis, L., Guarin, D., Bouvier, L., Taati, B., Yunusova, Y.: 3D video tracking technology in the assessment of orofacial impairments in neurological disease: clinical validation. J. Speech Lang. Hear. Res. **66**, 3151–3165 (2023). https://doi.org/10.1044/2023_JSLHR-22-00321
19. Novotny, M., Tykalova, T., Ruzickova, H., Ruzicka, E., Dusek, P., Rusz, J.: Automated video-based assessment of facial bradykinesia in de-novo Parkinson's disease. NPJ Digit. Med. **5**, 98 (2022). https://doi.org/10.1038/s41746-022-00642-5
20. Kim, H.J., et al.: Real-time shape tracking of facial landmarks. Multimed. Tools Appl. **79**, 15945–15963 (2018)
21. Dwivedi, K., Patel, K., Pandey, J.P., Garg, P.: An automatic robust deep learning and feature fusion-based classification method for early diagnosis of oral cancer using lip and tongue images. In: 2024 2nd International Conference on Disruptive Technologies (ICDT), pp. 391–395. IEEE (2024). https://doi.org/10.1109/ICDT61202.2024.10489266
22. Tran, D., Bourdev, L., Fergus, R., Torresani, L., Paluri, M.: Learning spatiotemporal features with 3D convolutional networks. In: 2015 IEEE International Conference on Computer Vision (ICCV), pp. 4489–4497. IEEE (2015)
23. Carreira, J., Zisserman, A.: Quo vadis, action recognition? A new model and the Kinetics dataset. In: IEEE Conference on Computer Vision and Pattern Recognition (CVPR) (2017). https://doi.org/10.1109/CVPR.2017.502
24. Kataoka, H., et al.: Would mega-scale datasets further enhance spatiotemporal 3D CNNs? arXiv preprint arXiv:2004.04968 (2020)
25. Mo, H., et al.: SFF-DA: spatiotemporal feature fusion for detecting anxiety non-intrusively. arXiv preprint arXiv:2208.06411 (2022)
26. Zhou, X., Wei, Z., Xu, M., Qu, S., Guo, G.: Facial depression recognition by deep joint label distribution and metric learning. IEEE Trans. Affect. Comput. **13**, 1605–1618 (2020)
27. Li, H., et al.: Enhancing facial classification and recognition using 3D facial models and deep learning. arXiv preprint arXiv:2312.05219 (2023)

DG-EER: A Domain Generalization Framework for EEG-Based Emotion Recognition

Xinghan Chen[1], Jing Li[1](✉), and Gaoxiang Ouyang[2]

[1] Tianjin University of Technology, Tianjin 300384, China
jing.li.2003@gmail.com

[2] State Key Laboratory of Cognitive Neuroscience and Learning, Beijing Normal University, Beijing 100875, China

Abstract. Emotion recognition based on Electroencephalography (EEG) is an important research area in affective computing. However, EEG signals usually exhibit significant individual differences, limiting the generalization ability of existing domain adaptation methods to unseen subjects. To this end, we propose a Domain-Generalized EEG Emotion Recognition framework (DG-EER) that learns domain-invariant representations for robust emotion recognition. During model training, we design a shared encoder in the source domain to capture domain-invariant features across different subjects. In the inference phase, the model only use the pre-trained encoder and a classifier to perform emotion recognition. Extensive experiments were conducted, and the proposed DG-EER achieved average classification accuracies of 75.16% and 76.83% on the valence and arousal dimensions of the DEAP dataset, respectively, and 88.05% on the SEED dataset. Moreover, our method reduces the impact of individual differences, thus enhancing its generalization ability in emotion recognition tasks.

Keywords: Electroencephalography · emotion recognition · individual differences · domain generalization

1 Introduction

Emotion refers to a state of mind, and its accurate and automatic recognition is essential for achieving intelligent human-computer interaction, personalized healthcare, and safety-related applications [1]. Compared to commonly used modalities such as facial expressions, eye movement, and texts, Electroencephalography (EEG) [2] can reflect an individual's emotion states more directly, enabling objective emotion analysis. As a valuable tool for understanding brain activities, EEG signals have been widely used in diverse research fields [3] such as autism diagnosis, motor imagery, and emotion recognition.

Advancements in machine learning and deep learning have contributed to notable improvements in EEG-based emotion recognition performance. However, EEG data are weak and non-stationary, and a variety of factors can lead to significant distribution disparities among EEG data from various subjects, such as devices, recording sessions,

H. Liu et al. (Eds.): CEI 2025, CCIS 2881, pp. 18–30, 2026.
https://doi.org/10.1007/978-981-95-9493-1_2

and environments [4]. Therefore, EEG-based emotion recognition models trained on source subjects often have limited generalization ability when applied to unseen subjects. In order to alleviate the distribution disparity of EEG data across various subjects, transfer learning was introduced in emotion recognition [5]. Generally, transfer learning improves the performance of target tasks by transferring knowledge from previously learned related tasks. However, a major challenge in transfer learning is domain shift, which refers to the difference in distributions between the source domain and target domain. Domain adaptation (DA), a widely adopted method in transfer learning, alleviates domain shift by aligning feature distributions extracted from both the source data and the target data. This method is commonly classified as Supervised DA, Semi-Supervised DA, and Unsupervised DA based on the availability of labels in the target domain. Therefore, a major limitation is that DA approaches depend on the target data during training. This limitation emphasizes the necessity of employing domain generalization (DG) strategies, which aim to extract domain-invariant features from different subjects, enabling the model to generalize to unseen target subjects without accessing their data during training.

Cross-subject DG can be categorized into three methods: i) Data Manipulation expands the training data through augmentation and transformation; ii) Representation Learning enables the model to achieve better adaptation across different domains by learning domain-invariant representations; iii) Learning Strategy fuses established approaches, such as meta-learning and ensemble learning, to enhance multi-domain training ability.

Data Manipulation increases the quantity and diversity of the training data to enhance the model's robustness, while Representation Learning promotes the model to concentrates on task-related features by minimizing distribution disparities from different subjects. However, the existing DG methods belonging to these two categories usually rely on complex training procedures or focus mainly on explicit feature alignment, which is insufficient for highly heterogeneous EEG signals. Therefore, we propose DG-EER, a novel DG framework for EEG-based emotion recognition that performs implicit feature alignment through cross-subject feature reconstruction and enhances data diversity through latent feature fusion. This design provides an effective mechanism for learning domain-invariant emotional representations, thus improving classification performance. This paper primarily provides the following contributions:

- We introduce DG into the EEG-based emotion recognition model to generalize on unseen target subjects, thus improving its robustness and applicability in real-world scenarios.
- We introduce a data augmentation technique based on the feature reconstruction across subjects to better mitigate the impact of insufficient source data;
- We design a shared encoder for all the source subjects and a multi-class subject discriminator to mitigate the issue of individual differences.

2 Related Work

2.1 EEG Classification with Deep Learning

In EEG signal analysis, deep learning usually involves three steps: i) preprocessing, ii) feature extraction, and iii) classification. In preprocessing, band-pass filtering, re-referencing, interpolation of bad channels, and removing artifact removal are usually applied. After preprocessing, features are extracted from the temporal, spatial, or frequency domains, which plays a crucial role in transforming preprocessed EEG signals into meaningful representations for classification. For instance, Hu et al. [6] proposed a novel Regional-asymmetric Adaptive Graph Convolutional Neural Network to extract spatial-temporal EEG features from both brain hemispheres for identifying autism spectrum disorder in children. Lin et al. [7] proposed HATNet, a hybrid attention-based transfer learning network that segments EEG signals into patches, and utilized a calibration-based strategy to enhance the detection performance of train drivers' states. Gao et al. [8] proposed a multi-scale fusion network by employing an attention mechanism for motor imagery, which integrated spatial, temporal, and spectral features to extract neural activity patterns.

2.2 Domain Adaptation for EEG-Based Emotion Recognition

As an important method in transfer learning, DA methods aim to learn domain-independent representations across EEG data in both source and target domains. Liu et al. [9] proposed a multi-branch capsule framework combined with adversarial DA to minimize the distribution discrepancies between source and target domains. Wang et al. [10] developed a Multi-source Selective Graph Domain Adaptation Network, which used DA to extract both subject-invariant and individual-specific features. Zhou et al. [11] proposed EEGMatch method, which employed a semi-supervised strategy for multi-domain adaptation to align data representations, thus mitigating the domain shift problem.

2.3 Domain Generalization for EEG-Based Emotion Recognition.

Compared to DA, DG aims to train a model that can generalize across unseen subjects by addressing distributional shifts in the training data. Wang et al. [12] proposed a Denoising Mixed Mutual Reconstruction model, where the model performs mutual reconstruction and applies mixed data augmentation to obtain subject-invariant features and enhance generalization across subjects. Chen et al. [13] introduced a Graph Domain Disentanglement Network that extracted common features from both graph connectivity and representations, and designed a domain-adaptive classifier aggregation module to enhance emotion prediction performance. Li et al. [14] proposed generalized contrastive partial label learning method, which integrated contrastive learning and DG to address label ambiguity and inter-subject variability.

3 Method

A detailed overview of the DG-EER framework (as shown in Fig. 1) is presented in this section, consisting of Feature Representation, Feature Masking, Feature Reconstruction, Domain Adversarial, and the overall training and inference process. To better formulate the domain generalization problem, we divide the dataset into the source domain X_s and the target domain X_t, where $X_s \cap X_t = \varnothing$.

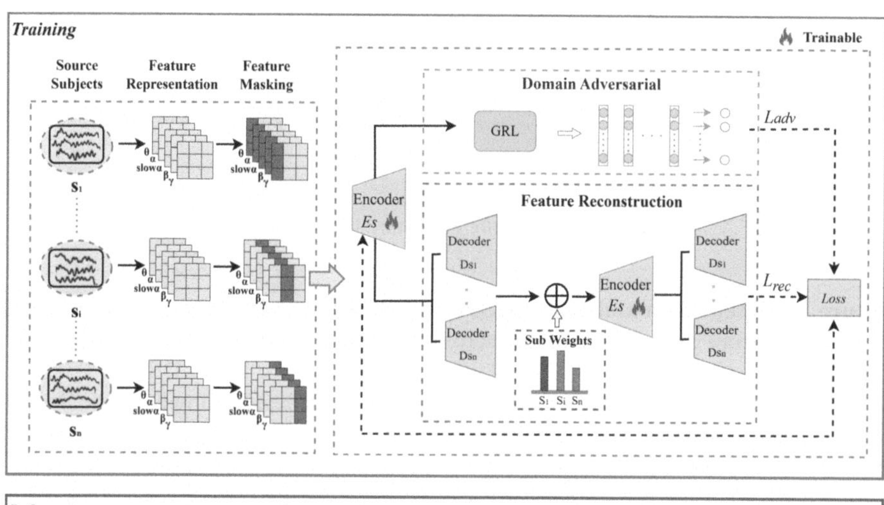

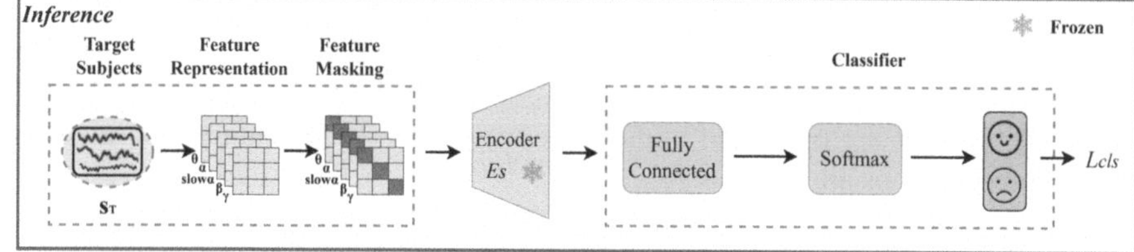

Fig. 1. The framework of DG-EER.

3.1 Training Phase

In the training phase, Differential Entropy (DE) and Power Spectral Density (PSD) features are obtained and fused to capture complementary information of different features. To improve the model's robustness and encourage the learning of domain-invariant representations, a masking technique is employed to randomly masks input features. This is followed by two modules: Domain Adversarial and Feature Reconstruction. The Domain Adversarial module utilizes adversarial learning to identify the domain of features [15]. For Feature Reconstruction, an encoder E_s is used to capture shared features for all the source subjects, and then we design N (the number of source subjects) Decoders $(D_{s_1}, \cdots, D_{s_n})$ for reconstructing features across different subjects within a same class.

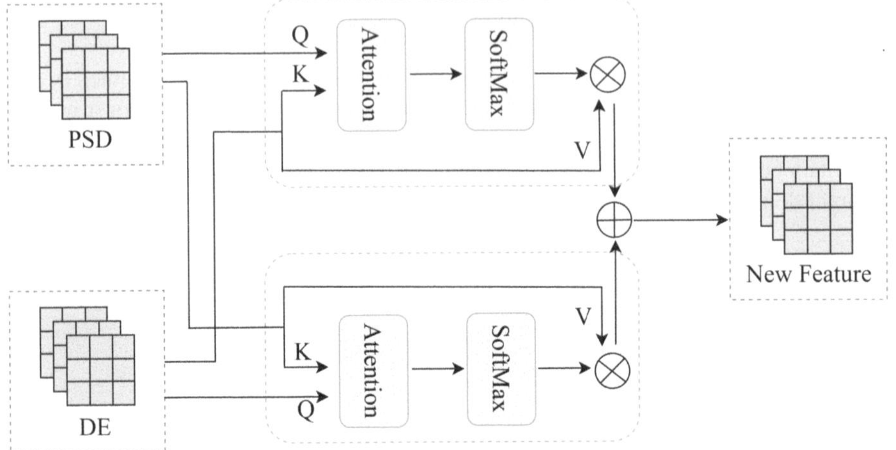

Fig. 2. The architecture of Feature Representation.

Feature Representation and Masking. As shown in Fig. 2, firstly, we extract DE and PSD features from each EEG channel across five frequency bands: θ (4–7 Hz), α (8–10 Hz), slow α (8–13 Hz), β (14–29 Hz), and γ (30–45 Hz). Then, DE and PSD are fused by applying attention across each frequency band. In detail, using the basic Scaled Dot-Product Attention mechanism, we designate the PSD as the value (V), and assign DE and PSD to the key (K) and query (Q) respectively, which is presented by Eq. (1):

$$Attention(Q, K, V) = softmax(\frac{QK^T}{\sqrt{d_k}})V \tag{1}$$

The DE features are processed in the same way as the PSD features, and the two feature representations are fused as $F_{fusion} \in R^{B*T*D}$:

$$F_{fusion}(DE, PSD) = Attention(DE, PSD, PSD) + Attention(PSD, DE, DE) \tag{2}$$

Here, B is batch size, T is time steps, and $D = R * C$ denotes the number of feature dimensions, where C denotes the number of channels and R denotes the number of frequency bands.

To learn domain-invariant representations, we employed a Bernoulli distribution to generate a mask matrix. This matrix is applied to the F_{fusion} via element-wise multiplication, and obtain the masked feature F_{mask}. The masking operation is defined as follows:

$$m \sim Bernoulli\,(1 \; - \; mask\_rate) \tag{3}$$

$$F_{mask} = F_{fusion} \odot m \tag{4}$$

where m is the mask matrix and $\odot$ denotes element-wise multiplication. This operation forces the model to rely not only on the visible features but also on the incomplete data, thereby making it more robust to noise and less sensitive to irrelevant features.

Feature Reconstruction. Due to the complex temporal and spatial structure of EEG data, traditional data augmentation techniques, such as noise injection or geometric transformations, are not well appropriate for EEG data. To alleviate this limitation, we design an encoder and multiple subject-specific decoders to generate mixed EEG features, thus enriching the feature space in a meaningful and task-relevant method.

The proposed data augmentation strategy consists of two stages, and the reconstruction losses at both stages are computed to guide the feature fusion and ensure the quality of reconstructed features. The entire process is described below.

At the first stage, both the encoder and decoders are constructed using multi-layer LSTM architectures. In each training iteration, a batch of EEG data from a source subject is encoded into latent emotional representations by the shared encoder. These representations are then fed into multiple decoders corresponding to different source subjects to reconstruct EEG features with the same emotion label but from different individuals. As defined in Eq. (5), $x_1^i \in R^{T*D}$ denotes the output of i-th decoder.

$$x_1^i = D_{s_i}(E_s(F_{mask})), i \in (1,2, \ldots, n) \tag{5}$$

Instead of directly using individual decoder outputs, we compute a weighted sum of these outputs to obtain a mixed feature x_{mix}, which linearly combines same-category features from different subjects and obtains subject-invariant features for specific emotions in the latent feature space without injecting noise. The weights w_i are dynamically determined based on the subject's reconstruction loss L_{rec1}^i at the first stage. The Mean Squared Error (MSE) is utilized to measure the discrepancy between generated features and those of the corresponding subject, $f^i \in R^{T*D}$ represents the original features of the i-th subject.

$$L_{rec1}^i = MSE(x_1^i, f^i), i \in (1,2, \ldots, n) \tag{6}$$

$$x_{mix} = \sum_{i=1}^{n} w_i * x_1^i \tag{7}$$

At the second stage, x_{mix} are reconstructed using the same encoder and the multi-decoder architecture. The reconstruction loss L_{rec2} measures the discrepancy between the reconstructed features and the corresponding subject-specific features, as seen in Eq. (9).

$$x_2^i = D_{s_i}(E_s(x_{mix})), i \in (1,2, \ldots, n) \tag{8}$$

$$L_{rec2} = \sum_{i=1}^{n} MSE(x_2^i, f^i) \tag{9}$$

where $x_2^i \in R^{T*D}$ represents the second-stage output of the i-th decoder.

Domain Adversarial. We design a multi-source subject discriminator based on the structure of Domain-Adversarial Neural Networks (DANN) [20]. This discriminator is a single-layer fully connected network, which is used to identify the origin of features.

This weakens the discriminator's ability to distinguish subjects, thus promoting the encoder to extract domain-invariant features.

$$D_{i'} = SD(E_s(F_{mask})) \tag{10}$$

$$L_{adv} = -\lambda D_i log(D_{i'}) \tag{11}$$

where *SD* is the subject discriminator, $D_{i'}$ denotes the prediction of *SD*, D_i denotes the i-th subject's domain label, the domain classification loss is L_{adv}.

3.2 Inference Phase

In the inference phase, the EEG data of the target domain undergo the same feature extraction process as in the training phase. After that, only the pre-trained encoder and an emotion classifier are used to implement emotion classification. We further optimize the model using the same input data as in the training phase to enhance its capability in emotion classification. After optimization, the model is evaluated on an unseen target subject.

3.3 Loss Function

To optimize the proposed DG-EER in the training phase, we define a loss function L_{total}:

$$L_{total} = \lambda_1 L_{rec2} + \lambda_2 L_{adv} \tag{12}$$

where λ_1 and λ_2 are the hyperparameters that balance the contributions of each loss term, tuned via grid search.

The classification loss L_{cls}, utilized in the inference phase, optimizes the emotion classifier by minimizing the cross-entropy computed from predicted labels *y'* and the ground truth *y*:

$$L_{cls} = cross\_entropy(y', y) \tag{13}$$

4 Experiments

4.1 Dataset

DEAP [21]: The dataset involves 32 participants, with EEG signals recorded using a 32-channel electrode cap. Participants rated their emotional responses on a scale from 0 to 9 across four dimensions: valence, arousal, dominance, and liking. Among these, valence and arousal are commonly used labels in emotion recognition tasks. Therefore, we also adopted these two labels in our experiments.

SEED [23]: The dataset contains EEG signals recorded from 15 participants (7 males and 8 females, with a mean age of 23.27 ± 2.37 years) using a 62-channel electrode cap. Participants watched 15 film clips, which evoked three emotional states: positive, neutral, and negative.

4.2 Implementation Details

The model was evaluated using a leave-one-subject-out (LOSO) cross-validation strategy, ensuring that each subject was tested individually while the others contributed to training. The overall performance was evaluated by computing the average accuracy and standard deviation across all the test individuals. During the training phase, a learning rate (lr) of 1e-3, a weight decay of 5e-4, a batch size of 256 and 200 epochs were used in the Adam optimizer. At the inference phase, the same optimizer was used with a lower lr of 1e-4, a weight decay of 0.01, and the same batch size and number of epochs.

4.3 Experiment Results and Analysis

To evaluate the emotion classification performance of DG-EER, we compare it with two DG methods, HSLT [16], TMLP + SRDANN [19], and other DA approaches, such as DA-CapsNet [9], MTLFuseNet [17], SPDNet [18], IDDA [24], and MCTL-SLAC [25] and show the average accuracy on the DEAP and SEED datasets.

HSLT [16]: It proposes a hierarchical spatial learning transformer that integrates multi-head self-attention mechanisms to robustly capture spatial relationships in different brain regions.

TMLP + SRDANN [19]: It combines Transposition Multi-Layer Perceptron with Sample-Reweighted to extract multi-channel EEG features and adaptively transfer discriminative knowledge across domains.

IDDA [24]: It integrates graph convolution with DA to dynamically learn intrinsic relationships between EEG channels, thereby aligning the feature distributions of source domains, target domains, and emotional sub-domains.

MCTL-SLAC [25]: It employs a Source Label Adaptive Correction strategy to mitigate domain discrepancies and reduces the negative effects of noisy labels by adaptively transforming source labels.

DA-CapsNet [9]: It integrates a multi-branch capsule network with adversarial DA to capture multi-scale emotional information.

MTLFuseNet [17]: It utilizes Variational Autocoder and Gated Recurrent Units to integrate deep latent representations of EEG data.

SPDNet [18]: It aligns both marginal and conditional distributions across different subjects' EEG data. This is achieved by leveraging symmetric positive definite (SPD) covariance matrices as features and incorporating prototype learning with Riemannian metrics.

As shown in Table 1, DG-EER achieves the best performance among all the compared models on the DEAP dataset, achieving an average accuracy of 75.16% for valence and 76.83% for arousal, which improves performance by 1.54% and 2.71% compared to the second-best method DA-CapsNet [9]. Regarding stability, DG-EER also shows the lowest standard deviation 3.57% for valence and 3.71% for arousal, which outperforms DA-CapsNet [9] by 1.41% and 0.96% in valence and arousal, respectively. Furthermore, we conducted experiments on the SEED dataset. As shown in Table 2, DG-EER also achieved the highest classification accuracy of 88.05%. For stability, DG-EER demonstrates a significant advantage, with a standard deviation of only 5.28%, which is 2.61%

lower than MCTL-SLAC [25]. These results demonstrate that our method not only outperforms other domain generalization methods, but also achieves better performance than domain adaptation methods, even though it is trained without any target domain data. This highlights the strong generalization ability and robustness of DG-EER for EEG-based emotion recognition across different subjects.

Table 1. Performance comparison of DG-EER with other methods on the DEAP dataset (%)

Method	Valence		Arouse	
	Acc	Std	Acc	Std
HSLT [16]	66.51	/	65.75	/
TMLP + SRDANN [19]	61.88	5.55	57.70	7.23
MTLFuseNet [17]	71.33	5.24	73.28	7.74
SPDNet [18]	66.47	8.75	69.79	11.93
DA-CapsNet [9]	73.62	4.98	75.25	4.67
DG-EER	**75.16**	**3.57**	**76.83**	**3.71**

Table 2. Performance comparison of DG-EER with other methods on the SEED dataset (%)

Method	Acc	Std
DA-CapsNet [9]	84.63	9.09
IDDA [24]	85.75	8.11
TMLP + SRDANN [19]	86.58	10.25
MCTL-SLAC [25]	87.30	7.89
DG-EER	**88.05**	**5.28**

In our ablation study, we evaluated the impact of key components in the DG-EER framework on the DEAP dataset, focusing on valence and arousal classification, and the results are shown in Table 2. The complete DG-EER achieved the highest performance, with an average accuracy of $75.16 \pm 3.57\%$ for valence and $76.83 \pm 3.71\%$ for arousal. Removing the Feature Masking technique resulted in a decrease of 0.48% in valence and 0.59% in arousal, indicating its effectiveness in enhancing the model's robustness. Furthermore, we simply perform a direct summation of the outputs from all decoders, without considering the reconstruction quality of mix features. A more significant drop was observed, with accuracy decreasing by 0.63% for valence and 0.95% for arousal. The largest performance decline occurred when both the Feature Masking technique and Weighted Mix features were removed, resulting in a drop of $1.24 \pm 0.24\%$ in valence

Table 3. Ablation study of DG-EER different components on the DEAP dataset(%)

Method	Valence		Arouse	
	Acc	Std	Acc	Std
DG-EER	**75.16**	**3.57**	**76.83**	**3.71**
w/o Feature Masking	74.68	3.59	76.24	3.63
w/o Weighted Mix	74.53	3.55	75.88	3.46
w/o both	73.92	3.81	75.45	3.94

and 0.95 ± 0.23% in arousal. This highlights the positive effect of both components on our model's performance improvement (Table 3).

Table 4. Ablation study of different hyperparameters on the DEAP dataset (%)

Hyperparameters	Valence		Arouse	
	Acc	Std	Acc	Std
$\lambda_1 = 1.0, \lambda_2 = 1.0$	74.10	3.58	75.91	3.77
$\lambda_1 = 0.5, \lambda_2 = 1.0$	73.47	3.83	75.66	3.81
$\boldsymbol{\lambda_1 = 1.0, \lambda_2 = 0.5}$	**75.16**	**3.57**	**76.83**	**3.71**

We conducted an ablation study to analyze the effects of different loss weight settings for reconstruction loss (λ_1) and domain classification loss (λ_2) in the pre-training phase. As shown in Table 4, the best performance is obtained with $\lambda_1 = 1.0$ and $\lambda_2 = 0.5$, with accuracies of 75.16% for valence and 76.83% for arousal. The results demonstrate that the weight of the reconstruction loss is important for learning emotional features, while the weight of the domain classification loss helps retain sufficient emotion-discriminative information.

To highlight the classification capabilities of DG-EER, we employed t-SNE [22] to visualize the feature distribution based on a randomly selected training set from the LOSO cross-validation in the valence dimension of the DEAP dataset. As shown in Fig. 3, the original features (as seen in (a)) exhibit significant overlap between the negative (red) and positive (blue) emotion classes, indicating poor class separability. In contrast, after the inference phase, as shown in (b), features from the same category become more tightly clustered, and the boundaries between categories become clearer. This suggests that our model can learn more discriminative representations for emotion classification.

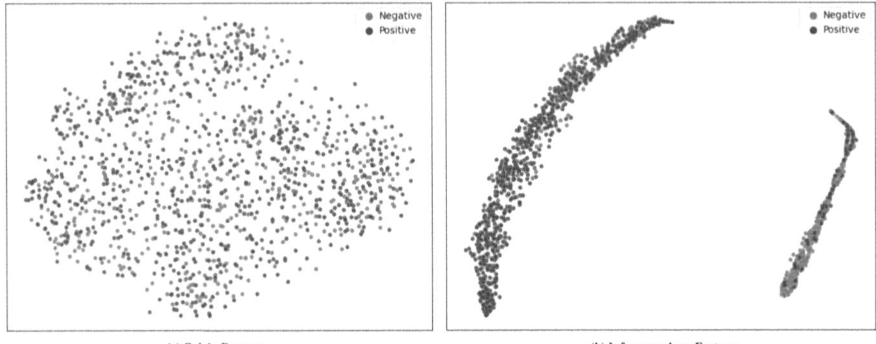

Fig. 3. Feature distribution visualization in the valence dimension of the DEAP dataset with t-SNE. (a) represents the original feature distribution, (b) shows the feature distribution after the inference phase (Color figure online).

5 Conclusion

In our work, we present a domain generalization framework for EEG-based emotion recognition, aiming to mitigate the impact of individual differences. Differing from traditional DA approaches that require access to target domain data, our model is trained only on subjects from source domains. By introducing a shared encoder to learn domain-invariant representations, the proposed method effectively reduces the influence of individual differences. Experimental results on the DEAP and SEED dataset exhibit that our method not only achieves competitive performance on valence and arousal classification tasks but also exhibits strong generalization ability across unseen subjects. These findings highlight the potential of our model to support more robust emotion recognition in real-world scenarios. We plan to extend our work to multi-modal settings, such as integrating EEG and eye-movement data. For each modality, a specific decoder can be designed to learn modality-invariant representations, thus improving classification performance.

Acknowledgments. This work was supported by National Natural Science Foundation of China under Grant 62373280, Natural Science Foundation of Tianjin (No. 25JCYBJC00600) and STI 2030-Major Projects (2021ZD0200500).

References

1. Dadebayev, D., Goh, W.W., Tan, E.X.: EEG-based emotion recognition: review of commercial EEG devices and machine learning techniques. King Saud Univ.-Comput. Inf. Sci. **34**(7), 4385–4401 (2022)
2. Andrea, B., Franceschiello, B., Murray, M.M.: Electroencephalography. Curr. Biol. **29**(3), R80–R85 (2019)
3. Li, J., et al.: Identification of autism spectrum disorder based on electroencephalography: a systematic review. Comput. Biol. Med. **170**, 108075 (2024)

4. Wan, Z., Yang, R., Huang, M., Zeng, N., Liu, X.: A review on transfer learning in EEG signal analysis. Neurocomputing **421**, 1–14 (2021)
5. Jayaram, V., Alamgir, M., Altun, Y., Scholkopf, B., Grosse-Wentrup, M.: Transfer learning in brain-computer interfaces. IEEE Comput. Intell. Mag. **11**(1), 20–31 (2016)
6. Hu, W., Jiang, G., Han, J., Li, X., Xie, P.: Regional-asymmetric adaptive graph convolutional neural network for diagnosis of autism in children with resting-state EEG. IEEE Trans. Neural Syst. Rehabil. Eng. **32**, 200–211 (2024)
7. Lin, S., Fan, C., Han, D., Jia, Z., Peng, Y., Kwong, S.: HATNet: EEG-based hybrid attention transfer learning network for train driver state detection. IEEE Trans. Cybern. **55**(5) (2025)
8. Gao, D., et al.: A multiscale feature fusion network based on attention mechanism for motor imagery EEG decoding. Appl. Soft Comput. **151**, 111129 (2024)
9. Liu, S., Wang, Z., An, Y., Li, B., Wang, X., Zhang, Y.: DA-CapsNet: A multi-branch capsule network based on adversarial domain adaption for cross-subject EEG emotion recognition. Knowl. Based. Syst. **283**, 111137 (2024)
10. Wang, J., Ning, X., Xu, W., Li, Y., Jia, Z., Lin, Y.: Multi-source selective graph domain adaptation network for cross-subject EEG emotion recognition. Neural Netw. **80**, 106742 (2024)
11. Zhou, R., et al.: EEGMatch: learning with incomplete labels for semisupervised EEG-based cross-subject emotion recognition. IEEE Trans. Neural Netw. Learn. Syst., 18 November 2024. Early Access. https://doi.org/10.1109/TNNLS.2024.3493425
12. Wang, Y., Zhang, B., Tang, Y.: DMMR: Cross-subject domain generalization for EEG-based emotion recognition via denoising mixed mutual reconstruction. Proc. AAAI Conf. Artif. Intell. **38**(1), 628–636 (2024)
13. Chen, B., Chen, C.P., Zhang, T.: GDDN: Graph domain disentanglement network for generalizable EEG emotion recognition. IEEE Trans. Affect. Comput. **15**(3), 1739–1753 (2024)
14. Li, W., Fan, L., Shao, S., Song, A.: Generalized contrastive partial label learning for cross-subject EEG-based emotion recognition. IEEE Trans. Instrum. Meas. **73**, 1–11 (2024)
15. Ma, B.Q., Li, H., Zheng, W.L., Lu, B.L.: Reducing the subject variability of EEG signals with adversarial domain generalization. In: Gedeon, T., Wong, K., Lee, M. (eds.) Neural Information Processing. ICONIP 2019. Lecture Notes in Computer Science, vol. 11953, pp. 30–42. Springer, Cham (2019). https://doi.org/10.1007/978-3-030-36708-4_3
16. Wang, Z., Wang, Y., Hu, C., Yin, Z., Song, Y.: Transformers for EEG-based emotion recognition: a hierarchical spatial information learning model. IEEE Sens. J. **22**(5), 4359–4368 (2022)
17. Li, R., et al.: MTLFuseNet: a novel emotion recognition model based on deep latent feature fusion of EEG signals and multi-task learning. Knowl. Based. Syst. **276**, 110756 (2023)
18. Wang, Y., Qiu, S., Ma, X., He, H.: A prototype-based SPD matrix network for domain adaptation EEG emotion recognition. Pattern Recognit. **110**, 107626 (2021)
19. Li, W., Hou, B., Li, X., Qiu, Z., Peng, B., Tian, Y.: TMLP+SRDANN: a domain adaptation method for EEG-based emotion recognition. Meas. **207**, 112379 (2023)
20. Ganin, Y., et al.: Domain-adversarial training of neural networks. J. Mach. Learn. Res. **17**(59), 1–35 (2016)
21. Koelstra, S., et al.: DEAP: A database for emotion analysis using physiological signals. IEEE Trans. Affect. Comput. **3**(1), 18–31 (2012)
22. Van der Maaten, L., Hinton, G.: Visualizing data using t-SNE. J. Mach. Learn. Res. **9**(11), 2579–2605 (2008)
23. Zheng, W.L., Lu, B.L.: Investigating critical frequency bands and channels for EEG-based emotion recognition with deep neural networks. IEEE Trans. Auton. Ment. Dev. **7**(3), 162–175 (2015)

24. An, Y., et al.: Cross-subject EEG emotion recognition based on interconnected dynamic domain adaptation. In: ICASSP 2024–2024 IEEE International Conference on Acoustics, Speech, and Signal Processing (ICASSP), pp. 12981–12985. IEEE (2024)
25. Zhu, L., Xu, M., Huang, A., Zhang, J., Tan, X.: Multiple class transfer learning framework with source label adaptive correction for EEG emotion recognition. Biomed. Signal Process. Control **104**, 107536 (2025)

Beyond Accuracy: A Review of Model and Data Trustworthiness in Audio-Visual Depression Recognition

Yuchen Pan[1], Hongxun Yao[1(✉)], Wuxin Shen[1], and Lang He[2]

[1] Harbin Institute of Technology, Harbin 150001, China
h.yao@hit.edu.cn
[2] Xi'an University of Posts and Communications, Xi'an 710121, China

Abstract. Depression is a pervasive global mental health disorder with significant societal impact. While AI-based audio-visual assessment tools offer a promising, objective, and scalable alternative to traditional diagnostics, their translation to clinical practice is blocked by a critical hurdle: **trust**. These tools must be demonstrably reliable, fair, explainable, and private. This paper provides a comprehensive review of the automated depression recognition field, uniquely framed through the lens of Trustworthy AI. We first survey the primary technical frameworks from unimodal handcrafted features to end-to-end multimodal fusion, establishing the technical foundation. We then conduct an in-depth analysis of the core pillars of trustworthiness, including **explainability** (moving from post-hoc visualization to interpretable-by-design methods), **reliability and fairness** (analyzing Uncertainty Quantification and the challenge of equitable reliability), and the non-trivial challenge of **privacy** (surveying approaches from intermediate features, Federated Learning, and hardware-level Deep Optics). We conclude that a holistic focus on trustworthiness, including generalization, multimodal explainability, and the privacy-efficacy trade-off, is the central challenge and the most critical direction for the field's future.

Keywords: Depression Recognition · Multimodal · Trustworthy Artificial Intelligence · Explainability · Privacy Preserving

1 Introduction

Depression disorder represents a significant public health challenge with profound implications for individual well-being and societal productivity. It is recognized as one of the most pervasive and debilitating mental health disorders globally. According to the World Health Organization (WHO), depression affects over 5.7% of people worldwide; furthermore, recent data reveals a concerning 28% growth rate in severe depression cases, manifesting a notable increase in incidence. Nevertheless, a mere 10% of afflicted individuals actively seek medical intervention [1]. The principal impediment is often the pervasive "stigma"

H. Liu et al. (Eds.): CEI 2025, CCIS 2881, pp. 31–56, 2026.
https://doi.org/10.1007/978-981-95-9493-1_3

associated with this condition, which can lead to fear of social judgment, discrimination, and a reluctance to self-identify. Furthermore, traditional diagnostic methods often rely on subjective patient self-reporting and clinical interviews. This process can be time-consuming, resource-intensive, and limited by the availability of trained mental health professionals, highlighting a critical need for more accessible and objective assessment tools.

In recent years, scholars have shown increasing interest in the fusion of AI healthcare, propelled by the rapid advancement of multimodal algorithms and deep learning-based technologies. Among these, the analysis of facial expressions and vocal patterns has emerged as a particularly promising avenue. The human face is a primary visual channel for non-verbal behavioral communication, broadcasting a rich stream of affective signals through muscle movements, gaze patterns, and expression dynamics [102]. Similarly, acoustic patterns offer powerful, language-independent insights. While linguistic content (*what* is said) is a powerful indicator, the non-verbal and para-verbal signals (*how* it is said) provide a rich, parallel stream of information, often considered as acoustic signals [132]. In depressive disorders, these signals are often characteristically altered, manifesting as blunted affect, reduced expressivity, or depressed facial postures and monotone vocal characteristics.

AI-driven solutions that can capture and interpret these subtle cues possess the potential to enhance the precision of clinical assessment and broaden access to early mental health support. They can offer objective, quantifiable metrics to supplement clinical judgment, potentially facilitating earlier and more accurate diagnosis. By enabling accessible, private, and automated screening (e.g., via a smartphone app), they can help mitigate the apprehension and societal stigma that deter individuals from seeking help. Concurrently, AI-enabled digital monitoring equips healthcare providers with more comprehensive, longitudinal patient data from naturalistic settings, tracking subtle changes over time and thereby augmenting the quality and personalization of treatment.

Despite this promise, the development of depression recognition algorithms faces significant hurdles, whether relying on audio signals [27,55,134], visual data [33,56,85], or audio-visual solutions [57,79]. The medical field and the public at large place a considerable and necessary emphasis on ensuring privacy and reliability. The sensitive nature of both biometric data and mental health information creates a significant ethical and technical challenge. Consequently, there is a growing demand for innovative approaches that can simultaneously execute depression recognition while safeguarding user privacy, and the given output should be explainable, rather than only a prediction number. The genesis of depression recognition as a substantial research issue can be traced back to the Audio-Visual Emotion Challenge and Workshop (AVEC). This competition, held over several years, featured sub-challenges related to audio-visual depression recognition in 2013 [112], 2014 [111], 2016 [110], 2017 [95], and 2019 [94]. In 2013 and 2014, the dataset was composed of video recordings of participants for depression recognition, first in a long and mixed interviewing task in 2013, which was then categorized into *Northwind* and *Freeform* tasks in 2014.

In 2016 and 2017, the competition used the Distress Analysis Interview Corpus - Wizard of Oz (DAIC-WOZ) [23], which was extended to the Extended Distress Analysis Interview Corpus (E-DAIC) [94] in 2019 with more samples. This series of challenges clearly illustrates the roadmap: in the earlier editions, recognition predominantly relied on complete facial images. However, the organizers adopted a heightened focus on privacy protection from 2016. Consequently, the DAIC dataset provided only essential biometric facial information, such as VGG facial features as visual data, thereby substituting full facial images. Similar to the AVEC data collection and organization, there have been several other open-source datasets that contribute to this task, such as D-Vlog [125], LMVD [31], and CMDC [139].

This review paper surveys the landscape of audio-visual based depression recognition, navigating its core methodologies and critical challenges. We place a particular focus on the components of Trustworthy AI, especially model explainability and privacy risk. We begin in Sect. 2 by examining the primary technical frameworks, from traditional handcrafted feature extraction to modern deep learning-based spatiotemporal and fusion models. In Sect. 3, we delve into the crucial challenge of model explainability, reliability, and fairness, which are vital components for clinical trust and adoption. Section 4 addresses the contemporary and non-trivial concern of privacy, exploring methods that attempt to balance diagnostic efficacy with robust data protection. Finally, Sect. 5 concludes the paper by summarizing the key challenges and outlining promising directions for future research in this impactful domain.

2 Audio-Visual Depression Recognition

The automated depression recognition from behavioral and acoustic cues is a fundamentally multimodal problem. This section reviews the primary technical frameworks for this task, which are typically divided into three domains: analysis of the audio signal, analysis of the visual signal, and methods for fusing these two modalities.

2.1 Audio-Based Recognition

Research on speech-based depression recognition has progressed from handcrafted descriptors to end-to-end deep representations, with a growing emphasis on attention, self-supervision, and multimodal fusion. Early work, grounded in the clinical sign of psychomotor retardation, treated depression as an altered coordination of the vocal tract. These approaches captured slowed and less synchronized articulation via articulatory trajectory estimates, acoustic-phonetic descriptors, and prosody [68,119]. Benchmark systems combined such features with traditional learners, including Support Vector Regression (SVR), Gaussian Mixture Models (GMM), and decision trees, to establish strong baselines for both classification and severity regression [111,112].

The shift to deep models introduced architectures like CNN-LSTM stacks, which jointly model local time-frequency patterns and long-range temporal dynamics, improving over shallow, hand-crafted pipelines [60]. Hybrid approaches subsequently combined learned and engineered cues, often using PCA or sparsity for compactness and generalization [29,66]. Concurrently, methodological studies addressed critical issues of aggregation, elicitation, and dataset reliability, such as using ℓ_p-norm pooling for evidence integration [77], optimizing speech-input length for speaker-independent inference [96], and auditing demographic or severity balance [127] to improve generalizability.

From 2020 onward, attention mechanisms and hierarchical designs became central. Examples include hierarchical attention transfer with attention autoencoders, and self-attention 3D log-Mel hybrids whose concatenated features are pooled and fed to SVR [132,133]. Time-domain architectures using dilated convolutions enlarged receptive fields, while efficient channel attention enhanced sensitivity to depression-related cues [6].

To mitigate challenges in small-data and cost-sensitive settings, some studies fused pretrained Speech Recognition (SR) and Speech Emotion Recognition (SER) embeddings in a hierarchical pipeline, which first classifies and then regresses severity, leveraging complementary vocal and affective information [17]. Parallel efforts emphasized robustness and regularization, alongside multi-resolution modulation-filtered cochleagrams to strengthen temporal modeling [82,88]. Traditional speech-technology baselines also remained informative, including i-vector/SVDA frameworks and MFCC-based RNNs, which provide competitive and interpretable points of comparison [69,93].

Recent work continues to push toward raw-waveform end-to-end learning and refined temporal-frequency fusion, exemplified by WavDepressionNet [76], TTFNet [10], attention-guided bi-directional models [55], and dense coordinate channel attention networks [134]. Meanwhile, self-supervised embeddings are being used to improve label efficiency. Emerging studies are also enriching acoustic data with transcribed speech, affect, and personality traits for severity estimation, signaling a shift toward an *acoustics-semantics-individual traits* paradigm [26,128].

Overall, the field has evolved from MFCC/prosody/articulatory proxies to attention-augmented representations, from shallow classifiers to hierarchical, multi-branch networks, and from preprocessed, handcrafted acoustic feature design to the end-to-end pipeline. With the recent progress of Large Language Models (LLMs), audio-based methods are also beginning to integrate semantic content with acoustic cues. However, audio-based depression recognition still faces open challenges in cross-corpus generalization, elicitation protocols, explainability, privacy, and principled fusion with lexical and person-centric information.

2.2 Visual-Based Recognition

In visual depression recognition approaches, the extraction of facial features encompasses two categories: handcrafted features and deep features, both of which have been extended to capture temporal dynamics.

Handcrafted features are typically designed by researchers who leverage domain knowledge, employing specialized operators to process images. Examples include geometric features (distances and angles between facial landmarks), appearance features (Local Binary Patterns (LBP) or Histogram of Oriented Gradients (HOG)), and specific metrics like the frequency and duration of Action Units (AUs) [32,38,116]. However, these features are often customized for specific low-level image patterns or for general-purpose facial recognition. Consequently, when applied to depression recognition, generic feature extraction algorithms may produce suboptimal results. While designing new operators specifically for depression is an option, it presents substantial challenges. Furthermore, even when combined with deep learning models [99,101], handcrafted features require a distinct pre-processing step. The necessary parameters must be manually set, making them difficult to integrate into an auto-differentiable, end-to-end learning framework.

Deep feature extractors possess the capability to autonomously learn particular patterns from extensive datasets. Typically, these are deep learning models, such as pre-trained CNN or ViT image encoders, paired with a regression head to predict depression severity. Early approaches applied 2D CNNs (e.g., VGG, ResNet) to single-frame facial images. These models were usually pretrained on large-scale face datasets to obtain basic facial representations and then fine-tuned on depression-related datasets to learn task-relevant features [30,136]. A major limitation of such static 2D models is their neglect of temporal information. For example, a person might exhibit a brief distressed expression in response to an unpleasant scene, but this may not be enduring. Individuals with depression, however, tend to maintain more long-term characteristic facial expressions. Integrating continuous video frames thus provides crucial temporal capability [33,56,114]. Beyond motion, facial videos can also be a source of physiological signals; notably, remote photoplethysmography (rPPG) has been studied as an effective signal for depression recognition [7,114].

In summary, visual-based depression recognition approaches can be divided into two main categories:

1. Employing handcrafted spatiotemporal feature extraction operators. In this approach, features are first extracted and then used for depression recognition via statistical analysis [37,116] or a deep learning model [101,126]. This branch is usually pretrain-free, as the expert-based feature extractor is the main component and the learning model often serves only as a data regressor.
2. Using end-to-end deep models. This category includes 2D-CNNs or 3D-models combined with spatiotemporal models and attention mechanisms. These models are often pretrained on large-scale facial and dynamic video datasets for the feature extractor, then fine-tuned on depression-specific datasets [3,85].

In this branch, the feature encoder and the regression head are learned simultaneously and automatically.

The video-based approach still faces several challenges. Some subtle micro-expressions related to depression require high-quality video capture, which can be costly for real-world deployment. Furthermore, illumination and head pose can cause significant changes in visual features, making model robustness in varied environments a persistent challenge. Finally, as will be discussed in the following sections, explainability and privacy remain critical concerns.

2.3 Audio-Visual Fusion

Given that both vocal and facial channels carry complementary affective information, a logical progression is to fuse them. Fusion models aim to create a more robust and accurate representation than either modality could provide alone. The fusion method is a critical design choice. According to the typical taxonomy, fusion strategies can be categorized as feature-level, decision-level, and model-level. However, it should be noted that the boundaries between these strategies are not always distinct.

Feature-Level (Early Fusion): In this approach, features from audio and visual streams are combined at the beginning of the pipeline. For example, hand-crafted audio features (MFCCs, Low-level descriptors (LLDs)) and visual features (AUs, facial landmarks) are concatenated into a single, large vector. This vector is then fed into a single classifier [4,22,40]. While simple, this method can be problematic as the modalities have different time scales and statistical properties, and concatenation can be a naive way of combining them which is challenging on the information discovery in single modality.
Decision-Level (Late Fusion): This method involves training separate, modality-specific models (e.g., one model for audio, one for video). The outputs or decisions from these models (e.g., their predicted depression scores) are then combined at the very end, often through simple averaging, a weighted sum, or a final integrated regression head [59,98,109,123]. This is a robust and common baseline, but it typically fails to capture any complex, non-linear interactions between the modalities (e.g., the synchrony of a smiling expression and a laugh).
Model-Level (Hybrid Fusion): This is the most complex and powerful approach, representing the focus of modern deep learning. Here, fusion occurs within the architecture of the model itself, allowing the model to learn complex intermodal relationships. This category includes methods like Cross-Modal Attention, where one modality's representation is used to interact with and attend to the most relevant parts of the other modality [12,28,46,83]. For instance, the audio model might learn to pay more attention to the visual features of the mouth region when speech is detected. Multimodal Transformers, which are now state-of-the-art, convert both audio and visual features into a common latent space (often represented as tokens) and process them jointly, allowing for deep, complex, and temporally-aware fusion. This approach is also a promising avenue for

Table 1. A systematic comparison of recent automated depression recognition methods on the AVEC dataset test sets. **M.**: Modality. **A/V**: Audio/Visual. **+T**: Includes text modality. **Dev set**: Reported on the development set.

(a) AVEC 2013

M.	Method	MAE↓	RMSE↓
A	AVEC 2013 Baseline [112]	10.35	14.12
	Two-Stage [59]	10.88	14.49
	PLSR [67]	9.14	11.19
	DCNN [29]	8.20	10.00
	Lp-norm [77]	7.48	9.79
	SAN-DCNN [133]	7.38	9.65
	Dis2DR (A) [83]	7.32	9.56
	FVCM [17]	7.32	8.73
	AGBiTNet [55]	7.29	9.45
	MFDS-VAN [87]	7.29	9.43
	MAFF [78]	7.14	9.50
	TTFNet [10]	7.08	8.93
	TDCA-Net [6]	6.90	9.22
	DCCANet [134]	6.78	8.47
	TFCAV [75]	6.26	8.32
	WavDepressionNet [76]	6.14	8.20
	DSDD [79]	6.09	8.27
	GMM [119] (Dev set)	5.75	7.42
V	AVEC 2013 Baseline [112]	10.88	13.61
	Sparse Coding [116]	8.22	10.27
	CCA [44]	7.86	9.72
	AD-DCNN [138]	7.58	9.82
	DPFV [32]	7.55	9.20
	RNN-C3D [3]	7.37	9.28
	MAFF [78]	7.32	8.97
	OpticalDR [84]	7.53	8.48
	VLDN-LSTM [108]	7.04	8.93
	DJ-LDML [137]	6.63	8.37
	DLGA-CNN [30]	6.59	8.39
	C3D-GAP [62]	6.40	8.26
	rPPG [7]	6.43	8.01
	LQGDNet [99]	6.38	8.20
	CNN-DDL [63]	6.30	8.25
	DepressNet [136]	6.20	8.28
	DAER [81]	6.28	8.13
	LMB [126]	6.28	7.54
	MDN [65]	6.24	7.55
	Behavior Primitives [101]	6.16	8.10
	STA-DRN [85]	6.15	7.98
	MTDAN [129]	6.14	8.08
	DMSN [16]	6.14	7.66
	LMTformer [36]	6.12	7.75
	Depressioner [72]	6.12	7.49
	EGDC [5]	6.09	8.05
	SE-TOV [80]	6.09	7.42
	PRA-Net [58]	6.08	7.59
	HMHN [51]	6.05	7.38
	LMS-VDR [124]	6.04	7.68
	MM-CRN [54]	6.04	7.61
	Dis2DR (V) [83]	6.04	7.50
	CFGMamba [56]	6.01	7.59
	MSN [64]	5.98	7.90
	Hi-Lo [131]	5.97	7.36
	Two-Stream [61]	5.96	7.97
	LSCAformer [34]	5.89	7.69
	LDBM [114]	5.71	6.99
	PTN [73]	5.62	7.36
	Depressformer [33]	5.49	7.47
	MLM-EOE [52]	5.49	6.84
	DepressionMLP [74]	5.43	7.49
	STE-Mamba [53]	5.27	7.26
	DSDD [79]	5.12	7.21
A-V	A-V System [41]	9.09	11.19
	MHH + PLSR [13]	-	10.62
	Fusion [67]	8.72	10.96
	CCA [44]	7.68	9.44
	FedDAAM [35]	6.78	8.61
	Two-Stage [59]	6.75	8.29
	TMFE-GFN [19]	6.60	9.00
	MAFF [78]	6.14	8.16
	AVA-DepressNet [86]	6.23	7.99
	FDFNet [46]	6.22	7.58
	Dis2DR (A-V) [83]	6.12	7.97
	MFMamba [57]	6.11	7.05
	VLDSP-TAP-MFB [109]	5.38	6.83
	DSDD [79]	5.19	6.48
	STE-Mamba [53]	5.08	6.94

(b) AVEC 2014

M.	Method	MAE↓	RMSE↓
A	AVEC 2014 Baseline [111]	10.04	12.57
	PLSR [39]	9.10	11.30
	SRI audio system [68]	8.83	11.10
	DCNN [29]	8.19	10.00
	Lp-norm [77]	8.02	9.66
	SAN-DCNN [133]	7.94	9.57
	MAFF [78]	7.65	9.13
	Dis2DR (A) [83]	7.63	9.28
	TFCAV [75]	7.49	9.25
	MFDS-VAN [87]	7.33	9.44
	AGBiTNet [55]	7.30	9.47
	TTFNet [10]	7.13	8.96
	TDCA-Net [6]	7.08	8.90
	i-vector + SVDA [69]	6.99	8.90
	FVCM [17]	6.80	8.82
	WavDepressionNet [76]	6.60	8.61
	DSDD [79]	6.22	8.14
	DCCANet [134]	6.17	7.54
V	AVEC 2014 Baseline [111]	8.86	10.86
	PLSR [39]	8.44	10.50
	AD-DCNN [138]	7.47	9.55
	OpticalDR [84]	7.89	8.82
	RNN-C3D [3]	7.22	9.20
	DPFV [32]	7.21	9.01
	VLDN-LSTM [108]	6.86	8.78
	ERBMA-Net [45]	6.80	8.18
	MAFF [78]	6.43	8.60
	rPPG [7]	6.57	8.49
	C3D-GAP [62]	6.59	8.31
	DJ-LDML [137]	6.59	8.30
	DLGA-CNN [30]	6.51	8.30
	DepressNet [136]	6.21	8.39
	MTDAN [129]	6.35	7.93
	Two-Stream [61]	6.20	7.94
	DeepFusion [9]	6.16	8.13
	CNN-DDL [63]	6.15	8.23
	DAER [81]	6.14	8.07
	LMB [126]	6.14	7.58
	LQGDNet [99]	6.08	7.84
	MDN [65]	6.06	7.65
	LMTformer [36]	6.05	7.97
	PRA-Net [58]	6.04	7.98
	HMHN [51]	6.01	7.60
	Depressioner [72]	6.01	7.56
	STA-DRN [85]	6.00	7.75
	MM-CRN [54]	5.99	7.59
	LMS-VDR [124]	5.98	7.59
	EGDC [5]	5.94	7.98
	Behavior Primitives [101]	5.95	7.15
	FacialPulse [113]	5.92	7.60
	Dis2DR (V) [83]	5.92	7.09
	LSCAformer [34]	5.91	7.55
	CFGMamba [56]	5.96	7.52
	SE-TOV [80]	5.87	7.39
	Hi-Lo [131]	5.85	7.23
	MSN [64]	5.82	7.61
	TSFFM [47]	5.75	7.91
	DMSN [16]	5.69	7.50
	DepressionMLP [74]	5.63	7.27
	Depressformer [33]	5.56	7.22
	DSDD [79]	5.52	6.80
	MLM-EOE [52]	5.51	7.22
	PTN [73]	5.41	7.12
	STE-Mamba [53]	5.38	7.24
	LDBM [114]	5.36	6.93
	DepMGNN [120]	4.99	6.28
A-V	AVEC 2014 Baseline [111]	7.89	9.89
	Fusion System [89]	8.99	10.82
	Model Fusion [98]	8.33	10.43
	Fisher Vector [37]	8.40	10.25
	PLSR fusion [39]	8.30	10.26
	LSTM-RNN [8]	7.91	9.98
	CCA [43]	7.69	9.61
	Meta knowledge [42]	7.10	9.19
	TMFE-GFN [19]	7.05	9.45
	Feature selection [25]	-	8.99
	FedDAAM [35]	6.77	8.59
	GMM + ELM [118]	6.31	8.12
	PLSR + LR [40]	6.14	7.43
	M-BAM [12]	5.78	7.47
	Dis2DR (A-V) [83]	5.45	6.61
	AVA-DepressNet [86]	5.32	6.83
	FAU-GF [21]	5.26	6.80
	MAFF [78]	5.21	7.03
	FDFNet [46]	5.21	6.49
	MFMamba [57]	5.16	6.71
	STE-Mamba [53]	5.10	6.77
	VLDSP-TAP-MFB [109]	5.03	6.16
	DSDD [79]	4.89	5.99

(c) DAIC-WOZ (E-DAIC)

M.	Method	MAE↓	RMSE↓
A	DAIC-WOZ Baseline [95]	5.72	7.78
	E-DAIC Baseline [94] (E-DAIC)	-	8.19
	CNN-GAN [115]	7.32	8.56
	Acoustic + RF [127] (E-DAIC)	5.77	6.78
	AFN [90]	5.67	6.55
	Acoustic + LR [127]	5.49	7.18
	DEPA [128] (Dev set)	5.48	6.31
	STFN [27] (E-DAIC)	5.38	6.29
	STFN [27]	5.38	6.36
	GSM [117] (Dev set)	5.36	6.74
	LLD + Fisher Vector [105]	5.30	6.34
	STE-Mamba [53]	5.27	6.79
	Random Forest [107]	5.22	6.17
	LSTM [2]	5.13	6.50
	TTFNet [10]	5.09	6.01
	TTFNet [10] (E-DAIC)	5.00	5.76
	Dis2DR (A) [83]	4.88	5.60
	STE-Mamba [53] (E-DAIC)	4.80	5.80
	DSDD [79]	4.62	5.61
	AGBiTNet [55]	4.27	5.35
	MFDS-VAN [87]	4.27	5.34
	HATN [132]	4.20	5.51
	MLAtt [92] (Dev set, E-DAIC)	-	5.11
	REPT [103]	4.11	4.94
	EmoAudioNet [82]	-	4.14
	HCAG [71] (+T)	2.94	3.80
V	DAIC-WOZ Baseline [95]	6.12	6.97
	E-DAIC Baseline [94]	-	8.01
	GSM [117] (Dev set)	5.88	7.13
	REPT [103]	5.36	6.72
	STE-Mamba [53] (E-DAIC)	4.89	6.28
	HOG-PCA [104]	4.89	6.23
	FDR + LDA [91]	4.64	5.98
	DepArt-Net [18]	4.61	5.78
	STE-Mamba [53]	4.58	5.99
	Dis2DR (V) [83]	4.51	5.88
	Behaviour-based [102] (Dev set)	4.37	5.84
	MLAtt [92] (Dev set, E-DAIC)	-	5.38
	DepressionMLP [74]	4.11	5.03
	DSDD [79]	4.09	5.40
	PTN [73]	3.84	5.08
A-V	DAIC-WOZ Baseline [95]	5.66	7.05
	E-DAIC Baseline [94]	-	6.37
	GSM [117] (Dev set)	5.52	6.62
	ANEW + GSR [15] (+T)	5.30	6.52
	STE-Mamba [53]	5.18	6.24
	DCNN-DNN-1 [122] (+T)	5.16	5.97
	STE-Mamba [53] (E-DAIC)	5.05	6.21
	AVA-DepressNet [86]	4.62	5.78
	Dis2DR (A-V) [83]	4.69	5.49
	FPT-Former [48] (E-DAIC)	4.58	4.80
	FDFNet [46] (E-DAIC)	4.41	5.10
	DCNN-DNN-2 [123] (+T)	4.36	5.40
	FDFNet [46]	4.25	5.34
	Two-stage [14] (+T)	3.98	5.11
	Topic Modeling [22] (+T)	3.96	4.99
	FAU-GF [21] (E-DAIC)	3.77	4.95
	FedDAAM [35]	3.68	4.71
	C-CNN [28] (Dev set)	3.67	-
	DSDD [79]	3.53	4.76

integrating semantic (linguistic) information from LLMs [20,106,130]. This could help address performance degradation caused by language differences. However, the integration of LLMs with behavioral and acoustic cues is still under development.

Multimodal approaches represent the main trend in depression recognition, often combining state-of-the-art findings from both audio and visual-based methods. However, the main challenges revolve around high computational cost, the need for high-quality and complete multimodal data, and the need for explainable predictions, especially regarding cross-modal interactions.

Finally, these various approaches, from single-modality handcrafted features to deep multimodal fusion models, are systematically cataloged and their performance comprehensively compared in Table 1.

3 Model Trustworthiness: Explainability, Reliability, and Fairness Depression Recognition

Can we trust the model's output? Is it explainable, reliable, and fair in its judgments?

The adoption of complex, deep learning models in a high-stakes clinical domain like mental health diagnostics is contingent not only on their accuracy but also on their transparency and reliability. For a clinician to trust and act upon an AI-generated assessment, the model's "black box" nature must be addressed. This need has given rise to a focus on Explainable Artificial Intelligence (XAI), which seeks to render model decisions comprehensible to human users. In the context of audio-visual depression recognition, this translates to a critical question: Which specific cues is the model using to arrive at its depression score, and do these cues align with clinical knowledge?

This section reviews the key pillars of building trust in these models: 1) post-hoc explainability, 2) interpretable-by-design models, and 3) the quantification of reliability and fairness.

3.1 Post-hoc Visualization and Saliency Methods

The most common approach to XAI in this domain is to apply post-hoc visualization techniques, which generate saliency or attention maps. These methods, such as Class Activation Mapping (CAM) [135] and its derivatives Grad-CAM [97], identify which parts of the input data most strongly influenced the model's final decision.

Several studies [3,65,85,136] have endeavored to use these techniques to visualize the features learned by deep learning depression recognition models. For visual data, this typically produces heatmaps that highlight specific facial regions. These efforts have successfully demonstrated that models learn to focus on clinically-relevant areas, such as the periorbital (eyes, eyebrows) or perioral (mouth) regions, to identify significant facial actions associated with depression. For instance, Fig. 1 shows the visualization results from STA-DRN [85] as a typical example of this analysis. Similarly, for the audio modality, attention weights can reveal which speech segments or acoustic events (e.g., pauses, specific word-level prosody) most contributed to the final score [76,78].

However, these visualization methods have a significant limitation. While they excel at answering where the model is looking, they provide little insight into why or what it has learned. A heatmap might highlight a key feature or region, but it cannot, by itself, explain the intricate relationship between a lack of smile dynamics or a specific vocal pitch, and the model's depression score. As such, a more nuanced understanding of the relationship between these regions and the model's reasoning remains an area of limited development. This refinement is essential to move beyond simple model validation and provide genuine, actionable insights for clinical advancement.

3.2 Interpretable-By-Design with Feature Disentanglement

A more recent and complex path to enhancing model explainability is through feature disentanglement. Rather than treating the model as a black box to be explained later, this approach aims to build models whose internal representations are inherently meaningful and separated by concept. In the context of multimodal depression recognition, this is a particularly powerful but challenging idea. An individual's audio-visual stream contains a massive entanglement of information:

1. **Identity**: The unique shape of a person's face or the fundamental pitch of their voice. This includes attributes such as gender and other personal identity information.
2. **Content**: The linguistic information being spoken, which is often independent of the acoustic features.
3. **Affect/Sentiment**: The emotional and physical state of the speaker (e.g., depression, fatigue, joy).

A robust depression model should, ideally, be invariant to identity and content, focusing only on the affective cues. Disentanglement aims to force the model to learn separate, non-overlapping representations for these factors. Recent research has begun to explore modality-level disentanglement [46,70,83], but this remains a nascent field.

The study of the interaction mechanism between modalities is even more scarce. A truly explainable system would not only disentangle features within each modality (e.g., separate speech content from vocal prosody) but also explain the fusion process itself. For example, how does the model learn to weigh the information from a flat, monotone voice against the information from a simultaneous subtle facial expression? In Dis2DR [83], this question is answered to a certain extent by revealing the modality homogeneous and heterogeneous mechanisms of depression recognition. Figure 2 shows an example of such research,

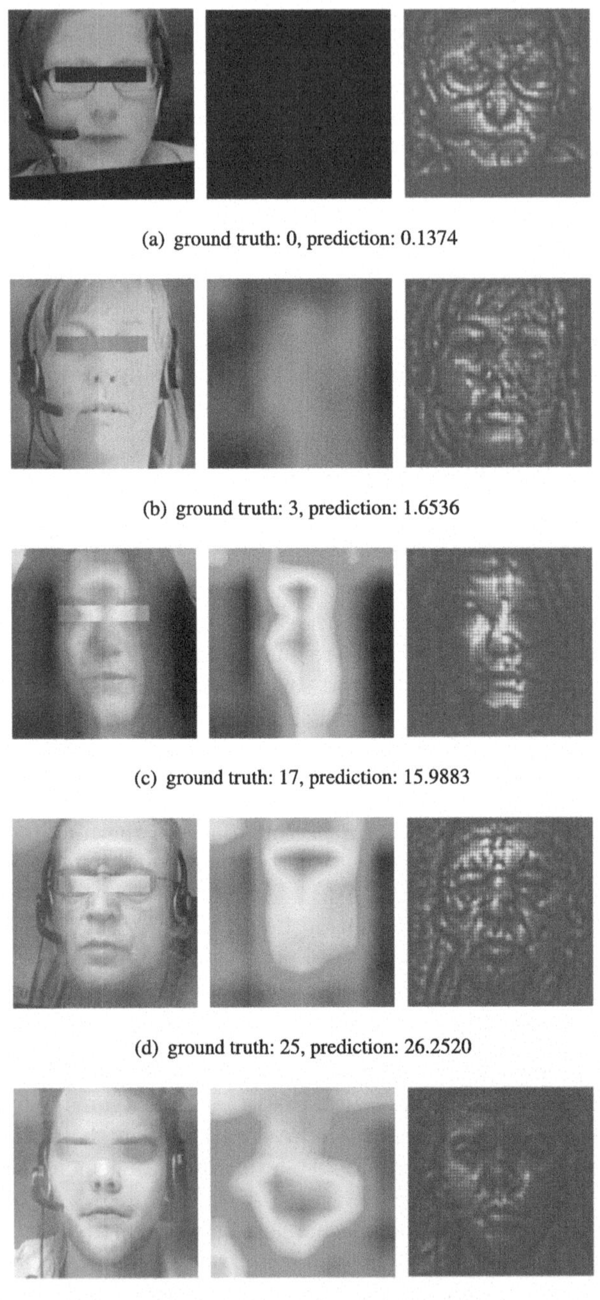

Fig. 1. Visualization analysis from STA-DRN [85]. *(Left)* CAM highlight broad facial regions contributing to the depression score (red indicates strong activation, blue indicates weak). *(Right)* Guided backpropagation maps reveal the specific pixel-level features (e.g., edges around the eyes and mouth, shown in yellow) that the model relies on within those regions.

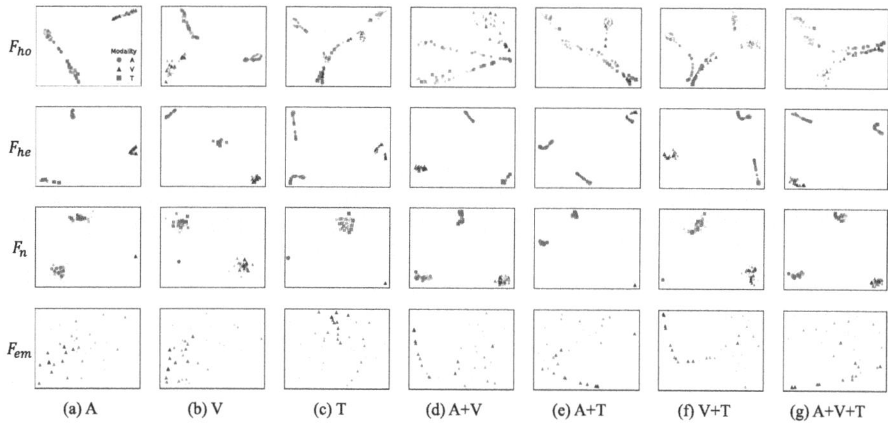

Fig. 2. Visualization of disentangled features from Dis2DR [83]. The model learns to separate modality-heterogeneous patterns from modality-homogeneous patterns across different modalities.

visualizing the disentangled features. The experimental results indicate that the text and visual modalities are the most crucial inputs, with the homogeneous feature (F_{ho}) space demonstrating a critical sensitivity to their absence. While F_{ho} effectively learns identical cross-modal representations that correlate strongly with depression severity, manifesting as tight clustering for severe cases and divergence for mild cases, the heterogeneous feature (F_{he}) space provides superior robustness. Specifically, F_{he} maintains proper representations even when a modality is missing, suggesting a powerful capability for handling incomplete data, while a high entanglement between audio and text modalities allows audio to implicitly compensate for missing textual information in the F_{ho} representation. However, research on this novel topic remains limited. Answering these questions is the next frontier for XAI and is crucial for understanding the complex, multimodal signature of depression.

3.3 Reliability and Fairness in Uncertainty Quantification

A distinct but complementary component of trustworthiness is predictive reliability. A model that provides a score without expressing its own confidence is clinically incomplete. A clinician needs to know if a depression score of "15" is a confident "15 ± 2" or a highly uncertain "15 ± 10". This is the domain of Uncertainty Quantification (UQ). UQ is vital as it provides clinicians with the necessary confidence measure for the model's prediction, enabling them to safely override uncertain assessments and preventing the model from being overconfident in a potentially life-altering diagnosis like severe depression.

Recently, achieving reliable depression predictions through UQ has attracted increasing attention [11,49,50]. The goal is to produce not just a single-point estimate (e.g., a score) but a valid, calibrated range or confidence interval. Methods such as Conformal Prediction [49] are gaining traction as they can provide such intervals with theoretical guarantees on their coverage.

Furthermore, it is crucial to investigate the algorithmic fairness of UQ. Fairness is paramount because diagnostic bias (e.g., against specific demographics like gender, age, or ethnicity) can lead to systematic underdiagnosis or misdiagnosis, denying vulnerable populations necessary care and worsening existing health disparities. Thus UQ in depression recognition should not only provide statistically valid confidence intervals globally but also ensure fair coverage rates across different demographic groups. Current UQ methods often produce disparate coverage rates across groups. This can lead to unfair predictions where majority groups are over-covered, resulting in excessively broad, clinically unhelpful intervals. While minority groups are under-covered, yielding dangerously overconfident and misleadingly narrow intervals. This is a subtle but dangerous form of bias, as the average reliability across the entire dataset may appear high, masking these severe group-level disparities. The work on Fair Uncertainty Quantification (FUQ) addresses this by introducing concepts like the Equal Opportunity of Coverage (EOC) [50]. This approach uses group-based analysis by sensitive attributes (e.g., gender, age) and a fairness-aware optimization strategy that works to equalize coverage rates, ensuring the model's reliability is equitable across demographic groups. This pursuit of fair and reliable predictions is essential for the ethical and responsible deployment of these technologies in diverse clinical populations.

4 Data Trustworthiness: Privacy-Preserving Depression Recognition

> Can we trust the system with our data? Is it private? Will it protect my identity?

The deployment of automated mental health assessment tools carries a profound privacy challenge. First, the depression assessment output of the model constitutes sensitive personal health information. Second, the raw video and audio of an individual input to the model is itself highly sensitive biometric data that can be used for re-identification. A robust framework must therefore protect both the user's diagnosis and their biometric identity.

With the growing emphasis on safeguarding data, research has moved beyond models that require raw audio-visual data. These efforts can be broadly categorized into methods that use intermediate with less-identifiable features, and methods that are structurally designed for privacy from the ground up.

4.1 Privacy-By-Processing: Using Intermediate Representations

A primary strategy is to remove identifiable information by processing the raw data into abstract and intermediate representations before analysis. The assumption is that these representations can preserve diagnostically relevant behavioral patterns while discarding biometric identifiers.

For visual data, this involves avoiding full face images. Instead, researchers have explored the utilization of non-image structural data, including facial landmarks (only 2D/3D coordinates of key facial points), Action Units (codified muscle activations), and gaze or head pose direction. This approach directly aligns with the later AVEC challenges after 2016, which provided only these features. However, current research predominantly centers on the temporal variations of these features, treating them as simple temporal data for analysis [18,28,101]. This can be a significant limitation, as it may miss crucial spatial relationships. In contrast, AVA-DepressNet [86] delved into the spatiotemporal characteristics of facial landmarks, considering the dynamic changes in their spatial interrelationships, and demonstrated the utility of this richer yet still privacy preserving representation.

A parallel approach exists for the audio modality. Instead of processing the raw waveform, which contains a unique and identifiable voiceprint [87], models can be trained on pre-extracted, low-level acoustic feature sets. These include prosodic features (pitch, energy) and spectral features (e.g., MFCCs). Like facial landmarks, these features are considered privacy-friendlier as they are more difficult to reverse engineer into a recognizable voice, thus preventing user identity or conversation content from being leaked. It is noteworthy that early research predominantly used such audio features for machine learning analysis [118,119]. With the rise of sequential deep learning models, end-to-end training on the raw waveform [27,76] has become common, which re-introduces the privacy risk of loading entire audio signals into an online or cloud-based AI assessment system.

4.2 Privacy-By-Design: Architectural and Hardware Solutions

While intermediate features offer a partial solution, a more robust line of inquiry focuses on building depression recognition systems that are inherently private by design, either at the software or hardware level.

Federated Learning (FL): One of the most prominent architectural solutions is FL. In this paradigm, the raw audio-visual data never leaves the user's local device (e.g., smartphone, laptop). A global model is sent to the device, trained locally on the user's private data, and only the resulting model updates (gradients) are sent back to a central server to be aggregated [24,35,121], rather than uploading any user data itself. This approach is a powerful solution for protecting raw data, though challenges in data heterogeneity and communication efficiency remain, which are also common issues in the broader FL field.

Hardware-Level Anonymization: A novel and cutting-edge paradigm for privacy protection is to intervene at the point of data capture itself. Given that digital data is vulnerable to leaks at any point in the processing pipeline, the core idea is to prevent the creation of digital data containing private information in the first place. This idea has led to the development of Deep Optics [100], which explores the joint design of a physical camera lens and a deep learning model. For depression recognition, this has led to frameworks like OpticalDR [84] as illustrated in Fig. 3, where the camera lens is optically optimized to perform a task-specific encryption. It is trained to physically distort the light from the scene, erasing identifiable facial features *before* the light ever hits the sensor, while simultaneously preserving the subtle, depression-related features. The resulting blurred image is incomprehensible not only to a human but also to state-of-the-art facial recognition systems, yet it is perfectly decodable by the jointly optimized neural network. This method provides an exceptionally strong, irreversible privacy guarantee at the hardware level.

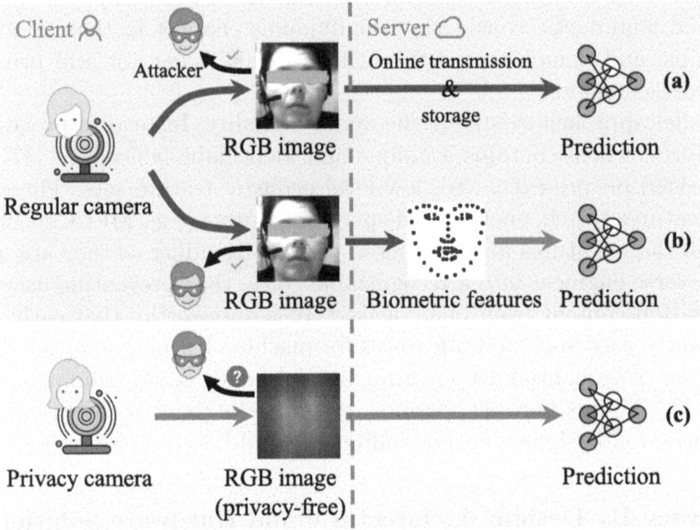

Fig. 3. The conceptual difference between traditional systems and the OpticalDR [84] framework. Red arrows represent data flows containing sensitive private information. Green arrows represent data flows where the private information has been removed.

4.3 The Privacy-Efficacy Trade-Off

Despite these advancements, research regarding privacy in audio-visual depression recognition remains relatively limited. The central challenge is the trade-off between the robustness of privacy protection and the effectiveness of depression recognition. Every privacy-enhancing step, from using abstract landmarks to applying optical distortion, carries an inherent risk of information loss.

This trade-off is the central emerging problem in privacy-preserving depression recognition. For instance, while a deep optics solution like OpticalDR [84] can effectively balance performance and privacy, making private information almost entirely unrecoverable while maintaining usable depression recognition performance. But it is not without costs. The resulting performance, while usable, still has a gap compared to the best state-of-the-art models that use full data. Furthermore, such end-to-end hardware solutions are often highly specific. They are hard to generalize, meaning that if the task or predictive labels change, the entire system must be re-trained or even re-designed from scratch. This lack of flexibility is a significant limitation for real-world deployment.

5 Conclusion

The field of automated depression recognition from audio-visual signals has witnessed several years of development, and has achieved notable performance. Research has evolved from static, single-modality feature engineering to complex, end-to-end spatiotemporal and multimodal fusion models. However, as this review has cataloged, performance on benchmark datasets is only the first step. Several emerging challenges must be addressed before these technologies can be responsibly translated into clinical practice.

1) Model robustness and generalization remain a fundamental challenge. The field's heavy reliance on small, homogeneous, and lab-collected datasets (AVEC and DAIC) limits the real-world applicability of current models. Future work must prioritize the collection of larger, more diverse, in-the-wild datasets [31,125] that capture a wider range of demographics and cultures. This is also a prerequisite for developing personalized models, which learn to track an individual's behavioral changes against their own baseline, rather than a population-level average.

2) The trustworthiness of these models is a critical and previously neglected area of research. For clinical adoption, a model must be transparent, reliable, and fair. For Explainability, the field is moving beyond simple CAM-based visualizations, which are limited to *where* a model is looking. Promising new directions, such as feature disentanglement [46,70,83], are beginning to explore the *why*, but this remains a nascent and highly complex area. For Reliability and Fairness, recent studies on UQ [49] and Fair UQ [11,50] represent a significant step forward. Ensuring that a model's confidence is both statistically valid and equitable across demographic groups is essential for ethical deployment.

3) Privacy and security necessitate a comprehensive, "privacy-by-design" approach related to data trustworthiness. Existing solutions such as using intermediate features [86], FL frameworks [24,35,121], and hardware-level solutions [84], all present a difficult trade-off between privacy robustness and model performance. This balance remains a central research problem. Moreover, it is worth noting that while visual privacy has received some attention, the specific challenges of audio privacy (e.g., voiceprint and content leakage from raw waveforms) and the complex privacy implications of multimodal fusion are almost entirely unstudied.

In conclusion, the future of automated depression recognition lies not in a singular pursuit of accuracy, but in a holistic approach that balances model performance with generalization, clinical trustworthiness, and robust privacy guarantees.

References

1. Mental Health Atlas 2024. World Health Organization, Geneva (2025)
2. Al Hanai, T., Ghassemi, M., Glass, J.: Detecting Depression with Audio/Text Sequence Modeling of Interviews. In: Interspeech, pp. 1716–1720 (2018)
3. Al Jazaery, M., Guo, G.: Video-based depression level analysis by encoding deep spatiotemporal features. IEEE Trans. Affect. Comput. **12**(1), 262–268 (2021). https://doi.org/10.1109/TAFFC.2018.2870884
4. Alghowinem, S., Goecke, R., Wagner, M., Epps, J., Hyett, M., Parker, G., Breakspear, M.: Multimodal depression detection: fusion analysis of paralinguistic, head pose and eye gaze behaviors. IEEE Trans. Affect. Comput. **9**(4), 478–490 (2018). https://doi.org/10.1109/TAFFC.2016.2634527
5. Bargshady, G., Goecke, R.: Estimating depression severity from long-sequence face videos via an ensemble global diverse convolutional model. In: 2023 International Conference on Digital Image Computing: Techniques and Applications (DICTA), pp. 296–303 (2023). https://doi.org/10.1109/DICTA60407.2023.00048
6. Cai, C., Niu, M., Liu, B., Tao, J., Liu, X.: TDCA-Net: Time-Domain Channel Attention Network for Depression Detection. In: Interspeech 2021, pp. 2511–2515 (2021). https://doi.org/10.21437/Interspeech.2021-1176
7. Casado, C.A., Cañellas, M.L., López, M.B.: Depression recognition using remote photoplethysmography from facial videos. IEEE Trans. Affect. Comput. **14**(4), 3305–3316 (2023). https://doi.org/10.1109/TAFFC.2023.3238641
8. Chao, L., Tao, J., Yang, M., Li, Y.: Multi task sequence learning for depression scale prediction from video. In: 2015 International Conference on Affective Computing and Intelligent Interaction (ACII), pp. 526–531 (2015). https://doi.org/10.1109/ACII.2015.7344620
9. Chen, Q., Chaturvedi, I., Ji, S., Cambria, E.: Sequential fusion of facial appearance and dynamics for depression recognition. Pattern Recogn. Lett. **150**, 115–121 (2021)
10. Chen, X., et al.: TTFNet: temporal-frequency features fusion network for speech based automatic depression recognition and assessment. IEEE J. Biomed. Health Inform. **29**(10), 7536–7548 (2025). https://doi.org/10.1109/JBHI.2025.3574864
11. Cheong, J., Bangar, A., Kalkan, S., Gunes, H.: U-Fair: Uncertainty-based Multimodal Multitask Learning for Fairer Depression Detection. In: Hegselmann, S., et al. (eds.) Proceedings of the 4th Machine Learning for Health Symposium. Proceedings of Machine Learning Research, vol. 259, pp. 203–218. PMLR (15–16 Dec 2025), https://proceedings.mlr.press/v259/cheong25a.html
12. Cholet, S., Paugam-Moisy, H., Regis, S.: Bidirectional associative memory for multimodal fusion: a depression evaluation case study. In: International Joint Conference on Neural Networks (IJCNN), pp. 1–6 (2019)
13. Cummins, N., Joshi, J., Dhall, A., Sethu, V., Goecke, R., Epps, J.: Diagnosis of depression by behavioural signals: a multimodal approach. In: ACM International Workshop on Audio/Visual Emotion Challenge (AVEC), pp. 11–20. Association for Computing Machinery, New York (2013)
14. Dai, Z., Zhou, H., Ba, Q., Zhou, Y., Wang, L., Li, G.: Improving depression prediction using a novel feature selection algorithm coupled with context-aware analysis. J. Affect. Disord. **295**, 1040–1048 (2021)
15. Dang, T., et al.: Investigating word affect features and fusion of probabilistic predictions incorporating uncertainty in AVEC 2017. In: ACM International Workshop on Audio/Visual Emotion Challenge (AVEC). pp. 27–35. Association for Computing Machinery, New York (2017)

16. de Melo, W.C., Granger, E., Lopez, M.B.: Facial expression analysis using decomposed multiscale spatiotemporal networks. Expert Syst. Appl. **236**, 121276 (2024)
17. Dong, Y., Yang, X.: A hierarchical depression detection model based on vocal and emotional cues. Neurocomputing **441**, 279–290 (2021)
18. Du, Z., Li, W., Huang, D., Wang, Y.: Encoding visual behaviors with attentive temporal convolution for depression prediction. In: 2019 14th IEEE International Conference on Automatic Face & Gesture Recognition (FG 2019), pp. 1–7 (2019). https://doi.org/10.1109/FG.2019.8756584
19. Fan, H., et al.: Transformer-based multimodal feature enhancement networks for multimodal depression detection integrating video, audio and remote photoplethysmograph signals. Inf. Fusion **104**, 102161 (2024)
20. Feng, S., Sun, G., Lubis, N., Wu, W., Zhang, C., Gasic, M.: Affect recognition in conversations using large language models. In: Kawahara, T., Demberg, V., Ultes, S., Inoue, K., Mehri, S., Howcroft, D., Komatani, K. (eds.) Proceedings of the 25th Annual Meeting of the Special Interest Group on Discourse and Dialogue, pp. 259–273. Association for Computational Linguistics, Kyoto, Japan, September 2024. https://doi.org/10.18653/v1/2024.sigdial-1.23, https://aclanthology.org/2024.sigdial-1.23/
21. Fu, C., et al.: Facial action units guided graph representation learning for multimodal depression detection. Neurocomputing **619**, 129106 (2025)
22. Gong, Y., Poellabauer, C.: Topic modeling based multi-modal depression detection. In: Proceedings of the 7th Annual Workshop on Audio/Visual Emotion Challenge, pp. 69–76. AVEC '17. Association for Computing Machinery, New York (2017). https://doi.org/10.1145/3133944.3133945, https://doi.org/10.1145/3133944.3133945
23. Gratch, J., et al.: The distress analysis interview corpus of human and computer interviews. In: Calzolari, N., Choukri, K., Declerck, T., Loftsson, H., Maegaard, B., Mariani, J., Moreno, A., Odijk, J., Piperidis, S. (eds.) Proceedings of the Ninth International Conference on Language Resources and Evaluation (LREC'14), pp. 3123–3128. European Language Resources Association (ELRA), Reykjavik, Iceland (May 2014), https://aclanthology.org/L14-1421/
24. Gupta, C., Khullar, V.: Modality independent federated multimodal classification system detached eeg, audio and text data for iid and non-iid conditions. Biomed. Signal Process. Control **108**, 107938 (2025)
25. Gupta, R., et al.: Multimodal prediction of affective dimensions and depression in human-computer interactions. In: Proceedings of the 4th International Workshop on Audio/Visual Emotion Challenge, pp. 33–40. AVEC '14. Association for Computing Machinery, New York (2014). https://doi.org/10.1145/2661806.2661810, https://doi.org/10.1145/2661806.2661810
26. Gön, K., Dibeklioğlu, H.: Affect and personality aided modeling of transcribed speech for depression severity estimation. IEEE Trans. Affect. Comput. **16**(3), 2334–2351 (2025). https://doi.org/10.1109/TAFFC.2025.3560476
27. Han, Z., et al.: Spatial–temporal feature network for speech-based depression recognition. IEEE Trans. Cognitive Dev. Syst. **16**(1), 308–318 (2024). https://doi.org/10.1109/TCDS.2023.3273614
28. Haque, A., Guo, M., Miner, A.S., Fei-Fei, L.: Measuring Depression Symptom Severity from Spoken Language and 3D Facial Expressions. arXiv e-prints arXiv:1811.08592, November 2018. https://doi.org/10.48550/arXiv.1811.08592
29. He, L., Cao, C.: Automated depression analysis using convolutional neural networks from speech. J. Biomed. Inform. **83**, 103–111 (2018)

30. He, L., Chan, J.C.W., Wang, Z.: Automatic depression recognition using cnn with attention mechanism from videos. Neurocomputing **422**, 165–175 (2021)
31. He, L., et al.: LMVD: A large-scale multimodal vlog dataset for depression detection in the wild. Inf. Fusion **126**, 103632 (2026)
32. He, L., Jiang, D., Sahli, H.: Automatic depression analysis using dynamic facial appearance descriptor and Dirichlet process fisher encoding. IEEE Trans. Multimedia **21**(6), 1476–1486 (2019). https://doi.org/10.1109/TMM.2018.2877129
33. He, L., Li, Z., Tiwari, P., Cao, C., Xue, J., Zhu, F., Wu, D.: Depressformer: leveraging video swin transformer and fine-grained local features for depression scale estimation. Biomed. Signal Process. Control **96**, 106490 (2024)
34. He, L., Li, Z., Tiwari, P., Zhu, F., Wu, D.: LSCAformer: long and short-term cross-attention-aware transformer for depression recognition from video sequences. Biomed. Signal Process. Control **98**, 106767 (2024)
35. He, L., Yang, W., Zhao, J., Chen, H., Jiang, D.: FedDAAM: federated domain adversarial learning with attention mechanism for privacy preserving multimodal depression assessment. IEEE Trans. Circuits Syst. Video Technol., p. 1 (2025). https://doi.org/10.1109/TCSVT.2025.3609776
36. He, L., Zhao, J., Zhang, J., Jiang, J., Qi, S., Wang, Z., Wu, D.: LMTformer: facial depression recognition with lightweight multi-scale transformer from videos. Appl. Intell. **55**(3) (Dec 2024)
37. Jain, V., Crowley, J.L., Dey, A.K., Lux, A.: Depression estimation using audiovisual features and fisher vector encoding. In: ACM International Workshop on Audio/Visual Emotion Challenge (AVEC), pp. 87–91. Association for Computing Machinery, New York (2014)
38. Jaiswal, S., Song, S., Valstar, M.: Automatic prediction of depression and anxiety from behaviour and personality attributes. In: 2019 8th International Conference on Affective Computing and Intelligent Interaction (ACII), pp. 1–7 (2019).https://doi.org/10.1109/ACII.2019.8925456
39. Jan, A., Meng, H., Gaus, Y.F.A., Zhang, F., Turabzadeh, S.: Automatic depression scale prediction using facial expression dynamics and regression. In: ACM International Workshop on Audio/Visual Emotion Challenge (AVEC), pp. 73–80. Association for Computing Machinery, New York (2014)
40. Jan, A., Meng, H., Gaus, Y.F.B.A., Zhang, F.: Artificial intelligent system for automatic depression level analysis through visual and vocal expressions. IEEE Trans. Cognitive Dev. Syst. **10**(3), 668–680 (2018)
41. Kächele, M., Glodek, M., Zharkov, D., Meudt, S., Schwenker, F.: Fusion of audiovisual features using hierarchical classifier systems for the recognition of affective states and the state of depression. In: International Conference on Pattern Recognition Applications and Methods (ICPRAM), pp. 671–678 (2014)
42. Kächele, M., Schels, M., Schwenker, F.: Inferring depression and affect from application dependent meta knowledge. In: Proceedings of the 4th International Workshop on Audio/Visual Emotion Challenge. p. 41–48. AVEC '14, Association for Computing Machinery, New York, NY, USA (2014).https://doi.org/10.1145/2661806.2661813, https://doi.org/10.1145/2661806.2661813
43. Kaya, H., Çilli, F., Salah, A.A.: Ensemble CCA for continuous emotion prediction. In: ACM International Workshop on Audio/Visual Emotion Challenge (AVEC), pp. 19–26. Association for Computing Machinery, New York (2014)

44. Kaya, H., Salah, A.A.: Eyes Whisper Depression: A CCA based Multimodal Approach. In: Proceedings of the 22nd ACM International Conference on Multimedia, pp. 961–964. MM '14, Association for Computing Machinery, New York, NY, USA (2014). https://doi.org/10.1145/2647868.2654978, https://doi.org/10.1145/2647868.2654978
45. Khan, M.T., Cao, Y., Shafait, F., Jun, W.: ERBMA-Net: Enhanced random binary multilevel attention network for facial depression recognition. IEEE Trans. Comput. Soc. Syst., 1–19 (2025). https://doi.org/10.1109/TCSS.2025.3596047
46. Li, S., et al.: Audio-visual Feature Disentanglement and Fusion Network for Automatic Depression Severity Prediction. IEEE Trans. Affective Comput., 1–15 (2025). https://doi.org/10.1109/TAFFC.2025.3611238
47. Li, X., et al.: TSFFM: depression detection based on latent association of facial and body expressions. Comput. Biol. Med. **168**, 107805 (2024)
48. Li, Y., et al.: FPT-former: a flexible parallel transformer of recognizing depression by using audiovisual expert-knowledge-based multimodal measures. Int. J. Intell. Syst. **2024**(1), 1564574 (2024)
49. Li, Y., Qu, S., Zhou, X.: Conformal depression prediction. IEEE Trans. Affect. Comput. **16**(3), 1814–1824 (2025). https://doi.org/10.1109/TAFFC.2025.3542023
50. Li, Y., Zhang, Z., Zhou, X.: Fair Uncertainty Quantification for Depression Prediction (2025). https://arxiv.org/abs/2505.04931
51. Li, Y., et al.: A facial depression recognition method based on hybrid multi-head cross attention network. Front. Neurosci. **17** (2023). https://doi.org/10.3389/fnins.2023.1188434, https://www.frontiersin.org/journals/neuroscience/articles/10.3389/fnins.2023.1188434
52. Lin, Z., Wang, Y., Zhou, Y., Du, F., Yang, Y.: MLM-EOE: Automatic depression detection via sentimental annotation and multi-expert ensemble. IEEE Trans. Affective Comput., 1–18 (2025). https://doi.org/10.1109/TAFFC.2025.3585599
53. Lin, Z., Wang, Y., Zhou, Y., Du, F., Yang, Y.: STE-Mamba: Automated multimodal depression detection through emotional analysis and spatio-temporal information ensemble. In: ICASSP 2025 - 2025 IEEE International Conference on Acoustics, Speech and Signal Processing (ICASSP), pp. 1–5 (2025). https://doi.org/10.1109/ICASSP49660.2025.10889512
54. Liu, J., Shang, Y., Yang, M., Lu, J., Shao, Z., Ding, H., Liu, T.: A multi-level and multi-scale context refinement network for video-based depression recognition. In: 2025 International Joint Conference on Neural Networks (IJCNN), pp. 1–8 (2025). https://doi.org/10.1109/IJCNN64981.2025.11228686
55. Liu, J., Shang, Y., Yang, M., Shao, Z., Ding, H., Liu, T.: Attention-guided bidirection temporal-aware network for speech-based depression recognition. Digital Sig. Process. **166**, 105359 (2025)
56. Liu, J., Shang, Y., Yang, M., Shao, Z., Ding, H., Liu, T.: CFGMamba: Cross frame group mamba for video-based depression recognition. Biomed. Signal Process. Control **110**, 108113 (2025)
57. Liu, J., Shang, Y., Yang, M., Shao, Z., Lu, J., Liu, T.: MFMamba: a multimodal fusion state space model for depression recognition. In: ICASSP 2025 - 2025 IEEE International Conference on Acoustics, Speech and Signal Processing (ICASSP), pp. 1–5 (2025). https://doi.org/10.1109/ICASSP49660.2025.10888951
58. Liu, Z., Yuan, X., Li, Y., Shangguan, Z., Zhou, L., Hu, B.: PRA-Net: Part-and-relation attention network for depression recognition from facial expression. Comput. Biol. Med. **157**, 106589 (2023)

59. Ma, X., Huang, D., Wang, Y., Wang, Y.: Cost-sensitive two-stage depression prediction using dynamic visual clues. In: Asian Conference on Computer Vision (ACCV), pp. 338–351. Springer, Cham (2017)
60. Ma, X., Yang, H., Chen, Q., Huang, D., Wang, Y.: DepAudioNet: An Efficient Deep Model for Audio based Depression Classification. In: Proceedings of the 6th International Workshop on Audio/Visual Emotion Challenge, pp. 35–42. AVEC '16. Association for Computing Machinery, New York (2016).https://doi.org/10.1145/2988257.2988267, https://doi.org/10.1145/2988257.2988267
61. Carneiro de Melo, W., Granger, E., Lopez, M.B.: Encoding temporal information for automatic depression recognition from facial analysis. In: ICASSP 2020 - 2020 IEEE International Conference on Acoustics, Speech and Signal Processing (ICASSP), pp. 1080–1084 (2020). https://doi.org/10.1109/ICASSP40776.2020.9054375
62. de Melo, W.C., Granger, E., Hadid, A.: Combining global and local convolutional 3D networks for detecting depression from facial expressions. In: 2019 14th IEEE International Conference on Automatic Face & Gesture Recognition (FG 2019), pp. 1–8 (2019).https://doi.org/10.1109/FG.2019.8756568
63. de Melo, W.C., Granger, E., Hadid, A.: Depression detection based on deep distribution learning. In: 2019 IEEE International Conference on Image Processing (ICIP), pp. 4544–4548 (2019).https://doi.org/10.1109/ICIP.2019.8803467
64. de Melo, W.C., Granger, E., Hadid, A.: A deep multiscale spatiotemporal network for assessing depression from facial dynamics. IEEE Trans. Affect. Comput. **13**(3), 1581–1592 (2022)
65. de Melo, W.C., Granger, E., López, M.B.: MDN: a deep maximization-differentiation network for spatio-temporal depression detection. IEEE Trans. Affect. Comput. **14**(1), 578–590 (2023)
66. Mendiratta, A., et al.: Automatic Detection of Depressive States from Speech, pp. 301–314. Springer, Cham (2018).https://doi.org/10.1007/978-3-319-56904-8_29, https://doi.org/10.1007/978-3-319-56904-8_29
67. Meng, H., Huang, D., Wang, H., Yang, H., AI-Shuraifi, M., Wang, Y.: Depression recognition based on dynamic facial and vocal expression features using partial least square regression. In: ACM International Workshop on Audio/Visual Emotion Challenge (AVEC), pp. 21–30. Association for Computing Machinery, New York (2013)
68. Mitra, V., et al.: The SRI AVEC-2014 evaluation system. In: ACM International Workshop on Audio/Visual Emotion Challenge (AVEC), pp. 93–101. Association for Computing Machinery, New York (2014)
69. Mobram, S., Vali, M.: Depression detection based on linear and nonlinear speech features in I-vector/SVDA framework. Comput. Biol. Med. **149**, 105926 (2022)
70. Mou, L., Zhen, S., Mao, S., Ma, N.: Disentangled Representation Learning via Transformer with Graph Attention Fusion for Depression Detection. In: Proceedings of the 1st International Workshop on Cognition-Oriented Multimodal Affective and Empathetic Computing, pp. 20–29. CogMAEC '25. Association for Computing Machinery, New York (2025). https://doi.org/10.1145/3746277.3760407, https://doi.org/10.1145/3746277.3760407
71. Niu, M., Chen, K., Chen, Q., Yang, L.: HCAG: a hierarchical context-aware graph attention model for depression detection. In: ICASSP 2021 - 2021 IEEE International Conference on Acoustics, Speech and Signal Processing (ICASSP), pp. 4235–4239 (2021). https://doi.org/10.1109/ICASSP39728.2021.9413486
72. Niu, M., He, L., Li, Y., Liu, B.: Depressioner: facial dynamic representation for automatic depression level prediction. Expert Syst. Appl. **204**, 117512 (2022)

73. Niu, M., Li, M., Fu, C.: PointTransform networks for automatic depression level prediction via facial keypoints. Knowl.-Based Syst. **297**, 111951 (2024)
74. Niu, M., Li, Y., Tao, J., Zhou, X., Schuller, B.W.: DepressionMLP: a multi-layer perceptron architecture for automatic depression level prediction via facial keypoints and action units. IEEE Trans. Circuits Syst. Video Technol. **34**(9), 8924–8938 (2024). https://doi.org/10.1109/TCSVT.2024.3382334
75. Niu, M., Liu, B., Tao, J., Li, Q.: A time-frequency channel attention and vectorization network for automatic depression level prediction. Neurocomputing **450**, 208–218 (2021)
76. Niu, M., Tao, J., Li, Y., Qin, Y., Li, Y.: WavDepressionNet: automatic depression level prediction via raw speech signals. IEEE Trans. Affect. Comput. **15**(1), 285–296 (2024). https://doi.org/10.1109/TAFFC.2023.3272553
77. Niu, M., Tao, J., Liu, B., Fan, C.: Automatic depression level detection via ℓ_p-norm pooling. In: Interspeech 2019. pp. 4559–4563 (2019). https://doi.org/10.21437/Interspeech.2019-1617
78. Niu, M., Tao, J., Liu, B., Huang, J., Lian, Z.: Multimodal spatiotemporal representation for automatic depression level detection. IEEE Trans. Affect. Comput. **14**(1), 294–307 (2023)
79. Niu, M., Wang, X., Gong, J., Liu, B., Tao, J., Schuller, B.W.: Depression scale dictionary decomposition framework for multimodal automatic depression level prediction. IEEE Trans. Circuits Syst. Video Technol. **35**(6), 6195–6210 (2025). https://doi.org/10.1109/TCSVT.2025.3533480
80. Niu, M., Zhao, Z., Tao, J., Li, Y., Schuller, B.W.: Selective element and two orders vectorization networks for automatic depression severity diagnosis via facial changes. IEEE Trans. Circuits Syst. Video Technol. **32**(11), 8065–8077 (2022). https://doi.org/10.1109/TCSVT.2022.3182658
81. Niu, M., Zhao, Z., Tao, J., Li, Y., Schuller, B.W.: Dual attention and element recalibration networks for automatic depression level prediction. IEEE Trans. Affect. Comput. **14**(3), 1954–1965 (2023). https://doi.org/10.1109/TAFFC.2022.3177737
82. Othmani, A., Kadoch, D., Bentounes, K., Rejaibi, E., Alfred, R., Hadid, A.: Towards robust deep neural networks for affect and depression recognition from speech. In: Del Bimbo, A., Cucchiara, R., Sclaroff, S., Farinella, G.M., Mei, T., Bertini, M., Escalante, H.J., Vezzani, R. (eds.) Pattern Recognition. ICPR International Workshops and Challenges, pp. 5–19. Springer Cham (2021)
83. Pan, Y., Jiang, J., Jiang, K., Liu, X.: Disentangled-multimodal privileged knowledge distillation for depression recognition with incomplete multimodal data. In: Proceedings of the 32nd ACM International Conference on Multimedia, pp. 5712–5721. MM '24. Association for Computing Machinery, New York (2024)
84. Pan, Y., Jiang, J., Jiang, K., Wu, Z., Yu, K., Liu, X.: OpticalDR: a deep optical imaging model for privacy-protective depression recognition. In: 2024 IEEE/CVF Conference on Computer Vision and Pattern Recognition (CVPR), pp. 1303–1312 (2024). https://doi.org/10.1109/CVPR52733.2024.00130
85. Pan, Y., Shang, Y., Liu, T., Shao, Z., Guo, G., Ding, H., Hu, Q.: Spatial–temporal attention network for depression recognition from facial videos. Expert Syst. Appl. **237**, 121410 (2024)
86. Pan, Y., Shang, Y., Shao, Z., Liu, T., Guo, G., Ding, H.: Integrating deep facial priors into landmarks for privacy preserving multimodal depression recognition. IEEE Trans. Affective Comput., 1–8 (2023)

87. Pan, Y., Shang, Y., Wang, W., Shao, Z., Han, Z., Liu, T., Guo, G., Ding, H.: Multi-feature deep supervised voiceprint adversarial network for depression recognition from speech. Biomed. Signal Process. Control **89**, 105704 (2024)
88. Peng, Z., Dang, J., Unoki, M., Akagi, M.: Multi-resolution modulation-filtered cochleagram feature for LSTM-based dimensional emotion recognition from speech. Neural Netw. **140**, 261–273 (2021)
89. Pérez Espinosa, H., Escalante, H.J., Villaseñor Pineda, L., Montes-y Gómez, M., Pinto-Avedaño, D., Reyez-Meza, V.: Fusing affective dimensions and audio-visual features from segmented video for depression recognition: INAOE-BUAP's participation at AVEC'14 challenge. In: ACM International Workshop on Audio/Visual Emotion Challenge (AVEC), pp. 49–55. Association for Computing Machinery, New York(2014)
90. Qureshi, S.A., Saha, S., Hasanuzzaman, M., Dias, G.: Multitask representation learning for multimodal estimation of depression level. IEEE Intell. Syst. **34**(5), 45–52 (2019)
91. Rathi, S., Kaur, B., Agrawal, R.K.: Enhanced depression detection from facial cues using univariate feature selection techniques. In: Pattern Recognition and Machine Intelligence, pp. 22–29. Springer, Cham (2019)
92. Ray, A., Kumar, S., Reddy, R., Mukherjee, P., Garg, R.: Multi-level attention network using text, audio and video for depression prediction. In: Proceedings of the 9th International on Audio/Visual Emotion Challenge and Workshop, pp. 81–88. AVEC '19. Association for Computing Machinery, New York (2019).https://doi.org/10.1145/3347320.3357697, https://doi.org/10.1145/3347320.3357697
93. Rejaibi, E., Komaty, A., Meriaudeau, F., Agrebi, S., Othmani, A.: MFCC-based recurrent neural network for automatic clinical depression recognition and assessment from speech. Biomed. Signal Process. Control **71**, 103107 (2022)
94. Ringeval, F., et al.: AVEC 2019 Workshop and Challenge: State-of-Mind, Detecting Depression with AI, and Cross-Cultural Affect Recognition. In: ACM International Workshop on Audio/Visual Emotion Challenge (AVEC), pp. 3–12. Association for Computing Machinery, New York (2019)
95. Ringeval, F., etal.: AVEC 2017: Real-Life Depression, and Affect Recognition Workshop and Challenge. In: ACM International Workshop on Audio/Visual Emotion Challenge (AVEC), pp. 3–9. Association for Computing Machinery, New York (2017)
96. Rutowski, T., Harati, A., Lu, Y., Shriberg, E.: Optimizing speech-input length for speaker-independent depression classification. In: Interspeech 2019, pp. 3023–3027 (2019). https://doi.org/10.21437/Interspeech.2019-3095
97. Selvaraju, R.R., Cogswell, M., Das, A., Vedantam, R., Parikh, D., Batra, D.: Grad-CAM: visual explanations from deep networks via gradient-based localization. In: 2017 IEEE International Conference on Computer Vision (ICCV), pp. 618–626 (2017). https://doi.org/10.1109/ICCV.2017.74
98. Senoussaoui, M., Sarria-Paja, M., Santos, J.a.F., Falk, T.H.: Model fusion for multimodal depression classification and level detection. In: Proceedings of the 4th International Workshop on Audio/Visual Emotion Challenge, pp. 57–63. AVEC '14, Association for Computing Machinery, New York (2014). https://doi.org/10.1145/2661806.2661819, https://doi.org/10.1145/2661806.2661819
99. Shang, Y., Pan, Y., Jiang, X., Shao, Z., Guo, G., Liu, T., Ding, H.: LQGDNet: a local quaternion and global deep network for facial depression recognition. IEEE Trans. Affect. Comput. **14**(3), 2557–2563 (2023)

100. Sitzmann, V., Diamond, S., Peng, Y., Dun, X., Boyd, S., Heidrich, W., Heide, F., Wetzstein, G.: End-to-end optimization of optics and image processing for achromatic extended depth of field and super-resolution imaging. ACM Trans. Graph. **37**(4), July 2018. https://doi.org/10.1145/3197517.3201333, https://doi.org/10.1145/3197517.3201333
101. Song, S., Jaiswal, S., Shen, L., Valstar, M.: Spectral representation of behaviour primitives for depression analysis. IEEE Trans. Affect. Comput. **13**(2), 829–844 (2022)
102. Song, S., Shen, L., Valstar, M.: Human behaviour-based automatic depression analysis using hand-crafted statistics and deep learned spectral features. In: 2018 13th IEEE International Conference on Automatic Face & Gesture Recognition (FG 2018), pp. 158–165 (2018). https://doi.org/10.1109/FG.2018.00032
103. Stepanov, E.A., et al.: Depression severity estimation from multiple modalities. In: 2018 IEEE 20th International Conference on e-Health Networking, Applications and Services (Healthcom), pp. 1–6 (2018)
104. Sun, B., Zhang, Y., He, J., Yu, L., Xu, Q., Li, D., Wang, Z.: A random forest regression method with selected-text feature for depression assessment. In: ACM International Workshop on Audio/Visual Emotion Challenge (AVEC), pp. 61–68. Association for Computing Machinery, New York (2017)
105. Syed, Z.S., Sidorov, K., Marshall, D.: Depression severity prediction based on biomarkers of psychomotor retardation. In: ACM International Workshop on Audio/Visual Emotion Challenge (AVEC), pp. 37–43. Association for Computing Machinery, New York (2017)
106. Tao, Y., Yang, M., Shen, H., Yang, Z., Weng, Z., Hu, B.: Classifying anxiety and depression through llms virtual interactions: a case study with chatgpt. In: 2023 IEEE International Conference on Bioinformatics and Biomedicine (BIBM), pp. 2259–2264 (2023). https://doi.org/10.1109/BIBM58861.2023.10385305
107. Tasnim, M., Stroulia, E.: Detecting depression from voice. In: Advances in Artificial Intelligence, pp. 472–478. Springer, Cham (2019)
108. Uddin, M.A., Joolee, J.B., Lee, Y.K.: Depression level prediction using deep spatiotemporal features and multilayer Bi-LTSM. IEEE Trans. Affect. Comput. **13**(2), 864–870 (2022). https://doi.org/10.1109/TAFFC.2020.2970418
109. Uddin, M.A., Joolee, J.B., Sohn, K.A.: Deep multi-modal network based automated depression severity estimation. IEEE Trans. Affect. Comput. **14**(3), 2153–2167 (2023). https://doi.org/10.1109/TAFFC.2022.3179478
110. Valstar, M., Gratch, J., Schuller, B., Ringeval, F., Lalanne, D., Torres Torres, M., Scherer, S., Stratou, G., Cowie, R., Pantic, M.: AVEC 2016: Depression, Mood, and Emotion Recognition Workshop and Challenge. In: Proceedings of the 6th International Workshop on Audio/Visual Emotion Challenge, pp. 3–10. AVEC '16, Association for Computing Machinery, New York (2016). https://doi.org/10.1145/2988257.2988258, https://doi.org/10.1145/2988257.2988258
111. Valstar, M., et al.: AVEC 2014: 3D Dimensional Affect and Depression Recognition Challenge. In: ACM International Workshop on Audio/Visual Emotion Challenge (AVEC), pp. 3–10. Association for Computing Machinery, New York (2014)
112. Valstar, M., et al.: AVEC 2013: The Continuous Audio/Visual Emotion and Depression Recognition Challenge. In: ACM International Workshop on Audio/Visual Emotion Challenge (AVEC), pp. 3–10. Association for Computing Machinery, New York (2013)

113. Wang, R., Huang, J., Zhang, J., Liu, X., Zhang, X., Liu, Z., Zhao, P., Chen, S., Sun, X.: FacialPulse: An Efficient RNN-based Depression Detection via Temporal Facial Landmarks. In: Proceedings of the 32nd ACM International Conference on Multimedia, pp. 311–320. MM '24, Association for Computing Machinery, New York (2024). https://doi.org/10.1145/3664647.3681546, https://doi.org/10.1145/3664647.3681546
114. Wang, Y., Lin, Z., Yang, C., Zhou, Y., Yang, Y.: Automatic depression recognition with an ensemble of multimodal spatio-temporal routing features. IEEE Trans. Affect. Comput. **16**(3), 1855–1872 (2025). https://doi.org/10.1109/TAFFC.2025.3543226
115. Wang, Z., Chen, L., Wang, L., Diao, G.: Recognition of audio depression based on convolutional neural network and generative antagonism network model. IEEE Access **8**, 101181–101191 (2020)
116. Wen, L., Li, X., Guo, G., Zhu, Y.: Automated depression diagnosis based on facial dynamic analysis and sparse coding. IEEE Trans. Inf. Forensics Secur. **10**(7), 1432–1441 (2015). https://doi.org/10.1109/TIFS.2015.2414392
117. Williamson, J.R., et al.: Detecting depression using vocal, facial and semantic communication cues. In: ACM International Workshop on Audio/Visual Emotion Challenge (AVEC), pp. 11–18. Association for Computing Machinery, New York (2016)
118. Williamson, J.R., Quatieri, T.F., Helfer, B.S., Ciccarelli, G., Mehta, D.D.: Vocal and facial biomarkers of depression based on motor incoordination and timing. In: ACM International Workshop on Audio/Visual Emotion Challenge (AVEC), pp. 65–72. Association for Computing Machinery, New York (2014)
119. Williamson, J.R., Quatieri, T.F., Helfer, B.S., Horwitz, R., Yu, B., Mehta, D.D.: Vocal biomarkers of depression based on motor incoordination. In: Proceedings of the 3rd ACM International Workshop on Audio/Visual Emotion Challenge, pp. 41–48. Association for Computing Machinery, New York (2013). https://doi.org/10.1145/2512530.2512531, https://doi.org/10.1145/2512530.2512531
120. Wu, Z., et al.: DepMGNN: matrixial graph neural network for video-based automatic depression assessment. In: Proceedings of the Thirty-Ninth AAAI Conference on Artificial Intelligence and Thirty-Seventh Conference on Innovative Applications of Artificial Intelligence and Fifteenth Symposium on Educational Advances in Artificial Intelligence. AAAI'25/IAAI'25/EAAI'25, AAAI Press (2025). https://doi.org/10.1609/aaai.v39i2.32153, https://doi.org/10.1609/aaai.v39i2.32153
121. Xu, X., Peng, H., Bhuiyan, M.Z.A., Hao, Z., Liu, L., Sun, L., He, L.: Privacy-preserving federated depression detection from multisource mobile health data. IEEE Trans. Industr. Inf. **18**(7), 4788–4797 (2022). https://doi.org/10.1109/TII.2021.3113708
122. Yang, L., Jiang, D., Xia, X., Pei, E., Oveneke, M.C., Sahli, H.: Multimodal measurement of depression using deep learning models. In: ACM International Workshop on Audio/Visual Emotion Challenge (AVEC), pp. 53–59. Association for Computing Machinery, New York (2017)
123. Yang, L., Sahli, H., Xia, X., Pei, E., Oveneke, M.C., Jiang, D.: Hybrid depression classification and estimation from audio video and text information. In: ACM International Workshop on Audio/Visual Emotion Challenge (AVEC), pp. 45–51. Association for Computing Machinery, New York (2017)
124. Yang, M., et al.: LMS-VDR: integrating landmarks into multi-scale hybrid net for video-based depression recognition. In: Lin, Z., et al. (eds.) Pattern Recognition and Computer Vision, pp. 299–312. Springer, Singapore (2025)

125. Yoon, J., Kang, C., Kim, S., Han, J.: D-vlog: Multimodal vlog dataset for depression detection. In: Proceedings of the AAAI Conference on Artificial Intelligence **36**(11), 12226–12234 (2022)
126. Yuan, X., Liu, Z., Chen, Q., Li, G., Ding, Z., Shangguan, Z., Hu, B.: Combining informative regions and clips for detecting depression from facial expressions. Cogn. Comput. (2023)
127. Zhang, L., Driscol, J., Chen, X., Hosseini Ghomi, R.: Evaluating acoustic and linguistic features of detecting depression sub-challenge dataset. In: Proceedings of the 9th International on Audio/Visual Emotion Challenge and Workshop, AVEC '19, pp. 47–53. Association for Computing Machinery, New York (2019). https://doi.org/10.1145/3347320.3357693, https://doi.org/10.1145/3347320.3357693
128. Zhang, P., Wu, M., Dinkel, H., Yu, K.: DEPA: Self-supervised audio embedding for depression detection. In: Proceedings of the 29th ACM International Conference on Multimedia, pp. 135–143. MM '21, Association for Computing Machinery, New York (2021). https://doi.org/10.1145/3474085.3479236, https://doi.org/10.1145/3474085.3479236
129. Zhang, S., et al.: MTDAN: a lightweight multi-scale temporal difference attention networks for automated video depression detection. IEEE Trans. Affect. Comput. **15**(3), 1078–1089 (2024). https://doi.org/10.1109/TAFFC.2023.3312263
130. Zhang, X., Liu, H., Xu, K., Zhang, Q., Liu, D., Ahmed, B., Epps, J.: When LLMs meets acoustic landmarks: An efficient approach to integrate speech into large language models for depression detection. In: Al-Onaizan, Y., Bansal, M., Chen, Y.N. (eds.) Proceedings of the 2024 Conference on Empirical Methods in Natural Language Processing, pp. 146–158. Association for Computational Linguistics, Miami, Florida, USA, November 2024. https://doi.org/10.18653/v1/2024.emnlp-main.8, https://aclanthology.org/2024.emnlp-main.8/
131. Zhao, J., Zhang, L., Cui, Y., Shi, J., He, L.: A novel image-data-driven and frequency-based method for depression detection. Biomed. Signal Process. Control **86**, 105248 (2023)
132. Zhao, Z., Bao, Z., Zhang, Z., Deng, J., Cummins, N., Wang, H., Tao, J., Schuller, B.: Automatic assessment of depression from speech via a hierarchical attention transfer network and attention autoencoders. IEEE J. Sel. Top. Sig. Process. **14**(2), 423–434 (2020). https://doi.org/10.1109/JSTSP.2019.2955012
133. Zhao, Z., Li, Q., Cummins, N., Liu, B., Wang, H., Tao, J., Schuller, B.W.: Hybrid Network Feature Extraction for Depression Assessment from Speech. In: Interspeech, pp. 4956–4960 (2020)
134. Zhao, Z., Liu, S., Niu, M., Wang, H., Schuller, B.W.: Dense coordinate channel attention network for depression level estimation from speech. In: Pattern Recognition: 27th International Conference, ICPR 2024, Kolkata, India, December 1–5, 2024, Proceedings, Part XIII, pp. 402–413. Springer, Heidelberg (2024). https://doi.org/10.1007/978-3-031-78201-5_26, https://doi.org/10.1007/978-3-031-78201-5_26
135. Zhou, B., Khosla, A., Lapedriza, A., Oliva, A., Torralba, A.: Learning deep features for discriminative localization. In: 2016 IEEE Conference on Computer Vision and Pattern Recognition (CVPR), pp. 2921–2929 (2016). https://doi.org/10.1109/CVPR.2016.319
136. Zhou, X., Jin, K., Shang, Y., Guo, G.: Visually interpretable representation learning for depression recognition from facial images. IEEE Trans. Affect. Comput. **11**(3), 542–552 (2020)

137. Zhou, X., Wei, Z., Xu, M., Qu, S., Guo, G.: Facial depression recognition by deep joint label distribution and metric learning. IEEE Trans. Affect. Comput. **13**(3), 1605–1618 (2022). https://doi.org/10.1109/TAFFC.2020.3022732
138. Zhu, Y., Shang, Y., Shao, Z., Guo, G.: Automated depression diagnosis based on deep networks to encode facial appearance and dynamics. IEEE Trans. Affect. Comput. **9**(4), 578–584 (2018). https://doi.org/10.1109/TAFFC.2017.2650899
139. Zou, B., et al.: Semi-structural interview-based Chinese multimodal depression corpus towards automatic preliminary screening of depressive disorders. IEEE Trans. Affect. Comput. **14**(4), 2823–2838 (2023). https://doi.org/10.1109/TAFFC.2022.3181210

Affective Evaluation of Aircraft Cockpit Interior in Complex Dynamic Environments

Lu Weihua[1(✉)], Liu Yuting[1], Liu Ziyue[1], Shao Xuying[1], Jing Yunfei[2], and Hu Jianbo[3]

[1] Nanjing University of Aeronautics and Astronautics, Nanjing, China
weihua.lu@nuaa.edu.cn

[2] China Eastern Airlines Jiangsu Limited, Nanjing, China

[3] Eastern Airlines Technic Co., Ltd. , Jiangsu Branch, Nanjing, China

Abstract. To mitigate aviation accidents attributable to human factors, this study develops an affective evaluation method for aircraft cockpit interiors in complex dynamic environments. A simplified model was constructed along the dimensions of mission timeline, phase, and scenario, and a Comprehensive Impact Index of Complex Dynamic Environments on Flight Emotions was defined. Criteria and method for pilot perceptual measurement were subsequently established. Following this, perceptible design features were characterized through flight simulation experiments replicating complex dynamic conditions, enabling collection of pilots' subjective and objective perceptual data. A BP neural network-based predictive model for cockpit interior evaluation was developed and validated. This work provides an evaluation methodology and experimental paradigm that better reflects real flight conditions, contributing to enhanced perceptual interaction in cockpit environments and supporting aviation safety.

Keywords: Affective Evaluation · Aircraft Cockpit Interior · Complex Dynamic Environment · Kansei Engineering · BP Neural Network

1 Introduction

The aircraft cockpit is the core interactive environment where pilots obtain information, control the aircraft, and execute tasks. Its design is crucial to flight safety and efficiency. Over 70% of global aviation accidents are linked to human factors [1], with pilots being the primary contributor [2]. A pilot's situational awareness and decision-making are thus vital to safety. Traditional cockpit design follows a function-centric, "human-adapting-to-machine" philosophy, focusing on predefined functions [3]. This leads to poor integration and ergonomics, causing challenges like unfriendly interfaces and high workload in non-routine situations, which can jeopardize safety [4]. With technological advances, cockpit design has shifted toward a human-centered, "machine-adapting-to-human" approach. Current research mainly follows physical logic, optimizing layout and displays, yet seldom addresses pilots' psychological states. However, in a confined cockpit, the interior ambiance significantly affects pilots' perception and performance during complex missions, and aids in accident prevention [5]. Pilots inherently seek

H. Liu et al. (Eds.): CEI 2025, CCIS 2881, pp. 57–72, 2026.
https://doi.org/10.1007/978-981-95-9493-1_4

cockpits that fulfill emotional connections and value realization, achieving harmony between themselves, the aircraft, and the environment. There is a clear need for innovative design methods that deepen insights into pilots' operational logic and integrate their emotional needs.

Scholars have explored aircraft cockpit interior design by integrating the methods and philosophies of Kansei Engineering [6, 7]. Their work primarily advances in two directions. On one hand, researchers have focused on establishing Kansei evaluation criteria and methods for cockpit interiors, addressing aspects such as styling semantics and layout optimization. For instance, Liu adopted the "average face" concept to extract key feature lines and average shapes from cockpit interior images. Using the semantic differential method, he evaluated design semantics, providing a reference for creative cockpit design [8]. Lu et al. constructed a three-dimensional Kansei space of Entity-Order-Atmosphere. By integrating subjective and objective data, a comprehensive Kansei evaluation system of business jet cockpit interior layout was established, thereby providing a basis for its optimization [9]. On the other hand, efforts are dedicated to constructing a Kansei evaluation and prediction model or system for aircraft cockpit interior design. For example, Wang et al. used images of the cockpit's T-shaped area as visual stimuli to collect Kansei evaluations. They deconstructed design elements using shape analysis and employed a neural network to model the relationship between Kansei evaluations and design elements, enabling the prediction of Kansei evaluation values for new design samples [10]. Chen et al. used a Kansei engineering model based on fuzzy set theory to evaluate cockpit color scheme images. They trained an intelligent cockpit color comprehensive evaluation system based on a support vector machine, providing decision support for the Kansei evaluation of cockpit interior colors [11].

The theoretical methods of Kansei engineering can effectively solve the affective evaluation and prediction problems of aircraft cockpit interior design space, layout, color, etc. Nevertheless, despite the attainment of phased progress in research on Kansei-driven aircraft cockpit interior design evaluation, the research framework remains incomplete. Current approaches to Kansei evaluation of user needs rely heavily on cockpit interior images, which cannot accurately replicate the actual flight experience. While Kansei evaluations based on static images represent the optimal approach under non-comprehensive simulation conditions where experimental cost control is a consideration, they still fall short of capturing the Kansei responses evoked during real flight conditions.

The aircraft cockpit is a highly complex operational platform with a confined space, dense interfaces, and integrated functions [12]. Real flight environments are dynamic, and pilot-cockpit interaction evolves across phases like takeoff, cruise, and landing. In these settings, pilots' focus shifts: during high workload, they concentrate on specific equipment, while in low workload, they notice the overall spatial ambiance [13]. Kansei also varies with the pilot's alertness. High-workload phases are critical, while low-workload cruise flights can induce fatigue and reduce vigilance, raising accident risks [14]. Cockpit design must therefore support pilots' optimal performance across all scenarios. Thus, Kansei evaluation must account for complex dynamic environments. A methodology suited to such conditions can identify design flaws under specific states, improve operational reliability and comfort, and ultimately enhance flight safety.

Based on the design philosophy of Kansei Engineering, this study examines the measurement methods and criteria for pilot affective evaluation under complex dynamic environments. Subjective and objective perceptual feedback from pilots is acquired through simulated flight experiments. Leveraging a BP neural network, this study realizes the prediction of affective evaluation using the perceptual feature elements of cockpit interior appearances, thereby providing enabling tools and methodological guidance for the optimization of aircraft cockpit interior design.

2 Complex Dynamic Flight Environments

The flight environment is defined as the external conditions under which an aircraft operates during flight, encompassing the natural environment, navigation environment, and system environment. It exhibits the characteristics of diversity, connectivity, variability, randomness, and irresistibility [15–17]. Given these characteristics, researchers have developed differing interpretations and proposed various definitions based on their distinct research objectives.

From the perspective of aircraft cockpit affective evaluation, this study reconstructs and proposes a complex dynamic environment system based on the "mission timeline, phase and scenario" characteristics, as shown in Fig. 1. Mission timeline serves as the measurement dimension to describe the sequence and duration of flight tasks, with flight phases and scenario both dependent on this temporal sequence. Under this framework, flight scenarios are defined as three categories: takeoff climb, cruise, and approach landing. Due to the variability of flight scenes, any flight phase may involve either high-load or low-load task modes.

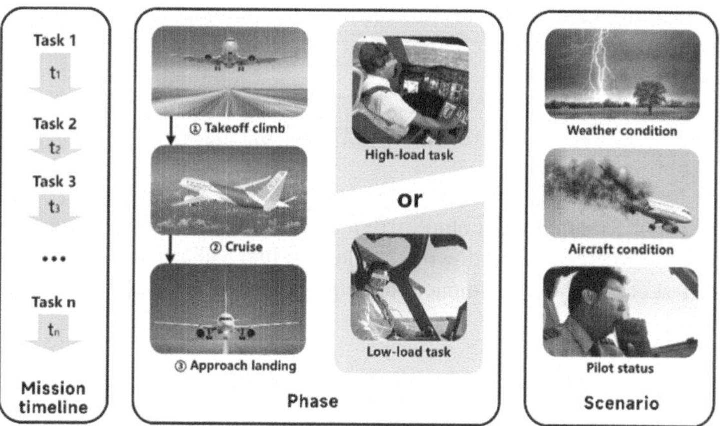

Fig. 1. Mission timeline-phase-scenario complex dynamic environment model.

Different complex dynamic environments exert distinct impacts on pilots' stress levels, emotional states, and situational awareness, and the corresponding affective evaluation methods for aircraft cockpit interiors also vary accordingly. To efficiently distinguish levels and design experiments, the *Comprehensive Impact Index of Complex Dynamic Environments on Flight Emotions* is proposed, which intuitively quantifies the influence of diverse complex dynamic flight environments on pilots' flight emotions. This metric holds important guiding significance for the design of experimental scenarios in cockpit interior affective evaluation research, enabling the acquisition of more targeted measurement data. Furthermore, it can assist relevant personnel in assessing pilots' flight emotions and operational states, and provides reference value for supplementing airworthiness regulations.

The three-dimensional space of the complex dynamic environment was constructed, in which the Comprehensive Impact Index on Flight Emotions is visualized in Fig. 2. The three-dimensional space comprises three axes: the X-axis (weather conditions), Y-axis (aircraft state), and Z-axis (pilot status). Specific conditions are mapped to scale values as follows:

- X-axis (x_0–x_5): normal weather, thunderstorms, low visibility, runway pollution, wind shear, and minor downburst.
- Y-axis (y_0–y_5): normal operation, engine failure, communication failure, landing gear retraction failure, engine rotation stall, and fuel leakage.
- Z-axis (z_0–z_2): normal status, mild fatigue, and severe fatigue.

Based on the subjective evaluations and decision-making analysis of 78 pilots, the influence weights of weather conditions, aircraft status, and pilot status on pilots' flight emotions were determined to be 20.4%, 27.2%, and 52.5% respectively.

Each configuration in this dynamic complex environment is represented as a sphere encompassing the flight phases of takeoff climb, cruise, and approach landing. The comprehensive impact of each scenario on pilot flying emotion is visualized through the sphere's color and diameter: colors closer to purple and larger diameters indicate greater impact. The environmental sphere, representing the comprehensive impact I of each complex dynamic environment configuration on pilots' flying emotions, is calculated using the following formula:

$$I = 0.204x + 0.272y + 0.525z \tag{1}$$

Among them, $x \in \{x_0, x_1, x_2, x_3, x_4, x_5\}$, $y \in \{y_0, y_1, y_2, y_3, y_4, y_5\}$, and $z \in \{z_0, z_1, z_2\}$. . For example, the complex dynamic environment configuration in which the weather encountered a small downburst, aircraft fuel leakage and severe pilot fatigue had the highest comprehensive impact on the pilot's flying emotion (0.802).

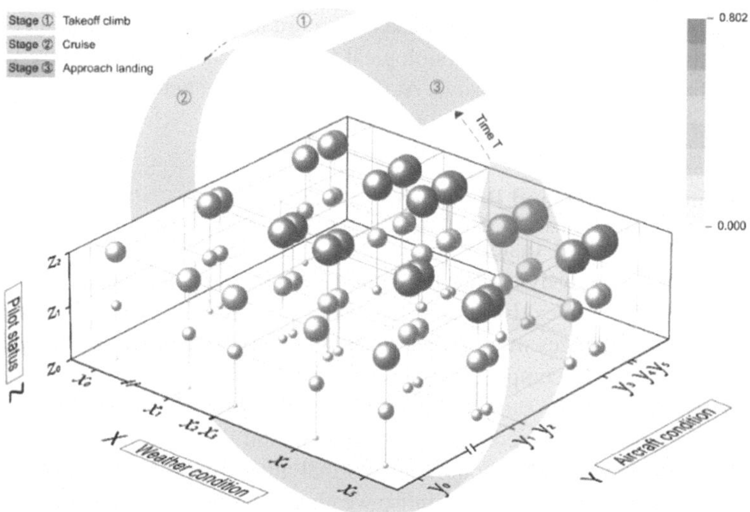

Fig. 2. Comprehensive impact index of complex dynamic environments on flight emotions.

3 Experimental Design for Affective Evaluation of Aircraft Cockpit Interior in Complex Dynamic Environments

3.1 Experimental Platform

Microsoft Flight Simulator 2020 is used together with operating equipment as a multi-dimensional perceptual interaction experiment platform for the cockpit to simulate the real flight environment to a certain extent. To control the influence of other variables on the perceptual evaluation of interior decorations, aircraft samples with similar fuselage sizes, cockpit functions and layouts, and performances were selected. Finally, 15 aircraft models were selected from multiple aviation brands to form a sample pool.

3.2 Affective Evaluation Method

In accordance with the pilot sensitivity measurement criteria for complex dynamic environment, subjective and objective measurement methods have been used to integrate multidimensional perceptual information. The subjective measurement tool used was the Pilot Affective Evaluation Comprehensive Scale, which integrates the NASA Task Load Index (NASA-TLX) [18], the Situation Awareness Rating Technique (SART) [19] and the Likert scales [20] of design satisfaction, all of which use a 7-point scale. Among them, the NASA-TLX is used to measure the psychological, physiological and time pressures of the subjects during the execution of the task. The SART was used to measure subjects' ability to perceive, understand and predict the surrounding environment and their own state. The supplemental Likert scale was used to measure subjects' satisfaction with the cockpit design, including vision, safety and comfort, to facilitate a more comprehensive consideration of the subjects' perceptual quality. The physiological measurement tool uses an ECG monitor to measure the heart rate to capture the fatigue state of the subjects and uses a portable eye tracker to record the line of sight and interest area of the subjects. Both methods of physiological measurement do not interfere with the experimental task and are less invasive. At the same time, the behavior of the subject is recorded via video for time calibration and alignment.

3.3 Experimental Tasks and Procedures

Experimental Scenes and Tasks

The experiment's complex dynamic environment configuration and task scheduling followed the proposed complex dynamic flight environment model. To control the experiment's duration, two stages more critical to flight safety were selected: takeoff/climb and approach/landing. To comprehensively examine the subjects' perceptual evaluation of the cockpit interior of the sample aircraft, there should be obvious differences in the comprehensive impact of the configured flight scene on the subjects' flying emotion: environment 1 (normal weather conditions, normal aircraft conditions, mild fatigue of the pilot) and environment 2 (low visibility weather conditions, normal aircraft conditions, severe fatigue of the pilot conditions). According to formula (1), the comprehensive impact of environment 1 and environment 2 on pilots' flying emotions are $I_1 = 0.259$ and $I_2 = 0.575$ respectively.

A total of 30 experimental tasks were generated by pairing 15 aircraft models with 2 environmental settings in a combinatorial manner. To control and differentiate between the two environments, the researchers set the subjects' states to transition from mild fatigue to severe fatigue. Subjects completed 15 flight tasks of different aircraft models in Environment 1 and Environment 2, numbered 1–30 sequentially.

Experimental Procedure

The experiment is arranged in a quiet and bright space without additional lighting, as shown in Fig. 3. There were 15 subjects in the experiment, all of whom were male undergraduates majoring in flight technology and had simulated flight experience. A Latin square was used to design the experimental tasks for each subject to eliminate the influence of task order on the experiment.

The specific process of the experiment was as follows: First, the researchers wore the Lepu ECG monitor TH12 and the portable eye tracker Tobbi Pro Glasses 3 for the subjects and calibrated them. Secondly, briefly explain to the participants the background, content, and precautions of the aircraft cockpit interior perception evaluation experiment. Third, the researchers configured the environment and aircraft models on the Microsoft Flight Simulator 2020 platform. Fourth, the subjects used the Tumast TCA flight rocker, throttle, flap, choke and rudder set to complete a flight task on an external VOC 32-inch fish screen display. The ECG monitor and eye tracker collected the physiological data of the subjects in the process of completing the task in real time, and the video recording of the GoPro 9 action camera behind the subjects was performed. Fifth, the subjects completed the paper pilot perceptual evaluation comprehensive scale. The third to fifth steps of the experiment were iterated until the subjects completed 30 experimental tasks. The entire experiment lasted approximately 110 min, and a timer was set to remind the beginning and end of each task with a bell to accurately control the experiment time and facilitate the alignment of the timeline for subsequent data.

After the experiment, we conducted brief interviews with each participant to record their subjective feelings and the basis for their scale ratings during the task, as a reference for explaining the mapping mechanism between the cockpit key styling line and subjective ratings.

Fig. 3. Experiment on the affective evaluation of aircraft cockpit interior.

4 Results and Analysis

4.1 Affective Evaluation Based on Subjective and Objective Data Analysis

Subject Status Verification

To verify the fidelity of pilot fatigue states in the experimental flight setup. The collected heart rate data from the experiment was segmented to calculate the subjects' cardiovascular load (CVL) during each task [21, 22]. The average CVL of 15 subjects in experimental tasks 1–15 (Environment 1) was in the range of 30%–60%, indicating a mildly fatigued state. In experimental tasks 16–30 (Environment 2), the average CVL is greater than 60%, which belongs to the severe fatigue state, which proves that the experimental parameter configuration conforms to the setting.

Subjective Assessment

Dimension weight.

To determine the weight of each dimension of the comprehensive pilot perceptual assessment scale (NASA-TLX, SART and Likert scale), 6 active pilots were invited to form an expert panel to conduct pair–pair comparisons of the impacts of workload, situational awareness and design satisfaction on pilots' flying emotions. Form a decision matrix. It was concluded that the influence weights of workload, situation awareness, and design satisfaction on pilots' flight emotions were 36.8%, 27.5%, and 35.7% respectively.

Environmental weight.

Pilots' performance and responses in harsh environments are particularly critical, as their situational awareness and decision-making capabilities are severely tested. These conditions more effectively reveal the impact of cockpit interior design on flight efficiency and safety. Therefore, different environments were assigned weights proportional to their severity relative to the comprehensive impact on flight emotions. This weighting scheme more objectively reflects the actual influence of various conditions on pilots. In this experiment, Environment 1 was assigned a weight of 36.4%, and Environment 2 a weight of 63.6%.

Subjective composite score.

The subjective composite score for each cockpit sample in each environment was computed as the weighted sum of the three subjective dimensions of the Pilot Affective Evaluation Comprehensive Scale, as presented in Table 1.

Table 1. Subjective scale scores.

Aircraft models	Environment 1				Environment 2				Composite score
	Workload	Situational awareness	Design satisfaction	Total score	Workload	Situational awareness	Design satisfaction	Total score	
Type 1	4.37	5.11	5.83	5.09	3.18	4.80	5.25	4.37	4.63
Type 2	3.53	4.13	3.80	3.79	3.06	3.56	3.39	3.32	3.49
Type 3	4.55	4.75	3.66	4.29	3.94	3.51	3.24	3.57	3.83
Type 4	3.26	3.70	4.75	3.91	3.20	3.42	4.70	3.80	3.84
Type 5	3.16	4.03	3.38	3.48	3.62	3.35	3.62	3.54	3.52
Type 6	5.07	4.11	4.24	4.51	4.61	4.03	3.96	4.23	4.33
Type 7	3.71	4.72	4.86	4.40	3.19	3.59	4.17	3.65	3.92
Type 8	5.57	4.97	5.45	5.36	5.41	3.21	5.42	4.81	5.01
Type 9	4.10	4.05	5.50	4.59	4.04	3.96	4.56	4.20	4.34
Type 10	4.40	3.04	3.37	3.66	4.15	5.10	4.85	4.65	4.29
Type 11	3.92	4.03	3.84	3.92	3.56	3.89	3.51	3.64	3.74
Type 12	4.26	3.29	4.88	4.21	3.24	3.45	4.05	3.58	3.81
Type 13	4.87	3.96	5.66	4.90	3.16	3.55	5.63	4.15	4.42
Type 14	5.03	5.13	4.07	4.71	4.43	5.32	4.76	4.79	4.76
Type 15	3.74	3.05	2.99	3.28	3.36	4.23	3.76	3.74	3.57

Objective Assessment

The eye movement heatmap is a visual tool used to show the subject's gaze point and duration on the screen. It is often used to analyze the subject's attention and interest points and to assess the subject's response to a specific task or interface. For 30 flight tasks, a superimposed eye movement heatmap of all the subjects was obtained, as shown in Fig. 4. The heatmap shows that the subjects not only pay attention to the information displayed on the instrument and screen during the flight but also pay attention to the interior design of the cockpit.

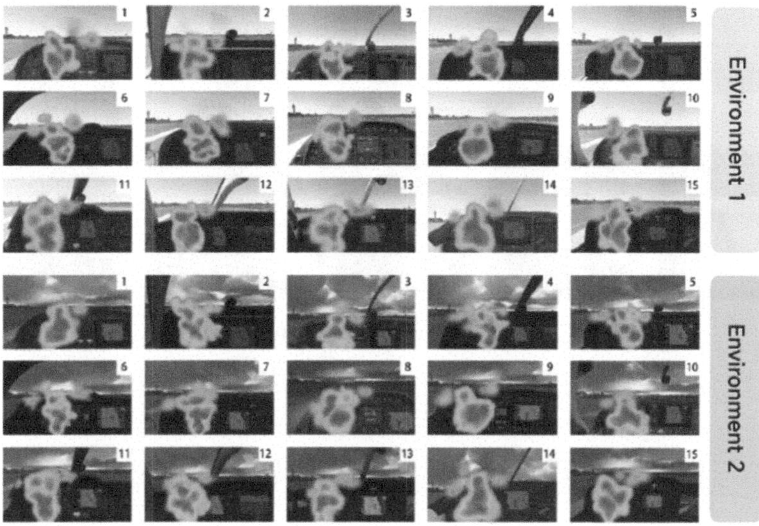

Fig. 4. Eye movement heatmap based on experimental tasks.

4.2 Decomposition of Design Elements in Aircraft Cockpit Interiors

Based on the bilateral symmetry of the aircraft cockpit, modeling lines were extracted exclusively from the left-half section for analysis, as illustrated in Fig. 5. A key styling line integrating both the common and distinctive shape characteristics across the 15 aircraft models was defined and parameterized, as shown in Fig. 6. The point in the lower left corner of the key styling line is defined as the starting point, marked as the origin A (0,0). The key styling line is scaled equally so that the horizontal coordinate of the end of the key styling line is 1, marked as point D. The direction from starting point A is defined as the leading side, and the direction from endpoint D is defined as the trailing side. The corner at the top left is defined as the main corner, which is in the visual center of gravity and determines the style and trend of the entire line. The starting point and end point of the main corner are defined as B and C respectively, and the maximum radius of curvature on the main corner is defined as K. The corner near starting point A is defined as curve at the origin, the swell near the end point D is defined as endpoint protrusion, and the width of endpoint protrusion on the X-axis is defined as u. The initial included angle between the line connecting starting point A and main corner starting point B and the X-axis is defined as θ_1, and the angle between the line connecting the main corner end point C and end point D and the X-axis is defined as θ_2.

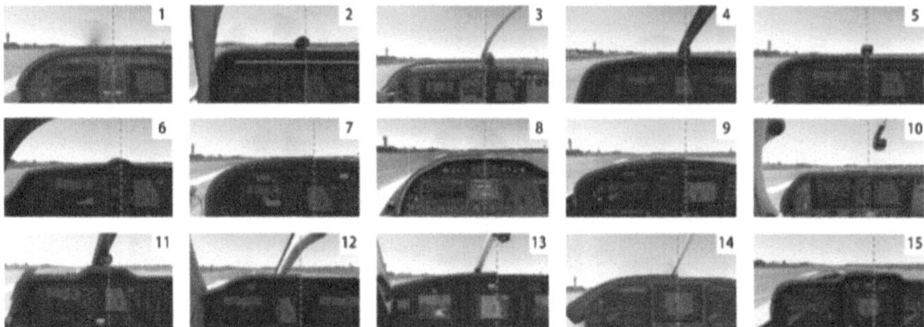

Fig. 5. Extraction of modeling lines from cockpits.

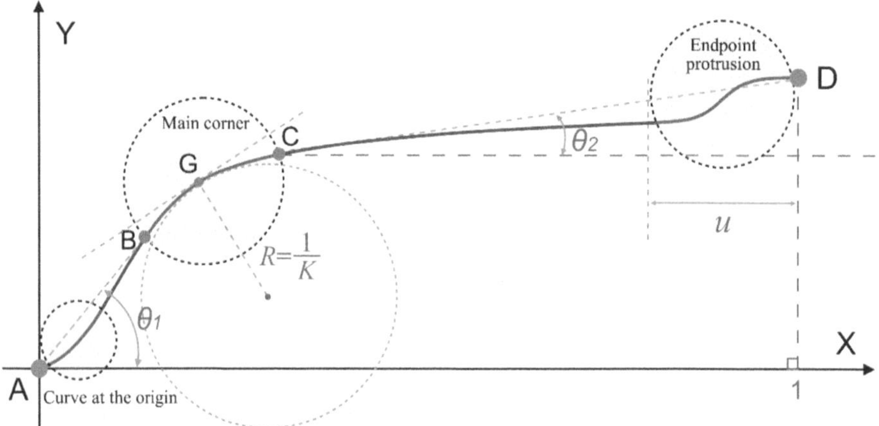

Fig. 6. Parameterization of the key styling line.

In light of their impact on aesthetics and pilot psychological state, this study groups the discernible exterior features of cockpit styling lines, colors, and materials into three categories (see Table 2). The key styling features include F1 to F7. Other styling line features include the glare shield stiffening rib F8 and the center windshield post F9. The presence of these structures varies across different aircraft models, with some models incorporating them and others not. Color feature F10 defines the most extensive area as the dominant hue, calibrated across nine brightness levels N1 to N9. Material feature F11 mainly involves panel materials composed of alloy and leather.

Table 2. Deconstruction of aircraft cockpit interior design elements.

Attribute	Code	Characteristic element	Level 1	Level 2	Level 3
Key styling line	F1	Initial included angle θ_1	$\theta_1 = 90°$	$45° \leq \theta_1 < 90°$	$0° < \theta_1 < 45°$
	F2	Curve at the origin	NO	Concave up	Concave Down
	F3	Leading line of main corner starting point B	NO	Straight line	Curve
	F4	Main bend maximum curvature radius K	$K > 2$	$1 < K \leq 2$	$K \leq 1$
	F5	Trailing line of main corner end C	Straight line	Curve	/
	F6	Endpoint protrusion width u	NO	$0 < u \leq 0.3$	$u > 0.3$
	F7	Angle between main corner θ_2	$\theta_2 > 0$	$\theta_2 = 0$	/
Other styling lines	F8	Windshield frame	NO	YES	/
	F9	Center windshield post	NO	YES	/
Color scheme	F10	Primary color lightness	Brightness N1-N3	Brightness N4-N6	/
Material	F11	Material	Alloy	Leather	/

4.3 Affective Evaluation Model Driven by BP Neural Network

Based on the BP neural network, a mapping relationship was established between the perceptual features of the cockpit appearance and the subjective scale scores. This model enables the prediction of pilots' perceptual feedback from the cockpit's exterior design features. The input layer of the network consists of the perceptual features, while the output layer corresponds to the total score of the pilot subjective scale.

Input Layer and Output Layer

On the basis of the nominal scale [23], the perceived feature elements of model samples are coded. According to Table 2, aircraft cockpit interior appearance has 4 characteristic attributes, each characteristic attribute is divided into different characteristic elements and categories, and each characteristic element corresponds to 3 digits or 2 digits according to the category. Thus, each model can be defined as a 27-bit Boolean code, and the total number of encoded bits is the sum of the number of element types of the perceived features of the cockpit appearance. The value of the corresponding bits of the characteristic element category is 1, and the value of the remaining digits is 0. For example, model Type 1 is encoded as 010100100001011001010100110.

Given the limited sample size of the aircraft cockpit experiment, K-fold cross-validation was adopted to maximize data utilization and reduce overfitting during BP neural network training and testing. This study includes 15 model samples. To maintain an appropriate ratio between the training set and test set, K was set to 5, implementing 5-fold cross-validation. The 15 models were randomly divided into 5 subsets in MATLAB. In each iteration, the Boolean codes of the remaining 12 samples after removing 3 test samples were used as the input layer, and the normalized comprehensive total scores of these samples (Table 1) served as the output layer.

The Number of Hidden Layers and Nodes

A single-hidden-layer BP neural network was adopted to simplify the model structure and accelerate the training process while maintaining performance. The number of hidden layer nodes was determined via a trial-and-error approach, aiming to minimize the node count without compromising generalization capability. The initial value was estimated using the following empirical formula:

$$m = \sqrt{n + l} + a \tag{2}$$

where m is the number of hidden layer nodes, l is the number of output layer nodes, n is the number of input layer nodes, and a is a constant between 1 and 10. Based on this formula, the initial number of hidden layer nodes was set to 7. Different node numbers were then successively tested to train the BP neural network. Results indicate that the training error decreased as the number of nodes increased from the initial value of 7. However, when the number of nodes reached 13 or more, the error stabilized, and further increases provided negligible improvement. Therefore, the number of hidden layer nodes was ultimately set to 13.

Other Parameters

The network was configured with the Levenberg-Marquardt algorithm as the training function, the learngdm() function for learning, and the logsig() function as the activation function. The mean squared error (MSE) was adopted as the error metric, with a target convergence error of 0.001 and a maximum of 100 training epochs.

4.4 Predictive Model Training and Testing

In each fold, one subset was sequentially selected as the test set, while the remaining 12 samples constituted the training set. Training was terminated once the error met the target criterion. The BP neural network achieved the required performance, with both the maximum and average absolute errors between the output and expected values being less than 0.001.

The trained BP neural network prediction model was tested for generalization capability. Subsets 1 to 5 were sequentially used as test sets, and the output values were compared with the normalized comprehensive total scores from the subjective scale. The corresponding test deviation values and deviation rates are presented in Table 3.

Table 3. Comparison between actual and predicted values of affective evaluation.

Test set	Test sample	True value	Predicted value	Deviation value	Deviation ratio
Subset 1	Type 1	0.661	0.684	−0.023	3.48%
	Type 6	0.618	0.599	0.020	3.24%
	Type 15	0.510	0.537	−0.027	5.29%
Subset 2	Type 2	0.499	0.533	−0.034	6.81%
	Type 10	0.613	0.650	−0.037	6.04%
	Type 14	0.681	0.714	−0.034	4.99%
Subset 3	Type 3	0.548	0.557	−0.010	1.82%
	Type 7	0.560	0.530	0.030	5.36%
	Type 9	0.620	0.644	−0.024	3.87%
Subset 4	Type 8	0.715	0.694	0.021	2.94%
	Type 11	0.534	0.506	0.028	5.24%
	Type 13	0.631	0.660	−0.029	4.60%
Subset 5	Type 4	0.548	0.530	0.018	3.28%
	Type 5	0.502	0.536	−0.033	6.57%
	Type 12	0.545	0.567	−0.022	4.04%

As shown in Table 3, the maximum deviation rate between predicted and actual values is 6.81%. The neural network predictions were denormalized and compared with the actual total scores from the subjective affective evaluation, with the results visualized in Fig. 7. The Pilot Affective Evaluation Comprehensive Scale employs a 7-point rating system, with a score of 4.2 (60% of the maximum) defined as the threshold for design evaluation. Scores below 4.2 indicate that the cockpit sample is considered to have an average interior design level, while scores above 4.2 reflect a favorable design that aligns with pilots' psychological expectations and needs. With the exception of Type 6, the predicted results for all 14 other samples are consistent with the actual evaluation outcomes, indicating that the BP neural network model has been successfully trained with good generalization capability and can serve as an effective predictive tool for Kansei evaluation of aircraft cockpit interior design.

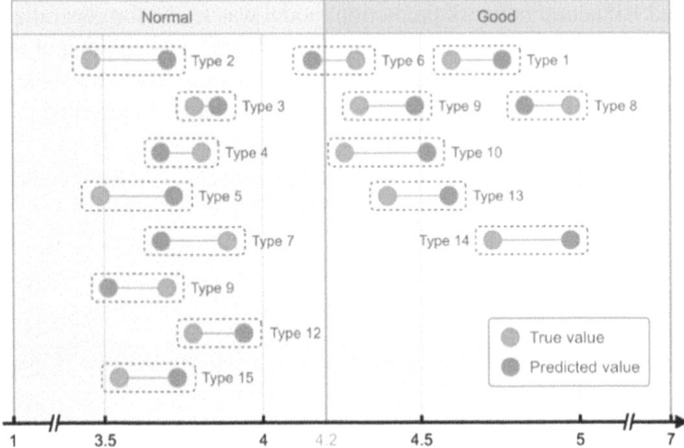

Fig. 7. Visual comparison of evaluated and BP neural network model predicted values.

5 Conclusions

Guided by behavioral logic, this study examines the factors and mechanisms influencing pilots' affective interaction with cockpit interiors. A simplified framework for complex dynamic flight environments was developed based on the three dimensions of "mission timeline, phase and scenario." A *Comprehensive Impact Index of Complex Dynamic Environments on Flight Emotions* was proposed to inform the configuration of flight environments in perceptual evaluation experiments. Using a flight simulation platform, perceptual interactions in aircraft cockpits under dynamic complex conditions were replicated. By integrating subjective and objective data, a BP neural network-based predictive model for the perceptual evaluation of cockpit interior design was constructed. This study provides a theoretical foundation and experimental methodology for evaluating and designing civil aircraft cockpit interiors in dynamic complex environments, contributing to both enhanced pilot experience and aviation safety.

As a preliminary investigation into affective evaluation under such conditions, this research acknowledges limitations due to the dynamic, multifaceted, and uncertain nature of pilot perceptual responses. Future work will focus on improving the simulation of diverse dynamic flight environments and refining the characterization of perceptual quality to achieve more accurate design evaluation.

Acknowledgment. This study was funded by National Natural Science Foundation of China (grant number 52275254).

Disclosure of Interests. The authors have no competing interests to declare that are relevant to the content of this article.

References

1. The Boeing Company: Statistical summary of commercial jet airplane accidents. https://skybrary.aero/sites/default/files/bookshelf/3198.pdf. Accessed 12 Nov 2025
2. Qiao, S.: Air Crash Apocalypse: Who is the Golden Key to Aviation Safety. Civil Aviation Press of China, Beijing (2018)
3. Zhao, C., Fan, R., Zhu, Z., Liu, H.: Civil Aircraft Cockpit Integrated Design and Airworthiness Verification. Shanghai Jiao Tong University Press, Shanghai (2020)
4. Şenol, M.B.: A new optimization model for design of traditional cockpit interfaces. Aircr. Eng. Aerosp. Technol. **92**, 404–417 (2020)
5. Parnell, K.J., Banks, V.A., Allison, C.K., Plant, K.L., Beecroft, P., Stanton, N.A.: Designing flight deck applications: combining insight from end-users and ergonomists. Cogn. Technol. Work **23**, 353–365 (2021)
6. Nagamachi, M.: Kansei engineering in consumer product design. Ergon. Des. **10**, 5–9 (2002)
7. Lu, W., Ye, C., Fang, Y., Čok, V., Petiot, J.F.: A systematic review of Kansei engineering in vehicle design. Digit. Eng. **3**, 100022 (2024)
8. Liu, G.: Research and application of commercial aircraft cockpit modeling design. Master's thesis, Shanghai Jiao Tong University, Shanghai (2015)
9. Lu, W., Jiang, G., Liu, Y., Zhang, Y., Zhang, Z.: Perceptual evaluation of business aircraft cockpit interior layout design. Comput. Integr. Manuf. Syst. **30**, 28–41 (2024)
10. Wang, L., Cao, Q., Mo, X., Yu, J., Li, B.: Study of users' Kansei on commercial aircraft cockpit interior design. J. Mech. Eng. **50**, 122–126 (2014)
11. Chen, Y., Yu, S., Chu, J., Yu, M., Chen, D.: Fuzzy emotional evaluation of color matching for aircraft cockpit design. J. Intell. Fuzzy Syst. **40**, 3899–3917 (2021)
12. Zhou, G., Xu, J., Ma, S., Zong, J., Shen, J., Zhu, H.: Review of key technologies for avionics systems integration on large passenger aircraft. Acta Aeronaut. Astronaut. Sin. **45** (2024)
13. Feng, C., Wanyan, X., Liu, S., Chen, H., Zhuang, D.: Study on situation awareness under different mental workloads. J. Northw. Polytech. Univ. **38**, 610–618 (2020)
14. Qian, C., et al.: Situation awareness discrimination based on physiological features for high-stress flight tasks. Aerospace **11**, 897 (2024)
15. Pei, X., Liu, J., Wang, X., Zhu, M., Zhang, L., Dan, Z.: Quasi-one-dimensional flow modeling for flight environment simulation system of altitude ground test facilities. Processes **10**, 377 (2022)
16. Yu, Z., Yue, Z., Liu, Y., Liu, W.: Function analysis of aircraft cargo door electro-hydraulic system in flight environment. Chin. J. Mech. Eng. **50**, 141–146 (2014)
17. Baumann, I., Trimmel, M.: Distribution of subjective assessments in a controlled aircraft environment. Aerosp. Sci. Technol. **25**, 93–101 (2013)
18. Said, S., et al.: Validation of the raw National Aeronautics and Space Administration Task Load Index (NASA-TLX) questionnaire to assess perceived workload in patient monitoring tasks: pooled analysis study using mixed models. J. Med. Internet Res. **22**, e19472 (2020)
19. Luximon, A., Goonetilleke, R.S.: Simplified subjective workload assessment technique. Ergonomics **44**, 229–243 (2001)
20. Zhang, X., Zhou, L., Savalei, V.: Comparing the psychometric properties of a scale across three Likert and three alternative formats: an application to the Rosenberg self-esteem scale. Educ. Psychol. Meas. **83**, 649–683 (2023)
21. Tang, H., Lee, B.G., Towey, D., Pike, M.: The impact of various cockpit display interfaces on novice pilots' mental workload and situational awareness: a comparative study. Sensors **24**(9), 2835 (2024)

22. Dias, M., et al.: Cardiovascular load assessment in the workplace: a systematic review. Int. J. Ind. Ergon. **96**, 103476 (2023)
23. Bove, G.: The homogeneity index as a measure of interrater agreement for ratings on a nominal scale. In: Grilli, L., Lupparelli, M., Rampichini, C., Rocco, E., Vichi, M. (eds.) Statistical Models and Methods for Data Science. CLADAG 2021. Studies in Classification, Data Analysis, and Knowledge Organization, pp. 15–25. Springer, Cham (2023). https://doi.org/10.1007/978-3-031-30164-3_2

Image Emotion Classification Through Chain of Thought Prompts

Yufei Xiao and Shangfei Wang(✉)

University of Science and Technology of China, Hefei 230026, Anhui, China
xyf730@mail.ustc.edu.cn, sfwang@ustc.edu.cn

Abstract. Existing methods for image emotion classification mainly rely on building large-scale networks that map visual features to emotion labels. However, as these networks grow in scale, they increasingly demand computational resources. Therefore, we propose a lightweight image emotion classification approach based on Chain of Thought (CoT) prompting. CoT introduces a novel paradigm in machine learning, leveraging specialized prompts to guide language models toward achieving appropriate outcomes. This paradigm has demonstrated promising few-shot performance across various natural language processing tasks but remains unexplored in the context of visual emotion understanding. Specifically, we first utilize Large Multimodal Models (LMMs) to generate reasoning processes that explain the emotional content in images. Then, we introduce a semantic similarity sampling mechanism to select the most relevant emotional reasoning examples for a given test sample, constructing appropriate CoT prompts to guide the LMM in step-by-step reasoning about emotional causes. Finally, we employ a self-consistency strategy to enhance the robustness of the reasoning process. Experimental results show that our approach outperforms mainstream methods on three widely used datasets, achieving superior accuracy in image emotion classification.

Keywords: Large Multimodal Models · Emotion Classification · Chain-of-Thought Reasoning

1 Introduction

Emotion is an abstract representation of the diverse expressions of human feelings. Image emotion classification is a key area within artificial intelligence and computer vision, aiming to categorize emotions based on visual cues in images. Currently, image emotion classification plays a crucial role in various application scenarios, such as social resource analysis, social media retrieval, and product recommendation systems.

In earlier studies, image emotion classification was often conceptualized as a conventional visual classification task [7,28]. Researchers mostly employed carefully designed visual feature extraction networks such as Convolutional

H. Liu et al. (Eds.): CEI 2025, CCIS 2881, pp. 73–88, 2026.
https://doi.org/10.1007/978-981-95-9493-1_5

Neural Networks (CNNs) [12], Residual Neural Networks (ResNets) [10], and Vision Transformers (ViTs) [9]. These networks capture latent representations to enhance the precision and effectiveness of image emotion classification.

With the advancement of Natural Language Processing (NLP), large-scale pre-trained models have increasingly become the mainstream architecture for NLP tasks, such as GPT-3 [3] and BERT [8]. These approaches have achieved competitive performance across various NLP downstream tasks. Subsequently, this methodology has been progressively extended to the field of computer vision, among which one of the most notable work is Contrastive Language-Image Pre-training (CLIP) [24]. Compared to traditional vision-only pre-training approaches, CLIP improves its generalization capabilities by aligning independent text and image encoders on a large-scale unsupervised dataset. This alignment facilitates the learning of more fine-grained visual concepts, making it suitable for a wide range of downstream language- vision tasks. Based on CLIP and other large language-vision pre-trained models, methods for image emotion classification have gradually evolved to leverage these models through fine-tuning.

In recent years, with the continual expansion of network sizes, Large Multimodal Models (LMMs) have emerged. Models such as BLIP2 [13], Flamingo [1], and LLaVA [17] have demonstrated exceptional performance in open-world visual understanding, capable of addressing multiple visual tasks including classification, segmentation, and captioning. In contrast, current LMMs remain in the early stages of emotional perception [14]. Due to their large network size, traditional fine-tuning methods consume substantial computational resources on LMMs. To fully leverage the few-shot learning potential of existing vision-based large models while avoiding substantial computational costs, we have introduced the Chain-of-Thought (CoT) prompting method, which has shown promising results in large language models (LLMs). Specifically, we propose a lightweight image emotion classification method based on CoT prompts. Our approach begins with the generation of emotional reasons. We utilize designed prompts that enable LMMs to comprehend the emotions of training examples. During the semantic similarity sampling phase, we first use a fine-tuned ViT encoder to map images into a high- dimensional emotional semantic feature space to obtain their feature representations. Subsequently, we employ cosine similarity to select training samples that are most semantically relevant to the test instance. To further enhance the quality of the CoT prompts, we have designed a voting prompt to guide the LMM in selecting a small number of samples that are most emotionally similar to the test image. Finally, we construct CoT prompts using the training examples and their corresponding emotional reasons determined during the voting phase and utilize these prompts to enable the LMM to generate the corresponding emotional labels.

Our proposed method is evaluated on three widely used benchmarks for image emotion classification, namely the EmoSet, WEBemo and FI datasets. Experimental results indicate that our method outperforms existing approaches, particularly surpassing the previous state-of-the-art methods on the WEBemo and FI dataset. Additionally, we conducted a series of ablation studies, the results of which demonstrate that the three key components of our method contribute to its overall performance.

The contributions of this work are summarized as follows:

(1) We propose a novel lightweight image emotion classification method based on CoT prompts, which avoids the substantial computational resources required for fine-tuning LMMs.

(2) To the best of our knowledge, this is the first work to integrate CoT prompting techniques with LMMs for image emotion classification tasks. This significantly enhances the emotional comprehension capabilities of LMMs.

(3) Experimental results on three popular emotional image datasets demonstrate that our proposed method outperforms the state-of-the-art methods in image emotion classification.

2 Related Work

Image emotion classification is a challenging task that requires understanding the subtle and complex emotional content embedded in visual data. Over the years, two main categories of approaches have been employed for this task: methods based on traditional neural networks and methods that leverage fine-tuning of pre-trained models.

2.1 Neural Network-Based Approaches

Traditional neural network-based methods for image emotion classification primarily focus on extracting emotional features using CNNs or Transformer architectures. Based on CNN architecture, Chen et al. [4] proposed DeepSentiBank, an enhanced visual emotion concept classification model trained on a vast dataset tagged with adjective-noun pairs. Zhao et al. [37] introduced a Polarity-consistent Deep Attention Network (**PDANet**) that integrates attention into a CNN with an emotion polarity constraint for fine-grained image emotion classification. Zhang et al. [36] proposed Weakly Supervised Emotion Intensity Prediction Networks(**WSEIPNet**). They leveraged emotion intensity learning to construct a deep neural network for image emotion recognition. Yang et al. [33] presented a stimuli-aware visual emotion analysis method termed **StimuliVEA**. He et al. [10] introduced a deep residual learning network(**ResNet**) to address the challenges of training very deep neural networks. Yang et al. [34] presented a novel approach to visual emotion analysis using weakly supervised coupled networks based on the ResNet backbone. Rao et al. [25] proposed a ResNet-based framework for classifying the emotional content of images using a multi-level region-based approach. She et al. [26] introduced Weakly Supervised Coupled Networks (**WSCNet**), which was a weakly supervised coupled convolutional network based on the backbone of ResNet101. It realized image emotion classification by coupling the global and local features according to the detected salient regions in the image.

Meanwhile, with the advent of the Transformer architecture and its exceptional performance in natural language processing (NLP) tasks, Dosovitskiy et al. [9] introduced Vision Transformer (ViT) to explore the application of Transformers to the field of computer vision. Following them, Liu et al. [15] explored the ViT architecture in the domain of image emotion classification. Xu et al. [30] leveraged the emotion hierarchy and the correlation between different affective levels and semantic levels to construct the Multi-level Dependent Attention Network (**MDAN**) with two branches. Pan et al. [22] introduced a novel multi-stage visual perception approach (**MSVPA**) for image emotion classification.

These methods excel in feature extraction and are well-suited for learning low-level and mid-level visual patterns. They demonstrate strong performance on specific tasks and do not rely on large scale pre-training datasets. However, these methods often lack the ability to model complex emotional relationships and contextual dependencies within images. Their scalability is limited by computational complexity, and their generalization performance across different datasets is relatively weak.

2.2 Fine-Tuning-Based Approaches

In recent years, with the rapid development of pre-trained networks, fine-tuning these networks to adapt to downstream tasks has increasingly become the paradigm for image emotion classification. Radford et al. [24] introduced an innovative approach termed Contrastive Language-Image Pre- training(**CLIP**) to pre-train visual models using natural language descriptions of images. This method enabled the model to understand and categorize new visual concepts described in natural language. Bondielli et al. [2] explored the application of the CLIP model in image emotion classification. Zhou et al. [38,39] proposed a simple approach, termed Context Optimization (**CoOp**), specifically for adapting CLIP-like vision-language models for downstream image recognition. Based on CoOp, Conditional Context Optimization (**CoCoOp**) extended CoOp by further learning a lightweight neural network to generate for each image an input-conditional token. Deng et al. [5] presented a prompt-based fine-tuning strategy, termed **SimEmotion**, to learn task-specific representations while preserving knowledge contained in CLIP. Xie et al. [29] proposed a visual instruction tuning approach **EmoViT** to enhance the emotion classification models. Deng et al. [6] proposed a novel prompt tuning method **PT-DPC** with diversified prompt composition, which conditions prompt on both the categories and image content. Xu et al. [31] introduced Multiple Views Prompt (**MVP**) to visual emotion analysis by leveraging emotional prompts with multiple views to enhance semantic emotional information.

These fine-tuning-based methods take advantage of extensive pre-training on different datasets to learn rich visual and language features. They have better semantic understanding capabilities and are also better in transferability and generalization. However, with the continual expansion of network sizes, the methods mentioned above require large-scale training and fine-tuning on specific network architectures, which leads to substantial consumption of computational resources. On the other hand, existing study [21] indicated that due to the generality of their pre-training data, current LMMs underperform specialized deep-learning models in the specific field of image emotion classification. To address these limitations, We propose a computationally lightweight method for image emotion classification based on CoT prompting. This approach aims to enhance classification accuracy by stimulating the LMM's ability to comprehend image emotions through the CoT mechanism.

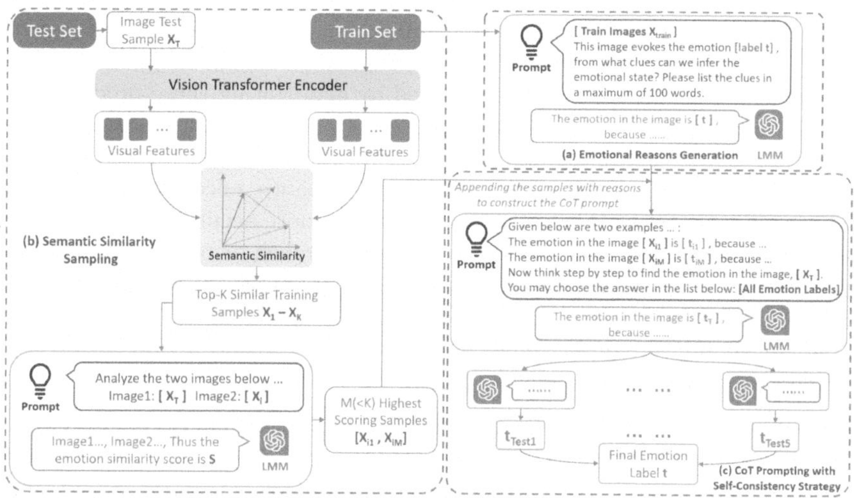

Fig. 1. The overall architecture of our proposed method. During (b) Semantic Similarity Sampling, given an input test image, the vision encoder initiates the process by extracting visual features. Then, after calculating the cosine similarity and LMM voting, we select a few examples from the train set that have the highest semantic similarity with the test image. These samples are subsequently interacting with the Emotional Reasons generated by (a). They will be used for constructing the CoT Prompts in (c).

3 Proposed Method

As illustrated in Fig. 1, we propose a lightweight image emotion classification method based on CoT prompting, including three main components: Emotional Reasons Generation, Semantic Similarity Sampling and CoT Prompting with Self-Consistency Strategy.

In particular, our approach initiates from the generation of emotional causes, utilizing well-designed CoT prompts to enable the LMM to comprehend the emotions of training examples. When provided with samples and corresponding emotional labels, the LMM typically generates sensible reasons for the emotions. During the Semantic Similarity Sampling phase, we first fine-tune a standard ViT model on the train set, using its encoder to measure the emotional semantic similarity in images. For a given test sample, we map it to a high-dimensional emotional semantic feature space using the ViT encoder to obtain its feature representation. Subsequently, we employ cosine similarity to select several training samples that are most semantically relevant. To further enhance the quality of the CoT prompts, we design a voting prompt to guide the LMM in selecting a few examples that are most emotionally similar to the test image from the selected samples. Finally, we construct the CoT prompts using the two training examples and their corresponding emotional reasons that are determined by the voting phase. These prompts encourage the LMM to explore multiple emotional clues within the images and to reveal the reasoning process leading to emotional labels. To further enhance the robustness of the proposed method, we employed a Self-Consistency Strategy during the prediction phase. This process involves using the same prompts to generate multiple predictions for the given test sample. The final emotional label is determined by aggregating these predictions.

By integrating these three components – Emotional Reasons Generation, Semantic Similarity Sampling, and CoT Prompting with Self-Consistency Strategy, our method utilizes the strengths of both semantic encoding and the generative capabilities of LMMs, thereby achieving a more accurate image emotion classification method. Furthermore, our overall approach involves training only a standard ViT model with a smaller number of parameters. Consequently, compared to traditional fine-tuning methods, our method reduces computational complexity, thereby becoming more lightweight.

3.1 Emotional Reasons Generation

The CoT prompting method has significant applications across various tasks. This reasoning approach enhances the LMM's inference capabilities on specific downstream tasks by transferring knowledge embedded in large pre- trained models through specifically designed prompts. This reduces the gap between pre-training and downstream tasks, whereby the knowledge contained in pre-training models is easily transferred to downstream tasks with only a few annotation examples. Specifically, we hope the LMM infers the latent cause of the emotion before answering the final emotion label t, instead of directly asking the LMM for the final result of the emotion. Therefore, we construct the prompt to generate the emotional reasons as follows:

> [Given Image X_{train}]
> This image evokes the emotion [Emotion Label t], from what clues can we infer the emotional state?
> Please list the clues in a maximum of 100 words.

The step can be formulated as:

$$C_{train} = Decoder_{LMM}(P(X_{train}, t)) \quad (1)$$

where C_{train} is the set of generated emotional reasons on the train set. $P()$ refers to the designed template of the prompt.

3.2 Semantic Similarity Sampling

As Liu et al. [18] have noted, the output of large pre-trained models is considerably sensitive to the chosen in-context examples, and carefully designed input data can significantly enhance the few-shot learning ability. Compared to the quantity of examples, the quality of examples has a greater impact on the model's performance. They suggest retrieving examples that are semantically similar to the test sample to formulate appropriate prompts. Therefore, we design a semantic similarity sampling pipeline to select several training samples that are most similar in emotional semantics to the test sample.

To be specific, the entire pipeline is divided into two steps. In the first step, we fine-tune a standard ViT model on the train set, and then utilize the encoder part of the model to measure semantic similarity between images. As the fine-tuning objective was based on the true emotion labels, the feature space associated with this encoder is relevant to emotional semantics. For a given test sample X_T, we map it into a high-dimensional semantic space using the trained encoder to obtain its feature representation. We then evaluate emotional semantic similarity by computing the cosine similarity between the feature representations of images. Finally, we choose the top-K semantically similar training samples $[X_1, X_2, ..., X_K]$. This step can be formulated as:

$$E_{train} = Encoder_{ViT}(X_{train}) \tag{2}$$

$$E_T = Encoder_{ViT}(X_T) \tag{3}$$

$$[X_1, X_2, ..., X_K] = argmax_{k=1}^{K}[cos(E_{train}, E_T)] \tag{4}$$

$$X_i \in X_{train}, i \in \{1, 2, ..., K\}$$

where $Encoder_{ViT}$ refers to the trained ViT encoder, E_{train} and E_T are the image encodings of the images in the train set and the test sample, respectively.

In the second step of the pipeline, we design a voting prompt to guide the LMM in conducting further similarity analysis on the K selected training samples:

> Analyze the two images below, then at the last line conclude "Thus the emotion similarity score is $\{s\}$",
> where s is an integer from 1 to 10.
> Image1: [Given Test Image X_T]
> Image2: [One of the Training Sample X_i]

This step can be formulated as:

$$[X_{i1}, ..., X_{iM}] = argmax_{k=1}^{M}[Decoder_{LMM}(P(X_T, X_k))] \tag{5}$$

where $[X_{i1}, ..., X_{iM}]$ is the chosen set of most similar to the test sample in terms of emotional semantics. $P()$ refers to the designed template of the voting prompt.

Following the completion of the steps above, we proceed to the construction of the CoT Prompts. In this phase, we sample instances $[X_{i1}, ..., X_{iM}]$ that demonstrate the highest semantic similarity to the test sampleX_T, along with their corresponding emotional reasons $[C_{i1}, ..., C_{iM}] \subset C_{train}$, to ensure the quality of the instances.

3.3 CoT Prompting with Self-Consistency Strategy

In the final phase of constructing the CoT prompts, we utilize the previously selected training samples $[X_{i1}, ..., X_{iM}]$, along with their corresponding emotional reasons $[C_{i1}, ..., C_{iM}]$, as few-shot examples in the prompts. This guides the LMM to generate the emotional label for the test sample X_T:

Given below are two examples of the emotions in the images and the causes for the emotions:
The emotion in the photo [X_{i1}] is [Emotional Label t_{i1}], because [C_{i1}]
...
The emotion in the photo [X_{iM}] is [Emotional Label t_{iM}], because [C_{iM}]
Now think step by step to find the emotion in the image, [X_T].
You may choose the answer in the list below: [All Emotional Labels]

This phase can be formulated as:

$$A_T = Decoder_{LMM}(P([X_{ij}, t_{ij}, C_{ij}]_{j=1}^{M}, X_T)) \tag{6}$$

where A_T represents the output text containing the predicted emotional label t_T. Then we extract t_T to serve as the predicted emotional response for the test sample X_T.

To enhance the robustness of our method, we further employ the Self-Consistency strategy [27] as the decoding strategy for the LMM. The Self-Consistency strategy innovatively enhances CoT prompts for complex reasoning tasks. Unlike traditional greedy decoding, this method leverages the principle that multiple valid reasoning approaches can converge to the correct solution by sampling different reasoning paths and selecting the most consistent answer. The Self-Consistency strategy aggregates various reasoning paths, not only mitigating the limitations of the greedy decoding, such as repetitiveness and local optimality, but also reducing the randomness of single-sample generation. This strategy closely aligns with human cognitive processes, where the confidence in the result increases as it is derived through various paths of reasoning.

To be specific, following the work of Wang et al. [27], we employ five distinct reasoning paths to determine the final emotional label. Each path provides a prediction for the emotional label t. With the Self-Consistency strategy, we select the emotional label with the highest voting number as the final label for the test sample X_T.

4 Experiments

4.1 Experimental Setup

Datasets We demonstrate the effectiveness of our method on the EmoSet [32], WEBEmo [23] and FI [35] datasets.

EmoSet is the largest dataset within the realm of visual emotion analysis. It comprises 3.3 million images with 118,102 of these meticulously annotated by human annotators, making it substantially larger and more comprehensive compared to other datasets. EmoSet includes a diverse range of images sourced from social networks and artistic collections, ensuring a balanced representation across different emotion categories. In this work, we have harnessed EmoSet-118K, which contains two types of annotations: eight categories and two polarities, denoted as EmoSet-8 and EmoSet-2, respectively.

WEBEmo dataset is a large-scale web-based image emotion dataset, structured according to Parrott's hierarchical model of emotions. The creators initiated the dataset by searching for each emotion-related keyword on internet platforms, resulting in the collection of approximately 300,000 weakly labeled images. They then removed the duplicate images and those with non-English tags, culminating in a final dataset comprising 268,000 images. Each image in the dataset is annotated with a weak label reflecting a three-tiered emotional classification, encompassing 25, 6, and 2 categories respectively. In this work, we utilize WEBEmo-2, WEBEmo-6, and WEBEmo-25 for the experiments.

FI dataset is a large-scale, strongly annotated image dataset for visual emotion analysis, sourced from Flickr and Instagram. The dataset comprises 23,308 strongly labeled images across eight emotion categories: Amusement, Awe, Contentment, Excitement, Anger, Disgust, Fear, and Sadness.

Following the work of the dataset papers [23,32,35], we split the data into 80% training set, 5% validation set and 15% test set for EmoSet-118K, 70% training set, 10% validation set and 20% test set for WEBEmo and 80% training set, 5% validation set, and 15% test set for FI.

Implementation Details In our experiments, we utilize a high-performance open-source LMM, specifically the LLaVa-NEXT-Mistral-7B model [16,17]. This model has outperformed most open-source LMMs in various capability tests. For the training of the ViT encoder, we employed the AdamW [20] as the optimizer over 6 training epochs, with an initial learning rate of 2×10^{-4} and a batch size of 16. The input images are resized to 224×224 with center-crop and normalization following the setting of the ViT image processor. All experiments were conducted on an NVIDIA RTX 4090 GPU with 24 GB CUDA memory. Additionally, we determine the values of the hyperparameters K and M through the grid search on the validation set. Our method performs best on the validation set when $K = 5$ and $M = 2$, respectively. Following the existing methods, we used accuracy and weighted F1 score as metrics to evaluate the efficacy of our proposed method.

4.2 Comparison Results

We compare our approach with the existing methods mentioned in the Related Work Section. These methods are categorized into two major groups. First, those based on traditional network architectures such as CNN, ResNet, and ViT, including **WSCNet** [26], **MRCNN** [25], **PDANet** [37], **WSEIPNet** [36], **StimuliVEA** [33], **MDAN** [30], **MSVPA** [22]. Second, those based on instruction fine-tuning large visual pre-trained models, such as **CoOp and CoCoOp** [38,39], **SimEmotion** [5], **PT-DPC** [6], **MVP** [31], **EmoVIT** [29].

The comparative experimental results are presented in Table 1. Due to the lack of data from other methods, we only compare the weighted F1 scores on the 8-category EmoSet. From the table, we obtain the following observations: our method achieves competitive results on the three datasets, particularly excelling on the WEBEmo and FI datasets, surpassing previous state-of-the-art methods. This demonstrates the efficacy of utilizing CoT prompts for image emotion classification. We have analyzed the distribution of samples in the EmoSet-8 test set. The results indicate an approximately 8% disparity between the categories with

Table 1. Comparison of different methods on EmoSet and WEBEmo datasets. The best and secondary performances are in bold and underlined, respectively.

Method	EmoSet			WEBEmo			FI
Number of Categories	8		2	25	6	2	8
	Acc	F1	Acc	Acc	Acc	Acc	Acc
AlexNet	0.6780	–	0.8928	0.2821	0.4866	–	0.5813
ResNet101	0.7487	–	0.9384	0.3214	0.5235	0.7817	0.6616
WSCNet	0.7632	–	0.9416	0.3275	0.5261	0.7943	0.7007
MRCNN	0.7539	–	0.9228	–	–	–	–
PDANet	–	–	–	0.3282	0.5346	0.8096	0.7213
WSEIPNet	–	–	–	0.3301	0.5388	0.8247	–
StimuliVEA	0.7840	–	0.9458	–	–	–	–
MDAN	0.7575	–	0.9371	0.3428	0.5565	0.8272	0.7641
CLIP	0.6976	0.6846	0.9074	<u>0.4065</u>	0.5642	0.8002	–
CoOp	0.7619	0.7539	0.9421	–	–	–	–
CoCoOp	0.8031	0.7863	0.9333	–	–	–	–
SimEmotion	0.7906	0.7894	0.9428	–	–	–	0.7962
PT-DPC	0.7713	0.7348	0.9246	–	–	–	0.7807
MVP	0.8192	<u>0.8047</u>	**0.9644**	–	–	–	–
MSVPA	–	–	–	0.3833	<u>0.5789</u>	<u>0.8277</u>	–
EmoVIT	**0.8336**	–	–	0.2112	–	–	0.6809
Ours	<u>0.8208</u>	**0.8161**	<u>0.9492</u>	**0.4504**	**0.6930**	**0.8613**	**0.7981**

the highest and lowest proportions, which suggests a relative imbalance for an eight-category dataset. Therefore, it is more appropriate to utilize the weighted F1 score to measure the performance of various methods. Our method surpasses the previous state-of-the-art methods in terms of the weighted F1 score on the EmoSet-8 dataset. This indicates that our approach benefits from the powerful few-shot learning capabilities of the LMM, enabling it to more effectively distinguish the differences between nuanced emotion categories. Notably, on the EmoSet dataset, our method generally outperforms approaches that involve instruction fine-tuning on large visual pre-trained models. This demonstrates that our method successfully enables the LMM to transfer a vast amount of generalized pre- trained knowledge to downstream image emotion classification tasks through the use of CoT prompts.

Compared with traditional image emotion classification methods based on neural networks and fine-tuning pre- trained networks, our method adopts a larger scale LMM. Through extensive pre-training on massive datasets, LMM shows excellent ability to understand longer contexts and capture complex image semantic relationships, thereby improving the performance of complex image emotion analysis. In addition, traditional methods usually rely heavily on high-quality, evenly distributed labeled data, and their performance is significantly affected by data scarcity. In contrast, LMM has been pre-trained on a wide range of general corpora. Therefore, it shows strong zero-shot and few-shot learning capabilities, as well as stronger generalization capabilities, and has achieved excellent performance on all datasets.

4.3 Computational Complexity Analysis

To more intuitively demonstrate the lightweight nature of our method, we compared it with the best-performing methods on the EmoSet-8 dataset, with results presented in Table 2. According to the Scaling Law [11], the computational cost of training one epoch can be estimated as $6ND$, where N represents the number of model parameters, and D denotes the number of tokens in the training set. For the EmoSet-8 dataset, we estimated the computational cost for training one epoch for these methods. Our method achieves competitive results with lower computational complexity. Particularly in comparison to EmoViT, our method reduces training consumption by several orders of magnitude, which underscores the effectiveness of our approach under a lightweight design.

Table 2. Comparison to best-performing methods on EmoSet-8 with training complexity

Methods	Total Training Parameters	Training Flops (Per Epoch)	Accuracy
MVP	$170.98M$	$1.94 \times 10^4 TFlops$	0.8192
EmoViT	$7.91B$	$8.96 \times 10^5 TFlops$	0.8336
Ours	$86.39M$	$9.79 \times 10^3 TFlops$	0.8208

4.4 Ablation Studies

We conducted ablation experiments on EmoSet-8, WEBEmo-6, and FI datasets. This choice is informed by the relatively extreme classification results of the binary and 25-category datasets, particularly where the binary classification accuracy approaches 90%. In contrast, the results for the chosen datasets are more balanced, making them more suitable for ablation studies. The results are presented in Table 3. We examined variant models in these experiments:

We replace the original CoT prompts with zero-shot prompts as illustrated below. This corresponds to the **Zero-shot** row in the table.

> [Given Test Image X_T]
> Think step by step to find the emotion in the image.
> You may choose the answer in the list below: [All Emotional Labels]

We random sample two training samples instead of the semantic similarity sampling pipeline, which is noted as **Random Sampling** in the table. We leverage the trained ViT Encoder to sample the top-M semantically similar training

Table 3. Ablation studies results on EmoSet-8 and WEBEmo-6 datasets. The best performances are in bold.

Method	EmoSet-8		WEBEmo-6		FI	
	Acc	F1	Acc	F1	Acc	F1
Zero-shot	0.5364	0.4004	0.5494	0.5146	0.6029	0.5786
Random Sampling	0.3556	0.3472	0.4612	0.4257	0.3964	0.3989
Top-M Sampling	0.7773	0.7729	0.6246	0.6068	0.6907	0.6879
w/o Self-Consistency	0.8039	0.7921	0.6704	0.6685	0.7695	0.7699
Only ViT Encoder	0.7309	0.7302	0.4755	0.4666	0.6465	0.6378
Baseline	**0.8208**	**0.8161**	**0.6930**	**0.6705**	**0.7891**	**0.7769**

samples and omit the voting phase to construct the CoT prompts, which is called **Top-M Sampling**. We generate only one path instead of five paths to determine the final emotional label. This corresponds to the **w/o Self-Consistency** row in the table. We only utilize the trained ViT Encoder to classify the image for comparison, which is termed as **Only ViT Encoder**.

Through the series of ablation studies, we observed that the removal of the Few-shot CoT prompt module leads to a significant decrease in model performance, approximately 30%. This underscores the pivotal role that Few-shot CoT prompts play in enhancing the model's capability to effectively process and comprehend emotional semantics in images. We noted that compared to the baseline, the disparity between accuracy and weighted F1 scores significantly increased under the zero-shot setting, indicating that these few-shot CoT prompts contribute to enhancing the model's ability to analyze and understand complex emotions. The performance of the model varies greatly under different sampling strategies. Notably, random sampling methods resulted in accuracy significantly lower than scenarios without sampling, indicating that the quality of examples has a substantial impact on the model's performance and that our proposed sampling pipeline greatly enhances the quality of CoT prompts. The elimination of the self- consistency strategy also impacted model performance, with a decrease of about 2%, suggesting that this strategy aids in diversifying the outputs generated by the LMM, thereby enhancing the accuracy of emotion classification. Finally, compared to using only the ViT encoder for classification, our method shows a significant improvement in accuracy, demonstrating that our approach does not solely rely on this encoder. Overall, these ablation studies collectively affirm the indispensable role of the main components proposed in our CoT-based image emotion classification task.

To determine the optimal value for the hyperparameters K and M, we conducted experiments on the validation sets of the EmoSet dataset. The experimental results are presented in Tables 4 and 5. We set the maximum value of K to 15, as excessively long context windows could potentially reduce the inference speed of large language models. The results indicate that the model achieves the best performance when K equals to 5 and M equals to 2.

Table 4. Ablation studies results of accuracy on the validation set of EmoSet-8 dataset. The best performances are in bold.

Accuracy	M = 1	M = 2	M = 3	M = 4	M = 5
K = 5	0.7659	**0.8194**	0.7909	0.8002	0.7785
K = 10	0.7329	0.7742	0.7841	0.7812	0.7868
K = 15	0.7392	0.7539	0.7832	0.7684	0.7829

Table 5. Ablation studies results of F1 score on the validation set of EmoSet-8 dataset. The best performances are in bold.

F1 score	M = 1	M = 2	M = 3	M = 4	M = 5
K = 5	0.7624	**0.8123**	0.7805	0.7886	0.7693
K = 10	0.7293	0.7694	0.7718	0.7697	0.7784
K = 15	0.7358	0.7431	0.7698	0.7591	0.7727

In addition, we investigated the impact of different image encoders on the model's performance, with the experimental results summarized in Table 6. For comparison, we employed two alternative encoders: **ResNet50** [10] and **Swin Transformer** [19]. ResNet50 is a deep convolutional neural network that is widely adopted for its robust performance on feature extraction tasks. Swin Transformer is a hierarchical vision transformer encoder that uses shifted windows for multi-scale feature representation, which makes it well-suited for dense prediction tasks. The results demonstrate that the model utilizing the ViT encoder outperforms those with other encoders. Consequently, we adopted the ViT encoder in our proposed method.

Table 6. Ablation studies results of image encoder on EmoSet-8 dataset. The best performances are in bold.

Encoder	Acc	F1
ResNet-50	0.7805	0.7729
Swin-Transformer	0.7962	0.7813
ViT(Ours)	**0.8208**	**0.8161**

4.5 t-SNE Visualization for Image Features

To further explore the qualitative results, we visualized the image features extracted from the ViT encoder using the t-SNE dimensionality reduction method. Due to space constraints, the main results are provided in Appendix A.

5 Conclusion

In this work, we propose a lightweight method for image emotion classification using CoT prompts. It effectively leverages the rich semantic content present in images through the use of the LMM. To enhance the few-shot learning capabilities of the LMM, our method automatically generates instance-specific prompts by searching for training samples that are semantically similar to the emotional semantics of the test instance. Compared to state-of-the-art methods, our proposed approach performs exceptionally well on three widely used datasets, encompassing binary and multi-class classifications, while consuming fewer computational resources.

Acknowledgement. This work was supported by National Natural Science Foundation of China 62376255.

References

1. Alayrac, J.B., et al.: Flamingo: a visual language model for few-shot learning. Adv. Neural. Inf. Process. Syst. **35**, 23716–23736 (2022)
2. Bondielli, A., Passaro, L.C., et al.: Leveraging clip for image emotion recognition. In: CEUR Workshop Proceedings, vol. 3015. CEUR-WS (2021)
3. Brown, T., et al.: Language models are few-shot learners. Adv. Neural. Inf. Process. Syst. **33**, 1877–1901 (2020)
4. Chen, T., Borth, D., Darrell, T., Chang, S.F.: DeepSentiBank: visual sentiment concept classification with deep convolutional neural networks. CoRR (2014)
5. Deng, S., et al.: SimEmotion: a simple knowledgeable prompt tuning method for image emotion classification. In: Bhattacharya, A., et al. (eds.) International Conference on Database Systems for Advanced Applications, pp. 222–229. Springer, Cham (2022). https://doi.org/10.1007/978-3-031-00129-1_15
6. Deng, S., et al.: Learning to compose diversified prompts for image emotion classification. Comput. Vis. Media, 1–15 (2024)
7. Deng, S., Wu, L., Shi, G., Zhang, H., Hu, W., Dong, R.: Emotion class-wise aware loss for image emotion classification. In: Proceedings of the First CAAI International Conference on Artificial Intelligence, CICAI 2021, Part I 1, Hangzhou, China, 5–6 June 2021, pp. 553–564. Springer, Cham (2021). https://doi.org/10.1007/978-3-030-93046-2_47
8. Devlin, J., Chang, M.W., Lee, K., Toutanova, K.: BERT: pre-training of deep bidirectional transformers for language understanding. In: Proceedings of the 2019 Conference of the North American Chapter of the Association for Computational Linguistics: Human Language Technologies, Volume 1 (Long and Short Papers), pp. 4171–4186 (2019)
9. Dosovitskiy, A., et al.: An image is worth 16x16 words: transformers for image recognition at scale. In: International Conference on Learning Representations (2021)
10. He, K., Zhang, X., Ren, S., Sun, J.: Deep residual learning for image recognition. In: Proceedings of the IEEE Conference on Computer Vision and Pattern Recognition, pp. 770–778 (2016)
11. Hoffmann, J., et al.: Training compute-optimal large language models. arXiv preprint arXiv:2203.15556 (2022)
12. Krizhevsky, A., Sutskever, I., Hinton, G.E.: ImageNet classification with deep convolutional neural networks. Adv. Neural Inf. Process. Syst. **25** (2012)

13. Li, J., Li, D., Savarese, S., Hoi, S.: BLIP-2: bootstrapping language-image pre-training with frozen image encoders and large language models. In: International Conference on Machine Learning, pp. 19730–19742. PMLR (2023)
14. Lian, Z., et al.: Explainable multimodal emotion reasoning. CoRR (2023)
15. Liu, C., Zhao, S., Luo, Y., Liu, G.: TransIEA: transformer-baseartd image emotion analysis. In: 2022 7th International Conference on Computer and Communication Systems (ICCCS), pp. 310–313. IEEE (2022)
16. Liu, H., et al.: LLaVA-NeXT: improved reasoning, OCR, and world knowledge, January 2024. https://llava-vl.github.io/blog/2024-01-30-llava-next/
17. Liu, H., Li, C., Wu, Q., Lee, Y.J.: Visual instruction tuning. Adv. Neural. Inf. Process. Syst. **36**, 34892–34916 (2023)
18. Liu, J., Shen, D., Zhang, Y., Dolan, W.B., Carin, L., Chen, W.: What makes good in-context examples for GPT-3? In: Proceedings of Deep Learning Inside Out (DeeLIO 2022): The 3rd Workshop on Knowledge Extraction and Integration for Deep Learning Architectures, pp. 100–114 (2022)
19. Liu, Z., et al.: Swin transformer: hierarchical vision transformer using shifted windows. In: Proceedings of the IEEE/CVF International Conference on Computer Vision, pp. 10012–10022 (2021)
20. Loshchilov, I., Hutter, F.: Decoupled weight decay regularization. In: International Conference on Learning Representations (2017)
21. Nadeem, M., Sohail, S.S., Javed, L., Anwer, F., Saudagar, A.K.J., Muhammad, K.: Vision-enabled large language and deep learning models for image-based emotion recognition. Cogn. Computat., 1–14 (2024)
22. Pan, J., Lu, J., Wang, S.: A multi-stage visual perception approach for image emotion analysis. IEEE Trans. Affect. Comput. (2024)
23. Panda, R., Zhang, J., Li, H., Lee, J.Y., Lu, X., Roy-Chowdhury, A.K.: Contemplating visual emotions: understanding and overcoming dataset bias. In: Ferrari, V., Hebert, M., Sminchisescu, C., Weiss, Y. (eds.) Proceedings of the European Conference on Computer Vision (ECCV), vol. 11206, pp. 579–595 (2018). https://doi.org/10.1007/978-3-030-01216-8_36
24. Radford, A., et al.: Learning transferable visual models from natural language supervision. In: International Conference on Machine Learning, pp. 8748–8763. PMLR (2021)
25. Rao, T., Li, X., Zhang, H., Xu, M.: Multi-level region-based convolutional neural network for image emotion classification. Neurocomputing **333**, 429–439 (2019)
26. She, D., Yang, J., Cheng, M.M., Lai, Y.K., Rosin, P.L., Wang, L.: WSCNet: weakly supervised coupled networks for visual sentiment classification and detection. IEEE Trans. Multimedia **22**(5), 1358–1371 (2019)
27. Wang, X., et al.: Self-consistency improves chain of thought reasoning in language models. In: The Eleventh International Conference on Learning Representations (2023)
28. Wu, L., Deng, S., Zhang, H., Shi, G.: Sentiment interaction distillation network for image sentiment analysis. Appl. Sci. **12**(7), 3474 (2022)
29. Xie, H., et al.: EmoVIT: revolutionizing emotion insights with visual instruction tuning. In: Proceedings of the IEEE/CVF Conference on Computer Vision and Pattern Recognition, pp. 26596–26605 (2024)
30. Xu, L., Wang, Z., Wu, B., Lui, S.: MDAN: multi-level dependent attention network for visual emotion analysis. In: Proceedings of the IEEE/CVF Conference on Computer Vision and Pattern Recognition, pp. 9479–9488 (2022)

31. Xu, Q., Wei, Y., Yuan, S., Wu, J., Wang, L., Wu, C.: Learning emotional prompt features with multiple views for visual emotion analysis. Inf. Fus. **108**, 102366 (2024)
32. Yang, J., Huang, Q., Ding, T., Lischinski, D., Cohen-Or, D., Huang, H.: EmoSet: a large-scale visual emotion dataset with rich attributes. In: Proceedings of the IEEE/CVF International Conference on Computer Vision, pp. 20383–20394 (2023)
33. Yang, J., Li, J., Wang, X., Ding, Y., Gao, X.: Stimuli-aware visual emotion analysis. IEEE Trans. Image Process. **30**, 7432–7445 (2021)
34. Yang, J., She, D., Lai, Y.K., Rosin, P.L., Yang, M.H.: Weakly supervised coupled networks for visual sentiment analysis. In: Proceedings of the IEEE Conference on Computer Vision and Pattern Recognition, pp. 7584–7592 (2018)
35. You, Q., Luo, J., Jin, H., Yang, J.: Building a large scale dataset for image emotion recognition: the fine print and the benchmark. In: Proceedings of the AAAI Conference on Artificial Intelligence, vol. 30 (2016)
36. Zhang, H., Xu, M.: Weakly supervised emotion intensity prediction for recognition of emotions in images. IEEE Trans. Multimedia **23**, 2033–2044 (2020)
37. Zhao, S., Jia, Z., Chen, H., Li, L., Ding, G., Keutzer, K.: PDANet: polarity-consistent deep attention network for fine-grained visual emotion regression. In: Proceedings of the 27th ACM International Conference on Multimedia, pp. 192–201 (2019)
38. Zhou, K., Yang, J., Loy, C.C., Liu, Z.: Conditional prompt learning for vision-language models. In: Proceedings of the IEEE/CVF Conference on Computer Vision and Pattern Recognition, pp. 16816–16825 (2022)
39. Zhou, K., Yang, J., Loy, C.C., Liu, Z.: Learning to prompt for vision-language models. Int. J. Comput. Vis. **130**(9), 2337–2348 (2022)

ReportFlow: Financial Deep Research Based on Multia-agent Collaboration

Qinghe Li[1], Yan Zhuang[1], Jiawen Deng[1(✉)], and Fuji Ren[1,2(✉)]

[1] University of Electronic Science and Technology of China, Chengdu, China
202321080626@std.uestc.edu.cn
[2] Shenzhen Institute for Advanced Study, UESTC, Shenzhen, China

Abstract. Financial research reports require structured analysis, multimodal presentation, and timely incorporation of external information. Automating this workflow remains difficult because current systems struggle to coordinate long-form reasoning, gather reliable evidence at scale, and generate consistent visual outputs. To address these limitations, we propose ReportFlow, a multi-agent system designed to automate the end-to-end creation of macroeconomic, industry, and company research reports. ReportFlow focuses on improving workflow coordination, information retrieval, and multimodal generation, enabling the system to operate in a manner closer to real-world research teams. It consists of three key components. The Dual Graph Multi-Agent Architecture organizes the overall workflow: a Parent Graph performs global planning, while multiple Sub Graphs generate report sections in parallel, ensuring structured and coherent content. The Enhanced Hybrid Retrieval Augmented Generation module integrates sparse retrieval, dense retrieval, and real-time web search, allowing the system to gather comprehensive and current evidence. The HTML-to-Image generation module converts model-generated HTML into rendered figures, producing consistent and high-quality charts. We evaluate ReportFlow on a custom dataset of professional financial reports and observe substantial improvements over baseline systems in factual accuracy, analytical completeness, and multimodal quality.

Keywords: Multi-agent systems · Financial · Deep Research

1 Introduction

Financial research reports are essential to modern investment pipelines, supporting macroeconomic analysis, industry assessment, and company-level evaluation. These reports influence the allocation of trillions of dollars annually and require rigorous reasoning, domain expertise, and multimodal presentation to communicate complex insights effectively. Despite recent advances in large language models, automating this process remains challenging due to the high stakes of financial decision making and the need for reliability, structure, and multimodality [10].

H. Liu et al. (Eds.): CEI 2025, CCIS 2881, pp. 89–103, 2026.
https://doi.org/10.1007/978-981-95-9493-1_6

Current systems face four key limitations. First, they lack effective mechanisms for integrating heterogeneous and time-sensitive financial data, including both structured market indicators and unstructured news streams, a persistent challenge in high-stakes domains [18]. Second, most systems support only text generation and cannot produce the charts or tables required for professional reporting. Third, single-pass generation prevents dynamic refinement of analytical plans, limiting the depth and adaptability of the resulting reports. Finally, factual inconsistencies and structural irregularities reduce the usability of automated outputs.

Deep research agents have emerged as a promising direction for addressing these issues [18]. By combining autonomous planning, Retrieval-Augmented Generation (RAG), and tool use, these systems offer improved analytical capability [2]. Commercial solutions such as OpenAI DeepResearch [11] and Gemini Deep Search [4] can produce preliminary report drafts but still fall short in multimodal generation, analytical depth, and end-to-end workflow reliability.

To overcome these limitations, we propose ReportFlow, a collaborative multi-agent system designed for professional-grade financial report generation. ReportFlow is guided by four system requirements: professionalism through domain-aware analysis modules; multimodality through robust visual generation; traceability via evidence-grounded RAG; and controllability that enables users to tune the workflow, integrate private data, and manage cost-time trade-offs.

ReportFlow is built around three core components. A Dual Graph Multi-Agent Architecture organizes the workflow into a global Parent Graph and multiple parallel Sub Graphs, improving analytical depth while reducing end-to-end generation time to approximately thirty minutes. An Enhanced Hybrid RAG [15] engine combines sparse retrieval, dense retrieval, and real-time web search via Perplexica to provide comprehensive and current financial information, significantly reducing hallucination rates. An HTML-to-Image multimodal module exploits the model's strength in HTML and CSS generation and uses a headless browser for rendering, achieving near-perfect reliability in producing high-quality charts.

We evaluate ReportFlow using the nine-dimension benchmark in the FinSight system [8]. ReportFlow demonstrates state-of-the-art performance, with substantial gains in information effectiveness and presentation quality.

Our main contributions are:

1. **A Dual Graph Multi-agent Architecture** that decomposes the reporting workflow into a globally coordinated Parent Graph and parallel Sub Graphs, enabling structured long-form reasoning and efficient end-to-end generation.
2. **An Enhanced Hybrid RAG Engine** that unifies sparse retrieval, dense retrieval, and real-time web search to provide comprehensive, up-to-date financial information while reducing hallucination.
3. **A Robust HTML-to-Image Multimodal Generation Scheme** that leverages HTML/CSS rendering instead of code-based plotting, achieving nearly 100% success in generating clear and consistent visualizations.

2 Related Work

2.1 Deep Research Systems

Deep Research Systems represent a paradigm shift from traditional information retrieval to comprehensive knowledge synthesis, characterized by their ability to conduct multi-round information searching and integration [18]. Currently, several technical trajectories have emerged in this domain: ReAct-based agents [20] (e.g., WebThinker [9]) employ "observation-thought-action" loops for iterative planning and execution; multi-agent systems (e.g., OWL [7] and Open Deep Research) focus on enhancing efficacy through collaborative problem decomposition and specialized processing. Commercial systems (e.g., OpenAI Deep Research [11], Grok Deep Research [6]), alongside open-source and free systems like DeepSeek, have jointly propelled rapid market development, recently augmented by platforms such as Gemini/Research [4], which features verifiable citations and multi-angle exploratory capabilities.

Despite significant advancements, existing frameworks exhibit notable limitations in two critical areas: multimodal processing and domain-specific application [19]. Owing to the text-centric nature of report generation workflows and the lack of native chart generation capabilities in underlying models, reports produced by current systems generally lack essential visual elements such as charts and diagrams. Furthermore, these systems demonstrate inadequate adaptation in professional domains like finance, particularly exhibiting limited capacity to support professional-grade chart generation and integrate real-time market data, resulting in a substantial gap between system outputs and professional requirements [10].

2.2 Retrieval-Augmented Generation (RAG) in Finance

Retrieval-Augmented Generation has become a central method for grounding language models in factual and current information. This is particularly important in finance, where accuracy is essential and relevant information changes rapidly [1]. Standard RAG pipelines that rely on a single dense retriever often struggle in this domain [17], prompting a shift toward hybrid retrieval that combines sparse keyword-based search and dense semantic search.

Financial tasks present additional challenges because they require the integration of diverse data sources, including structured indicators, regulatory documents, and real-time news. Recent work has begun addressing these needs, such as the use of agent-driven RAG pipelines and advanced retrieval models like Multi-HyDE for financial question answering [5].

ReportFlow replaces code generation with a fully HTML/CSSbased workflow. Instead of emitting Python, the model produces self-contained markup that a headless browser deterministically renders into images. This HTML-to-Image pipeline avoids the variability of executing model-generated code and provides a stable, reliable method for producing high-quality visual content.

3 The ReportFlow System

3.1 Overall Architecture

ReportFlow is designed as a four-layer decoupled architecture, as shown in Fig. 1. This separation allows for the independent optimization and maintenance of business logic (Application), process control (Architecture), factual basis (Data), and core capabilities (Tools).

1. **Application Layer:** The user interface responsible for receiving user requests (e.g., "Generate a company report for SenseTime") and routing them to the appropriate agent graph.
2. **Data Layer:** The Data Engine (see Sect. 3.2), which aggregates professional data from sources like AKShare, Eastmoney, and the World Bank, and supports private knowledge base integration.
3. **Architecture Layer:** The system's "core brain," which is the Dual-Graph architecture (see Sect. 3.3) implemented on LangGraph. It controls the end-to-end report generation workflow.
4. **Tool Layer:** Provides core capabilities, primarily the Enhanced Hybrid RAG Engine (see Sect. 3.4) and the HTML2Picture Visualization Engine (see Sect. 3.5).

Fig. 1. The Four-Layer System Architecture of ReportFlow.

3.2 Data Layer

Reliable information is central to producing high-quality analytical output. The Data Layer provides validated and traceable data through a standardized processing pipeline that includes extraction, classification, cleaning, unification, and validation. A caching mechanism stores previously queried results to reduce retrieval time and computational cost.

Different data channels support company-level, industry-level, and macroeconomic analysis. The system retrieves company fundamentals such as financial statements and ownership structures, constructs peer comparison groups, and organizes sector-level information through aggregated web search to avoid naming inconsistencies across data sources. For macroeconomic analysis, the system extracts core indicators such as GDP, CPI, and PMI, supported by specialized modules for global economic comparison and risk assessment. Table 1 summarizes the data sources and processing methods used across the system (Fig. 2).

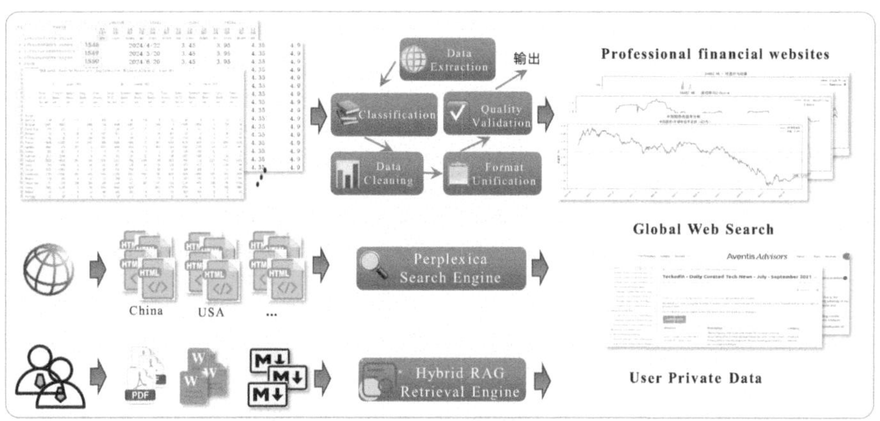

Fig. 2. Data Engine Layer of ReportFlow.

3.3 Dual-Graph Multi-agent Architecture

The core of the system is a Dual Graph Multi-Agent Architecture that structures the reasoning workflow. Inspired by the division of labor in human research teams, a Parent Graph is responsible for global planning, while multiple Sub Graphs operate in parallel on specific sections.

The Parent Graph interprets user requests, generates a structured plan, assigns subtasks to Sub Graphs, monitors their progress, and synthesizes their results into a coherent final output. Each Sub Graph performs an iterative process of retrieval, analysis, writing, and visualization focused on its assigned topic.

Table 1. Data Sources and Processing Methods

Data Category	Source(s)	Frequency	Data Format
Company Data			
Financials	AKShare	T+1	Excel/CSV
Co. Information	Eastmoney, THS	Real-time	JSON
News/Opinion	Google Search (Playwright)	Real-time	HTML
Peer Reports	Financial Websites	Daily	PDF
Macro Data			
GDP	World Bank	Quarterly	Excel
Inflation (CPI)	National Statistics Bureaus	Monthly	Excel
Interest Rates	Central Bank Websites	Real-time	CSV
Policy Reports	Government Websites	Irregular	HTML/PDF
Market Data			
Stock/Indices	Exchange Websites	Real-time	JSON

This design produces two important advantages. First, parallel execution reduces the overall processing time, enabling the system to generate comprehensive reports efficiently. Second, context management is improved by limiting each Sub Graph to the information required for its own section. Only the final distilled outputs are returned to the Parent Graph, reducing token usage and mitigating the context overload that often arises in long-form generation tasks (Fig. 3).

3.4 Enhanced Hybrid RAG Engine

To ensure the credibility and factual rigor of generated reports, ReportFlow incorporates an Enhanced Hybrid RAG Engine that integrates three complementary retrieval mechanisms to construct a robust knowledge foundation:

1. **BM25** [14] **Sparse Retrieval:** Built on an inverted index, this component is highly effective at exact keyword matching. It is employed to query a local corpus of financial documents and accurately locate paragraphs containing domain-specific terminology, particular corporate entities, and key financial ratios.
2. **FAISS** [13] **Vector Retrieval:** This dense retrieval component leverages pre-trained financial-domain semantic encoders to embed both queries and documents into a shared vector space. By capturing semantic relatedness, it enables queries such as "profitability" to retrieve passages discussing, for example, "net profit margin," thereby expanding the coverage beyond literal keyword overlap.
3. **Perplexica** [3] **Real-Time Search:** This module exposes agents to a real-time web search engine (an open-source alternative to Perplexity AI). It is

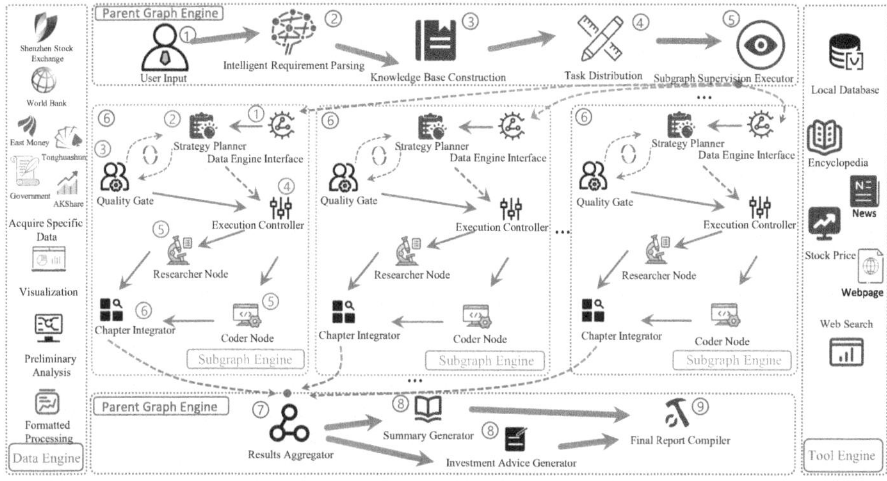

Fig. 3. The Dual-Graph Multi-Agent Collaborative Framework.

crucial for acquiring up-to-date market developments, regulatory and policy changes, and news events that are not yet reflected in the static knowledge base (FIg. 4).

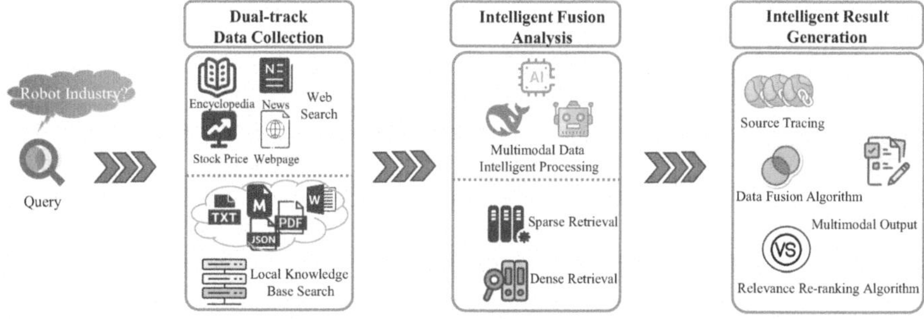

Fig. 4. Enhanced Hybrid RAG Engine.

3.5 Enhanced Visual Content Generation

Charts and tables are essential for communicating analytical results. Instead of generating executable plotting code, which is often unreliable, the system adopts an HTML-based visualization pipeline. When a visualization is required, the language model produces a self-contained HTML and CSS representation of the figure. A headless browser renders this content and produces a final image through a controlled screenshot process. This method avoids execution failures common in code-based approaches and produces consistent visual outputs.

For structured data such as multi-year financial summaries, a deterministic script generates charts directly, and the model interprets the resulting visualization rather than constructing it. This combination ensures robust and efficient visual content generation (Fig. 5).

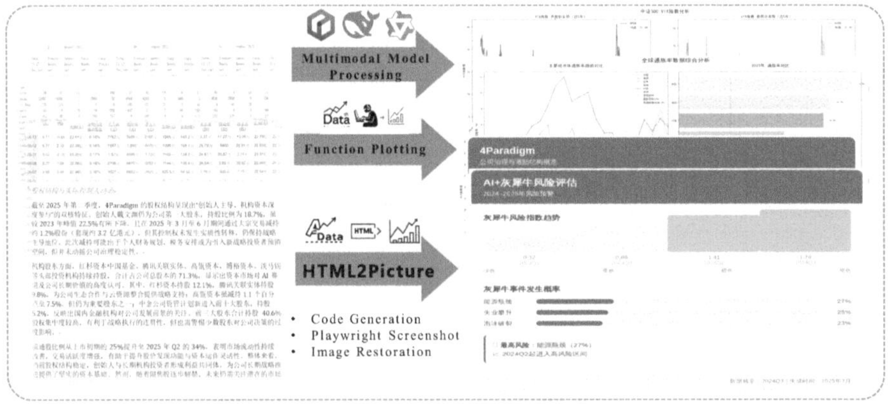

Fig. 5. Enhanced visual content generation.

3.6 Controllability and Stability Design

The system provides several mechanisms to balance cost, time, and analytical depth. Users can adjust the number of iterations, choose faster or more thorough generation modes, specify custom report structures, and incorporate private data sources. Stability is maintained through comprehensive error handling, retry strategies for tool calls, active monitoring of Sub Graph processes, and a caching layer that reduces repeated data acquisition.

These design choices allow the system to operate reliably under diverse conditions while offering flexibility for different user needs.

4 Experimental Evaluation

We conducted a series of experiments to evaluate ReportFlow's performance against state-of-the-art baselines.

4.1 Experimental Setup

Dataset: Due to the scarcity of public benchmarks for end-to-end financial report generation, we constructed a high-quality evaluation set. Our methodology was inspired by the work [16], which demonstrated the construction of a dataset for summarizing financial reports from both text and tables. We selected 30 research tasks, of which 10 each for macroeconomic, industry, and company analysis. For each task, we procured a "golden standard" reference report, typically 20+ pages with rich multimodal content, from a professional investment institution.

Evaluation Metrics: We adopted the comprehensive 9-dimensional automated evaluation benchmark and LLM-as-judge methodology [8] on the FinSight system. This framework provides a multi-faceted assessment across three core dimensions, with each metric scored on a 10-point scale:

1. **Factual Accuracy:**
   - **Conclusion Consistency (Cons.):** Whether the model's conclusions align with the reference report.
   - **Textual Faithfulness (Faith.):** Whether facts are supported by reliable sources and citations.
   - **Text-Image Coherence (T-I.):** Whether textual descriptions match the data presented in charts.
2. **Information Effectiveness:**
   - **Information Richness (Rich.):** The number of unique information points covered.
   - **Key-point Coverage (Cover.):** Coverage of the reference report's key arguments and data.
   - **Analytical Insight (Insight.):** Whether the report provides deep analysis beyond simple fact-listing.
3. **Presentation Quality:**
   - **Structural Logic (Logic.):** Clarity and coherence of the report's organization.
   - **Language Professionalism (Lang.):** Use of appropriate financial terminology and tone.
   - **Chart Expressiveness (Vis.):** The quality, clarity, and relevance of generated visualizations.

Baseline Systems: We compared ReportFlow against two categories of baselines:

1. **LLM + Search Tools:** Standard large models with web access:
   - GPT-4 w/Search
   - Claude-4.1 w/Search
   - DeepSeek-R1 w/Search
2. **Deep Research Agents:** Commercial systems optimized for long-form research:
   - Grok Deep Search [6]
   - OpenAI DeepResearch [11]
   - Perplexity Deep Research [12]
   - Gemini 2.5 Pro DR [4]

Our backbone model uses Qwen3-235B-A22B-Instruct. The maximum input length is set to 128K, and the maximum output length is set to 16K. For evaluation, we use the multimodal model Gemini-2.5-Pro as our evaluation model.

4.2 Main Results

Table 2 presents the comprehensive performance comparison across all nine metrics. ReportFlow achieves the highest average score (7.52), significantly outperforming all baselines.

Table 2. Performance Comparison on 9-Dimensional Metrics. Scores are averaged across all tasks, 1–10 scale.

Model	Factual			Analytical			Presentation			Avg.
	Cons.	Faith.	T-I.	Rich.	Cover.	Insight	Logic	Lang.	Vis.	
LLM with Search Tools										
GPT-4 w/ Search	5.42	6.68	3.30	6.15	4.05	5.71	6.95	5.10	3.12	5.16
Claude-4.1 w/ Search	4.90	5.00	2.85	5.30	4.78	4.55	6.30	5.65	2.05	4.60
DeepSeek-R1 w/ Search	5.85	5.10	2.60	7.40	6.25	7.20	7.00	6.95	2.30	5.63
Deep Research Agents										
Grok Deep Search	4.20	5.50	3.95	5.25	3.40	4.70	5.60	4.91	4.12	4.63
OpenAI DeepResearch	5.75	7.20	5.05	6.50	6.60	5.80	7.10	6.70	4.80	6.16
Perplexity Deep Research	3.95	5.70	4.10	4.20	2.90	3.40	5.15	4.05	3.80	4.14
Gemini 2.5 Pro DR	**7.25**	6.60	4.80	7.30	7.90	7.70	7.80	**7.98**	4.10	6.83
ReportFlow (Ours)	6.90	**7.55**	**6.12**	**7.35**	**8.40**	**7.86**	**8.10**	7.50	**7.88**	**7.52**

The results clearly demonstrate ReportFlow's superiority. Compared to the strongest baseline, Gemini 2.5 Pro DR (6.83), ReportFlow (7.52) shows a significant improvement. The advantage is particularly pronounced in two dimensions: (1) **Presentation Quality:** ReportFlow's score in Chart Expressiveness (Vis.) is 7.88, compared to a mere 4.10 for Gemini 2.5 Pro DR and 4.80 for OpenAI DeepResearch. This quantitative result provides conclusive evidence for the success of our HTML2Picture strategy. Baselines, which either produce no images or low-quality, simplistic charts, fail to meet the professional standard. (2)**Information Effectiveness:** ReportFlow achieves the highest scores in Key-point Coverage (8.40) and Analytical Insight (7.86). This indicates that our Enhanced Hybrid RAG Engine and specialized data modules are highly effective at gathering comprehensive information and supporting deep analysis, avoiding the omissions common in other systems.

4.3 Ablation Study

To validate the contribution of ReportFlow's key components, we conducted an ablation study. We evaluated two degraded versions of our system: (1) w/o Hybrid RAG, which removes the BM25 and FAISS retrievers, relying only on web search, and (2) w/o HTML2Picture, which disables the HTML generation scheme, relying only on structured data plotting and thus producing no charts for unstructured analysis.

Table 3. Ablation Study of ReportFlow's Core Components. The scores are averaged by dimension.

Model Variant	Factual	Info	Present
Full ReportFlow	6.86	7.87	7.83
w/o Hybrid RAG (Search only)	6.30 (↓)	6.00 (↓)	6.50 (↓)
w/o HTML2Picture (Text/Structured only)	6.70 (↓)	7.66 (↓)	7.13 (↓)

Table 3 shows that: (1) **Removing Hybrid RAG** causes a catastrophic drop in Information Effectiveness (7.87 → 6.00) and a significant drop in Factual Accuracy (6.86 → 6.30). This shows that web search alone is insufficient. The internal knowledge base, accessed via hybrid BM25/FAISS search, is critical for providing the foundational data, key-point coverage, and factual grounding necessary for a deep analysis. (2) **Removing HTML2Picture** does not significantly impact the factual or information scores, as the analysis is still present in the text. However, it causes a sharp decline in Presentation Quality (7.83 → 7.13). This isolates the component's value: the HTML2Picture scheme is directly responsible for the professional, multimodal quality of the final report, dramatically improving its readability and expressiveness.

4.4 Qualitative and Statistical Analysis

In this section, we performed a statistical analysis of the artifacts generated by ReportFlow to understand the scale of its output. As shown in Table 4, the generated reports are substantial, averaging 73 pages and including a high density of references, searches, and multimodal elements (Table 4).

This stands in stark contrast to baseline systems. Many "Deep Research" agents produce outputs that are effectively long-form text answers, often with 0 images and only 3–4 simple tables. ReportFlow's ability to generate an average of 28 complex images and 12 tables per report, resulting in a 73-page document, demonstrates that its output is structurally and qualitatively closer to a human-authored professional report than any of the baseline systems.

Table 4. Statistical Analysis of Generated Report Artifacts.

Metric/Report	Average Value
Average Page Count	73
Average Reference Count	323
Average Web Searches	46
Average Image Count	28
Average Table Count	12

5 Conclusion

We presented ReportFlow, a system for reliable long-form financial report generation. Its four-layer architecture and dual-graph multi-agent workflow enable structured planning, parallel chapter generation, and efficient context management. The hybrid retrieval engine combines sparse, dense, and real-time search to ensure factual grounding, while the HTML-based visualization pipeline provides a robust solution for generating charts without relying on code execution. The system also offers user controls over cost, depth, content, and data sources, supported by stability mechanisms for practical deployment. Together, these components form a scalable and dependable framework for producing data-driven, visually rich professional reports.

Acknowledgment. This work was supported by Sichuan Science and Technology Program (Grant No.2024YFG0006), the National Natural Science Foundation of China (Grant No. U24A20250), and the Fundamental Research Funds for the Central Universities (No. ZYGX2024Z005).

Disclosure of Interests. The authors have no competing interests to declare that are relevant to the content of this article.

Appendix

(See Fig. 6)

4Paradigm(06682.HK) 深度研究报告

报告日期： 2025 年 07 月 23 日

第 1 章：投资摘要

增持，目标价 23.50 港元。核心依据为公司在中国企业级 AI 平台市场确立的领先地位及 SaaS 化转型带来的盈利改善趋势。

4Paradigm 是专注于企业级人工智能决策的领先平台厂商，以 **Sage AI 平台**为核心，形成"平台+行业解决方案"的双轮驱动模式，尤其在金融领域占据约 22%市场份额，服务超 80%国内头部银行。公司正加速向平台化、订阅化转型，2023 年平台类收入占比达 50%-60%，**订阅制收入占比升至 45%**，客户留存率达 92%，显示出强客户粘性。财务上，2023 年营收 18.7 亿元，同比增长 67%；毛利率提升至 70%-75%，经营性现金流**历史性转正**。预计 2024-2025 年收入 CAGR 维持在 35%-45%，有望于 2025 年实现 Non-GAAP 盈利。估值采用 **DCF 与相对法结合**，综合得出合理价值区间为 18.0–30.0 港元，**目标价 23.50 港元**（对应基准情景）。主要催化剂包括：**非金融行业拓展加速、订阅收入占比突破 50%、2024 年盈利拐点兑现。**

主要风险包括：**客户集中度较高，前十大客户贡献 62%收入；行业竞争加剧，面临华为云、阿里云 PAI 等头部厂商挤压；AI 监管政策趋严，数据合规成本上升。**

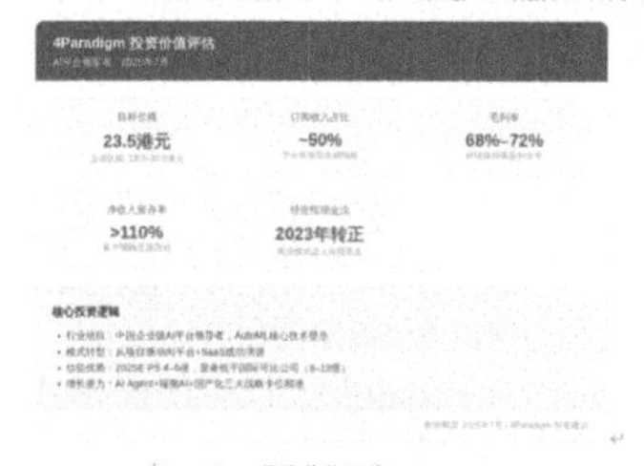

4Paradigm 投资价值评估

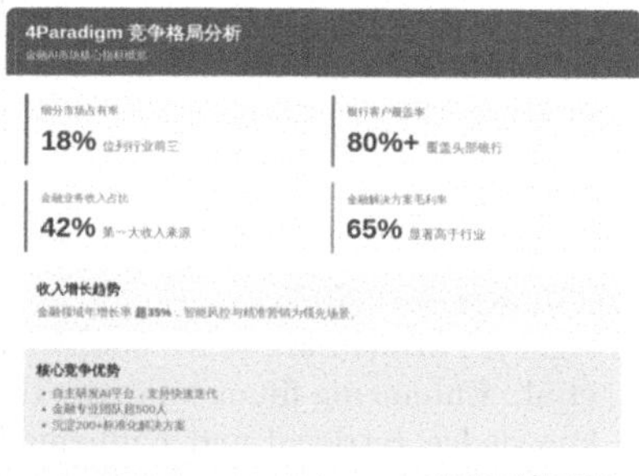

4Paradigm 核心指标

注：此图表展示了 4Paradigm 在客户留存、收入结构、研发投入等方面的核心运营与财务指标。

- 风险管理体系与可持续发展
- *业务与财务风险*

客户集中度风险仍存，前五大客户收入占比虽未披露，但 KA 客户贡献 60%-70%营收，头部 10 家客户贡献约 40%总收入，构成主要风险点。应收账款占 2023 年上半年营收的 48.5%，周转天数偏高，现金流压力较大。需加强客户信用管理与回款跟踪，优化供应链流程。

- *技术与合规风险*

公司需应对《生成式人工智能服务管理暂行办法》等监管政策影响，加强数据安全、算法可解释性与 AI 伦理治理框架建设。对第三方云计算资源与 GPU 算力存在依赖，中美科技脱钩背景下算力获取的可持续性需持续关注。

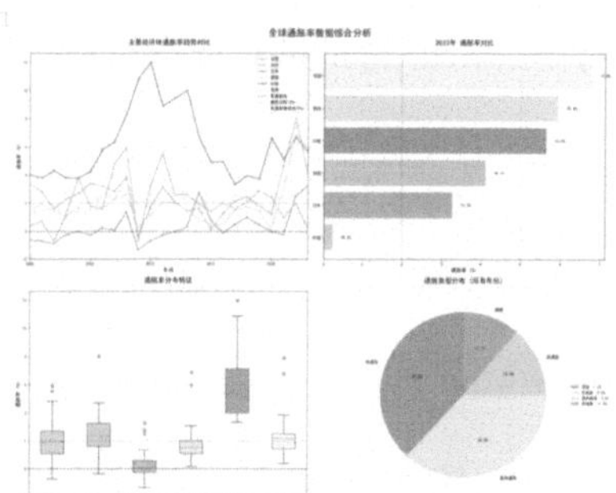

全球通胀格局呈现"西高东低"特征。2023 年，中国 CPI 仅录得 0.23%，接近通缩边缘，凸显内需不足的深层矛盾。而美国、德国、英国通胀率分别达 4.12%、5.95%、6.79%，主因能源价格冲击与工资-物价螺旋。中国 PPI 已连续多月负增长，工业品价格持续下行，若不及时干预，可能陷入"债务-通缩"螺旋。

- 六、货币政策传导机制与金融支持能力分析
- *（一）M2 与社融结构演变：从"总量驱动"到"结构优化"*

尽管 M2 增速从 2023 年的 9.7%趋稳，但社融结构显著优化。科技金融占新增社融比重达 18%，其中 AI 相关融资占其 35%。非信贷融资占比提升，科创板 IPO 数量年均增长 22%（2023–2024），缓解银行信贷依赖。企业中长期贷款占比提升，与 AI 研发周期（3–5 年）匹配度增强。

- *（二）结构性货币政策工具实施效果*
  - **科技创新再贷款：**长三角、粤港澳、京津冀合计占投放总量 60%以上，平均放款周期缩短至 7 个工作日。
  - **设备更新再贷款：**累计投放超 3000 亿元，约 38%用于智能化改造与算力基础设施升级，直接服务于"人工智能+制造"。

- *三、市场情绪：由谨慎转向积极，风险偏好明显回升*

市场情绪是资产价格波动的重要驱动因素。2023–2025 年，随着"人工智能+"政策持续推进与资本市场改革预期升温，投资者情绪显著回暖，风险偏好明显提升。

（一）中证 300 VIX 指数中枢下移，情绪趋于稳定

中证 300 VIX 指数过去五年平均值为 19.89，最新值为 20.37，处于正常波动区间（15–25）。高达 91.2%的交易日落在该区间，仅 7.3%进入高波动期（≥25），极端恐慌（≥35）仅出现 2 天，峰值达 41.19。VIX 呈现长期下降趋势（五年降幅达 34%），反映监管完善、机构占比提升与市场韧性增强。

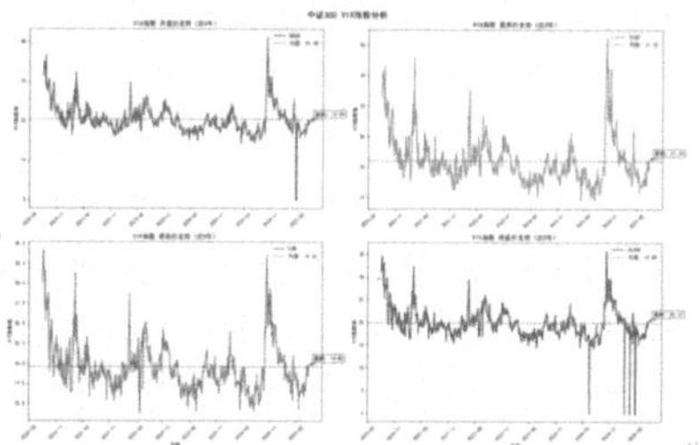

中证 300 VIX 指数分析

当前 VIX 接近均值，既无过度乐观，也无恐慌情绪，处于**情绪均衡状态**。其作为逆向指标，当持续低于 15 时提示市场可能过热，突破 25 则预示风险溢价上升，可考虑波动率对冲或逢低布局。

（二）资金流向印证情绪回暖：科技+金融双轮驱动

近 20 日所有行业均实现净资金流入，总流入达 492.7 亿元，市场呈现普涨格局。其中：

- **证券行业净流入 182 亿元**，居首位，资金流效率高达 23.45%，反映资本市场改革预期强烈；

Fig. 6. The final company report of The 4Paradigm (part).

References

1. Asai, A., Wu, Z., Wang, Y., Sil, A., Hajishirzi, H.: Self-rag: Learning to retrieve, generate, and critique through self-reflection (2024)
2. Bruzzone, A., Giovannetti, A., Genta, G., Cefaliello, D.: Generative ai and retrievalaugmented generation (rag) in an agent-based simulation framework for urban planning. In: Proceedings of the International Multidisciplinary Modeling & Simulation Multiconference (I3M) (2023)
3. Contributors, P.: Perplexica. https://github.com/ItzCrazyKns/Perplexica (2025), gitHub repository
4. Gemini: Gemini deep research. https://gemini.google/overview/deep-research (2025), accessed: 2025
5. George, R., Srinivasan, A.G., Joe, J.K., MR, H., Kant, H., Vimalkanth, R., Suresh, S., et al.: Enhancing financial rag with agentic ai and multi-hyde: A novel approach to knowledge retrieval and hallucination reduction. In: Proceedings of The 10th Workshop on Financial Technology and Natural Language Processing. pp. 19–32 (2025)
6. Grok: Grok 3 beta – the age of reasoning agents. https://x.ai/news/grok-3 (2025), accessed: 2025
7. Hu, M., Zhou, Y., Fan, W., Nie, Y., Xia, B., Sun, T., Ye, Z., Jin, Z., Li, Y., Chen, Q., et al.: Owl: Optimized workforce learning for general multi-agent assistance in real-world task automation. arXiv preprint arXiv:2505.23885 (2025)
8. Jin, J., Zhang, Y., Xu, Y., Qian, H., Zhu, Y., Dou, Z.: Finsight: Towards real-world financial deep research. arXiv preprint arXiv:2510.16844 (2025)
9. Li, X., Jin, J., Dong, G., Qian, H., Wu, Y., Wen, J.R., Zhu, Y., Dou, Z.: Webthinker: Empowering large reasoning models with deep research capability. arXiv preprint arXiv:2504.21776 (2025)
10. Nie, Y., Kong, Y., Dong, X., Mulvey, J.M., Poor, H.V., Wen, Q., Zohren, S.: A survey of large language models for financial applications: Progress, prospects and challenges. arXiv preprint arXiv:2406.11903 (2024)
11. OpenAI: Introducing deep research. https://openai.com/index/introducing-deep-research (2025), accessed: 2025
12. Perplexity: Perplexity deep research. https://www.perplexity.ai (2025), accessed: 2025
13. Research, F.A.: Faiss: Facebook ai similarity search. https://github.com/facebookresearch/faiss (2025), gitHub repository
14. Robertson, S., Zaragoza, H., et al.: The probabilistic relevance framework: Bm25 and beyond. Foundations and Trends® in Information Retrieval **3**(4), 333–389 (2009)
15. Sawarkar, K., Mangal, A., Solanki, S.R.: Blended rag: Improving rag (retriever-augmented generation) accuracy with semantic search and hybrid query-based retrievers. In: 2024 IEEE 7th international conference on multimedia information processing and retrieval (MIPR). pp. 155–161. IEEE (2024)
16. Wang, Z., Jiang, Z., Zhang, X., Soon, J., Zhang, J., Xiaoyao, W., Du, H.: Beyond pure text: Summarizing financial reports based on both textual and tabular data. In: IJCAI. pp. 5233–5241 (2023)
17. Weller, O., Boratko, M., Naim, I., Lee, J.: On the theoretical limitations of embedding-based retrieval. arXiv preprint arXiv:2508.21038 (2025)
18. Xu, R., Peng, J.: A comprehensive survey of deep research: Systems, methodologies, and applications. arXiv preprint arXiv:2506.12594 (2025)

19. Yang, Z., Pan, B., Wang, H., Wang, Y., Liu, X., Zhu, M., Zhang, B., Chen, W.: Multimodal deepresearcher: Generating text-chart interleaved reports from scratch with agentic framework. arXiv preprint arXiv:2506.02454 (2025)
20. Yao, S., Zhao, J., Yu, D., Du, N., Shafran, I., Narasimhan, K.R., Cao, Y.: React: Synergizing reasoning and acting in language models. In: The eleventh international conference on learning representations (2022)

MH-ECR: A Multi-hop Reasoning Framework for Interpreting Emotions Causes in Conversations

Kexin Meng, Jiawen Deng(✉), Yan Zhuang, Yitao Wang, Ruiting Hu, and Fuji Ren(✉)

School of Computer Science and Engineering, University of Electronic Science and Technology of China, Chengdu, China
renfuji@uestc.edu.cn

Abstract. Interpreting the causes of emotions in dialogues is vital for emotion models aiming to comprehend human sentiments. Current research often simplifies this task to causal emotion entailment (CEE), which focus only on identifying causal utterances without providing interpretable explanations. To address this limitation, we introduce a **M**ulti-**h**op **E**motion **C**ause **R**easoning (MH-ECR) framework. Leveraging the chain-of-thought reasoning capability of large language models (LLMs), this framework incorporates context theory from linguistics to guide the extraction and reasoning about critical information. Using this framework, we construct a **C**onversation **E**motion **C**ause **R**easoning Dataset (CECR-Data) containing the reasoning chains generated by prompting the LLMs. Additionally, we have fine-tuned Llama2-7B on the CECR-Data to develop MH-ECReasoners that are tailored for interpreting emotion causes. Experimental results show that our model successfully handles the traditional CEE task and provides a comprehensive understanding of dialogue content while accurately inferring the specific causes of emotions.

Keywords: Conversation Emotion Entailment · Large Language Model · Multi-hop Reasoning

1 Introduction

Understanding emotions is crucial for effective human communication, and identifying the causes of emotions within conversations can significantly improve a model's grasp of human sentiments [1]. By pinpointing the root reasons behind emotions, models can effectively decode the causality behind these emotional responses. [2]. Therefore, emotion cause interpretation in conversation is very important. The target of this process is shown in Fig. 1.

To gain deeper insights into emotions, the task of causal emotion entailment (CEE) garners considerable attention. Introduced by [3], CEE involves analyzing a dialogue to determine which utterances are responsible for the emotions

H. Liu et al. (Eds.): CEI 2025, CCIS 2881, pp. 104–118, 2026.
https://doi.org/10.1007/978-981-95-9493-1_7

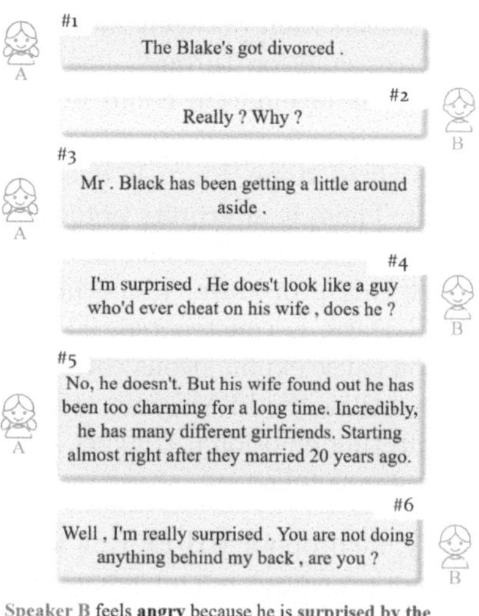

Fig. 1. Target of emotion cause interpretation: In the conversation above, we aim to analyze the entire dialogue to explain the reasons behind speaker B's anger.

expressed in the conversation. Research efforts, including KBCIN [4], PAGE [5], and TSAM [6], have utilized graph-based models to evaluate pairs of utterances. A number of datasets have also been introduced to identify emotion causes, including RECCON [3], integrated from DailyDialog and IEMOCAP and Emo-Know [7], which is extracted from Twitter.

Despite these advancements, there are notable limitations. The standard CEE task focuses solely on identifying causal utterances through binary classification models, which often lacks interpretability. Additionally, current generative language models struggle to accurately analyze and identify the specific utterances that trigger emotions due to insufficient domain-specific knowledge in their training data [8]. Existing emotion-related models also fall short, as they generally do not incorporate reasoning processes, leading to results that lack interpretability and depth. The available emotion cause datasets are also inadequate for addressing these issues. RECCON dataset [3] only annotates specific emotion-triggering phrases, which can sometimes be difficult to understand. Emo-Know dataset is limited to sentence level analysis and doesn't facilitate the analysis of conversations.

To tackle these challenges, we develop an innovative approach grounded in chain-of-thought (CoT) [9] and multi-hop reasoning, guided by the context theory [10] of conversational linguistics. By analyzing the broader macro context and specific micro context of conversations, our MH-ECR framework can provide a comprehensive perspective on the causes of emotions. The macro context refers to the background and topic of the dialogue, while the micro context focuses on the specific content of the conversation between the two speakers. For instance, if a speaker chooses to express emotion through insinuation or sarcasm rather than direct language, this cause of emotion could be hidden within the micro context.

Our framework includes three steps. First, it dissects the macro and micro contexts of the conversation. Then, it interprets potential emotion causes based on these contexts. Finally, it recognizes utterance indices according to the interpretation. To further assist this procedure, a specialized dataset for emotion cause interpretation, CECR-Data, is constructed. This dataset details the reasoning processes and emotion cause explanations corresponding to our analytical path. Using this data set, we utilize the LLMs generation capabilities to fine-tune a model dedicated to interpreting emotional triggers.

Our main contributions are as follows:

- Guided by context theory, we propose MH-ECR: a multi-hop reasoning framework for interpreting emotion causes in conversations.
- Based on MH-ECR framework, we develop a dataset for emotion causes inferring, including data on reasoning processes and interpretations of emotion causes.
- We introduce a model for multi-hop reasoning emotion cause interpretation based on Llama2-7B. Extensive experiments demonstrate that our model can comprehensively understand conversation content and infer the specific causes of particular emotions.

2 Related Work

2.1 Causal Emotion Entailment

[3] introduced the task of recognizing emotion causes in conversations, along with two subtasks: Causal Span Extraction (CSE) and Causal Emotion Entailment (CEE). Their dataset includes emotion labels for each utterance and causal span annotations for non-neutral utterances, indicating specific phrases or sentences in the dialogue history that triggered the speaker's emotion. [29] introduced a social commonsense knowledge (CSK) enhanced conversational graph for context modeling, akin to the approaches by [4] and [5]. [4] developed a CSK-intensified attention-based graph model, while [5] constructed an RGCN considering sequential relationships between utterances. [6] proposed a two-stream attention model to simulate emotional influences within conversations. Despite their effectiveness in identifying emotion-triggering utterances, these models lack interpretability.The Emo-Know dataset [7] also tackles emotion cause extraction by annotating each tweet's emotion and the spans causing it. This highlights the need for a more granular dataset for emotion cause identification in conversations.

2.2 CoT and Multi-hop Reasoning

Chain of Thought (CoT) [9] have proven highly effective in solving complex problems. CoT facilitates step-by-step reasoning by breaking down complex problems into manageable sub-problems. Recent advancements in CoT include generating and selecting consistent reasoning paths [11], automating prompt creation [12], and optimizing prompt selection [13]. The Tree of Thought (ToT) framework [14] further extends CoT by employing a tree search strategy, allowing backtracking and multi-path exploration for improved problem-solving.

Multi-hop reasoning leverages the output of one reasoning step as input for the next, facilitating stricter supervision of intermediate results and making it ideal for tasks requiring the synthesis of multiple pieces of evidence. The HotpotQA dataset [15] exemplifies the application of multi-hop reasoning. Recent research [16] applies multi-hop reasoning to LLMs for sentiment analysis of product reviews, achieving notable results.

3 Multi-hop Emotion Cause Reasoning Framework

Based on the concept of CoT [9], we propose a conversation emotion cause reasoning path. In this multi-hop reasoning path, each step of reasoning builds upon the previous one. Compared to single-step CoT generation, this method can supervise and adjust the model's intermediate output, which enhances the model's understanding of the conversation.

3.1 Task Definition

For a conversation C with t utterances, the corresponding emotions e_i for each utterance u_i are represented as $\{[u_1, e_1], [u_2, e_2], \ldots, [u_t, e_t]\}$. The speaker of i-th utterance is $s_i \in \{s_1, s_2\}$.

Given the n-th utterance and its corresponding emotion $[u_n, e_n]$, our goal is to explain the detailed causes of emotion e_n, and identify which specific utterances in the conversation (including itself) cause speaker s_n to feel e_n.

3.2 MH-ECR Path

Building upon the standard CEE task, our approach focus on providing corresponding explanations, detailing why these utterances elicited the speaker's emotion. Therefore, We offer a multi-hop emotion cause reasoning (MH-ECR) path to elucidate the underlying reasons for the speaker's emotions.

Explainable Multi-hop Reasoning Prompts By adding reasoning steps that promote conversation understanding, a model can gain a better comprehension of the dialogue, thereby achieving better results in extracting emotional causes. This reasoning path consists of three main steps, each of which relies

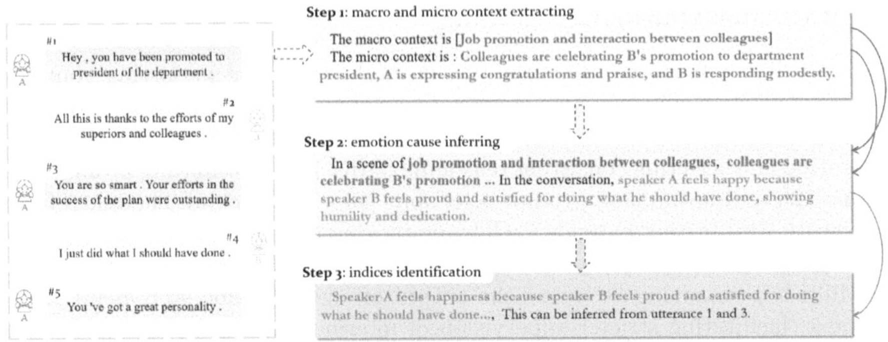

Fig. 2. Reasoning Path of MH-ECR Framework. Dashed arrows represent the three reasoning steps. Solid arrows indicate the transmitting of relevant dialogue information, including macro and micro contexts as well as emotion interpretation.

on the results of the previous step. Below are the prompts for each step of our reasoning path:

Step 1: Given the conversation C, the last utterance U of the dialogue, the speaker S of the last utterance, and the emotion E_{us} of the speaker, we first summarize the macro and micro contexts of the dialogue. Guided by the context theory of [10,17], we use contextual information to help the model extract key elements from the dialogue. The macro context, summarized in a brief phrase, includes factors such as the overall background, social status of the interlocutors, and the occasion of the dialogue. The micro context is detailed in a paragraph, summarizing the specific content and sequence of the conversation. The reasoning for this step is defined as follows:

$$P_1 : (C, U, S, E_{us}) \rightarrow (C_{\text{macro}}, C_{\text{micro}}) \tag{1}$$

Output: C_{macro} is the macro context of conversation C, and C_{micro} is the micro context of conversation C.

In this process, we divide the conversation into two levels for summarization: macro context and micro context.

Step 2: After extracting the macro context C_{macro} and micro context C_{micro} of conversation C, it is necessary to analyze the whole conversation to identify the specific reasons behind the speaker S's emotion E_{us}. This step of reasoning is defined as follows:

$$P_2 : (C, U, S, E_{us}, C_{\text{macro}}, C_{\text{micro}}) \rightarrow (R_{us}) \tag{2}$$

Output: R_{us} represents the model's explanation of the speaker S's emotion in the utterance U.

In this step, by integrating the dialogue content with the macro and micro contexts extracted in the previous step, the model is capable of generating an emotion interpretation of U.

Step 3: After obtaining the emotion interpretation R_{us} of the speaker S's utterance U, we will map this interpretation to specific utterances in the conversation that directly triggered the speaker's emotion. This step of reasoning is defined as follows:

$$P_3 : (C, U, S, E_{us}, R_{us}) \rightarrow (I_{us}) \quad (3)$$

Output: I_{us} is the indices of utterances that cause emotion E_{us} according to R_{us}.

In this step, the model uses R_{us}, the interpretation generated in the previous step regarding why speaker S experienced the corresponding emotion. The model will review the entire dialogue history to identify the specific utterance that caused the emotion E_{us}. The entire reasoning process is illustrated in Fig. 2.

Testaments for MH-ECR Paths We first conduct a pilot study on the proposed reasoning paths. Using our reasoning paths to guide one of the most advanced LLM, GPT-4o, we validate the effectiveness of the paths. The detailed procedures will be described in the Experiments section.

4 Construction of CECR-Data

According to the MH-ECR framework proposed in the previous section, we construct a **C**onversation **E**motion **C**ause **R**easoning Dataset (CECR-Data). This dataset is intended for supervised training of generative language models to enhance their emotion reasoning capabilities. The process of constructing the dataset is illustrated in Fig. 3.

4.1 Selection of Reasoning Paths

To tackle complex problems, enhancing the reasoning capabilities of LLMs can significantly improve their interpretability and accuracy [18]. This approach ensures that the decision-making process of the model is transparent, trustworthy, and amenable to human oversight and correction. By developing structured reasoning paths, our objective is to advance LLM reasoning.

We propose three reasoning paths to improve the identification of emotional causes:

Path 1 involves directly extracting the cause of the emotion from the original dialogue. This straightforward approach leverages the inherent information within the dialogue itself without additional contextual processing.

Path 2 involves summarizing the conversation to obtain an initial understanding of its content. Based on this summary and the original dialogue, we then explain the cause of the emotion. This method provides a concise overview, facilitating a clearer identification of emotional triggers.

Path 3 builds on context theory, as proposed by Dutch linguist Teun A. van Dijk [10,17]. This path involves extracting both the macro and micro contexts of

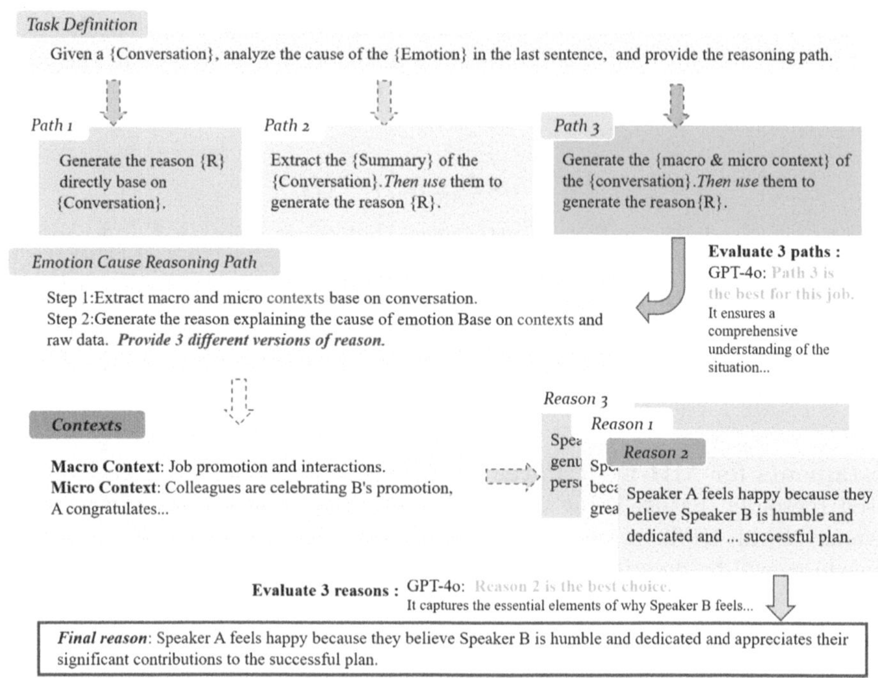

Fig. 3. The Process of Construction of CECR-Data using ToT: For this task, we propose three potential paths. After evaluating each option, Path 3 is identified as the most suitable. Following steps of Path 3, we create two types of contextual information, then develope three different versions of emotion interpretation and select the most appropriate one.

the dialogue. The emotional cause is then inferred by integrating these contextual elements with the original dialogue.

By employing these reasoning paths, we aim to enhance the ability of LLMs to understand and interpret emotional causes in conversations more effectively.

4.2 Generation of Inference Data Using ToT

Tree of Thoughts [14] framework introduces a branching structure that allows for more complex and nuanced reasoning processes. As a result, ToT is better suited for data generation. Therefore, we used this approach to construct a dataset for MH-ECR paths based on RECCON-dd dataset. First, we employed GPT-4o to evaluate the feasibility of three proposed paths. After evaluation by GPT-4o, path 3 shows best performance for considering the complete context and specific causal spans, leading us to use it for generating inference data.

After determining the prompt path to be used, we first generate the macro and micro contexts for each conversation. Referring to the idea of generating branches of the ToT first and then pruning, we let GPT-4o generate three different versions of emotion interpretation based on the prompt as branches of the tree. This allows the model to analyze the dialogue content as thoroughly as possible and generate more comprehensive and reasonable answers. Then, GPT-4o compares these three reasons, select the most appropriate one and add to our dataset.

Compared to the original RECCON dataset, our extended conversation emotion cause reasoning dataset includes the following content: the macro and micro contexts of dialogues, and the inferred reasons of the corresponding emotion.

4.3 Evaluation of CECR-Data Quality

Based on the structure of CECR-Data and methods outlined by [7], we evaluate the quality of CECR-Data using four indicators: relevance, fluency, consistency, and coherence. Relevance assesses whether the intermediate steps align with their definitions. Fluency examines the readability and grammatical accuracy. Consistency checks for contradictions with the dialogue content. Coherence evaluates the logical flow between sentences.

We randomly selected 150 samples and had three postgraduate students with relevant linguistic expertise rate the two intermediate steps on these four indicators, using a scale from 1 (lowest) to 5 (highest). The result is shown in Table 1. The evaluation scores for the CECR-Data indicate high overall quality across all indicators.

Table 1. Human Evaluation Scores of CECR-Data.

Indicator	Rel	Flu	Con	Coh
Contexts_{old}	4.75	4.77	4.87	4.79
Reason_{old}	4.48	4.87	4.36	4.55
Contexts_{new}	4.79	4.83	4.91	4.80
Reason_{new}	4.53	4.90	4.45	4.57

4.4 Training of MH-ECReasoner

After constructing the CECR-Data, we employ it to train the MH-ECReasoner model to enhance the capability for emotion reasoning in dialogues. Following the multi-hop training method proposed by [16], we fine-tune LLaMA2-7B [19], a highly capable LLM developed by Meta. In the training period, the output of each step served as the input of the next, ensuring the correctness of each intermediate step. Specifically, we aggregate the loss values of the three steps as the final loss function.

5 Experiments

5.1 Dataset

Our base dataset is RECCON-dd dataset [3]. The original data for the RECCON-dd comes from DailyDialog [20], a multi-turn dialogue dataset containing conversations in everyday scenarios. RECCON-dd contains over 1,000 dialogues and more than 10,000 utterance-cause pairs. The RECCON dataset also annotates the sentences and phrases that cause the emotion in the whole conversation for every sample, and marks them as causal spans.

Firstly, we cleaned the original dataset by removing all non-neutral emotion utterances that did not have a causal span. Then, following our data construction method, we used GPT-4o to automatically generate intermediate reasoning steps for non-neutral utterances in the training set. The distribution of the entire training set, validation set, and test set of CECR-Data is shown in Table 2.

Table 2. Statistics for Train, Validation, and Test Sets.

Statistics	Train	Valid	Test
Positive Causal Pairs	7,027	328	1,767
Negative Causal Pairs	20,646	838	5,330
Unique Conversations	834	47	225
Utterances	8,043	200	2,384

5.2 Evaluation Metrics

Evaluating emotion interpretations generated by the model requires suitable and accurate metrics. [21] divides evaluations into reference-based and reference-free scenarios. In our work, it is necessary to refer to the conversation and causal spans provided by the original dataset. Besides, we also need to consider the model's overall understanding and analysis of the dialogue content. Therefore, we combine reference-based and reference-free perspectives to evaluate from multiple angles.

LLM Evaluation While acknowledging conventional metrics including accuracy, fluency and consistency, we find that these metrics are insufficient for assessing the model's comprehensive dialogue interpretation skills. In response to this limitation, we have introduced new measures to ensure thorough evaluation. Below are all the evaluation metrics:

- Correlation (Cor): Whether the generated reason contradicts the original conversation and contains any hallucination.

- Identification (Ide): Whether the generated reason is sufficiently related to the causal spans.
- Detailedness (Det): Whether the reason provides a detailed description of the event that causes the emotion. It should concentrate on the specific reasons that trigger the emotion, rather than simply summarizing the entire dialogue.
- Fluency (Flu): Whether the generated reason is fluent, readable, and has no grammatical errors.
- Consistency (Con): Whether the generated reason is consistent with the content and background of the dialogue.
- Clarity (Cla): Whether the generated reason is clear and easy to understand without being vague.

[22] state that GPT-4 is capable of ranking models' outputs in a manner that aligns reasonably closely with human judgment across various tasks. Therefore, we use GPT-4o to evaluate these six indicators, with scores ranging from 1 (worst) to 10 (best). The whole prompt is shown in Appendix.

Automatic Evaluation We also employ automated metrics to evaluate our model. We use the causal spans from the original dataset as the golden answer to measure BLEU, ROUGE, and Distinct metrics. For the utterance indices from the final step of reasoning, we evaluate them by calculating their F1 scores.

Table 3. Results of different models using LLM Evaluation (BLEU, ROUGE, Distinct) and Automatic Evaluation (Correlation, Identification, Detailedness, Fluency, Consistency, Clarity). The ROUGE and Distinct score is the sum of all test sets.

Method	Size	Bleu	Rouge-1	Rouge-L	Distinct	Cor	Ide	Det	Flu	Con	Cla
Fine-tuned emotion LLMs											
EmoLLaMA	7B	**0.60**	172.9	142.1	927.9	6.24	6.01	5.69	8.22	6.50	7.39
ECR-Chain	7B	0.12	144.6	124.7	701.1	5.41	4.78	5.82	7.35	6.01	5.86
Advanced general LLMs											
LLaMA2-7B-chat	7B	0.34	175.1	152.8	1009.2	4.55	4.28	3.63	6.79	4.58	5.53
LLaMA3-8B	8B	0.25	157.7	131.2	969.3	7.01	6.72	6.36	8.93	7.16	8.20
ChatGPT3.5	-	0.29	207.2	173.3	1013.4	7.69	7.63	6.00	9.28	7.86	8.68
Claude-3	-	0.38	199.2	169.0	999.1	7.85	7.78	6.52	9.33	7.95	8.82
MH-ECReasoners											
MH-ECR Path 1	7B	0.33	**310.0**	**284.5**	**1019.3**	7.52	7.40	6.44	9.12	7.48	8.54
MH-ECR Path 2	7B	0.34	279.1	253.5	1017.7	7.59	7.48	6.52	9.20	7.62	8.62
MH-ECR Path 3	7B	0.35	233.1	201.9	1018.6	**7.91**	**7.80**	**6.84**	**9.38**	**7.98**	**8.89**

5.3 Testaments for MH-ECR Paths

Before training MH-ECReasoner, we verify our reasoning paths' validity through a pilot study using the generative language model, GPT-4o. We apply our reasoning paths to guide its inferring process. After generating the reasons, GPT-4o assesses its own performance across three reasoning paths. To ensure the originality of the model, we employ zero-shot prompting for each reasoning path. Table 4 shows the reasoning scores achieved by GPT-4o across three reasoning paths.

Table 4. Evaluation of three paths.

Method	Cor	Ide	Det	Flu	Con	Cla
Path 1	8.03	8.07	6.86	9.41	8.25	8.98
Path 2	8.27	8.19	7.07	9.45	**8.50**	9.18
Path 3	**8.34**	**8.30**	**7.28**	**9.48**	8.47	**9.19**

The results indicate that the reasons generated by Path 2 and Path 3 are significantly superior to those generated by Path 1, especially in detailedness, correlation and consistency, which is the exact indicators that reflect accuracy of identified causes, showing the model has learned through the intermediate step. Furthermore, the generated reasons of Path 3 surpass those of Path 2 in five metrics, demonstrating that the use of context theory helps the model to understand dialogues from a more comprehensive perspective, thereby resulting in more accurate and reasonable emotion reasoning. This result validates the effectiveness of our MH-ECR framework.

5.4 Training Setups of MH-ECReasoner

Following prior research [23], we select LLaMA2-7B as the base model for fine-tuning. Due to computational constraints, we apply LoRA fine-tuning [24] for supervised training. Our training batch size is set to 16, with a learning rate of 1e-4. We train for 3 epochs on one 80G A100 GPU and select the model that performs best on the validation set for evaluation on the test set. Experiments are conducted across three different paths.

5.5 Evaluation for MH-ECReasoner

The evaluation results of emotion interpretation are in Table 3. The fine-tuned MH-ECReasoner shows significant improvements across all six metrics compared to other models. Among them, the model using Path 3 demonstrates substantial enhancements in all metrics compared to the other two paths, indicating the effectiveness of this path.

There is a progressive enhancement of six indices from Path 1 to Path 3, illustrating that the reasoning paths we proposed significantly improved the performance of the model. Compared with Paths 1 and 2, the most notable improvements are the first three indices: correlation, identification, and detailedness. These indices are measured in reference-based scenario. This suggests that our

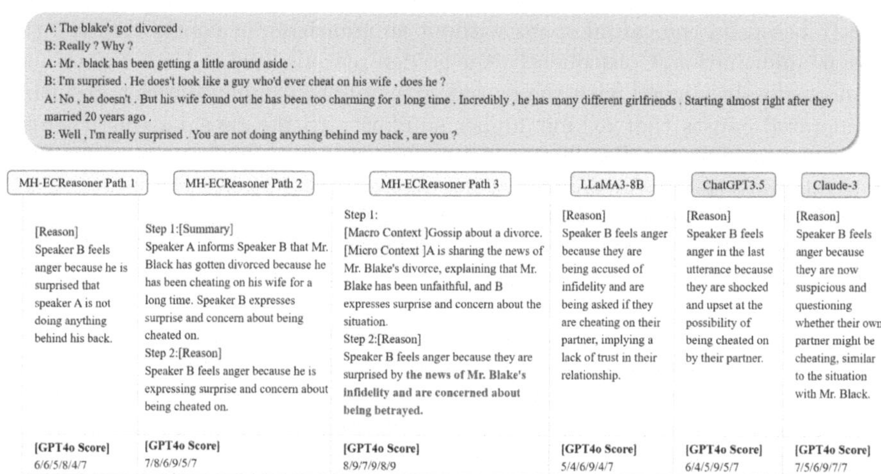

Fig. 4. Case Study of Interpreting Conversation Emotion Cause.

reasoning paths and CECR-Data effectively aids the model in comprehensively understanding dialogue content and analyzing emotion causes.

In comparison with other LLMs, such as fine-tuned emotion LLMs EmoLLaMA [25] and ECR-Chain [26], and advanced general LLMs like ChatGPT3.5 and Claude-3, our model exhibits notable improvements, particularly in terms of detailedness and identification. This is attributed to the limitation in LLMs that tend to summarize the whole conversation as the emotion cause, while neglecting the root reason which authentically triggers emotions. Such limitations result in overly-generic descriptions that fail to align with the causal span of original datasets thereby leading to low scores in identification and detailedness. Furthermore, some of these LLMs focus only on the last utterance, neglecting conversation history and hence resulting in a reduction in Correlation scores. In the examples we provided in Fig. 4, it can be observed that both LLaMA3-8B and ChatGPT3.5 models exhibit these issues. The reason in Step 1 is the misinterpretation of dialogue, while Step 2 fails to sufficiently incorporate conversation content. In contrast, Step 3, by extracting the context, is able to deduce the genuine emotion causes while incorporating the dialogue background.

Automatic Evaluation Using the causal spans from the original dataset as the ground truth, metrics such as BLEU score, ROUGE-1 f1, ROUGE-L f1, and Distinct total are employed to measure the similarity between the generated causes and the causal spans in Table 3.

In the automated evaluation of generated causes, the MH-ECReasoner demonstrates superior performance compared to other LLMs across all metrics except for BLEU. Notably, the MH-ECReasoner utilizing Path 1 achieves the highest scores in both ROUGE and Distinct metrics. We attribute this to the fact that during the generation of reasoning data, Path 1 constructs its data directly based on the causal spans without summarizing or contextualizing the dialogue information. Consequently, the golden reasons used in Path 1's training are more closely aligned with the causal spans of the original dataset, resulting in generated causes that exhibit higher similarity to the causal spans, thereby achieving higher ROUGE and Distinct scores. However, Path 1 does not effectively integrate the overall content of the dialogue, leading to lower scores in the LLM evaluation compared to Path 2 and Path 3.

We also calculated the F1 score of the utterance indices from the final step of reasoning against the ground truth in the dataset.

Table 5. F1-Scores of Different Models in CEE Task.

Method	Neg-f1	Pos-f1	Macro-f1
RankCP	**97.30**	33.00	65.15
KEC	95.74	66.76	**81.25**
TSAM	90.48	**70.00**	80.24
KBCIN	89.65	68.59	79.12
PAGE	95.58	65.75	80.67
ECR-Chain	89.87	67.70	78.79
MH-ECR Path 1	95.39	66.03	<u>80.71</u>
MH-ECR Path 2	95.44	65.14	80.29
MH-ECR Path 3	95.17	63.87	79.52

As shown in Table 5, our model exhibits excellent performance in identifying utterance indices in the standard Causal Event Extraction (CEE) task. Among our models, Path 1 achieves the best results, primarily due to its training data being directly generated from causal spans.

6 Conclusion

We propose MH-ECR, combining Chain-of-Thought and Multi-Hop Reasoning for interpretable emotional cause analysis. Using three reasoning paths and CECR-Data for supervised training, MH-Reasoner outperforms advanced LLMs in identifying emotional causes and CEE tasks, enhancing understanding of human emotions and supporting context-aware conversational AI.

7 Limitations

Identifying emotions with too many causes can be challenging. Additionally, our current model identifies emotion causes without post-processing. We recognize these limitations and plan to address them in future work.

Acknowledgment. This work was supported by Sichuan Science and Technology Program (Grant No. 2024YFG0006), the National Natural Science Foundation of China (Grant No. U24A20250), and the Fundamental Research Funds for the Central Universities (No. ZYGX2024Z005).

References

1. Xia, R., Ding, Z.: Emotion-Cause Pair Extraction: A New Task to Emotion Analysis in Texts. In: Proceedings of the 57th Annual Meeting of the Association for Computational Linguistics (ACL 2019), pp. 1003–1012 (2019)
2. Gao, J., et al.: Improving empathetic response generation by recognizing emotion cause in conversations. In: Findings of the Association for Computational Linguistics: EMNLP 2021, pp. 807–819 (2021)
3. Poria, S., et al.: Recognizing emotion cause in conversations. Cogn. Comput. **13**, 1317–1332 (2021)
4. Zhao, W., Zhao, Y., Li, Z., Qin, B.: Knowledge-bridged causal interaction network for causal emotion entailment. In: Proceedings of the AAAI Conference on Artificial Intelligence, vol. 37(11), pp. 14020–14028 (2023)
5. Gu, X., Lou, R., Sun, L., Li, S.: PAGE: a position-aware graph-based model for emotion cause entailment in conversation. In: ICASSP 2023 IEEE International Conference on Acoustics, Speech and Signal Processing (ICASSP), pp. 1–5. IEEE (2023)
6. Zhang, D., Yang, Z., Meng, F., Chen, X., Zhou, J.: TSAM: a two-stream attention model for causal emotion entailment. In: Proceedings of the 29th International Conference on Computational Linguistics, pp. 6762–6772 (2022)
7. Nguyen, M., Samaradivakara, Y., Sasikumar, P., Gupta, C., Nanayakkara, S.: EMO-KNOW: a large scale dataset on emotion-cause. In: Findings of the Association for Computational Linguistics: EMNLP 2023, pp. 11043–11051 (2023)
8. Singh, S., Caragea, C., Li, J.J.: Language models (mostly) do not consider emotion triggers when predicting emotion. In: Proceedings of NAACL 2024 (Short Papers), pp. 603–614 (2024)
9. Wei, J., et al.: Chain-of-thought prompting elicits reasoning in large language models. Adv. Neural. Inf. Process. Syst. **35**, 24824–24837 (2022)
10. Van Dijk, T.A.: Society and Discourse: How Social Contexts Influence Text and Talk. Cambridge University Press (2009)
11. Wang, X., et al.: Self-consistency improves chain of thought reasoning in language models. In: The Eleventh International Conference on Learning Representations (ICLR 2023) (2023)
12. Zhang, Z., Zhang, A., Li, M., Smola, A.: Automatic chain of thought prompting in large language models. In: The Eleventh International Conference on Learning Representations (ICLR 2023) (2023)
13. Diao, S., Wang, P., Lin, Y., Pan, R., Liu, X., Zhang, T.: Active prompting with chain-of-thought for large language models. In: Proceedings of the 62nd Annual Meeting of the Association for Computational Linguistics (ACL 2024), pp. 1330–1350 (2024)
14. Yao, S., Yu, D., Zhao, J., Shafran, I., Griffiths, T., Cao, Y., Narasimhan, K.: Tree of Thoughts: Deliberate Problem Solving with Large Language Models. Advances in Neural Information Processing Systems **36** (2024)

15. Yang, Z., Qi, P., Zhang, S., Bengio, Y., Cohen, W., Salakhutdinov, R., Manning, C.D.: HotpotQA: a dataset for diverse, explainable multi-hop question answering. In: Proceedings of EMNLP 2018, pp. 2369–2380 (2018)
16. Fei, H., Li, B., Liu, Q., Bing, L., Li, F., Chua, T.-S.: Reasoning implicit sentiment with chain-of-thought prompting. In: Proceedings of the 61st Annual Meeting of the Association for Computational Linguistics (ACL 2023) (2023)
17. Van Dijk, T.A.: Discourse and Context: A Sociocognitive Approach. Cambridge University Press (2008)
18. Huang, J., Chang, K.C.-C.: Towards reasoning in large language models: a survey. In: Proceedings of the 61st Annual Meeting of the Association for Computational Linguistics (ACL 2023) (2023)
19. Touvron, H., et al.: LLaMA 2: Open Foundation and Fine-Tuned Chat Models. arXiv preprint arXiv:2307.09288 (2023)
20. Li, Y., Su, H., Shen, X., Li, W., Cao, Z., Niu, S.: DailyDialog: a manually labelled multi-turn dialogue dataset. In: Proceedings of the Eighth International Joint Conference on Natural Language Processing (IJCNLP 2017), pp. 986–995 (2017)
21. Li, Z., Xu, X., Shen, T., Xu, C., Gu, J.-C., Tao, C.: Leveraging Large Language Models for NLG Evaluation: A Survey. arXiv preprint arXiv:2401.07103 (2024)
22. Sottana, A., Liang, B., Zou, K., Yuan, Z.: Evaluation Metrics in the Era of GPT-4: Reliably Evaluating Large Language Models on Sequence-to-Sequence Tasks. In: Proceedings of the 2023 Conference on Empirical Methods in Natural Language Processing (EMNLP 2023) (2023)
23. Zhang, Y., et al.: DialogueLLM: Context and Emotion Knowledge-Tuned Large Language Models for Emotion Recognition in Conversations. arXiv preprint arXiv:2310.11374 (2024)
24. Hu, E.J., et al.: LoRA: Low-Rank Adaptation of Large Language Models. arXiv preprint arXiv:2106.09685 (2021)
25. Liu, Z., Yang, K., Zhang, T., Xie, Q., Yu, Z., Ananiadou, S.: EmoLLMs: A Series of Emotional Large Language Models and Annotation Tools for Comprehensive Affective Analysis. arXiv preprint arXiv:2401.08508 (2024)
26. Huang, Z., Zhao, J., Jin, Q.: ECR-chain: advancing generative language models to better emotion-cause reasoners through reasoning chains. In: Larson, K. (ed.) Proceedings of the Thirty-Third International Joint Conference on Artificial Intelligence (IJCAI-24), pp. 6288–6296 (2024). 10.24963/ijcai.2024/695
27. Hwang, J.D., et al.: (comet-) ATOMIC 2020: On Symbolic and Neural Commonsense Knowledge Graphs. In: Proceedings of the AAAI Conference on Artificial Intelligence, vol. 35(7), pp. 6384–6392 (2021)
28. Weston, J., Chopra, S., Bordes, A.: Memory Networks. arXiv preprint arXiv:1410.3916 (2014)
29. Li, J., et al.: Neutral utterances are also causes: enhancing conversational causal emotion entailment with social commonsense knowledge. In: De Raedt, L. (ed.) Proceedings of the Thirty-First International Joint Conference on Artificial Intelligence (IJCAI-22), pp. 4209–4215
30. Scarselli, F., Gori, M., Tsoi, A.C., Hagenbuchner, M., Monfardini, G.: The Graph Neural Network Model. IEEE Trans. Neural Networks **20**(1), 61–80 (2008)
31. Wang, J., et al.: Is ChatGPT a Good NLG evaluator? a preliminary study. In: Proceedings of the 4th New Frontiers in Summarization Workshop, pp. 1–11. Association for Computational Linguistics (2023)

CARE: Collaborative Cognitive Reframing in Large Language Models via Reasoning for Psychological Counseling

Ruiting Hu[1], Jiawen Deng[1(✉)], Yue Li[2], Zheng Hu[1], Lirong Qiu[3], Kexin Meng[1], Guotai Huang[1], and Fuji Ren[1(✉)]

[1] School of Computer Science and Engineering, University of Electronic Science and Technology of China, Chengdu, China
{dengjw,renfuji}@uestc.edu.cn

[2] School of Information and Communication Engineering, University of Electronic Science and Technology of China, Chengdu, China

[3] Mental Health Education Center, University of Electronic Science and Technology of China, Chengdu, China

Abstract. Cognitive reframing, a core cognitive behavioral therapy (CBT) technique, has been widely recognized as an effective psychological intervention. However, clients often exhibit negative or resistant attitudes during treatment, posing a persistent challenge even for state-of-the-art large language models (LLMs) in cognitive reframing. To address this challenge, we propose the **C**ognitive Reframing **A**ssistant with **R**eflective **E**ngagement (CARE), which dynamically adapts to the user's evolving state. Specifically, as a user's cognition of an event evolves, their emotions change accordingly. By capturing these shifts, CARE helps users recognize and adjust negative thinking patterns, to alleviate emotional distress through structured multi-hop reasoning steps. Moreover, we introduce a novel metric, COG-DEBATE, to evaluate the effectiveness of cognitive reframing intuitively. Experimental results demonstrate that CARE outperforms baseline models, increasing the success rate of cognitive reframing by over 40%, effectively fostering independent thinking. Artificial experiments further show that our approach is highly effective in encouraging positive emotions (The code and data will be made public after the paper is accepted.).

Keywords: Cognitive Reframing · Large Language Models · Multi-hop Reasoning · Psychological Counseling

1 Introduction

Low-intensity CBT interventions have been proven to be highly effective in self-help formats [1]. People's feelings and actions are determined not by the situation itself but by how they interpret it [2,3]. By addressing irrational thoughts, CBT significantly improves both emotional and behavioral outcomes. For example,

H. Liu et al. (Eds.): CEI 2025, CCIS 2881, pp. 119–133, 2026.
https://doi.org/10.1007/978-981-95-9493-1_8

when a patient thinks, *"If I fail this exam, my life will be ruined,"* CBT would help them challenge negative thinking patterns and recognize, *"The exam is not the only measure of success; doing my best is enough,"* thereby reducing anxiety.

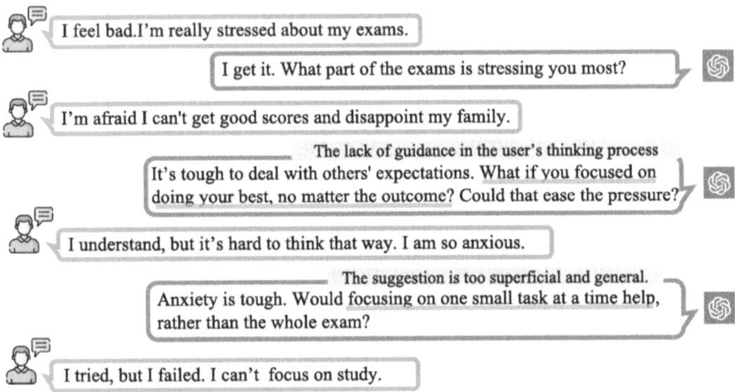

Fig. 1. LLMs struggle with client resistance. As shown, GPT-4o skips the cognitive exploration and offers superficial suggestions.

CBT does not simply replace negative thoughts with positive ones [2,4]. Instead, its objective is to assist individuals in shifting their cognitive evaluations from unhealthy, maladaptive patterns to evidence-based, adaptive ones. In other words, cognitive reframing emphasizes the crucial role of the client's active engagement in the process of cognitive change rather than simply relying on the direct suggestions provided by the therapist [5].

Impressed by the remarkable performance of LLMs, recent research has demonstrated that LLMs have the ability to provide mental health support [6,7]. A common approach involves collecting conversational data from real doctor-patient interactions, which is subsequently rewritten or expanded to train closed-source models (e.g., Smilechat [8], Mechat [9], ChatCounselor [10]). Empirical research from Harvard has shown that the quality of cognitive reframing generated by GPT outperforms that of 85% human therapists [11]. HealMe [12] emphasizes the importance of user autonomy in cognitive reframing and is effective for users who cooperate actively. CACTUS [13] extends cognitive reframing to multi-turn dialogues by setting a predefined CBT plan before counseling. However, in real-world therapy, users' attitudes and behaviors can vary significantly: some may engage actively, while others may exhibit passive avoidance, which puts higher demands on the therapist's ability [10]. Furthermore, we find that users with negative or resistant attitudes are particularly challenging for existing LLMs (Fig. 1).

Cognitive reframing is a structured, collaborative process, which involves three core stages: identifying irrational thoughts, critically evaluating their rationality, and collaborating to develop alternative explanations [14]. Given the structured nature of this task, we carefully design CARE to implement the process step by step.

To facilitate the automation of counselor evaluation, we propose a chain of thought that mimics the user's cognitive process. Considering the privacy issues in psychological counseling, we further construct a multi-turn dialogue dataset based on the above methods. Both automatic and human evaluations demonstrate that, compared to baselines, our approach significantly boosts performance. Specifically, our contributions are as follows:

1. We propose a novel framework that mitigates the difficulties LLMs face in cognitive reframing tasks by employing multi-hop reasoning to help users better understand and manage emotional distress.
2. We design a cognitive chain that comprehensively simulates an individual's thought process, and propose a novel metric to measure the effectiveness of cognitive reframing, facilitating the automation of counselor evaluations.
3. Given the privacy concerns, we construct CareGiver, a multi-turn dialogue dataset consisting of 1,507 dialogues, which provides materials for training open-source LLMs.

2 Related Work

Cognitive reframing is a widely recognized emotion regulation strategy that effectively reduces negative emotions [2,11]. Previous research [15,16] focuses on generating high-quality cognitive reframing with unhelpful thoughts and associated situations is given, providing valuable resources for subsequent research. [8] aims to support psychological counseling trainees in acquiring relevant CBT skills through the construction of patient cognitive models.

In recent years, artificial intelligence technologies, particularly LLMs, have been employed to address the shortage of psychological resources and enhance the accessibility and quality of mental health care [17,18]. The CBT-LLM [9], based on the PsyQA dataset [19], incorporates structured CBT intervention strategies. The system designed by [20] guides thousands of participants in identifying cognitive traps and reframing negative thoughts, thereby validating the effectiveness of LLMs in cognitive reframing. HealMe [12] utilizes a three-step framework to assist clients in discovering alternative perspectives. CACTUS [13] is the first to extend cognitive reframing tasks to multi-turn interactions, addressing a gap in psychological data and providing new insights into this field. However, whether based on fixed turn numbers or predefined strategies, these studies limit the model's ability to adapt to diverse users in real-world scenarios.

3 Method

3.1 Problem Definition

Cognitive reframing can help individuals address problems and alleviate their emotional distress by transforming negative thinking patterns [2]. The client holds an unhelpful thought, denoted as T_i, and the counselor's objective is to help the client reframe T_i into a more adaptive thought R_i through dialogue.

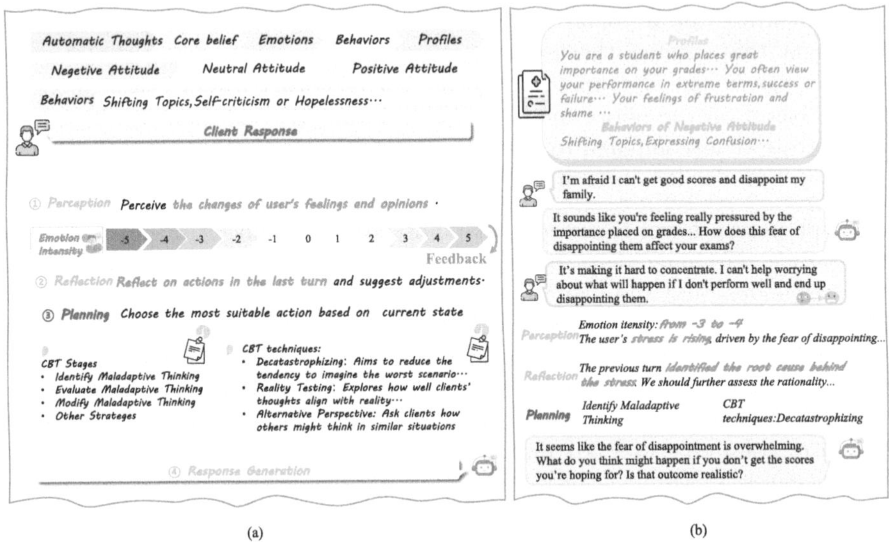

Fig. 2. (a) The overall framework of CARE. CARE adapts its intervention strategies by incorporating feedback from changes in the user's emotional and cognitive state. (b) An example dialogue illustrating how CARE applies this process in practice.

3.2 CARE

The ABC theory from [3] posits that emotions are not caused by the event itself but by the individual's interpretation and evaluation of the event. Therefore, changes in emotional state and expressed cognitions provide signals to evaluate whether an intervention is effective. CARE (Fig. 2), a multi-step reasoning framework, monitors the user's evolving cognitive and emotional state, reflects on the outcomes of previous interventions, and adaptively applies CBT strategies to facilitate gradual cognitive reframing. Through this sequential reasoning process, the agent guides self-exploration that gradually shifts the user's cognitive patterns. Specifically, CARE conducts cognitive reframing through the following four reasoning steps:

Step 1: Perception. CARE begins by inferring the current emotional and cognitive state of the user based on the context of the dialog. To capture emotional valence, we define an emotion intensity score ranging from -5 (highly negative) to 5 (highly positive). This quantified emotional assessment, together with a description of the user's thoughts, forms the evidential basis for subsequent reasoning.

Step 2: Reflection. CARE reflects on the previous intervention by examining how the user's current state differs from the prior turn. Explicit shifts in expressed opinions provide direct cognitive feedback, while changes in emotional intensity offer implicit signals of evolving appraisals. This reflection step updates the system's representation of the user's cognitiveemotional trajectory and offeres recommendations regarding the strategies for the this turn.

Step 3: Planning. Based on the analysis above, CARE selects the next therapeutic action in a structured manner. Cognitive reframing typically proceeds through three phases—*identification*, *evaluation*, and *modification* of maladaptive thinking [14]. To operationalize these phases, the Planning module decomposes therapeutic reasoning into four stages:

1. **Identify Maladaptive Thinking:** Help the user distinguish between situations, thoughts, and feelings, and identify specific automatic thoughts associated with strong negative emotions.
2. **Evaluate Maladaptive Thinking:** Guide the user in examining the accuracy, usefulness, and logical consistency of their thoughts, assessing whether they are evidence-based or overly generalized.
3. **Modify Maladaptive Thinking:** Collaborate with the user to generate alternative explanations, such as balanced interpretations, realistic assessments of feared outcomes, or concrete coping strategies.
4. **Other Strategies:** When negative affect remains high, prioritize empathetic validation, emotional support, and active listening to stabilize affect before deeper cognitive work.

To support these stages, CARE integrates a set of CBT techniques selected with guidance from psychological experts, including Pie Chart Technique, Reality Testing, Pros and Cons Analysis, Efficiency Evaluation, Continuum Technique, Decatastrophizing, Alternative Perspective, Changing Rules to Wishes, Behavior Experiment, Systematic Exposure, and Problem-Solving Skills Training [13]. The selected techniques guide the direction for the final response generation.

Step 4: Response. Depending on the inferred state, reflective evaluation, and the selected CBT technique, CARE generates an empathetic and therapeutically grounded response. The response guides the user toward alternative interpretations, challenges maladaptive beliefs, or constructs more balanced evaluations, completing one full cycle of the CARE reasoning process.

3.3 Client Simulation

We adopt the methodology of the PATIENT-ϕ framework [8], in which simulated clients are grounded in Cognitive Conceptualization Diagrams (CCDs) developed under the guidance of licensed therapists. Following this approach, we construct client profiles through a chain of cognitive processes that mirrors clinical conceptualization practices. Building on Beck's Cognitive Theory, where core beliefs can be categorized into 18 distinct types [2], we ensure that each simulated client

Table 1. The categories of core beliefs.

3 major categories	18 fine-grained categories
HELPLESS	I am ineffective in accomplishing tasks.
	I am incompetent and helpless.
	I am powerless, vulnerable, and at risk of harm.
	I am a failure.
	I am defective.
	I cannot protect myself.
	I am less capable than others.
	I am unable to meet expectations.
UNLOVABLE	I am unlovable.
	I am unattractive.
	I am undesirable and unwanted.
	I am bound to be rejected.
	I am bound to be abandoned.
	I am bound to be alone.
WORTHLESS	I am morally bad.
	I am a sinner.
	I am dangerous, toxic, crazy, and evil.
	I don't deserve to live.

is anchored in a clinically meaningful belief structure in Table 1. By explicitly modeling these cognitive pathways, the simulated client can exhibit more stable unhelpful thinking patterns. After inferring the core belief that underlies a given automatic thought, we further infer the emotional and behavioral responses that such a thought is likely to trigger, ultimately yielding a coherent profile (Fig. 2).

Notably, prior studies have shown that GPT-based simulated patients tend to display overly positive or compliant attitudes that fail to reflect the variability of real-world clients [13]. To mitigate this bias, we incorporate a broader spectrum of behavioral styles following the taxonomy in [21]. Specifically, we define three overarching attitudinal orientations–*positive*, *neutral*, and *negative*. Each orientation corresponds to different dialogue behaviors that shape how the simulated client responds to interventions. For negative attitudes, we introduce six behavior patterns including topic shifting, defensiveness, resistance, self-criticism, emotional withdrawal, and pessimistic interpretation. These behaviors reflect common challenges observed in psychotherapy sessions and enable simulated clients to exhibit more realistic resistance or disengagement. Positive users, in contrast, adopt behaviors such as active cooperation, open self-disclosure, and willingness to explore alternative viewpoints. Neutral users do not receive additional behavioral instructions and are free to respond naturally.

Through the integration of (1) unhelpful thinking patterns, (2) cognitive processdriven profile, and (3) attitudinally grounded behavior, our simulated clients better approximate the diversity and complexity of real-world therapy participants. To further enhance ecological validity, we do not impose a fixed number of dialogue turns; instead, simulated users may voluntarily terminate the conversation at any moment, reflecting the open-ended nature of actual therapeutic interactions.

3.4 COG-DEBATE

We propose a novel metric to intuitively measure the effectiveness of cognitive reframing. In addition, cognitive reframing is a debate-like conversational process. During a debate, two or more people hold different points of view about a given topic and strive to change others' viewpoints, attitudes, or behaviors through conversation [22]. Similarly, cognitive reframing involves the client and the counselor discussing their different interpretations of the same event. After the debate, the winner is determined by the audience based on which side they ultimately agree the most. Inspired by this, we proposed the **COG-DEBATE** metric, which compares the final viewpoint of the user with the initial two thoughts to determine whether cognitive reframing is successful.

As shown in Fig. 3, the client and the counselor engage in a dialogue based on the given unhelpful thought and reframed thought, respectively. After counseling: First, we extract and summarize the client's final thought. In CBT practice, a feedback stage is typically conducted at the end of each counseling session, during which the therapist asks the client what they have gained from the session. Following this protocol, after each simulated counseling conversation, we first prompt the simulated client to reflect on whether their thoughts or emotions have changed. Next, we combine the simulated client's self-summarized reflection with the full dialogue history and feed them into an evaluation LLM to derive the user's Final Thoughts. The resulting Final Thoughts Fi is then used in the COG-DEBATE metric to determine whether the cognitive reframing has been achieved. We use the evaluation LLM to compare this Final Thought Fi with both the Unhelpful Thought Ti and the Reframed Thought Ri to judge which the Final Thought is closer to: If it is closer to Ri, cognitive reframing is considered successful. If it is closer to Ti, cognitive reframing is considered unsuccessful. If neither, the topic is considered deviated, and cognitive reframing is unsuccessful.

4 Dataset Construction

To construct high-quality cognitive reframing dialogues, we begin with the PATTERNREFRAME dataset [15], which contains 10k unhelpful thoughts labeled with their corresponding cognitive distortion types, along with 27k reframed thoughts. Since each unhelpful thought is paired with multiple candidate reframes, we follow [16] in selecting the most specific and empathetic

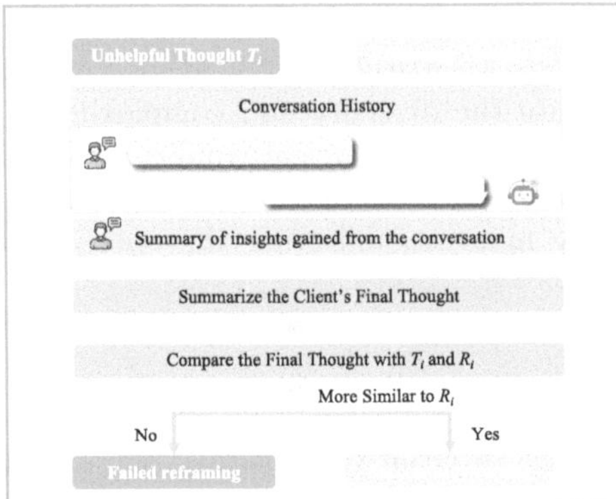

Fig. 3. COG-DEBATE Metric. Compare the Final Thought Fi with both the Unhelpful Thought (Ti) and the Reframed Thought (Ri). If Fi is closer to Ri, we regard this cognitive restructuring as a success.

reframed thought, as these responses tend to be more acceptable and therapeutically effective for users. Each selected (Unhelpful Thought, Reframed Thought) pair serves as the seed for generating a full multi-turn cognitive reframing dialogue between a simulated client and counselor.

Given the privacy-sensitive nature of psychological counseling, real-world deployment often favors local or open-source solutions [13]. Following this motivation, we randomly sample 2,000 unhelpful thoughts from PATTERNREFRAME and generate 2,000 corresponding dialogues to construct a dataset for training locally deployed models. The therapist role is implemented using the GPT-4o with CARE reasoning framework, while the client role is simulated using GPT-4o-mini to reduce computational overhead.

The raw dialogues undergo a two-stage quality filtering procedure to ensure both behavioral realism and therapeutic validity.

Stage 1 User Performance Filtering. The simulated client's performance is evaluated along following dimensions, each scored as 0 (unmet) or 1 (satisfied): **Personality Consistency:** The user's personality traits must remain coherent with the initial CCD-based profile, without contradictions. **Attitude Consistency:** The user's expressed attitude must align with the assigned condition. Only dialogues in which all criteria receive a score of 1 are retained. This step removes 38 dialogues that exhibit inconsistencies such as unrealistic compliance, contradictory emotional expressions, or meta-role shifts.

Stage 2 Cognitive Reframing Effectiveness Filtering. For the remaining dialogues, we apply the COG-DEBATE metric to automatically evaluate whether cognitive reframing has been successfully achieved. Only dialogues that exhibit effective reframing are preserved.

After applying both filtering stages, a total of 1,507 high-quality dialogues remain, forming the **CareGiver** dataset. The average dialogue contains 16.66

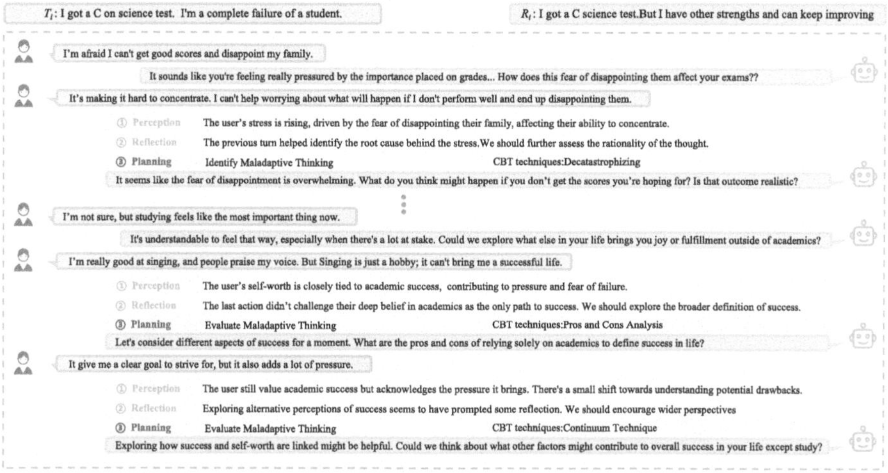

Fig. 4. A demonstration of cognitive reframing between a user with negative attitudes (blue) and GPT-4o + *CARE* (orange). Compared to the base model in Fig. 1, the counselor with CARE offers a deeper and more specific analysis, encouraging the user to gradually recognize his strengths beyond academic performance. (Color figure online)

turns, with an average counselor response length of 46.72 words. Additionally, we select another 100 unhelpful thoughts from to construct a test set.

5 Experiments

5.1 Baseline Methods

We compare our method against two categories baselines: (1)**Off-the-shelf LLMs.** Given the high demands of the output formatting capability, we choose GPT-4o[1], GPT-4o-mini[2], and Gemini[3] 1.5 Pro as the baseline models. (2)**fine-tuend LLMs.** We take the Llama 3.1 model with 8 billion parameters as the base model and fine-tune it on psychological counseling datasets, including Esconv [23], Psych8k [10], and CACTUS [13], respectively.

5.2 Implementation Details

We utilize the official APIs for closed-source models. Moreover, we obtain the weight of Meta's Llama-3.1-8B-Instruct from Hugging Face. Llama3 is fine-tuned using Low-Rank Adaptation (LoRA) [24], a parameter-efficient technique that reduces both GPU memory usage and computational costs. The learning rate is set to 1×10^{-4}, the batch size to 16, and the model is trained for a maximum

[1] https://platform.openai.com/docs/models#gpt-4o.
[2] https://platform.openai.com/docs/models#gpt-4o-mini.
[3] https://ai.google.dev/gemini-api/docs/models/gemini#gemini-1.5-pro.

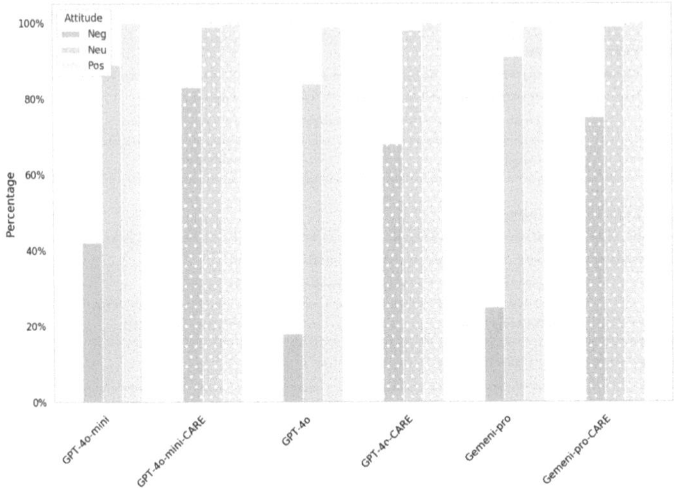

Fig. 5. Success rate for users with different attitudes.

of 5 epochs, with the best checkpoint selected based on performance on the validation set. The LoRA rank is set to 8, and the alpha parameter is set to 16. To accommodate the length of multi-turn dialogues, the cut-off length is set to 2048, ensuring the model can handle longer input sequences effectively.

5.3 Automatic Evaluation

Evaluation of Users with Different Attitudes To demonstrate the effectiveness of CARE, we conduct experiments on users with different attitudes. The

Table 2. Results of automated evaluation of simulated users with negative attitudes. EmoR denotes Emotion Resonance.

Model	Type	Success Rate	Specificity	EmoR	Persuasiveness	Guidance
GPT-4o-mini	Close	42%	4.35	4.02	3.50	4.10
GPT-4o-mini+*CARE*	Close	**83%**	**4.40**	4.20	**3.68**	**4.70**
GPT-4o	Close	18%	3.88	3.76	2.96	3.46
GPT-4o+*CARE*	Close	68%	4.13	**4.25**	3.38	4.54
Gemeni-pro	Close	25%	3.93	3.66	3.12	3.70
Gemeni-pro+*CARE*	Close	75%	4.23	4.24	3.60	4.46
Llama3	Open	58%	4.07	4.01	3.32	4.06
Llama3+*Esconv*	Open	6%	1.35	1.40	1.21	1.24
Llama3+*Psych8k*	Open	78%	4.11	4.11	3.30	4.50
Llama3+*CACTUS*	Open	61%	3.97	4.06	3.28	4.42
Llama3+*CareGiver*	Open	81%	4.28	4.17	3.66	4.67

success rate of cognitive reframing is evaluated by COG-DEBATE (Fig. 5), which compares the final thought after counseling to the initial unhelpful thought and reframed thought. CARE variants significantly outperforms the baselines: For users with positive or neutral attitudes, existing LLMs can already effectively address their issues. However, when equipped with CARE, the success rate further increases, approaching 100%. For users with negative attitudes, however, the base models perform poorly. Notably, all the CARE variants excel in transforming unhelpful thoughts with an improvement of 50%, substantially enhancing base models.

Results on Users with Negative Attitudes To further explore the challenges in users with negative or resistant attitudes, we extend the scope of the experiment. We utilize a set of metrics to comprehensively assess the counselor's ability [25]. Specifically, we employ G-Eval [26] to evaluate four criteria in a Likert scale (15): **Specificity** evaluates the limitations of LLMs in providing generalized responses; **Emotional Resonance** assesses the user's emotional experience; **Guidance** measures the user's level of active engagement; **Persuasiveness** evaluates the overall effectiveness.

As shown in Table 2, it is evident that when equipped with CARE, all closed-source models show significant improvement across almost all metrics, where the GPT-4o-mini with CARE achieves the highest scores in four out of five metrics. In comparison to the baselines, the CARE variants exhibit competitive Guidance scores, indicating that CARE effectively encourages active engagement in reflective thinking. For fine-tuned models, the Psych8k and CACTUS datasets result in slight improvements. Surprisingly, the Esconv dataset leads to a sharp decline in performance, suggesting that not all psychological counseling datasets are suitable for cognitive reframing tasks. Notably, our CareGiver consistently outperforms all baseline datasets by a significant margin, particularly in addressing users' specific issues and effectively guiding them in self-exploration. Moreover, the effectiveness indicated by Persuasiveness does not completely align with the Success Rate, showing the limitations of LLMs as evaluators. We also use the same client and unhelpful thinking pattern as in Fig. 1 to illustrate how the CARE variants engage in cognitive restructuring. Compared to the baseline, the CARE variant offers a more comprehensive analysis, which encourages the user to engage in deeper reflection, gradually recognizing the limitations of their prior thinking (Fig. 4).

5.4 Artificial Experiments

To further assess the effectiveness of the model in real-world psychological counseling, we recruit 12 volunteers with similar ages and temperaments. These participants engage in conversations with four different models, each deployed on the same server. The models are randomly assigned to three volunteers each. We evaluate the models' performance with two methods: the Positive and Negative Affect Schedule (PANAS scale) [27], which measures changes in emotional

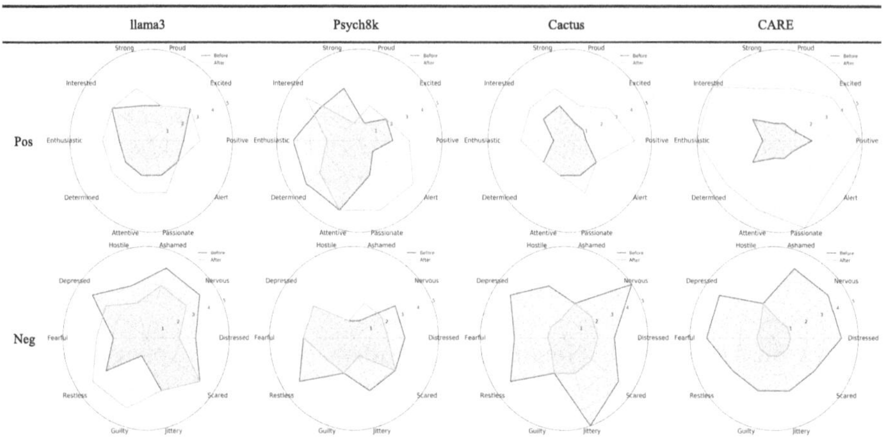

Fig. 6. Visualization of emotional changes in users before and after interacting with different models. Blue represents initial emotional states, while orange shows emotions after the conversation. (Color figure online)

states, and five traditional criterion used in psychological counseling evaluations [12].

Visulization of PANAS Scale Changes The PANAS scale is widely used to assess emotional states over a specified period, consisting of 10 positive and 10 negative emotions. Participants rate the intensity of each emotion based on their current emotional experience, using a scale from 1 to 5, where 1 denotes "not applicable" and 5 denotes "strongly applicable." The effectiveness of cognitive reframing is determined by measuring changes in participants' positive and negative emotions before and after the conversation.

Figure 6 presents the changes in PANAS scale scores for four representative participants. It is observed that Llama3 has a limited effect on emotional regulation. However, after fine-tuning, all three models effectively alleviated negative emotions. Notably, CareGiver brings the most significant improvement in positive emotions, leading to the best overall results. Similar trends are observed in the PANAS scale scores of the other participants.

Human Ratings. After psychological counseling [20], participants are usually invited to rate the counselor's performance. We ask volunteers to rate from 5 aspects based on a Likert scale (1–5, where 1 represents "strongly disagree" and 5 represents "strongly agree"), including Helpfulness, Empathy, Reasonableness, Memorability, Learnability.

The CareGiver fine-tuned model outperforms all other models across all criteria, particularly excelling in **Helpfulness**, **Memorability**, and **Learnability**, demonstrating significant effectiveness and the potential to continuously improve the user's maladaptive cognition. (Table 3).

User 1 reports that Llama3 fails to capture the key points, providing scattered responses with numerous questions that make it difficult for him to determine how to respond. User 2 mentions that while the suggestions from Psych8k appear correct, the questions are superficial and do not engage the user effectively. In contrast, CARE guides the user through increasingly in-depth questions and provides practical, actionable suggestions, ultimately helping the user identify the root cause of their issue.

Table 3. Human evaluation results.

Model	Helpfulness	Empathy	Reasonableness	Memorability	Learnability
Llama3	2.56	3.00	3.11	2.67	2.67
+Psych8k	3.00	3.67	4.00	4.00	2.89
+CACTUS	3.33	3.78	3.89	3.67	3.22
+CareGiver	**4.33**	**4.11**	**4.33**	**4.56**	**4.00**

6 Ablation Study

We perform an ablation study to determine the contribution of each module in CARE to the overall cognitive restructuring process. CARE consists of two primary modules: the Feedback module, which includes Perception and Reflection, and the Planning module, which integrates psychological knowledge. An ablation study was conducted to evaluate these two modules. We respectively remove each of these two modules for performance comparison.

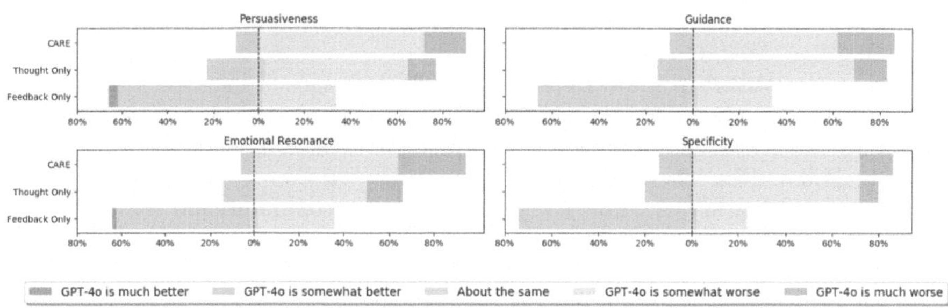

Fig. 7. Distribution of compared results, with GPT-4o as the base model. X-axis: percentage of examples falling into each specific level; Y-axis: different variants of CARE. Evaluation is conducted across five levels.

The results highlight the crucial role of CBT knowledge in guiding the model's interventions (Fig. 7). Notably, compared to the baselines, the model with only the Feedback module performs even worse. This suggests that without psychological guidance, the model lacks a clear direction for adjustment, ultimately reducing its effectiveness.

7 Conclusion

Given the structured nature of cognitive reframing, we introduce CARE, a user-centered assistant that can dynamically understand and adapt to users evolving cognitive and emotional states. By incorporating psychological techniques, CARE offers users detailed and insightful analyses that promote self-exploration, gradually shifting their cognitive patterns. Additionally, we introduce COG-DEBATE, a novel evaluation metric that intuitively measures the success of cognitive reframing. Both automated and human experimental results highlight CARE's significant effectiveness, particularly for users with negative or resistant attitudes.

Acknowledgements. This work was supported by Sichuan Science and Technology Program (Grant No. 2024YFG0006), the National Natural Science Foundation of China (Grant No. U24A20250), and the Fundamental Research Funds for the Central Universities (No. ZYGX2024Z005).

References

1. Shafran, R., Myles-Hooton, P., Bennett, S., Öst, L.-G.: The concept and definition of low intensity cognitive behaviour therapy. Behav. Res. Ther. **138**, 103803 (2021)
2. Beck, J.S.: Cognitive behavior therapy: Basics and beyond. Guilford Publications (2020)
3. Ellis, A.: Rational emotive therapy. In: Albert Ellis Revisited, pp. 25–37. Routledge (2013)
4. Beck, A.T., Dozois, D.J.A.: Cognitive therapy: current status and future directions. Annual Rev. Med. **62**(1), 397–409 (2011)
5. Johnco, C., Wuthrich, V.M., Rapee, R.M.: The influence of cognitive flexibility on treatment outcome and cognitive restructuring skill acquisition during cognitive behavioural treatment for anxiety and depression in older adults: Results of a pilot study. Behav. Res. Ther. **57**, 55–64 (2014)
6. Chiu, Y.Y., Sharma, A., Lin, I.W., Althoff, T.: A computational framework for behavioral assessment of llm therapists. arXiv preprint arXiv:2401.00820 (2024)
7. Trott. Can large language models help augment english psycholinguistic datasets? Behavior Research Methods, pp. 1–19 (2024)
8. Wang, R., et al. Patient-ψ: Using large language models to simulate patients for training mental health professionals. arXiv preprintarXiv:2405.19660 (2024)
9. Na, H.: Cbt-llm: a chinese large language model for cognitive behavioral therapy-based mental health question answering. *arXiv preprint* arXiv:2403.16008 (2024)
10. Liu, J.M., Li, D., Cao, H., Ren, T., Liao, Z., Wu, J.: Chatcounselor: A large language models for mental health support. corr abs/2309.15461 (2023)
11. Li, J.Z., Herderich, A., Goldenberg, A.: Skill but not effort drive gpt overperformance over humans in cognitive reframing of negative scenarios (2024)

12. Xiao, M., et al.: Harnessing cognitive reframing in large language models for psychotherapy. arXiv preprintarXiv:2403.05574 (2024)
13. Lee, S., et al.: Cactus: towards psychological counseling conversations using cognitive behavioral theory. arXiv preprint arXiv:2407.03103 (2024)
14. Wenzel, A.: Basic strategies of cognitive behavioral therapy. Psychiatric Clinics **40**(4), 597–609 (2017)
15. Maddela, M., Ung, M., Xu, J., Madotto, A., Foran, H., Boureau, Y.-L.: Training models to generate, recognize, and reframe unhelpful thoughts. arXiv preprint arXiv:2307.02768 (2023)
16. Sharma, A., et al.: Cognitive reframing of negative thoughts through human-language model interaction. arXiv preprint arXiv:2305.02466 (2023)
17. Demszky, D., et al.: Using large language models in psychology. Nature Reviews Psychology **2**(11), 688–701 (2023)
18. Sharma, A., Lin, I.W., Miner, A.S., Atkins, D.C., Althoff, T.: Human-ai collaboration enables more empathic conversations in text-based peer-to-peer mental health support. Nature Machine Intelligence **5**(1), 46–57 (2023)
19. Sun, H., Lin, Z., Zheng, C., Liu, S., Huang, M.: Psyqa: a Chinese dataset for generating long counseling text for mental health support. *arXiv preprint* arXiv:2106.01702 (2021)
20. Sharma, A., Rushton, K., Lin, I.W., Nguyen, T., Althoff, T.: Facilitating self-guided mental health interventions through human-language model interaction: A case study of cognitive restructuring. In: Proceedings of the CHI Conference on Human Factors in Computing Systems, pp. 1–29 (2024)
21. Li, A., et al.: Understanding client reactions in online mental health counseling. arXiv preprint arXiv:2306.15334 (2023)
22. Fogg, B.J.: Persuasive technology: using computers to change what we think and do. Ubiquity **2002**(December), 2 (2002)
23. Liu, S., Zheng, C., Sabour, S., Huang, M.: Towards emotional support dialog systems, Orianna Demasi (2021)
24. Hu, E.J., et al.: Lora: low-rank adaptation of large language models. arXiv preprint arXiv:2106.09685 (2021)
25. Chen, M., et al.: The future of cognitive strategy-enhanced persuasive dialogue agents: new perspectives and trends. Front. Comp. Sci. **19**(5), 195315 (2025)
26. Liu, Y., Iter, D., Xu, Y., Wang, S., Xu, R., Zhu, C.: G-eval: Nlg evaluation using gpt-4 with better human alignment. arXiv preprint arXiv:2303.16634 (2023)
27. Watson, D., Clark, L.A., Tellegen, A.: Development and validation of brief measures of positive and negative affect: the panas scales. J. Personality Soc. Psychol. **54**(6), 1063 (1988)

Fine-Grained Attention Enhancement for Mitigating Hallucinations in LVLMs

Jidong Yang, Hongxun Yao(✉), Xi Chen, and Shouxu Jiang

Faculty of Computing, Harbin Institute of Technology, Harbin, China
h.yao@hit.edu.cn

Abstract. Large vision-language models (LVLMs) have achieved impressive performance on tasks such as visual question answering and image captioning, yet they still suffer from hallucinations, producing descriptions that conflict with the visual input. Prior efforts to mitigate hallucinations often rely on data-centric strategies or specialized fine-tuning, which require large-scale annotations or costly retraining. More recent training-free methods adjust attention at the modality level but largely ignore fine-grained objectregion grounding. In this work, we analyze hallucinations through the lens of cross-modal attention and show that, during decoding, LVLMs tend to collapse onto a few visually global tokens, while progressive encoding compresses visual evidence into global tokens that are easily overridden by language priors. To address this, we propose a training-free framework that (i) leverages CLIP patch embeddings and early-layer attention maps to reweight decoder cross-attention in an object-centric, fine-grained manner, and (ii) introduces an auxiliary decoding branch with masked global tokens for contrastive decoding, effectively reducing hallucinations without additional training.

Keywords: Hallucination · LVLMs · Training-free

1 Introduction

In recent years, the rapid advancement of large vision-language models (LVLMs) has driven significant progress in scene understanding. While these models demonstrate strong capabilities in tasks such as visual question answering and image captioning, they exhibit a critical weakness in scene understanding: a tendency to generate descriptions that are inconsistent with the actual visual content, as shown in Fig. 1(a), a phenomenon known as hallucination.

Hallucinations are commonly attributed to factors such as noisy training data, misalignment between visual and textual representations, and the inherent complexity of interpreting fine-grained scene contexts. To mitigate this, researchers have proposed data-centric strategies and specialized fine-tuning techniques. However, these approaches often require large-scale, high-quality annotated data or computationally expensive model retraining, limiting their scalability. As a result, training-free methods have gained increasing attention.

H. Liu et al. (Eds.): CEI 2025, CCIS 2881, pp. 134–148, 2026.
https://doi.org/10.1007/978-981-95-9493-1_9

For instance, PAI [14] observes that LVLMs tend to over-rely on textual history and compensates by strengthening attention to visual tokens. However, PAI uniformly increases the weight of all visual tokens at the modality level, without enforcing finer-grained alignment between specific visual regions and the generated text. As shown in Fig. 1(b), we find that during decoding the model often fails to attend to the primary objects and the spatial layout of the scene. Instead, it tends to collapse onto a few visually uninformative background tokens that effectively act as global sink tokens. These global tokens encode only high-level, coarse visual semantics and miss many fine-grained object and relation details. When the model over-relies on such incomplete visual summaries, language priors can easily fill in missing details, leading to hallucinated descriptions.

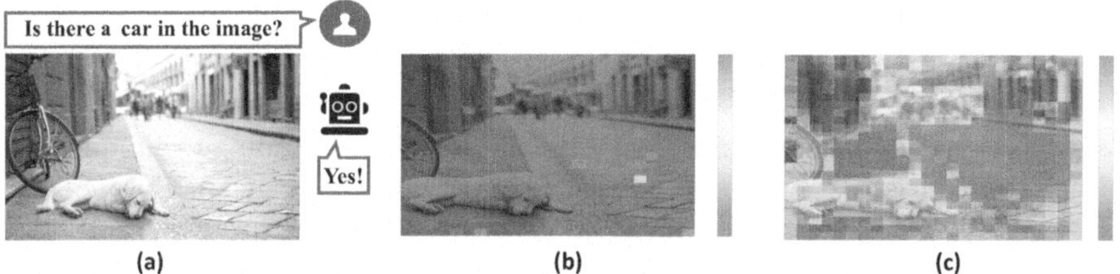

Fig. 1. (a) Illustration of a hallucinated response produced by an LVLM. (b) Decoder attention map at an early layer (3rd layer). (c) Visual encoder attention map at an early layer (3rd layer).

To address this issue, we propose a **F**ine-Grained **A**ttention **E**nhancement (FAE) mechanism that explicitly strengthens object-centric visual grounding during the decoding stage while reducing the model's reliance on global sink tokens. Specifically, since most LVLMs adopt CLIP as the visual encoder, and CLIP's patch embeddings and early-layer attention maps capture rich spatial structure and highlight salient objects, as shown in Fig. 1(c), we leverage these signals to reweight the decoder's cross-attention in a fine-grained manner. This encourages the decoder to focus on object-centric regions and their spatial relationships, rather than on background sink tokens. In addition, we observe that as encoding proceeds, visual information is progressively compressed into a small number of global visual tokens that concentrate high-level semantics. We treat these global tokens as the main interface through which language priors can override fine-grained visual evidence. To disentangle the effect of language priors, we introduce an auxiliary decoding branch in which these global tokens are masked, yielding a text-priordominated generation. By performing contrastive decoding between the visually grounded branch and this text-prior branch, we bias the final output toward hypotheses that are simultaneously likely under strong visual grounding and less supported by pure language priors, thereby mitigating hallucinations induced by over-reliance on textual information.

Our main contributions are summarized as follows:

- We analyze hallucinations in LVLMs from the perspective of cross-modal attention and propose a training-free, object-centric attention enhancement mechanism that leverages CLIP patch embeddings and early-layer attention maps to enhance fine-grained visual grounding.
- We design a dual-branch contrastive decoding framework, where a visually grounded branch is contrasted with a text-priordominated branch (obtained by masking global sink tokens), effectively reducing hallucinations without additional training.
- We evaluate our method using CHAIR, POPE, and MME evaluation metrics to assess its performance in image description and VQA tasks comprehensively.

2 Related Work

2.1 Large Vision-Language Models

Recent progress in both pre-training [1,16] and instruction-tuning techniques [15, 21] has substantially improved the capabilities of large language models (LLMs) such as LLaMA [20] and Vicuna [17], which in turn has catalyzed advances in large vision-language models (LVLMs). The CLIP [18] and BLIP [10] families learn joint imagetext representations and have become standard backbones for a broad range of multimodal applications. Building on these foundations, models like LLaVA [13], InstructBLIP [3], and Qwen-VL [22] enable users to interact with LVLMs through image and text prompts. Despite these developments, current LVLMs still exhibit prominent hallucination behaviors, frequently generating descriptions that are inconsistent with the visual input.

2.2 Mitigation of LVLM Hallucinations

To mitigate hallucinations, a variety of approaches have been explored. A major cause of hallucination has been attributed to dataset bias and the mismatch between visual and textual knowledge. Consequently, improving data filtering strategies [12] and enhancing the quality of annotations [5] have been regarded as key directions. Other works [24,25] introduce auxiliary data or adversarial samples to stress-test models and improve robustness. In parallel, several studies advocate additional alignment training [7], architectural refinements [2], or leveraging external models to provide richer visual information [6]. However, these solutions typically require substantial retraining or modification of large models, making them time-consuming and computationally expensive.

This has motivated a growing interest in training-free methods. VCD [9] adopts a contrastive decoding strategy that compares outputs conditioned on different visual inputs to suppress hallucinated content. PAI [14] tackles overreliance on textual context by globally amplifying the attention weights of visual tokens during generation. Similarly, CODE [8] mitigates hallucinations by replacing visual tokens with the model's own initial predictions and performing contrastive decoding between these alternatives. Meanwhile, VAF [23] shows that intermediate decoder layers play a crucial role in hallucination formation and can be explicitly regularized. Nonetheless, most of these training-free approaches focus on relatively coarse-grained adjustments to decoding or attention, without explicitly modeling fine-grained visual evidence when constraining hallucinations.

3 Method

3.1 Preliminaries

The overall framework of large visionlanguage models (LVLMs) is typically composed of three key modules: an image encoder, a feature projector, and a language decoder. Both the image encoder and the language decoder are usually pre-trained on large-scale datasets. The encoder transforms the input image into a set of visual tokens, which are subsequently projected into the textual embedding space through the projector. This alignment enables the fusion of image and text tokens, forming a unified token sequence that serves as input to the language decoder. The decoder then produces textual outputs by attending to these fused representations.

In most LVLM architectures, the LLaMA is adopted as the backbone language decoder. After projection, the visual tokens are concatenated with textual tokens and passed into the LLaMA layers for multimodal reasoning. Within each transformer layer, multiple attention heads perform self-attention operations on the fused sequence, maintaining a consistent input dimensionality across layers as follows:

$$O_h = A_h V_h, \quad A_h^{softmax} = \text{softmax}\left(\frac{Q_h K_h^\top}{\sqrt{d_k}}\right). \tag{1}$$

Each attention head h computes attention using its own parameterized projections of the input sequence, namely the queries $Q_h \in \mathbb{R}^{n \times d_k}$, keys $K_h \in \mathbb{R}^{n \times d_k}$, and values $V_h \in \mathbb{R}^{n \times d_k}$, where$n$ denotes the sequence length and d_k is the hidden dimension. The output of the head, $O_h \in \mathbb{R}^{n \times d_k}$, is obtained by applying the attention weights $A_h^{softmax} \in \mathbb{R}^{n \times n}$ to the value matrix. Each row of $A_h^{softmax}$ represents the attention distribution over all tokens, allowing the model to selectively emphasize different parts of the input and capture complementary contextual information across multiple heads. For an LVLM parameterized by θ, given an instructional input $\mathcal{X}$ and a visual input $\mathcal{V}$, the model predicts a probability distribution for the next token $y \in \mathbb{R}^v$ which can be formatted as:

$$\begin{aligned} y_t &\sim p_\theta\left(y_t \mid \mathcal{X}, \mathcal{V}, \mathcal{H}\right), \\ &\propto softmax(\text{logit}_\theta\left(y_t \mid \mathcal{X}, \mathcal{V}, \mathcal{H}\right)). \end{aligned} \tag{2}$$

where y_t refers to the token predicted at the current time step t, and $\mathcal{H}$ represents the history of all tokens generated prior to t, i.e., $\mathcal{H} = \{y_1 \cdots y_{t-1}\}$.

3.2 Overall Architecture

Our goal is to mitigate hallucinations by guiding the model to focus on the key objects in the image and enhancing the alignment between the generated textual content and the visual information. To this end, we introduce a simple yet effective mechanism that, at inference time, strengthens patch-level attention on the primary objects in the image and mitigates hallucinations arising from the model's over-reliance on attention sink tokens, which leads it to overlook other relevant visual content. An overview of our FAE is shown in Fig. 2. In our framework, we begin by enhancing the decoder's interpretability and focus through the **Attention Enhance (AE)** module, which refines the attention matrices to strengthen the model's emphasis on primary objects within the input image. Prior to decoding, we further optimize the visual inputs during the image-encoding stage using the **Global Token Mask (GTM)** module. GTM generates a deeply fused attention map to detect and suppress visual tokens associated with attention sinks, ensuring that only informative visual features are preserved. These filtered visual representations are then integrated with textual features and passed into the decoder, where the dual-branch design–one branch operating on the original visual tokens–works jointly with AE to achieve more robust and semantically aligned decoding.

3.3 Attention Enhancement

In LVLMs, response generation proceeds in an autoregressive manner, where each output token is conditioned on the input image, the instruction, and all previously generated tokens. This sequential process is implemented by a multi-layer attention-based decoder that produces a vocabulary distribution at each decoding step. Our goal is to exploit the CLIP visual encoder's ability to focus on primary objects and preserve spatial structure in its shallow layers–an ability that has been widely leveraged for open-vocabulary semantic segmentation–to strengthen the model's attention to salient targets in the image and improve its understanding of the overall scene layout.

When producing the t-th token in the decoding sequence, each attention head receives a combined input consisting of three parts: the instruction embedding $\mathcal{X} = [x_1, ..., x_a]$, the visual embedding $\mathcal{V} = [v_1, ..., v_b]$, and the contextual embedding of previously generated tokens $\mathcal{H} = [h_1, ..., h_c]$. Here, the visual representation $\mathcal{V}$ corresponds to the output processed by the projector module. Formally, the hidden states at step t can be described as:

$$X_t = concat(\mathcal{X}[1:m], \mathcal{V}, \mathcal{X}[m+1:a], \mathcal{H}), \tag{3}$$

where $\mathcal{X}[1:m]$ denotes the first m tokens within the instruction sequence.

During decoding, each attention head dynamically allocates attention across these components to construct the representation of the current token. Our method aims to strengthen the model's focus on visual information. To this end, we identify the attention weights associated with the visual tokens for the current decoding step, apply a fine-grained adjustment, and subsequently re-normalize the attention distribution via a softmax operation.

Given an input image, during the forward pass of the visual encoder we also extract the fused attention matrix of the CLS token from early layers:

$$\hat{A}(i) = \sum_{l=1}^{k} \hat{A}_l(i), \tag{4}$$

where l indicates the layer index, and i denotes the i-th image token.

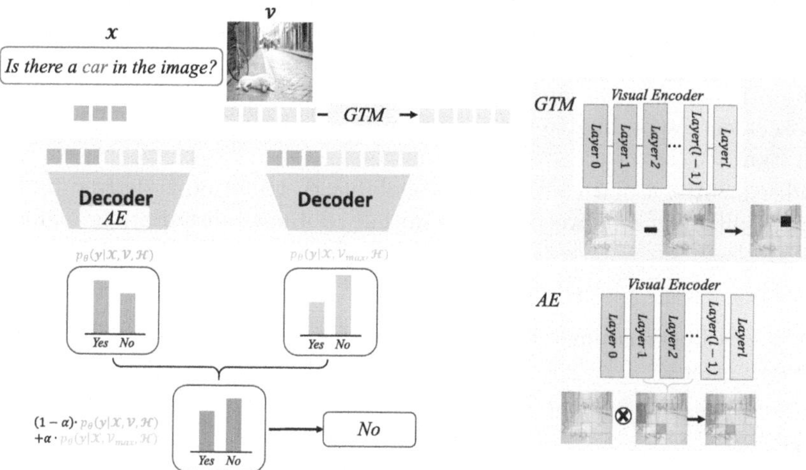

Fig. 2. In the FAE framework, the encoding stage first processes an input image using GTM to obtain a deeply fused attention map. This map is used to identify and mask global tokens. The remaining visual features are then fused with textual features and passed to the decoder. Furthermore, during decoding, AE extracts shallow-layer attention maps from the visual encoder and uses them to adjust the decoder's attention weights, enabling the model to focus more effectively on the primary content of the image.

Then, during the decoding phase of the decoder, we extract the attention weights $A(i)$ for the image tokens corresponding to the currently generated token, before the softmax operation. Considering that the main objects in the image should receive more attention, we identify the key visual tokens according to Eq. (4), and then increase the attention weight of those tokens. Therefore, the attention map is modified as follows:

$$A_i \leftarrow A_i + \alpha \cdot \hat{A}(i) \cdot |A(i)|, \tag{5}$$

where the hyperparameter α determines the magnitude of the applied intervention. After modifying the attention weights, a softmax operation is employed to re-normalize the attention distribution across all tokens during the update of encoded hidden states. This adjustment is performed iteratively for each token generation step and remains agnostic to the decoding strategy adopted.

3.4 Global Token Mask

As illustrated in Fig. 3, our analysis reveals that the model places high attention on global visual tokens during text generation. However, this leads the model to overlook finer details in the image, which are then compensated for by textual priors, thereby increasing the risk of hallucinations. To alleviate this phenomenon, we propose a masking strategy that selectively suppresses global visual tokens. Specifically, during the encoding of visual information, we extract the fused attention matrix $\tilde{A}(i)$ from the deep layers and identify the top-k high-attention indices Ω. The image representation $\mathcal{V}$ is then modified by removing the tokens corresponding to the indices in Ω, resulting in the transformed representation $\mathcal{V}'$.

Subsequently, a new contrastive probability distribution is derived by leveraging the differences between the two initially obtained distributions as follows:

$$\tilde{y}_t = (1+\gamma) \cdot p_\theta(y|\mathcal{X}, \mathcal{V}, \mathcal{H}) - \gamma \cdot p_\theta(y|\mathcal{X}, \mathcal{V}', \mathcal{H}), \tag{6}$$

where γ is a hyperparameter that balances the degree of contrast between the two distributions.

4 Experiments

4.1 Experiment Setups

Baselines. We assess the effectiveness of our method by evaluating it across three different models. To better understand the influence of image feature tokens processed by different projectors, we selected two models with linear projectors, LLaVA-1.5 and Qwen-VL, alongside one model that utilizes resamplers, InstructBlip. All experiments were conducted using the default hyperparameters provided in the open-source implementations of these models.

Implementation Details. Since different models have varying image token lengths, leading to different levels of image neglect, we adjusted the alignment with the image sequence length of each model. Specifically, we set $\alpha = 0.8$, $\gamma = 0.5$ for LLaVA-1.5, $\alpha = 0.5$, $\gamma = 0.5$ for Qwen-VL, $\alpha = 0.6$, $\gamma = 0.5$ resampler models InstructBlip.

4.2 Evaluation Metrics

CHAIR [19] is a standard metric for assessing hallucinations in image captioning systems. For each image, a reference set of ground-truth object labels

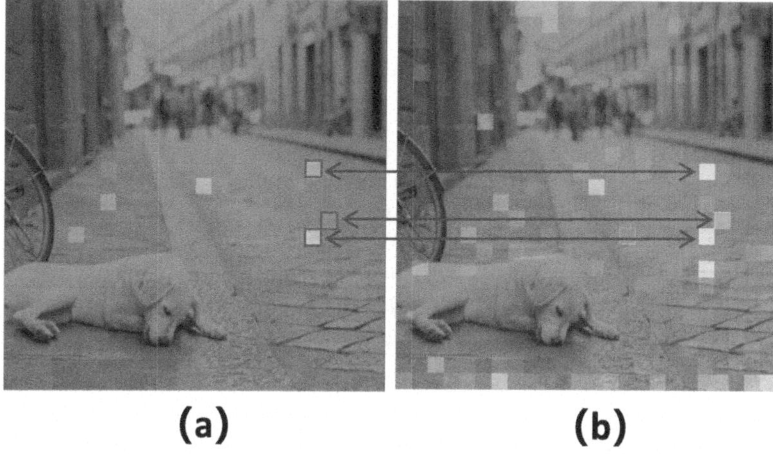

Fig. 3. Figure (a) shows the deep-layer attention map of the visual encoder, and Figure (b) shows the deep-layer attention map of the decoder. It can be observed that the decoder allocates heavily attention on the global tokens produced by the encoder.

is prepared. Any object mentioned in a caption that is absent from this reference set is counted as a hallucinated object. CHAIR reports two complementary scores–instance-level (CHAIR_I) and sentence-level (CHAIR_S)–defined as:

$$\text{CHAIR}_I = \frac{|\{\text{hallucinated objects}\}|}{|\{\text{all mentioned objects}\}|}, \tag{7}$$

$$\text{CHAIR}_S = \frac{|\{\text{captions with hallucinated objects}\}|}{|\{\text{all captions}\}|}. \tag{8}$$

Our experiments are conducted on the MSCOCO 2014 validation dataset. The model generates image captions under the prompt "Please describe the image in detail." To ensure comparability, we follow the evaluation configuration used in PAI [14] for analyzing hallucinations in long text generation.

POPE [11] is a benchmark specifically designed for evaluating hallucinations in the Visual Question Answering (VQA) setting. It detects object-level hallucinations through binary questions such as "Is there a <object> in the image?", where <object> is sampled from one of three categories–**random**, **popular**, or **adversarial**. In our experiments, we select 500 images from the COCO dataset and associate six queries with each image under every POPE split. Model performance on object recognition is assessed using both **accuracy** and **F1 score**.

MME [4] is a broad benchmark that examines LVLMs across multiple dimensions, comprising ten perception-oriented subtasks and four cognition-oriented subtasks. Following VCD [9], we use the **existence** and **count** subsets to quantify object-level hallucinations, and the **position** and **color** subsets to assess attribute-level hallucinations. Results are measured using the official metrics, **accuracy** and **accuracy+**.

4.3 Experimental Results

Results on CHAIR. The experimental results are presented in Table 1.

Table 1. CHAIR hallucination evaluation results on three LVLMs. CHAIR is employed as the evaluation metric, where a smaller number indicates fewer hallucinations. The best results are highlighted in bold.

Method	LLaVA		InstrctBlip		Qwen-VL	
	$CHAIR_S$ ↓	$CHAIR_I$ ↓	$CHAIR_S$ ↓	$CHAIR_I$ ↓	$CHAIR_S$ ↓	$CHAIR_I$ ↓
Nucleus	52.8	17.2	50.8	15.7	23.6	9.6
VCD [9]	54.2	17.4	46.4	13.3	23.4	9.3
PAI [14]	48.8	14.7	49.8	14.2	22.3	8.7
VAF [23]	46.3	15.1	43.8	12.9	19.3	7.1
Ours	**45.6**	**13.7**	**42.9**	**11.5**	**17.4**	**6.2**

In the CHAIR metric, we compared our method with three other training-free approaches, PAI, VCD and CODE. Both PAI and VCD require only a single forward pass, whereas our method and CODE necessitate two forward passes during inference. Our method achieved the best results across all three models, demonstrating the positive impact of enhancing attention weights for important visual tokens. Notably, our method shows the greatest improvement on Qwen-VL, suggesting that dynamic attention adjustment during inference is crucial for models with stronger multimodal pretraining capabilities.

Results on POPE. In contrast to the CHAIR evaluation, POPE adopts a VQA-style format, where model responses are brief and generally start with "yes" or "no". As a result, the **Refine** strategy becomes less applicable in the context of VQA tasks. Therefore, we only employ the **Enhance** and **Mask** strategies in our experiments. The results, as shown in Table 2, under the random, popular, and adversarial settings, demonstrate that our approach achieves the best improvement across all three models. Similar to the results on CHAIR, our method shows more significant improvement on the Qwen-VL model.

Results on MME Hallucination. Given the consistent performance trends observed across the evaluated LVLMs, we present LLaVA-1.5 as a representative example. As illustrated in Fig. 4, the integration of FAE consistently mitigates object hallucination errors. This enhancement yields stable performance improvements across perception-oriented benchmarks while preserving the fundamental recognition capabilities of the base models. These findings indicate that FAE strengthens visual grounding by directing the model's attention toward salient visual tokens. In contrast to POPE's exclusive focus on object existence, the MME framework encompasses both object-level and attribute-level hallucination assessment. The observed improvements in Existence and Count metrics demonstrate FAE's efficacy in facilitating more accurate perception of visual

Table 2. Quantitative comparison on POPE. The best results are highlighted in bold.

Setting	Method	LLaVA		InstrctBlip		Qwen-VL	
		Acc↑	F1↑	Acc↑	F1↑	Acc↑	F1↑
Random	Nucleus	83.5	83.7	81.4	81.0	84.1	81.2
	VCD [9]	85.7	85.9	83.5	82.9	86.5	84.6
	PAI [14]	85.3	85.6	83.2	82.6	85.7	84.1
	VAF [23]	85.7	86.2	83.7	83.4	84.8	84.3
	Ours	**86.5**	**86.7**	**84.2**	**84.0**	**87.2**	**85.8**
Popular	Nucleus	81.5	81.9	78.4	78.6	83.6	80.7
	VCD	83.1	84.3	80.3	80.4	85.5	83.9
	PAI	82.1	82.9	79.9	79.5	85.0	83.4
	VAF	83.3	84.1	80.9	81.5	87.0	85.2
	Ours	**84.5**	**85.7**	**82.8**	**82.3**	**87.3**	**85.5**
Adversarial	Nucleus	76.1	77.2	77.4	77.8	83.3	80.4
	VCD	77.8	79.4	77.9	78.3	84.1	82.2
	PAI	76.7	78.8	77.4	78.0	84.3	82.6
	VAF	78.3	79.6	78.4	78.7	84.0	82.6
	Ours	**78.8**	**80.7**	**79.1**	**79.7**	**85.6**	**84.0**

entities and their associated attributes. This suggests that the proposed mechanism effectively counterbalances language-prior biases, thereby achieving broader hallucination mitigation. Furthermore, performance gains on the position task substantiate that our strategy enhances the model's capacity for spatial structure comprehension.

4.4 Analyze

To evaluate the effectiveness of our approach, we conduct comprehensive ablation studies using LLaVA-1.5 and InstructBLIP as representative LVLM baselines. Nucleus sampling is employed as the primary decoding strategy to systematically examine the impact of our proposed mechanism on long-form image caption generation. For quantitative assessment, we adopt the CHAIR metric to measure hallucination rates, with detailed results presented in Table 3.

During inference, two hyperparameters, α and γ, are introduced to modulate the strength of visual attention reinforcement in the **AE** and **GTM** modules, respectively. As illustrated in Table 4, different LVLMs architectures respond distinctively to variations in amplification magnitude. When the values of α are set too low, the model tends to produce descriptions containing spurious or hallucinatory objects. In contrast, overly large values of α may impair the linguistic coherence and overall fluency of the generated responses. Furthermore,

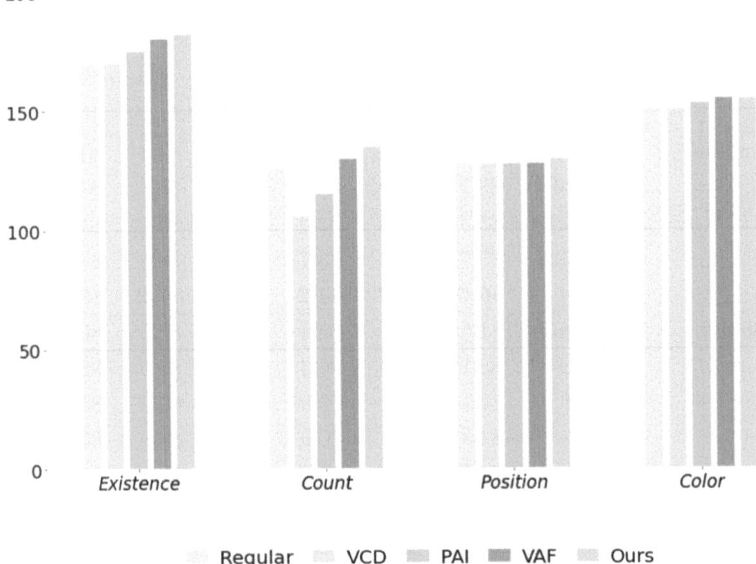

Fig. 4. MME results on LLaVA-1.5. FAE leads to consistent enhancement in LVLMs' perception capacities while preserving their cognition competencies.

Table 3. Ablation studies of the proposed three mechanisms. The best results are highlighted in bold.

AE	GTM	LLaVA		InstructBLIP	
		$CHAIR_S$ ↓	$CHAIR_I$ ↓	$CHAIR_S$ ↓	$CHAIR_I$ ↓
✗	✗	52.8	17.2	50.8	15.7
✓	✗	50.2	15.7	48.3	14.4
✗	✓	48.2	14.6	45.6	13.8
✓	✓	**45.6**	**13.7**	**42.9**	**11.5**

we incorporate γ as a balancing coefficient to mediate the contribution between predictions obtained from standard and masked visual inputs.

We further investigate the effect of the hyperparameter k, which determines the number of attention layers selected in our method. The experimental results are shown in Fig. 5. For the AE module, we integrate attention maps from the shallow layers $[1, k]$ of the visual encoder, while for GTM, we select attention maps from the deep layers $[23 - k, 23]$. The results demonstrate that the choice of k has minimal impact on performance, as the attention maps from shallow layers consistently highlight primary objects and spatial structures in the image, while the global tokens remain identical in deep-layer attention maps.

As shown in Fig. 6, we present the original attention map of LLaVA, the shallow-layer attention map of its visual encoder, and the attention map of

Table 4. Hyperparameter analysis for α and γ on three Models. The best results are highlighted in bold.

LLaVA				InstructBLIP				Qwen-VL			
α	γ	CHAIR_S	CHAIR_I	α	γ	CHAIR_S	CHAIR_I	α	γ	CHAIR_S	CHAIR_I
-	-	52.8	17.2	-	-	50.8	15.7	-	-	23.6	9.6
0.7	0.4	47.5	15.1	0.5	0.4	43.9	13.7	0.4	0.4	19.6	8.3
0.8	0.4	47.2	15.8	0.6	0.4	45.1	13.9	0.5	0.4	19.3	7.2
0.9	0.4	46.9	15.2	0.7	0.4	44.6	14.3	0.6	0.4	18.5	7.8
0.7	0.5	46.2	14.6	0.5	0.5	43.3	12.9	0.4	0.5	18.7	7.1
0.8	**0.5**	**45.6**	**13.7**	**0.6**	**0.5**	**42.9**	**11.5**	**0.5**	**0.5**	**17.4**	**6.2**
0.9	0.5	45.9	14.2	0.7	0.5	43.6	12.6	0.6	0.5	18.2	7.5
0.7	0.6	46.3	14.8	0.5	0.6	44.7	13.1	0.4	0.6	18.9	7.9
0.8	0.6	47.0	14.5	0.6	0.6	44.9	13.6	0.5	0.6	18.3	8.8
0.9	0.6	46.5	15.2	0.7	0.6	46.2	14.3	0.6	0.6	19.7	9.3

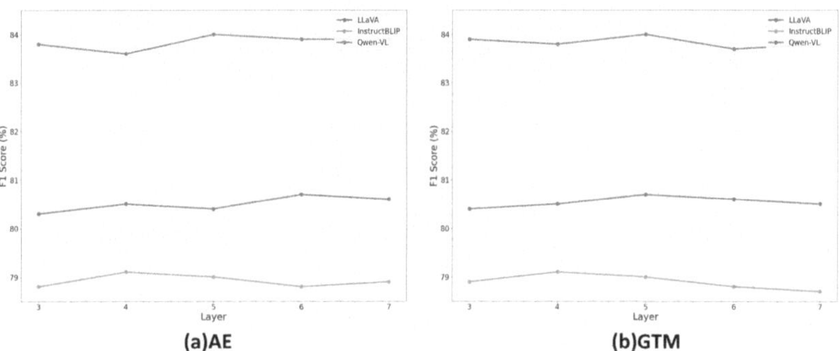

Fig. 5. Experimental results of selecting different layers in AE and GTM.

LLaVA after the intervention of our AE module. When prompted with the instruction "Please help me describe the image in detail.", our attention-intervention method enables the model to focus more accurately on the primary objects in the image, thereby reducing the risk of hallucination.

To evaluate the computational performance, we measure token throughput (token/s) and decoding latency (ms/token) for different methods on an NVIDIA 4090 GPU, as summarized in Table 5. Although our method introduces additional computational overhead due to the modified attention map compared with VCD, this overhead is negligible relative to the overall computation. In contrast, CODE incurs substantially higher computational cost because it requires an additional caption-generation pass.

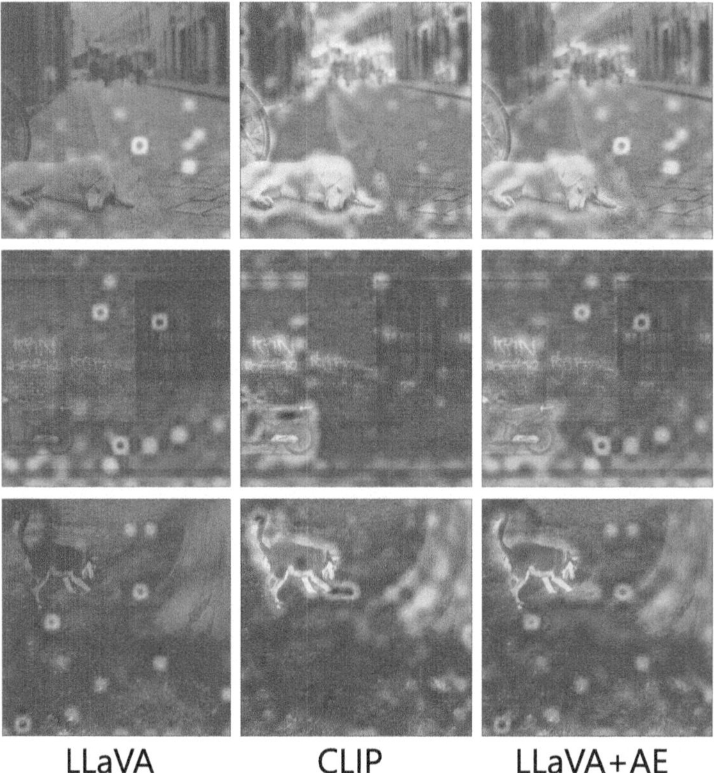

Fig. 6. Visualization of the self-attention maps for LLaVA with and without AE, where the CLIP represents the shallow-layer attention of the visual encoder.

Table 5. Computational analysis on decoding throughput and latency.

Method	Token throughput (tokens/s)↑	Decoding latency (ms/token)↓
VCD	16.11	62.06
PAI	15.95	62.79
CODE	12.67	78.93
Ours	15.80	62.67

5 Conclusion

We tackle hallucination in Large Vision-Language Models (LVLMs) by proposing a training-free Fine-Grained Attention Enhancement (FAE) mechanism. Existing approaches often fail to align visual regions with textual descriptions, leading to over-reliance on global tokens and language priors. Our method leverages CLIP's early-layer attention maps to enhance object-level spatial awareness and employs contrastive decoding to reduce prior dominance. Experiments on multiple benchmarks show that FAE effectively mitigates hallucination while maintaining strong performance on standard vision-language tasks. Its training-free nature enables easy integration across different LVLM architectures without extra data or costly fine-tuning.

Limitations: FAE introduces extra computation due to processing intermediate attention maps, and attention interventions can sometimes slightly disrupt global textual coherence.

Future Work: We plan to analyze the contribution of individual attention heads to hallucination and explore adaptive attention strategies to improve the balance between visual grounding and textual fluency.

Acknowledgments. This research was supported by the National Natural Science Foundation of China (No. 62476069).

References

1. Brown, T., et al.: Language models are few-shot learners. Adv. Neural. Inf. Process. Syst. **33**, 1877–1901 (2020)
2. Chen, Z., et al.: Internvl: scaling up vision foundation models and aligning for generic visual-linguistic tasks. In: Proceedings of the IEEE/CVF Conference on Computer Vision and Pattern Recognition, pp. 24185–24198 (2024)
3. Dai, W., et al.: Instructblip: towards general-purpose vision-language models with instruction tuning. Adv. Neural. Inf. Process. Syst. **36**, 49250–49267 (2023)
4. Fu, C., et al.: Mme: a comprehensive evaluation benchmark for multimodal large language models. In: The Thirty-ninth Annual Conference on Neural Information Processing Systems Datasets and Benchmarks Track (2025)
5. Gunjal, A., Yin, J., Bas, E.: Detecting and preventing hallucinations in large vision language models. In: Proceedings of the AAAI Conference on Artificial Intelligence, vol. 38, pp. 18135–18143 (2024)
6. Jain, J., Yang, J., Shi, H.: Vcoder: versatile vision encoders for multimodal large language models. In: Proceedings of the IEEE/CVF Conference on Computer Vision and Pattern Recognition, pp. 27992–28002 (2024)
7. Jiang, C., et al.: Hallucination augmented contrastive learning for multimodal large language model. In: Proceedings of the IEEE/CVF Conference on Computer Vision and Pattern Recognition, pp. 27036–27046 (2024)
8. Kim, J., Kim, H., Yeonju, K., Ro, Y.M.: Code: contrasting self-generated description to combat hallucination in large multi-modal models. Adv. Neural. Inf. Process. Syst. **37**, 133571–133599 (2024)
9. Leng, S., et al.: Mitigating object hallucinations in large vision-language models through visual contrastive decoding. In: Proceedings of the IEEE/CVF Conference on Computer Vision and Pattern Recognition, pp. 13872–13882 (2024)
10. Li, J., Li, D., Xiong, C., Hoi, S.: Blip: bootstrapping language-image pre-training for unified vision-language understanding and generation. In: International Conference on Machine Learning, pp. 12888–12900. PMLR (2022)
11. Li, Y., Du, Y., Zhou, K., Wang, J., Zhao, W.X., Wen, J.R.: Evaluating object hallucination in large vision-language models. In: Proceedings of the 2023 Conference on Empirical Methods in Natural Language Processing, pp. 292–305 (2023)

12. Liu, F., Lin, K., Li, L., Wang, J., Yacoob, Y., Wang, L.: Mitigating hallucination in large multi-modal models via robust instruction tuning. In: The Twelfth International Conference on Learning Representations (2023)
13. Liu, H., Li, C., Wu, Q., Lee, Y.J.: Visual instruction tuning. Adv. Neural. Inf. Process. Syst. **36**, 34892–34916 (2023)
14. Liu, S., Zheng, K., Chen, W.: Paying more attention to image: a training-free method for alleviating hallucination in lvlms. In: European Conference on Computer Vision, pp. 125–140. Springer (2025)
15. Mishra, S., Khashabi, D., Baral, C., Hajishirzi, H.: Cross-task generalization via natural language crowdsourcing instructions. In: Proceedings of the 60th Annual Meeting of the Association for Computational Linguistics (Volume 1: Long Papers), pp. 3470–3487 (2022)
16. Ouyang, L., et al.: Training language models to follow instructions with human feedback. Adv. Neural. Inf. Process. Syst. **35**, 27730–27744 (2022)
17. Peng, B., Li, C., He, P., Galley, M., Gao, J.: Instruction tuning with gpt-4. arXiv preprint arXiv:2304.03277 (2023)
18. Radford, A., et al.: Learning transferable visual models from natural language supervision. In: International Conference on Machine Learning, pp. 8748–8763. PmLR (2021)
19. Rohrbach, A., Hendricks, L.A., Burns, K., Darrell, T., Saenko, K.: Object hallucination in image captioning. arXiv preprint arXiv:1809.02156 (2018)
20. Touvron, H., et al.: Llama: open and efficient foundation language models. arxiv. arXiv preprint arXiv:2302.13971 (2023)
21. Wei, J., et al: Finetuned language models are zero-shot learners. arXiv preprint arXiv:2109.01652 (2021)
22. Yang, A., et al.: Qwen2. 5 technical report. arXiv preprint arXiv:2412.15115 (2024)
23. Yin, H., Si, G., Wang, Z.: Clearsight: visual signal enhancement for object hallucination mitigation in multimodal large language models. In: Proceedings of the Computer Vision and Pattern Recognition Conference, pp. 14625–14634 (2025)
24. Yu, Q., et al.: Hallucidoctor: mitigating hallucinatory toxicity in visual instruction data. In: Proceedings of the IEEE/CVF Conference on Computer Vision and Pattern Recognition, pp. 12944–12953 (2024)
25. Zhang, J., Wang, T., Zhang, H., Lu, P., Zheng, F.: Reflective instruction tuning: Mitigating hallucinations in large vision-language models. In: European Conference on Computer Vision, pp. 196–213. Springer (2025)

Progressive Enhancement for Emotional Speech Captioning

Hailiang Yao[1,2(✉)], Bin Liu[2,3], Shun Chen[2,3], Zhuofan Wen[2,3], and Ziping Zhao[1]

[1] Tianjin Normal University, Tianjin, China
zhaoziping@tjnu.edu.cn
[2] Institute of Automation, MAIS, CASIA, Beijing, China
2311090059@stu.tjnu.edu.cn, liubin@nlpr.ia.ac.cn,
{chenshun2023,wenzhuofan2023}@ia.ac.cn
[3] School of Artificial Intelligence, UCAS, Beijing, China

Abstract. Speech emotion understanding has garnered significant attention in recent years due to advances in audio large language models (ALLMs). While existing methods perform well on emotion classification tasks, the inherent dynamic nature of emotions and their reliance on subtle acoustic cues present a core challenge: how to simulate the human reasoning process for understanding complex and evolving emotional states. To address this, we propose a novel Progressive Emotion Reasoning Framework, in which the reasoning process is guided by both paralinguistic and linguistic information. This framework enhances the emotional comprehension capability of ALLMs through a progressive strategy, centered around a three-stage fine-tuning process: first, injecting linguistically and paralinguistically rich emotional cues prior to model reasoning; second, performing emotion-based curriculum fine-tuning; and finally, generating high-quality speech emotion descriptions through interpretable reasoning steps. Furthermore, we have established a foundational data infrastructure and introduced the first paralinguistic-centric speech emotion dataset, which includes multi-dimensional annotations such as paralinguistic features, emotion labels, and text transcripts, providing a critical resource for advancing speech emotion understanding research. Experimental results demonstrate that our method achieves leading and competitive performance on speech emotion understanding and description tasks, offering a novel perspective for the field.

Keywords: Speech Emotion · Caption · Audio LLMs

1 Introduction

Speech serves as the most natural medium for human communication. Its value lies not only in conveying textual information but also in carrying rich paralinguistic cues–such as emotion, tone, and speaker attributes. These cues collectively reveal the true intent behind an utterance and guide appropriate responses.

H. Liu et al. (Eds.): CEI 2025, CCIS 2881, pp. 149–162, 2026.
https://doi.org/10.1007/978-981-95-9493-1_10

The deep integration of linguistic and paralinguistic signals enables the development of human-computer dialogue systems [1,4,14,18,27,31,34] capable of empathy beyond pure text-based interaction, thereby further advancing speech large language models.

However, most mainstream ALLMs [5,8,12,23,30,32] primarily focus on general tasks such as question-answering, instruction-following, or speech-to-text conversion, largely overlooking the emotional states embedded in speech. These models often infer speaker states solely from textual content, failing to perform fine-grained discrimination based on emotional tones and speaking styles. This leads to discrepancies between generated speech descriptions and actual emotional content. The root of this limitation lies in the fact that existing speech emotion datasets rarely capture the stylistic dynamics in speech effectively. The scarcity of such data makes it difficult for researchers to leverage paralinguistic information–a straightforward yet effective form of annotation–thus restricting its potential in speech emotion description.

Inspired by recent research on reasoning models R1 [19], which excel at solving complex tasks by integrating reasoning processes with model operations while providing interpretable rationales, we are prompted to ask: Can linguistic and paralinguistic information, through effective interaction, jointly enhance speech emotion understanding? To address this question, we propose a novel framework–Progressive Emotion Reasoning Framework(PERF). This framework achieves progressive enhancement through three stages: first, acoustic information guidance; second, emotion-based curriculum fine-tuning; and finally, interpretable emotion reasoning. It aims to synergistically utilize both linguistic and paralinguistic information from the input speech to achieve more accurate speech emotion descriptions. To further support model training, we designed a data management pipeline to automatically generate high-quality paralinguistic descriptions covering key attributes such as pitch, energy, and speaking rate. Based on this pipeline, we constructed Emo-Para, a paralinguistic-centric speech emotion dataset, providing a foundation for preliminary curriculum fine-tuning.

The contributions of this study can be summarized as follows: (1) We propose PERF, an emotion reasoning framework collaboratively guided by linguistic and paralinguistic information. This framework integrates fine-tuning with emotion reasoning, achieving fine-grained and interpretable emotion understanding from speech data. (2) We construct and release the Emo-Para dataset. It contains transcriptions, emotion labels, and detailed paralinguistic annotations, serving as a comprehensive data infrastructure to advance speech emotion analysis research.

2 Related Work

Audio Large Language Models (ALLMs)

The integration of large language models with audio systems has achieved remarkable progress across multiple key dimensions in recent years [2,5,6,9,20,22]. A series of advanced models have demonstrated powerful multi-task and cross-domain generalization capabilities, adapting to diverse audio processing tasks.

The Pengi [13] model pioneered this field with its versatile text-generation approach to audio tasks, creating a unified architecture that processes audio and text inputs to generate textual outputs. Without task-specific modifications, it achieves state-of-the-art performance on both open-ended tasks like audio captioning and closed-ended tasks including sound event detection. SALMONN [33] extends this capability by integrating speech and general audio signals within a multimodal framework, demonstrating emergent abilities in audio storytelling and cross-modal reasoning without explicit training. This represents significant progress toward AI systems with comprehensive auditory perception. Qwen-Audio [11] further advances the field through large-scale pre-training on over 30 audio task types, achieving outstanding performance in acoustic scene classification, speech emotion recognition, and audio captioning. Its multi-task framework effectively handles cross-task interference, setting new benchmarks in general audio understanding.

Speech Emotion Caption (SEC)

Speech Emotion Caption aims to generate nuanced natural language descriptions of emotional states from speech signals, moving beyond conventional discrete emotion classification. SECap established this paradigm by systematically formulating the task of representing speech emotions through textual descriptions.

Technically, SEC has evolved from traditional [7,16,35,36,39] feature-based pipelines to an integrated "perception-understanding-generation" approach using audio large language models. Models like MiDashengLM [15] achieve breakthrough performance through end-to-end alignment between audio modalities and emotional descriptions, enabling deep semantic fusion.

Modern SEC systems employ self-supervised audio encoders (e.g., Wav2Vec 2.0) [3] that learn context-aware representations incorporating both speech content and paralinguistic features. These representations provide robust foundations for emotional semantic understanding. Furthermore, unified frameworks integrating speech transcription, audio description, and music comprehension facilitate cross-modal learning, enabling coherent generation of contextual emotion captions.

3 Methodology

This section details our proposed Progressive Emotion Reasoning Framework. As illustrated in Fig. 1, our approach comprises three core stages: 1) Dual-modality Information Extraction, 2) Emotion-Centric Curriculum Fine-tuning, and 3) Chain-of-Thought Reasoning and Caption Generation. The framework is designed to systematically guide audio large language models to perform human-like emotion reasoning based on acoustic attributes, ultimately generating rich and credible emotion captions.

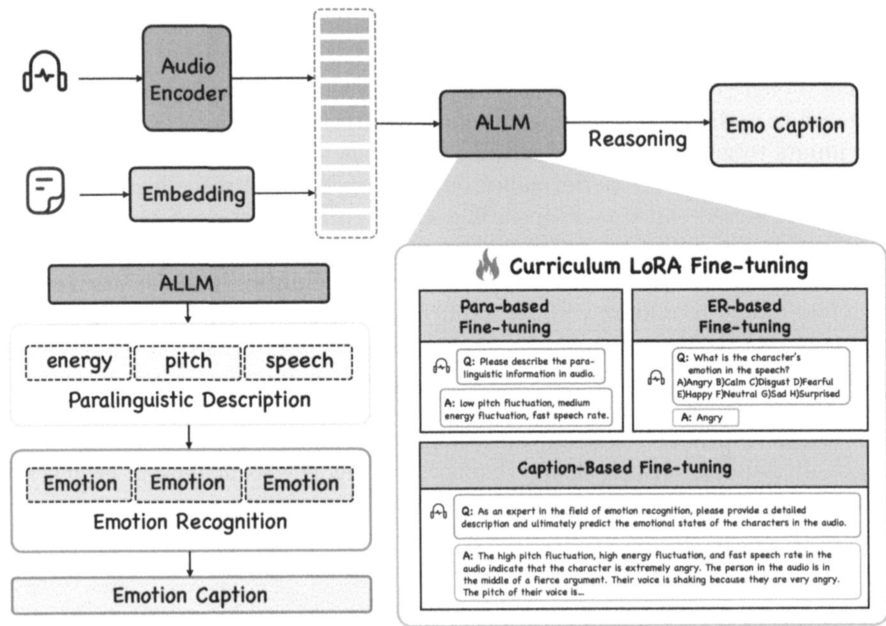

Fig. 1. Progressive Emotion Reasoning Framework(PERF)

3.1 Dual-Modality Information Extraction

The primary objective of this stage is to extract two crucial types of information from raw audio signals–linguistic content and paralinguistic cues–to establish the foundation for subsequent emotion understanding and reasoning. Given a raw audio input, we first transform it into dense sequential audio representations using a pre-trained audio encoder.

During the extraction process, linguistic information corresponding to the semantic content in the audio is typically represented as text sequences and encoded into semantic vectors through a text encoder. In the fine-tuning stage, we guide the model to align audio representations with textual semantic representations via cross-modal attention mechanisms. Simultaneously, paralinguistic information, serving as crucial carriers of emotional expression, is primarily characterized by three acoustic attributes: pitch, energy, and speaking rate. Pitch reflects intonation variations, energy corresponds to speech intensity, and speaking rate is measured by the number of syllables per unit time. These features are regressed from audio representations using specialized neural projection heads or signal processing methods. Finally, both linguistic and paralinguistic information are integrated into a multimodal input context and fed into the subsequent large language model for joint reasoning and emotion caption generation.

3.2 Emotion-Centric Curriculum Fine-Tuning

To efficiently and stably inject emotional knowledge into the pre-trained Audio Large Language Model (ALLM), we design a three-stage curriculum learning paradigm that exclusively employs parameter-efficient LoRA (Low-Rank Adaptation) technology. For a pre-trained model with parameters Θ, LoRA constrains its weight update ΔW to a low-rank decomposition: $\Delta W = BA$, where B, A are trainable adapter parameters and rank $= r \ll D$. This significantly reduces training overhead.

The entire curriculum fine-tuning process consists of three progressive stages:

Paralinguistic-Based Fine-Tuning: To establish a direct mapping from raw audio to quantized acoustic attributes. We construct a dataset $\mathcal{D}_p = \{(A_i, P_i)\}$, where P_i represents the ground truth paralinguistic information for audio A_i. In this stage, we only fine-tune the LoRA adapter $\Delta\Theta_p$ connected to the audio encoder. We employ the Smooth L1 loss:

$$\mathcal{L}_p = \frac{1}{N}\sum_{i=1}^{N} \text{SmoothL1}(\text{ALLM}(A_i; \Theta + \Delta\Theta_p), P_i) \tag{1}$$

This stage enables the model to acquire "auditory perception" capabilities, allowing it to accurately identify physical characteristics of sound.

Emotion Recognition-Based Fine-Tuning: To teach the model to recognize discrete emotion categories based on acoustic attribute perception.

Method: We use an emotion classification dataset $\mathcal{D}_e = \{(A_i, y_i)\}$, where y_i represents the one-hot encoded emotion label. We introduce a new LoRA adapter $\Delta\Theta_e$ and apply it to the deep network layers of the model.We employ the cross-entropy loss:

$$\mathcal{L}_e = -\frac{1}{N}\sum_{i=1}^{N} y_i \log(\text{Softmax}(\text{ALLM}(A_i; \Theta + \Delta\Theta_p + \Delta\Theta_e))) \tag{2}$$

This stage is performed while keeping the Stage 1 adapter $\Delta\Theta_p$ frozen, ensuring that emotion recognition is built upon a solid foundation of acoustic perception.

Caption-Based Fine-Tuning: To integrate the capabilities from the previous two stages and guide the model to generate natural, fluent, and detailed emotional description texts. We utilize our constructed emotion description dataset $\mathcal{D}_c = \{(A_i, C_i)\}$, where $C_i = \{c_1^i, c_2^i, ..., c_T^i\}$ represents high-quality emotional description text. We introduce a third LoRA adapter $\Delta\Theta_c$, primarily applied to the language model head. We employ the auto-regressive language modeling loss:

$$\mathcal{L}_c = -\frac{1}{N}\sum_{i=1}^{N}\sum_{t=1}^{T} \log P(c_t^i | A_i, c_{<t}^i; \Theta + \Delta\Theta_p + \Delta\Theta_e + \Delta\Theta_c) \tag{3}$$

Finally, through adapter fusion, we integrate the knowledge from all three stages into the complete model, with parameters:

$$\Theta_{\text{final}} = \Theta + \Delta\Theta_p + \Delta\Theta_e + \Delta\Theta_c \tag{4}$$

3.3 Chain-of-Thought Reasoning and Caption Generation

During the inference phase, we not only require the model to generate the final emotion caption but also guide it to demonstrate the complete reasoning chain through carefully designed prompts, significantly enhancing the model's interpretability.

Given a test audio sample $\mathbf{A}_{test}$, we construct the following prompt:

"Analyze the provided audio clip step-by-step.

First, carefully identify and describe the paralinguistic information of the speech, such as speaking rate, energy, and pitch.

Then, based on this information, determine the speaker's emotional state.

Finally, synthesize the analysis to form a comprehensive emotion caption."

Leveraging the knowledge acquired during fine-tuning, the model autoregressively generates text comprising three components:

$$\mathbf{O} = [\text{Paralinguistic Analysis}; \text{Emotion Judgment}; \text{Emotion Caption}] \tag{5}$$

This chain-of-thought reasoning process $P(\mathbf{O}|\mathbf{A}_{\text{test}}, \text{Prompt}; \mathbf{\Theta}_{\text{final}})$ intuitively demonstrates how the model progressively reasons from low-level acoustic features to high-level semantics and emotion captions, making the decision-making process transparent and trustworthy.

4 Para-EmoData: A Paralinguistic-Centered Speech Emotion Dataset

To support the model training and performance evaluation in this study, we have integrated and constructed a comprehensively annotated, novel speech emotion dataset. This dataset merges multiple high-quality open-source resources and employs a standardized automatic annotation pipeline to generate fine-grained multimodal annotations (Fig. 2).

4.1 Dataset Composition and Sources

This dataset integrates four publicly available, high-quality speech emotion datasets to ensure diversity in language types and contextual backgrounds. Specifically, it includes English datasets: RAVDESS-Speech [28] and SAVEE [21], as well as Chinese datasets: MER2023 [24] and MER2024 [25]. Through systematic integration, the resulting corpus comprehensively covers bilingual content (Chinese and English), various recording environments, and diverse speaker styles, providing a robust data foundation for model training.

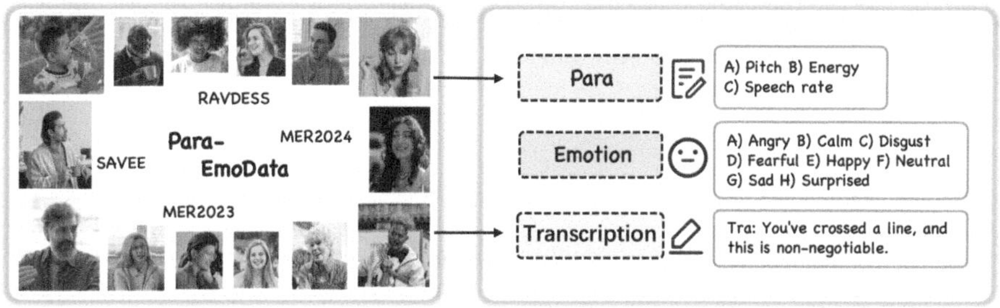

Fig. 2. Data Curation Pipeline of the Para-EmoData.

4.2 Unified Annotation Pipeline

To ensure annotation consistency and reproducibility, we designed an automated pipeline that generates three core annotations for each audio clip:

Text Transcription: Utilizing the Whisper V3 [30] speech recognition model for unified transcription, ensuring high accuracy;

Paralinguistic Information Annotation: Automatically generating paralinguistic descriptions through three steps: feature extraction (pitch, energy, speaking rate), discretization into categorical classes (low/medium/high), and structured description generation;

Emotion Labels: Unifying original emotion labels into standardized emotion categories.

This pipeline ensures consistent annotation quality, providing a reliable foundation for model training.

4.3 Data Statistics and Characteristics

The dataset constructed through the above process possesses the following characteristics:

Comprehensive Multimodal Annotations: Each sample includes audio signals, text transcription, emotion labels, and structured paralinguistic descriptions, perfectly aligning with the requirements of the proposed progressive training framework.

High Annotation Quality and Strong Consistency: Automated annotation using Whisper V3 and standardized signal processing tools effectively avoids subjective bias and the high costs associated with manual annotation.

Support for Interpretability Analysis: The discretized paralinguistic information not only serves as model input but also facilitates the visualization and understanding of the model's decision-making process, enhancing reasoning transparency.

4.4 Discussion

The dataset constructed in this study provides a crucial data foundation for speech emotion captioning tasks. Its core contribution lies in transforming raw audio signals into structured, semantically-rich multimodal information, thereby effectively supporting end-to-end learning from low-level acoustic perception to high-level emotion reasoning.

5 Experimental

We conducted systematic experiments on our custom Para-EmoData test set, selecting SALMONN [33], AudioFlamingo2 [17], GLM4 [38], SECap [37], Qwen-Audio [11], and Qwen2-Audio [10] as baseline models for comparison with our proposed method. To accommodate the free-form generation nature of large models, we employed a unified setup where each model generates emotion captions for input audio. Subsequently, we utilized DeepSeek R1 [19] to automatically extract specific emotion labels from the generated text, with quantitative results presented in Table 1.

To further provide an intuitive evaluation of the generated emotion captions, we conducted supplementary experiments on EMOSpeech - a dataset containing human-annotated speech emotion descriptions. Given the inherent challenges in directly assessing the semantic quality of generated content, we introduced BLEU-1 [29], ROUGE-1 [26], and Fluency as evaluation metrics, with results shown in Table 2.

Table 1. Performance comparison of different models on Para-EmoData

Model	RAVDESS			SAVEE			MER2023			MER2024		
	WA	UWA	F1	WA	UWA	F1	WA	UWA	F1	WA	UWA	F1
GLM4	12.50	12.78	10.43	21.46	19.05	14.67	47.93	45.74	38.59	48.92	47.86	40.03
SALMONN	15.83	16.41	10.23	17.08	16.19	12.38	44.77	40.26	35.60	47.39	47.03	38.01
FLamingo2	17.08	16.47	11.16	22.50	19.40	15.17	32.12	29.68	24.63	34.23	33.18	26.14
SECap	27.46	26.03	18.09	26.04	24.40	18.83	42.71	40.15	34.88	43.03	42.56	35.29
Qwen-Audio	71.18	72.01	58.99	66.67	62.74	56.58	45.50	42.20	35.64	44.57	45.94	44.57
Qwen2-Audio	70.42	69.73	58.65	56.87	55.48	49.14	43.56	41.82	35.07	40.98	40.18	31.38
PERF(our)	75.38	74.91	62.05	67.42	63.79	57.20	50.66	46.13	36.87	52.54	49.31	44.98

5.1 Performance Analysis

To validate the effectiveness of the proposed progressive emotion reasoning framework, we designed a series of comparative experiments. All experiments employed uniform prompts requiring models to generate complete emotion captions, while strictly adhering to the official recommended parameter settings for each baseline model to ensure fair comparison.

Table 1 presents the performance comparison of different models across four speech emotion recognition datasets, evaluated using Weighted Accuracy (WA), Unweighted Accuracy (UWA), and F1 score.

In-depth analysis of the results in Table 1 reveals the following key findings:

Table 2. Performance comparison of different models on natural language generation metrics(↑: higher is better, ↓: lower is better)

Model	Fluency↓	BLEU↑	Rouge↑
SALMONN	92.47	17.83	13.59
FLamingo	98.25	11.76	9.42
GLM4	91.38	18.94	15.07
Qwen	82.14	29.06	21.96
Qwen2	80.53	31.89	22.14
SECap	75.94	35.98	25.50
PERF(our)	74.61	38.27	27.35

Table 3. Performance comparison with different component combinations(IE: Information Extraction, CL: Curriculum Fine-tuning, RC: Reasoning Caption)

Components			Metrics		
IE	CL	RC	Fluency↓	BLEU↑	Rouge↑
			79.45	32.18	21.73
✓			78.62	33.91	22.04
✓	✓		76.29	36.07	25.36
✓	✓	✓	74.61	38.27	27.35

Linguistic foundation impacts cross-lingual generalization: Models GLM4 and SALMONN, primarily trained on Chinese corpora, performed relatively well on Chinese datasets (MER2023/2024), with GLM4 achieving 48.92% WA on MER2024. However, their performance significantly declined on English datasets (RAVDESS/SAVEE), where WA fell below 28%, revealing limitations in cross-lingual emotion understanding.

General-purpose models show deficiencies in specialized tasks: AudioFlamingo2, as a general audio-language model, demonstrated strong performance in cross-modal tasks but performed poorly in emotion recognition (achieving only 17.08% and 22.50% WA on RAVDESS and SAVEE, respectively), indicating that general audio capabilities cannot be directly translated into precise emotion analysis.

Diverse training data provides advantages: The Qwen series models, leveraging highly diverse training data across languages and tasks, exhibited strong and robust performance on English datasets (with Qwen-Audio achieving 71.18% and 66.67% WA on RAVDESS and SAVEE, respectively) while maintaining competitiveness on Chinese datasets, validating the importance of large-scale pre-training for building general audio models.

Our framework demonstrates superior effectiveness and universality: The proposed method achieved the best or highly competitive performance across all baseline models, maintaining leadership on English datasets while achieving the most significant improvements on Chinese datasets (reaching 52.54% WA on MER2024). This strongly validates that the progressive emotion reasoning framework, through phased curriculum learning, systematically enhances the model's ability to extract emotional cues and perform reasoning, demonstrating excellent generalization across different languages and datasets.

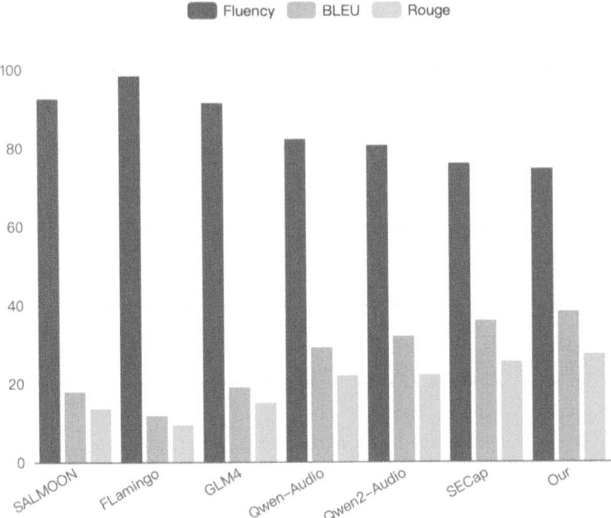

Fig. 3. Performance Analysis Visualization

5.2 Generation Quality

To systematically evaluate the quality of emotion description texts generated by the models, we conducted experiments on the Chinese dataset EMOSpeech, employing Fluency, BLEU, and ROUGE as evaluation metrics. The experimental results are presented in Table 2, with visualizations provided in Fig. 3 for more intuitive representation.

Analysis of Table 2 reveals that general-purpose large language models (such as SALMONN, FLamingo, and GLM4) demonstrate relatively limited performance on this task. Their generated texts show deficiencies in both semantic matching (evidenced by low BLEU and ROUGE scores) and linguistic fluency (indicated by high Fluency values), reflecting inherent limitations of general models in integrating audio understanding with fine-grained emotion description generation. In contrast, specialized audio captioning models exhibit progressive improvement across metrics. Our proposed model, based on the progressive emotion reasoning framework, achieves optimal balance across all indicators–achieving the lowest Fluency score (74.61) while attaining the highest BLEU (38.27) and ROUGE (27.35) scores. This demonstrates its comprehensive advantages in generating descriptions with superior fluency, semantic accuracy, and detail restoration capabilities.

5.3 Ablation Study

Furthermore, we present ablation study results of the proposed components in Table 3. The findings indicate that the model performs weakest when no additional modules are incorporated, highlighting the necessity of specialized design for this task. Introducing only the information extraction module yields certain improvements, demonstrating the fundamental role of high-quality feature representation in task understanding. When combined with the curriculum fine-tuning strategy, the model performance improves significantly, indicating that the systematic training process can effectively integrate and utilize multimodal features. Finally, the model incorporating the complete reasoning mechanism (fourth row) achieves optimal performance across all metrics, particularly attaining the lowest Fluency score (74.61) and the highest BLEU (38.27) and ROUGE (27.35) scores. This validates the crucial role of the chain-of-thought reasoning mechanism in guiding the model to generate fluent and semantically accurate descriptions. The modules exhibit clear synergistic enhancement effects.

5.4 Comprehensive Discussion

The experimental results demonstrate that our proposed progressive emotion reasoning framework achieves leading performance on two key tasks: emotion recognition (as shown in Table 1) and emotion caption generation (as shown in Table 2). The ablation study confirms the necessity and synergistic effects of individual components within the framework. The framework successfully shifts the model's focus from merely generating fluent text to producing high-quality descriptions that are both fluent and rich in accurate emotional information, achieving simultaneous improvements in both performance and interpretability.

6 Conclusion

This paper addresses the core challenge of accurately describing dynamic emotional states in speech emotion understanding tasks by proposing a progressive framework for enhancing acoustic and emotion attributes in speech captioning. Through systematic integration of linguistic and paralinguistic information, we have constructed a three-stage emotion reasoning pipeline comprising dual-modality information extraction, emotion-centric curriculum fine-tuning, and interpretable chain-of-thought reasoning. Additionally, we have constructed and released Para-EmoData, the first large-scale speech emotion dataset centered on paralinguistic information, providing an important data foundation for subsequent related research. Experimental results demonstrate that our proposed method achieves leading performance across multiple benchmarks. In emotion classification tasks, the model exhibits excellent generalization capability in cross-lingual scenarios. For emotion caption generation tasks, the model-generated texts outperform existing baseline methods in fluency, semantic accuracy, and detail restoration.

7 Limitations

Although this study has made significant progress in speech emotion captioning tasks, several limitations remain. First, while our constructed dataset covers bilingual environments (Chinese and English), its scale and scenario diversity require further expansion, particularly in cross-cultural emotional expressions and speech samples under noisy conditions. Furthermore, the model's reasoning capability remains constrained by the knowledge boundaries of pre-trained language models, potentially leading to inaccuracies when processing complex or contradictory emotions. Finally, the current methodology primarily relies on multi-stage fine-tuning techniques, and future work should explore feasible technical improvements, including developing more efficient multimodal fusion methods, investigating emotion understanding in low-resource scenarios, and advancing more interpretable affective computing frameworks.

Acknowledgments. The authors have no competing interests to declare that are relevant to the content of this article.

References

1. Achiam, J., et al.: Gpt-4 technical report. arXiv preprint arXiv:2303.08774 (2023)
2. Ao, J., et al.: Speecht5: unified-modal encoder-decoder pre-training for spoken language processing. arXiv preprint arXiv:2110.07205 (2021)
3. Baevski, A., Zhou, Y., Mohamed, A., Auli, M.: wav2vec 2.0: a framework for self-supervised learning of speech representations. Adv. Neural Inf. Process. Syst. **33**, 12449–12460 (2020)
4. Bai, J., et al.: Qwen technical report. arXiv preprint arXiv:2309.16609 (2023)
5. Borsos, Z., et al.: Audiolm: a language modeling approach to audio generation. IEEE/ACM Trans. Audio Speech Lang. Process. **31**, 2523–2533 (2023)
6. Borsos, Z., Sharifi, M., Vincent, D., Kharitonov, E., Zeghidour, N., Tagliasacchi, M.: Soundstorm: efficient parallel audio generation. arXiv preprint arXiv:2305.09636 (2023)
7. Cai, X., Yuan, J., Zheng, R., Huang, L., Church, K.: Speech emotion recognition with multi-task learning. In: Interspeech, vol. 2021, pp. 4508–4512. Brno (2021)
8. Chen, S., et al.: Vall-e 2: neural codec language models are human parity zero-shot text to speech synthesizers. arXiv preprint arXiv:2406.05370 (2024)
9. Chen, S., et al.: Wavlm: large-scale self-supervised pre-training for full stack speech processing. IEEE J. Sel. Top. Sig. Process. **16**(6), 1505–1518 (2022)
10. Chu, Y., et al.: Qwen2-audio technical report. arXiv preprint arXiv:2407.10759 (2024)
11. Chu, Y., et al.: Qwen-audio: advancing universal audio understanding via unified large-scale audio-language models. arXiv preprint arXiv:2311.07919 (2023)
12. Copet, J., et al.: Simple and controllable music generation. Adv. Neural. Inf. Process. Syst. **36**, 47704–47720 (2023)
13. Deshmukh, S., Elizalde, B., Singh, R., Wang, H.: Pengi: an audio language model for audio tasks. Adv. Neural. Inf. Process. Syst. **36**, 18090–18108 (2023)
14. Devlin, J., Chang, M.W., Lee, K., Toutanova, K.: Bert: pre-training of deep bidirectional transformers for language understanding. In: Proceedings of the 2019 Conference of the North American Chapter of the Association for Computational Linguistics: Human Language Technologies, Volume 1 (Long and Short Papers), pp. 4171–4186 (2019)

15. Dinkel, H., et al.: Midashenglm: efficient audio understanding with general audio captions. arXiv preprint arXiv:2508.03983 (2025)
16. Ghosh, S., Laksana, E., Morency, L.P., Scherer, S.: Representation learning for speech emotion recognition. In: Interspeech, pp. 3603–3607 (2016)
17. Ghosh, S., et al.: Audio flamingo 2: an audio-language model with long-audio understanding and expert reasoning abilities. arXiv preprint arXiv:2503.03983 (2025)
18. Gu, A., Dao, T.: Mamba: Linear-time sequence modeling with selective state spaces. In: First Conference on Language Modeling (2024)
19. Guo, D., et al.: Deepseek-r1: incentivizing reasoning capability in llms via reinforcement learning. arXiv preprint arXiv:2501.12948 (2025)
20. Hsu, W.N., Bolte, B., Tsai, Y.H.H., Lakhotia, K., Salakhutdinov, R., Mohamed, A.: Hubert: Self-supervised speech representation learning by masked prediction of hidden units. IEEE/ACM Trans. Audio Speech Lang. Process. **29**, 3451–3460 (2021)
21. Jackson, P., Haq, S.: Surrey Audio-Visual Expressed Emotion (savee) Database. University of Surrey, Guildford, UK (2014)
22. Kong, Z., Goel, A., Badlani, R., Ping, W., Valle, R., Catanzaro, B.: Audio flamingo: a novel audio language model with few-shot learning and dialogue abilities. arXiv preprint arXiv:2402.01831 (2024)
23. Leng, Y., et al.: Prompttts 2: describing and generating voices with text prompt. arXiv preprint arXiv:2309.02285 (2023)
24. Lian, Z., et al.: Mer 2023: multi-label learning, modality robustness, and semi-supervised learning. In: Proceedings of the 31st ACM International Conference on Multimedia, pp. 9610–9614 (2023)
25. Lian, Z., et al.: Mer 2024: semi-supervised learning, noise robustness, and open-vocabulary multimodal emotion recognition. arXiv preprint arXiv:2404.17113 (2024)
26. Lin, C.Y.: Rouge: a package for automatic evaluation of summaries. In: Text Summarization Branches Out, pp. 74–81 (2004)
27. Liu, A., et al.: Deepseek-v3 technical report. arXiv preprint arXiv:2412.19437 (2024)
28. Livingstone, S.R., Russo, F.A.: The ryerson audio-visual database of emotional speech and song (ravdess): a dynamic, multimodal set of facial and vocal expressions in north american english. PLoS ONE **13**(5), e0196391 (2018)
29. Papineni, K., Roukos, S., Ward, T., Zhu, W.J.: Bleu: a method for automatic evaluation of machine translation. In: Proceedings of the 40th annual meeting of the Association for Computational Linguistics, pp. 311–318 (2002)
30. Radford, A., Kim, J.W., Xu, T., Brockman, G., McLeavey, C., Sutskever, I.: Robust speech recognition via large-scale weak supervision (2022). https://doi.org/10.48550/ARXIV.2212.04356, https://arxiv.org/abs/2212.04356
31. Radford, A., Wu, J., Child, R., Luan, D., Amodei, D., Sutskever, I., et al.: Language models are unsupervised multitask learners. OpenAI blog **1**(8), 9 (2019)
32. Rubenstein, P.K., et al.: Audiopalm: a large language model that can speak and listen. arXiv preprint arXiv:2306.12925 (2023)
33. Sun, G., et al.: video-salmonn: speech-enhanced audio-visual large language models. arXiv preprint arXiv:2406.15704 (2024)
34. Touvron, H., et al.: Llama: open and efficient foundation language models. arXiv preprint arXiv:2302.13971 (2023)
35. Vaswani, A., et al.: Attention is all you need. In: Advances in Neural Information Processing Systems, vol. 30 (2017)

36. Wang, Y., Shen, G., Xu, Y., Li, J., Zhao, Z.: Learning mutual correlation in multimodal transformer for speech emotion recognition. In: Interspeech, pp. 4518–4522. Cary, NC (2021)
37. Xu, Y., et al.: Secap: speech emotion captioning with large language model. In: Proceedings of the AAAI Conference on Artificial Intelligence, vol. 38, pp. 19323–19331 (2024)
38. Zeng, A., et al.: Glm-4-voice: towards intelligent and human-like end-to-end spoken chatbot. arXiv preprint arXiv:2412.02612 (2024)
39. Zou, H., Si, Y., Chen, C., Rajan, D., Chng, E.S.: Speech emotion recognition with co-attention based multi-level acoustic information. In: ICASSP 2022-2022 IEEE International Conference on Acoustics, Speech and Signal Processing (ICASSP), pp. 7367–7371. IEEE (2022)

Capturing Topic Contributions for Text-Audio Depression Assessment

Min Hu, Zheng Guo(✉), Xiaohua Wang, Yan Xing, Jiaoyun Yang, Ning An, and Aoqiang Zhu

Hefei University of Technology, Hefei, China
2023170740@mail.hfut.edu.cn

Abstract. Depression is a common mental health issue, and due to limited medical resources, many patients find it difficult to receive timely diagnosis and treatment. In recent years, automated depression assessment based on multimodal information has gradually become a research focus. However, most studies have only focused on multimodal feature extraction and fusion while ignoring the topic-specific differential characteristics across subjects, which play a crucial role in enhancing assessment performance. To address this, this paper proposes a multimodal depression assessment method based on topic modeling and introduces a text-language joint topic modeling model named the Capturing Topic Contributions Network (CTCNet). The aim of CTCNet is to capture the contributions of different topics to depression assessment and improve the assessment performance. First, to solve the problem of losing key depression information in long sequences, this paper propose a topic modeling-based attention mechanism to evaluate the importance of different topics, guiding the model to focus on key depressive information within topics. Then, to better capture critical depression-related information within each topic, this paper employ a multi-dimensional large-kernel convolution module to extract comprehensive depression features from multiple dimension. Furthermore, a dynamic adaptive decision-making mechanism is introduced in the modality fusion module to selectively emphasize key features for fine-grained fusion. Extensive experiments on the DAIC-WOZ and E-DAIC datasets demonstrate that CTCNet significantly improves depression assessment performance, achieving state-of-the-art results.

Keywords: Attention Mechanism · Capturing Topic Contributions Network · Dynamic Adaptive Fusion · Multimodal Depression Assessment · Topic Modeling

1 Introduction

Depression is a severe mental health disorder that affects emotions, cognition, and behavior, with widespread impacts on individuals, families, and society [15,40]. Its rising prevalence [14] highlights the need for early detection and intervention. Traditional depression assessments, reliant on subjective and

H. Liu et al. (Eds.): CEI 2025, CCIS 2881, pp. 163–177, 2026.
https://doi.org/10.1007/978-981-95-9493-1_11

time-intensive face-to-face interviews, are increasingly limited by scarce medical resources and accessibility issues. Recently, advancements in deep learning have enabled automated, accurate, and efficient depression detection, offering a promising alternative to traditional methods.

Deep learning has significantly improved the efficiency and accuracy of depression detection by learning implicit patterns from data. Pan et al. [20] proposed a voiceprint adversarial network that combines long- and short-term acoustic features with raw audio waveforms to capture spatiotemporal features associated with depression. Teng et al. [32] employed a multi-modal, multi-task approach to analyze emotional expression in individuals with depression. However, these methods often suffer from data imbalance and critical information loss due to sequence padding or truncation. To address this, studies [28,31] have used BiLSTM and GRU networks to better capture contextual information. Nevertheless, these approaches often ignore topic-specific differences, which are crucial for inferring psychological states.

Although topic modeling-based methods [10,12] have shown promise in extracting depression features, they rely on fixed interview questions, limiting the data used for training. This paper proposes an improved approach combining text and audio responses for topic modeling, enabling a more comprehensive analysis. A topic attention mechanism is designed to capture the relationship between emotional expression and depression across topics, reflecting a subject's internal state more accurately and holistically.

This paper proposes the CTCNet model for depression detection, leveraging variations in emotional expression across interview topics to extract key depression-related features (Fig. 1). The model consists of three core modules: the topic attention module, the multi-dimensional convolution module, and the modality fusion module. The topic attention module, designed for topic modeling, analyzes the importance of topics and their relationships to capture depression-related information more effectively. The multi-dimensional convolution module extracts features across topic, channel, and feature dimensions, enabling a deeper and more comprehensive understanding of depressive symptoms. To enhance feature fusion, a dynamic adaptive decision fusion method is introduced, selectively emphasizing depression-related features for optimal performance. The contributions of this paper are summarized as follows.

1) This paper proposes a text-language joint topic modeling model, named Capturing Topic Contributions Network (CTCNet), which aims to capture the contributions of different topics to depression assessment and enhance evaluation performance.
2) This paper designs a topic attention module based on topic modeling to assess the importance of different topics. This module focuses on the topic dimension by analyzing depressive information within topics and inter-subject correlations, thereby capturing the significance of specific topics.
3) This paper introduces a multi-dimensional convolution module to decouple and model the relationships among topics, channels, and features. This mod-

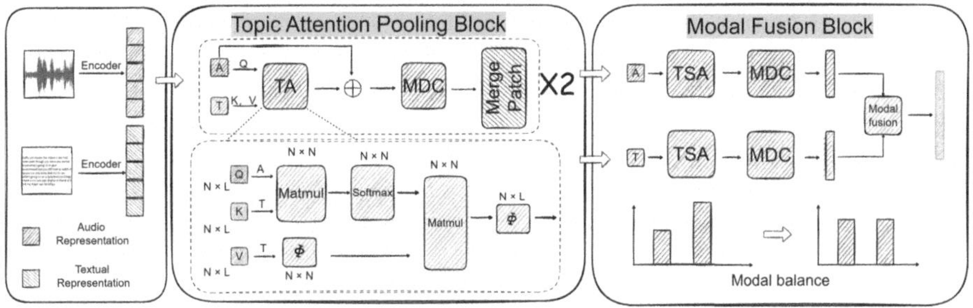

Fig. 1. Overall architecture diagram of CTCNet. The structures of TA and TSA are identical; the difference is that TA represents cross-modal topic attention, while TSA represents single-modal topic attention.

ule effectively captures critical depressive features within topics, enhancing the depth and comprehensiveness of information extraction.

4) This paper introduces a dynamic adaptive decision fusion method to refine the feature fusion process. This strategy enables the model to obtain complementary information across modalities, perform diverse fine-grained feature fusion tasks, and enhance its generalization capabilities, thereby improving the accuracy and reliability of depression detection.

2 Method

2.1 Learning Textual and Audio Modality

The semantic information in text plays a crucial role in understanding an individual's psychological state and emotions. Utilizing pre-trained models to extract textual features is effective in depression detection tasks. Therefore, this paper introduce the pre-trained Sent2Vec model [18] to capture the emotional semantics embedded in textual data. Additionally, due to the uncertainty of interview questions, participants may exhibit varying emotional states over the course of long interviews. To better identify the importance of different responses, this paper incorporates the concept of topic modeling. This paper select M responses from their interview text and correspondingly select M audio samples as input. The textual data of the i-th topic is denoted as $\mathrm{S_i}(\mathrm{i}=1,2,\cdots,\mathrm{M})$, each topic consists of a textual response and its corresponding audio data. Therefore, the textual data of M topics can be represented as: $\mathrm{S_t}=\{\mathrm{S_1},\ \mathrm{S_2},\cdots,\ \mathrm{S_M}\}$. This paper extract textual features using the Sent2Vec model, with the extraction process formulated as follows:

$$\mathrm{X_T} = \mathrm{Embedding}\ (\mathrm{S_t})\,. \tag{1}$$

This paper extracts paralinguistic information related to depression from audio data to complement textual information. Additionally, pre-trained models can learn rich feature representations, which help improve the generalization ability of the model. To this end, we introduce the pre-trained Wav2Vec 2.0 model [2] to capture the emotional polarity in audio data [36]. Based on the timestamps of the topic textual data, we segment the corresponding audio data. The i-th audio segment can be represented as: $\mathrm{A_i}$. Thus, the M audio segments can be represented as: $\mathrm{A_a} = \{\mathrm{A_1},\ \mathrm{A_2}, \cdots,\ \mathrm{A_M}\}$. Next, we extract features using the Wav2Vec 2.0 model, which is formulated as follows:

$$\mathrm{X_A} = \text{ Embedding } (\mathrm{A_a}), \tag{2}$$

where $X_m \in \mathbb{R}^{N \times L}$, $m \in \{A, T\}$, N and L represent the number of topics, feature dimensions, respectively.

2.2 Topic Attention Module

Each topic contains different types of information, and participants exhibit varying emotional states accordingly. As a result, the importance of information within each topic also differs. For example, the response *"I couldn't drive, I couldn't sleep, I couldn't eat, um, I... I couldn't do anything, I was completely..."* clearly reflects the participant's mental state, whereas *"I would say going to college right after high school"* provides significantly less emotional information. Based on this observation, we introduce a topic attention mechanism to learn and quantify the importance of each topic. To enable the model to capture the weight relationships across modalities in the topic dimension and dynamically adjust the significance of different modalities, we develop a cross-modal TA module. In each TAPB, the TA module uses the mapped features of one modality as the query, while the mapped features of the other modality serve as the key and value. Taking the audio branch as an example (as shown in Fig. 1), the audio features are projected into the query space, while the textual features are projected into the key and value spaces. This design facilitates effective cross-modal interactions, ensuring that the model not only extracts critical information but also attends to the emotional states and importance of different topics. Through this topic attention mechanism, the model can dynamically adjust the influence of different modalities across various topics, thereby capturing key emotional cues in depression detection more accurately. The specific formulation is as follows:

$$Q = X_A W_Q,\ K = X_T W_K, \tag{3}$$

where $X_m \in \mathbb{R}^{N \times L}$ is input features, $m \in \{A, T\}$. $W_Q \in \mathbb{R}^{L \times d}$ and $W_K \in \mathbb{R}^{L \times d}$ are projection matrix. The dimension d represents the module's size. Next, we compute the relevance scores between the query (Q) and the key (K) and transform them into a probability distribution using the softmax function. This approach differs from other attention mechanisms because the output sequence of the TA module needs to retain complete topic information. During computation, Q, K, and V are responsible for operations across the topic dimension of different modalities. Specifically, V undergoes a mapping process followed by a transpose operation to ensure that computations occur along the topic dimension. This design effectively preserves topic information from different modalities during fusion, enhancing the model's ability to capture emotional cues. Through this mechanism, we not only obtain the importance of each topic across different modalities but also ensure that the complete topic information is retained in the final output. The specific calculation formula is as follows:

$$\hat{V} = X_T W_V, \tag{4}$$

$$X_{A,\text{atten}} = \left(\text{Softmax}\left(\frac{QK^T}{\sqrt{d}}\right)\hat{V}^T\right)W_{\text{atten}}, \tag{5}$$

where $W_V \in \mathbb{R}^{L\times N}$, $W_{atten} \in \mathbb{R}^{N\times L}$ is projection matrix. $\hat{V}^T \in \mathbb{R}^{N\times N}$, the first N represents the feature dimension, while the second N denotes the topic dimension. The i-th column corresponds to the i-th topic, and each weighting operation is performed on that specific topic. The TA module is responsible for cross-modal topic-level integration. By computing across the topic dimension of different modalities, this mechanism not only enables each topic to incorporate relevant information from corresponding topics in other modalities but also effectively captures the importance of each topic. This design ensures that when handling multimodal data, the model can fully leverage the complementary nature of different emotional information, thereby improving the accuracy and reliability of depression detection.

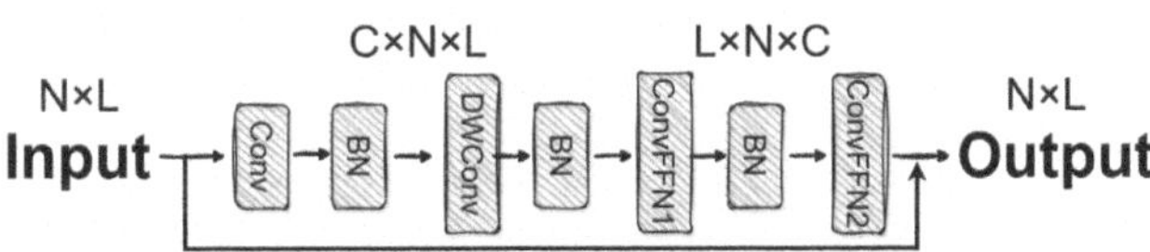

Fig. 2. Structure diagram of the MDC module. The ConvFFN consists of two PWConv layers and a Batch Normalization (BN) layer, where C, N, and L represent channel, topic, and feature dimensions, respectively.

2.3 Multi-dimensional Convolution Module

In the Multidimensional Convolution (MDC) module, Depthwise Convolution (DWConv) is responsible for capturing the correlations between different topics within the same modality, while the Convolutional Feedforward Network (ConvFFN) focuses on learning depression-related features along the channel and feature dimensions. This design aims to decouple the three types of relationships among topics, channels, and features [16], thereby extracting more effective depression-related features. As shown in Fig. 2, this study enhances the two-dimensional spatial features of audio and text into three-dimensional spatial features by adding a channel dimension, which helps the model better capture correlations across different dimensions. In this design, convolution operations are applied separately for channel and feature modeling to capture inter-channel and inter-feature relationships. Before extracting depression-related features from the feature and channel dimensions, it is necessary to first learn the correlations between topics. Specifically, the text features are expanded by adding a channel dimension and processed through one-dimensional convolution. This design not only enhances the model's representation capability but also ensures that multimodal data comprehensively account for interactions across different dimensions. The specific formula is as follows:

$$X_{m,\mathrm{Emb}} = \mathrm{Conv1d}(\mathrm{unsqueeze}(X_m)), \tag{6}$$

where $X_{M,\mathrm{Emb}} \in \mathbb{R}^{N \times C \times L}$, $M \in \{A, T\}$, N, C and L represent the topic, channel, and feature dimensions, respectively. The model can capture hierarchical topic features along the channel dimension. By increasing the channel dimension, the model can integrate more comprehensive depression-related information, thereby significantly enhancing its representational capability. In this study, DWConv is employed to model inter-topic relationships, which requires modeling topic correlations within the same channel. To achieve this, the channel and topic dimensions are first reordered to ensure that inter-topic relationships can be effectively captured during DWConv. This adjustment not only optimizes data organization but also enhances the model's flexibility and efficiency in capturing hierarchical topic features. By adopting this approach, the model can more precisely identify complex depression-related features, further improving its performance. The specific processing steps and formulas are as follows:

$$X_{m,\mathrm{Dwc}} = \mathrm{DWConv}(\mathrm{reshape}(X_{m,\mathrm{Emb}})), \tag{7}$$

where $X_{m,\mathrm{Dwc}} \in \mathbb{R}^{C \times N \times L}$, $\mathrm{reshape}(\cdot) \in \mathbb{R}^{C \times N \times L}$. Reordering the channel and topic dimensions can effectively prevent information mixing across different topic dimensions during the DWConv process. This design focuses on extracting features along the topic dimension. Next, we apply 2-D convolution to model the channel and feature dimensions separately, aiming to capture inter-channel and inter-feature dimensions. This process not only helps extract more effective depression-related features but also enhances the model's sensitivity to underlying patterns in multi-dimensional data. By doing so, the model can achieve a more comprehensive understanding and representation of depression-related information, thereby improving overall performance. The specific processing steps and formulas are as follows:

$$X_{m,\mathrm{c}} = \mathrm{ConvFFN1}(\mathrm{BN}(X_{m,\mathrm{Dwc}})), \tag{8}$$

$$X_{m,\mathrm{l}} = \mathrm{ConvFFN2}(\mathrm{reshape}(X_{m,\mathrm{c}})), \tag{9}$$

where $X_{m,\mathrm{c}} \in \mathbb{R}^{C \times N \times L}$, $ConvFFN1$ is responsible for modeling the channel dimension. $X_{m,\mathrm{l}} \in \mathbb{R}^{L \times N \times C}$, $\mathrm{reshape}(\cdot) \in \mathbb{R}^{L \times N \times C}$, $ConvFFN2$ is responsible for modeling the feature dimension.

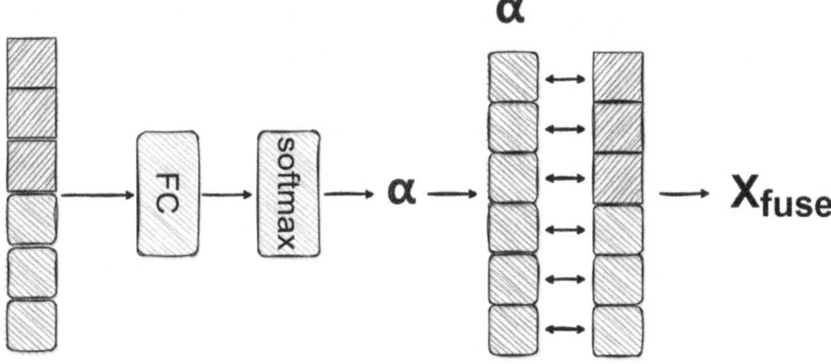

Fig. 3. Structure diagram of Modal Fusion.

2.4 Multi-modal Fusion

Previously, decision-level fusion methods mainly included two approaches: one directly concatenates features from different modalities within a single layer, while the other concatenates features that integrate multiple modalities with those from a single modality. Although these methods have achieved certain success in modality fusion, they still fail to effectively address the issue of modality imbalance. To prevent the model from overemphasizing or underemphasizing a specific modality, which could lead to modality bias, this paper introduce a dynamic adaptive decision fusion process in MF [8]. This process computes dynamic weights for multimodal output features, selectively emphasizing relevant features to optimize the overall model performance. Additionally, the TA module integrates cross-modal multi-level features. As the network deepens, these cross-modal features continuously fuse, enhancing interactions between modalities while compensating for potential information loss. As shown in Fig. 3, this paper concatenate features from different modalities and compute the dynamic weight α, with the specific formula as follows:

$$\alpha = \text{Softmax}(W(\text{Concat}[X_A, X_T]) + \text{bias}). \tag{10}$$

By dynamically generating the weight α for modality fusion features, this paper can adaptively emphasize relevant features, significantly optimizing the model's performance. However, directly performing weighted modality fusion at the model level is not sufficient to fully capture effective depression-related features. To address this, we further introduce dynamic weight computation at the feature level to refine the feature fusion process. This approach enables the model to handle different fine-grained tasks and enhances its generalization ability. By computing dynamic weights for these features and adjusting the fusion strategy accordingly, the model can flexibly extract key depression-related features. This refined feature fusion mechanism not only improves the model's performance on specific tasks but also strengthens its generalization to unseen data. The final fusion prediction formula is as follows:

$$X_{\text{fuse}} = \alpha \odot (\text{Concat}[X_A, X_T]). \tag{11}$$

Here, X_{fuse}, X_T and X_A represent the modality fusion feature, the feature vector of the text modality, and the feature vector of the audio modality, respectively. $\odot$ denotes the Hadamard product. This feature fusion approach refines the feature integration process and enhances the model's generalization ability. Additionally, it helps mitigate the challenges posed by class imbalance.

3 Experiment

3.1 Dataset

This paper employ two datasets to evaluate the performance of CTCNet: the DAIC-WOZ dataset [34] and the E-DAIC dataset [23]. The DAIC-WOZ dataset is part of the Distress Analysis Interview Corpus (DAIC), while the E-DAIC dataset is an extended version of DAIC-WOZ, developed by International Communication Technology (ICT) [11]. Both datasets primarily consist of clinical interview recordings designed to support the diagnosis of psychological distress conditions such as anxiety, depression, and post-traumatic stress disorder. The corpus includes Oz interviews [5] conducted by a virtual animated interviewer named Ellie, controlled by a real human interviewer in another room. Specifically, the DAIC-WOZ dataset is divided into three subsets: 107 samples for training, 35 for validation, and 47 for testing. Among them, 57 participants are diagnosed with depression, while 132 are non-depressed. The E-DAIC dataset contains data from 275 participants, also split into three subsets: 163 for training, and 56 each for validation and testing. By comparing and analyzing these two datasets, we can comprehensively evaluate the effectiveness and robustness of CTCNet in depression detection.

3.2 Data Preprocessing and Implementation Details

To address timestamp mismatches between transcript text and audio files in the DAIC-WOZ dataset, we adjusted timestamps using preprocessing code from Bailey et al. [3], ensuring synchronization. Given the absence of textual records for questions in the E-DAIC dataset, each participant's response (combining text and audio) is treated as an independent topic. 40 topics are randomly selected from each transcript, with input dimensions of (40,768) derived using the pretrained Sent2Vec model [18] to capture emotional semantics. For audio data, segments corresponding to the chosen text topic timestamps are selected. Utilizing the pretrained Wav2Vec 2.0 model [2], emotional valence information is extracted from the audio, resulting in audio features of size (40,768).

3.3 Comparison With Other Methods

In this section, we present the experimental results of the proposed method and compare it with other depression detection methods based on text, audio, text-audio, and text-audio-visual modalities. For the DAIC-WOZ dataset, most previous studies only performed performance evaluation on the validation set.

Table 1. Comparison of Model Performance on the DAIC-WOZ Dataset. The best results are indicated in bold, while the second-best results are underlined.

Methods	Modality	MAE ↓	RMSE ↓
Zhang et al. [39]	A	4.75	5.73
Zhao et al. [30]	A	4.83	**5.34**
Fang et al. [7]	A	5.21	6.13
Han et al. [13]	A	5.10	5.91
Pan et al. [20]	A	**4.27**	**5.34**
Pan et al. [21]	A	4.88	5.60
Hu et al. [17]	A	4.87	5.80
Ours	A	4.53	5.48
Stepanov et al. [29]	T	4.88	5.83
Al et al. [1]	T	5.18	6.38
Roharian et al. [25]	T	4.98	6.05
Niu et al. [19]	T	**3.73**	**4.80**
Zhang et al. [39]	T	4.25	5.61
Ours	T	3.86	5.12
Al et al. [19]	A+T	4.97	6.27
Roharian et al. [29]	A+T	5.18	6.40
Wei et al. [38]	A+T+V	4.92	5.86
Zhang et al. [39]	A+T+V	4.48	5.57
Pan et al. [21]	A+T+V	4.28	5.33
Ours	A+T	**3.62**	**4.71**

To ensure a fair and reasonable comparison of model performance, this study randomly split 10% of the samples from the training set [42] as a validation set for hyperparameter tuning and tested on this validation set. For the E-DAIC dataset, the original data partition was used. To simultaneously compare the performance of single-modal models in depression detection, this study adjusted the model and built a single-modal depression assessment backbone network. The output of this backbone network was flattened and input into the regression layer to obtain depression prediction results for the corresponding modality. Tables 1 and 2 show the comparison results of single-modal and multi-modal methods on the DAIC-WOZ and E-DAIC datasets, respectively. When using only the audio modality for depression assessment, the proposed method showed highly competitive prediction performance compared to previous state-of-the-art methods. Similarly, when using only the text modality for depression assessment, the proposed method also demonstrated excellent performance. At the same time, it was observed that the prediction results of the single audio modality model were generally lower than those of the single text modality model. This phenomenon indicates that, although previous text or audio single-modal depression detection methods have somewhat improved performance, a single modality still cannot fully capture an individual's emotional and psychological state, leading to inaccurate assessment results.

Table 2. Comparison of Model Performance on the E-DAIC Dataset. The best results are indicated in bold, while the second-best results are underlined.

Methods	Modality	CCC ↑	MAE ↓	RMSE ↓
Fan et al. [6]	A	0.045	–	8.19
Makiuchi et al. [24]	A	0.048	–	6.88
Uddin et al. [33]	A	–	–	<u>5.78</u>
Han et al. [13]	A	–	<u>5.38</u>	6.29
Hu et al. [17]	A	<u>0.262</u>	–	6.23
Ours	A	**0.382**	**4.23**	**5.36**
Ray et al. [22]	T	**0.67**	<u>4.02</u>	**4.73**
Steijn et al. (Method 3) [35]	T	<u>0.62</u>	–	6.06
Steijn et al. (Method 5) [35]	T	0.53	–	5.37
Sadeghi et al. [26]	T	–	4.26	5.36
Tank et al. [31]	T	0.474	4.589	5.896
Ours	T	0.503	**3.83**	<u>4.86</u>
Fan et al. [6]	A+T	0.43	4.39	5.91
Makiuchi et al. [24]	A+T	0.403	–	6.11
Wang et al. [37]	A+T	–	<u>3.35</u>	<u>4.55</u>
Pan et al. [20]	A+T	<u>0.467</u>	4.28	5.34
Saggur et al. [27]	A+T+V	0.457	–	5.36
Fang et al. [7]	A+T+V	–	–	5.17
Teng et al. (Method 3) [32]	A+T+V	0.466	5.21	–
Ours	A+T	**0.683**	**3.18**	**4.21**

For text and audio multi-modal depression assessment, the proposed method achieves state-of-the-art prediction performance on both datasets, outperforming existing multi-modal depression detection methods. This demonstrates the efficiency of using topic modeling for depression detection. For example, Wei et al. [41] used a ConvBiLSTM backbone network, and Pan et al. [9] proposed the Multi-Feature Deep Supervised Voiceprint Adversarial Network (MFDS-VAN) to extract depression information. However, these methods treat all topics as a whole, ignoring the differences between topics, and thus fail to capture the correlations between topics and the complete depression information within topics. The proposed TA module focuses on the importance of different topics along the topic dimension, dynamically adjusting weights to capture the correlations between topics and the depression information within each topic. In feature fusion, Hu et al. [4] used interactive feature fusion by recursively fusing cross-modal depression features across layers. Wei et al. [41] employed Subattention, a weighted fusion method for different modality features. Compared to other direct feature fusion methods, these approaches alleviate the issue of excessive reliance on single-modality features for single-layer feature fusion. However, they overlook the model bias caused by modality imbalance and the loss of key features. This study introduces the cross-modal TA module for multi-modal information interaction in TAPB, and incorporates a dynamic adaptive decision fusion process in MFB. This process calculates dynamic feature weights through multi-modal output features, selectively emphasizing relevant features, thereby improving model evaluation accuracy.

4 Results and Discussion

4.1 Different Feature Extraction Methods

To further demonstrate the superiority of our proposed topic modeling-based CTCNet, we replaced our MDC module with the feature extraction module from previous methods and trained the model on the DAIC-WOZ and E-DAIC datasets. The experimental results are shown in Table 3. The results indicate that our method outperforms previous approaches. This is because the MDC module adds a channel dimension to the input, which better helps the model capture the correlations across different dimensions in the data. Additionally, by using large-kernel convolutions, it more effectively captures long-term dependencies in the data. The MDC module decouples the modeling of the three relationships–topic, channel, and feature–and captures more effective depressive features. This allows it to capture depressive information within topics and the weight relationships between topics along the topic dimension.

Table 3. Comparison of Backbone Network Ablation Experiments.

Backbone Ablation	DAIC-WOZ		E-DAIC	
Method	MAE ↓	RMSE ↓	CCC ↑	RMSE ↓
GRU	4.51	5.43	0.412	5.99
LSTM	4.43	5.52	0.416	5.91
ConvBiLSTM	4.30	5.45	0.427	5.82
BiLSTM	4.38	5.35	0.454	5.66
BiLSTM with Attention	4.11	5.19	0.430	5.80
Ours	**3.62**	**4.71**	**0.683**	**4.21**

Table 4. Comparison of Multimodal Feature Fusion Methods.

Fusion Ablation	DAIC-WOZ		E-DAIC	
Method	MAE ↓	RMSE ↓	CCC ↑	RMSE ↓
FWA	3.86	5.09	0.646	4.53
AttFN	4.36	5.48	0.602	4.68
Subattention Fusion	3.82	4.98	0.626	4.60
DCAF	4.14	5.19	0.619	4.97
Adaptive Late-Fusion	4.08	5.14	0.628	4.64
Ours	**3.62**	**4.71**	**0.683**	**4.21**

4.2 Different Multimodal Fusion Methods

We replaced the feature fusion method used in previous multimodal approaches with the dynamic adaptive decision fusion method proposed in this study. The experimental results are shown in Table 4. The results indicate that the dynamic adaptive decision fusion approach presented in this study is more efficient. This is because directly performing weighted fusion of modalities at the model level cannot fully capture efficient depression-related features. Therefore, by further calculating dynamic feature-level weights, the model dynamically captures key depression features from different modalities during training, refining the feature fusion process and improving the model's depression prediction performance.

Table 5. Results of Different Attention Selections.

Attention Operation	DAIC-WOZ		E-DAIC	
Method	MAE ↓	RMSE ↓	CCC ↑	RMSE ↓
Self-attention	4.02	5.37	0.620	4.93
Cross-attention	3.89	5.06	0.643	4.52
Topic-atten	**3.62**	**4.71**	**0.683**	**4.21**

4.3 Different Attention Mechanisms

Our method is based on topic modeling, and to allow the attention module to compute on the topic dimension, we designed TA. To demonstrate the effectiveness of TA, we compared it with Cross-attention and Self-attention, and the results are shown in Table 5. The results indicate that in our network, the TA we designed outperforms both Cross-attention and Self-attention. This is because the computation in TA is performed entirely on the topic dimension, enabling the attention mechanism to focus more on the features of the topic dimension, better identifying the topic weight relationships, and thus more effectively capturing the depressive information in the topic dimension.

5 Conclusion

In this paper, a topic modeling-based multi-modal depression assessment model, CTCNet, leverages text and audio modalities to enhance evaluation accuracy. The core of CTCNet is a topic modeling-based attention mechanism that focuses on depression-related key information. To capture depression features effectively, the MDC module decouples relationships between topics, channels, and features. Additionally, a dynamic adaptive decision fusion mechanism enhances depression assessment performance by emphasizing key features.

CTCNet surpasses existing methods on the DAIC-WOZ and E-DAIC datasets, proving its multi-modal superiority. It excels with long time-series and cross-modal data, surpassing single-modality approaches. To handle missing modalities, future work aims to supplement absent visual features for a more comprehensive depression detection framework.

Acknowledgments. This study was funded by the National Key Research and Development Program of China under Grant 2023YFC3604704.

References

1. Al Hanai, T., Ghassemi, M.M., Glass, J.R.: Detecting depression with audio/text sequence modeling of interviews. In: Interspeech, pp. 1716–1720 (2018)
2. Baevski, A., Schneider, S., Auli, M.: vq-wav2vec: self-supervised learning of discrete speech representations. arXiv preprint arXiv:1910.05453 (2019)
3. Bailey, A., Plumbley, M.D.: Gender bias in depression detection using audio features. In: 2021 29th European Signal Processing Conference (EUSIPCO), pp. 596–600. IEEE (2021)
4. De Melo, W.C., Granger, E., Hadid, A.: A deep multiscale spatiotemporal network for assessing depression from facial dynamics. IEEE Trans. Affect. Comput. **13**(3), 1581–1592 (2020)
5. DeVault, D., et al.: Simsensei kiosk: a virtual human interviewer for healthcare decision support. In: Proceedings of the 2014 International Conference on Autonomous Agents and Multi-Agent Systems, pp. 1061–1068 (2014)
6. Fan, W., He, Z., Xing, X., Cai, B., Lu, W.: Multi-modality depression detection via multi-scale temporal dilated cnns. In: Proceedings of the 9th International on Audio/Visual Emotion Challenge and Workshop, pp. 73–80 (2019)
7. Fang, M., Peng, S., Liang, Y., Hung, C.C., Liu, S.: A multimodal fusion model with multi-level attention mechanism for depression detection. Biomed. Signal Process. Control **82**, 104561 (2023)
8. Fu, X., et al.: Balanced multimodal learning: an integrated framework for multi-task learning in audio-visual fusion (2024)
9. Gao, F., Yang, Y., Wang, J., Sun, J., Yang, E., Zhou, H.: A deep convolutional generative adversarial networks (dcgans)-based semi-supervised method for object recognition in synthetic aperture radar (sar) images. Remote Sens. **10**(6), 846 (2018)
10. Gong, Y., Poellabauer, C.: Topic modeling based multi-modal depression detection. In: Proceedings of the 7th Annual Workshop on Audio/Visual Emotion Challenge, pp. 69–76 (2017)

11. Gratch, J., et al.: The distress analysis interview corpus of human and computer interviews. In: LREC, vol. 14, pp. 3123–3128. Reykjavik (2014)
12. Guo, Y., Zhu, C., Hao, S., Hong, R.: Automatic depression detection via learning and fusing features from visual cues. IEEE Trans. Comput. Soc. Syst. **10**(5), 2806–2813 (2022)
13. Han, Z., et al.: Spatial-temporal feature network for speech-based depression recognition. IEEE Trans. Cogn. Dev. Syst. **16**(1), 308–318 (2023)
14. Hawton, K., i Comabella, C.C., Haw, C., Saunders, K.: Risk factors for suicide in individuals with depression: a systematic review. J. Affect. Disord. **147**(1-3), 17–28 (2013)
15. Herrman, H., et al.: Time for united action on depression: a lancet-world psychiatric association commission. Lancet **399**(10328), 957–1022 (2022)
16. Howard, A.G., et al.: Mobilenets: efficient convolutional neural networks for mobile vision applications. arXiv preprint arXiv:1704.04861 (2017)
17. Hu, M., Liu, L., Wang, X., Tang, Y., Yang, J., An, N.: Parallel multiscale bridge fusion network for audio-visual automatic depression assessment. IEEE Trans. Comput. Soc. Syst. (2024)
18. Moghadasi, M.N., Zhuang, Y.: Sent2vec: a new sentence embedding representation with sentimental semantic. In: 2020 IEEE International Conference on Big Data (Big Data), pp. 4672–4680. IEEE (2020)
19. Niu, M., Chen, K., Chen, Q., Yang, L.: Hcag: a hierarchical context-aware graph attention model for depression detection. In: ICASSP 2021-2021 IEEE International Conference on Acoustics, Speech and Signal Processing (ICASSP), pp. 4235–4239. IEEE (2021)
20. Pan, Y., Jiang, J., Jiang, K., Liu, X.: Disentangled-multimodal privileged knowledge distillation for depression recognition with incomplete multimodal data. In: Proceedings of the 32nd ACM International Conference on Multimedia, pp. 5712–5721 (2024)
21. Pan, Y., et al.: Multi-feature deep supervised voiceprint adversarial network for depression recognition from speech. Biomed. Signal Process. Control **89**, 105704 (2024)
22. Ray, A., Kumar, S., Reddy, R., Mukherjee, P., Garg, R.: Multi-level attention network using text, audio and video for depression prediction. In: Proceedings of the 9th International on Audio/Visual Emotion Challenge and Workshop, pp. 81–88 (2019)
23. Ringeval, F., et al.: Avec 2019 workshop and challenge: state-of-mind, detecting depression with ai, and cross-cultural affect recognition. In: Proceedings of the 9th International on Audio/visual Emotion Challenge and Workshop, pp. 3–12 (2019)
24. Rodrigues Makiuchi, M., Warnita, T., Uto, K., Shinoda, K.: Multimodal fusion of bert-cnn and gated cnn representations for depression detection. In: Proceedings of the 9th International on Audio/Visual Emotion Challenge and Workshop, pp. 55–63 (2019)
25. Rohanian, M., Hough, J., Purver, M., et al.: Detecting depression with word-level multimodal fusion. In: Interspeech, pp. 1443–1447 (2019)
26. Sadeghi, M., et al.: Exploring the capabilities of a language model-only approach for depression detection in text data. In: 2023 IEEE EMBS International Conference on Biomedical and Health Informatics (BHI), pp. 1–5. IEEE (2023)
27. Saggu, G.S., Gupta, K., Arya, K., Rodriguez, C.R.: Depressnet: a multimodal hierarchical attention mechanism approach for depression detection. Int. J. Eng. Sci. **15**(1), 24–32 (2022)

28. Sanchis-Segura, C., Cruz-Gómez, Á.J., Esbrí, S.F., Tirado, A.S., Arnett, P.A., Forn, C.: Multiple sclerosis and depression: translation and adaptation of the spanish version of the chicago multiscale depression inventory and the study of factors associated with depressive symptoms. Arch. Clin. Neuropsychol. **38**(5), 724–738 (2023)
29. Stepanov, E.A., et al.: Depression severity estimation from multiple modalities. In: 2018 IEEE 20th International Conference on E-Health Networking, Applications and Services (healthcom), pp. 1–6. IEEE (2018)
30. Sun, H., Wang, H., Liu, J., Chen, Y.W., Lin, L.: Cubemlp: an mlp-based model for multimodal sentiment analysis and depression estimation. In: Proceedings of the 30th ACM International Conference on Multimedia, pp. 3722–3729 (2022)
31. Tank, C., Pol, S., Katoch, V., Mehta, S., Anand, A., Shah, R.R.: Depression detection and analysis using large language models on textual and audio-visual modalities. arXiv preprint arXiv:2407.06125 (2024)
32. Teng, S., Chai, S., Liu, J., Tateyama, T., Lin, L., Chen, Y.W.: Multi-modal and multi-task depression detection with sentiment assistance. In: 2024 IEEE International Conference on Consumer Electronics (ICCE), pp. 1–5. IEEE (2024)
33. Uddin, M.A., Joolee, J.B., Sohn, K.A.: Deep multi-modal network based automated depression severity estimation. IEEE Trans. Affect. Comput. **14**(3), 2153–2167 (2022)
34. Valstar, M., et al.: Avec 2016: Depression, mood, and emotion recognition workshop and challenge. In: Proceedings of the 6th International Workshop on Audio/Visual Emotion Challenge, pp. 3–10 (2016)
35. Van Steijn, F., Sogancioglu, G., Kaya, H.: Text-based interpretable depression severity modeling via symptom predictions. In: Proceedings of the 2022 International Conference on Multimodal Interaction, pp. 139–147 (2022)
36. Wagner, J., et al.: Dawn of the transformer era in speech emotion recognition: closing the valence gap. IEEE Trans. Pattern Anal. Mach. Intell. **45**(9), 10745–10759 (2023)
37. Wang, C., et al.: A multi-modal feature layer fusion model for assessment of depression based on attention mechanisms. In: 2022 15th International Congress on Image and Signal Processing, BioMedical Engineering and Informatics (CISP-BMEI), pp. 1–6. IEEE (2022)
38. Wei, P.C., Peng, K., Roitberg, A., Yang, K., Zhang, J., Stiefelhagen, R.: Multimodal depression estimation based on sub-attentional fusion. In: European Conference on Computer Vision, pp. 623–639. Springer (2022)
39. Zhang, P., Wu, M., Dinkel, H., Yu, K.: Depa: self-supervised audio embedding for depression detection. In: Proceedings of the 29th ACM International Conference on Multimedia, pp. 135–143 (2021)
40. Zhang, W., Mao, K., Chen, J.: A multimodal approach for detection and assessment of depression using text, audio and video. Phenomics **4**(3), 234–249 (2024)
41. Zhao, Z., Wang, K.: Unaligned multimodal sequences for depression assessment from speech. In: 2022 44th Annual International Conference of the IEEE Engineering in Medicine & Biology Society (EMBC), pp. 3409–3413. IEEE (2022)
42. Zhou, Z., Guo, Y., Hao, S., Hong, R.: Hierarchical multifeature fusion via audio-response-level modeling for depression detection. IEEE Trans. Comput. Soc. Syst. **10**(5), 2797–2805 (2022)

EMAA: Towards Explainable Multimodal Affective Analysis

JiaQi Zhang[1,2], JunJia Feng[1,2], ShiYi Zhou[1,2], YuTing Sun[3], and Lin Shang[1,2](✉)

[1] State Key Laboratory of Novel Software Technology, Nanjing University, Nanjing, China
[2] School of Computer Science, Nanjing University, Nanjing, China
{522024330119,fengjunjia,shiyizhou}@smail.nju.edu.cn, shanglin@nju.edu.cn
[3] The Marketing Service Center of State Grid Jiangsu Electric Power Co., Ltd., Nanjing, China
372362290@qq.com

Abstract. Recent methods for affective analysis have made progress in polarity prediction. However while they work to generate accurate natural language explanations, the transparency and user trust is limited–especially in complex, multi-aspect social media scenarios. To bridge this gap, we propose a method named EMAA(Explainable Multimodal Affective Analysis), a two-stage framework that integrates explanation generation into aspect-based sentiment analysis, combining self-training with direct preference optimization. Additionally, we develop a filter model to automatically evaluate and select high-quality explanations, thereby significantly improving the reliability of training data. Experiments on benchmark datasets show that our method outperforms the baselines in both classification accuracy and explanation quality. Furthermore, we demonstrate that high-quality explanations can improve the robustness and interpretability of sentiment classifications.

Keywords: Affective analysis · Natural language explanation · Multimodal sentiment data fusion technology · Preference optimization

1 Introduction

Explainable Multimodal Affective Aanalysis (EMAA) aims to identify sentiment polarities toward specific aspects by integrating information from multiple modalities such as text and images. This task has broad application potential in scenarios such as social media monitoring, brand analysis, and human-computer interaction. Despite the notable progress in multimodal affective analysis, most existing approaches primarily focus on predicting sentiment polarity labels, while largely neglecting the reasoning process that underlies such predictions. This limitation is especially pronounced in aspect-level analysis, where fine-grained sentiment reasoning is essential.

H. Liu et al. (Eds.): CEI 2025, CCIS 2881, pp. 178–193, 2026.
https://doi.org/10.1007/978-981-95-9493-1_12

In particular, current multimodal sentiment explanation methods are often confined to the sentence or overall level, failing to establish explicit mappings between individual aspects and their corresponding sentiments. However, in real-world applications such as social media, users frequently mention multiple aspects within a single post and express different sentiments toward each. This poses a significant challenge to both the granularity and accuracy of sentiment explanations. Furthermore, existing methods generally lack mechanisms for controlling or evaluating the quality of generated explanations, and little is known about whether high-quality explanations can actually improve downstream sentiment classification performance.

To address these issues, we propose EMAA, a novel framework for explainable multimodal affective analysis. We introduce a new task as shown in Fig. 1 that incorporates natural language explanation into EMAA, and design a unified two-stage training paradigm. In the first stage, we combine self-training with supervised fine-tuning to enhance the model's ability to generate high-quality explanations. In the second stage, we introduce a preference learning mechanism that leverages an automatically constructed preference dataset to further improve explanation quality. Additionally, a filter model is developed to automatically evaluate and prioritize high-quality explanations, leading to a notable improvement in the reliability of training data.

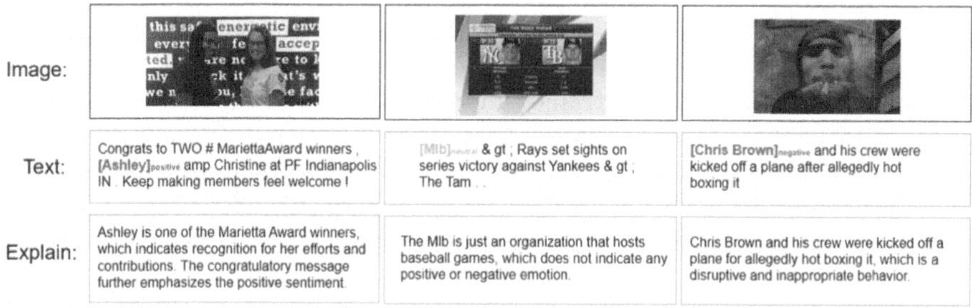

Fig. 1. Examples of EMAA with natural language explanation.

Experimental results demonstrate that our method consistently outperforms existing models across several benchmark multimodal datasets, achieving superior performance in semantic similarity, natural language quality, and sentiment polarity classification. Moreover, empirical analysis confirms that high-quality explanations can effectively enhance the accuracy and robustness of downstream sentiment classification, validating the practical value of explanation generation in the context of EMAA.

2 Related Work

In recent years, advances in multimodal learning and large language models have sparked growing interest in enhancing the accuracy of multimodal affective analysis tasks. From the perspective of modality alignment, researchers have explored methods such as modality fusion, cross-modal transformation, and unified processing via multimodal large language models (MLLMs). Fusion-based methods [1–5] typically employ learnable attention modules to enable interaction between modalities, effectively capturing inter-modal associations. Cross-modal transformation approaches [6,7] aim to project different modalities into a shared semantic space, which is especially effective when auxiliary modalities are used to enrich the primary one. The emergence of multimodal large language models (MLLMs) has made it a standard practice to perform sentiment classification by harnessing their strong semantic capabilities and extensive world knowledge. Techniques such as prompt engineering [8–10] and instruction tuning [11,12] are commonly used to further enhance the affective analysis capabilities of these models in multimodal settings.

Further, researchers have begun to investigate the causal relationship between sentiment causes and sentiment recognition, aiming to improve the explainability of EMAA. Lian et al. [13] first introduced the EMER task, which focuses on generating detailed natural language explanations for emotion recognition outputs. They further proposed AffectGPT [14], which is trained in stages on EMER datasets with varying annotation granularity, thereby optimizing the generation of emotion descriptions. Hu et al. [15] reformulated emotion recognition and cause analysis as a masked prediction problem, using causal prompt templates to handle both subtasks in a unified manner. In the dialogue domain, Li et al. [16] proposed the Emotion Deducing Explanation in Dialogues (EDEN) task, which requires models not only to recognize emotions in dialogues but also to reason about their causes. Experimental results show that large language models outperform traditional pre-trained models on this task, and can be further enhanced through instruction tuning to activate emotional reasoning capabilities. In another line of work, Zheng et al. [17] introduced the Explainable Multimodal Depression Recognition for Clinical Interviews (EMDRC) task, targeting depression detection in clinical interviews. They designed the PhqMML training framework, which combines a novel dataset with a multimodal model to achieve both high performance and interpretability in mental health prediction.

While these studies have demonstrated the potential of generative explanations in multimodal affective tasks, most of them focus on sentence-level or holistic emotion representation, without addressing the fine-grained alignment between explanations and individual aspects. In real-world scenarios, especially on social media, users often express different sentiments toward multiple aspects within a single post. Existing approaches typically struggle to establish accurate mappings between sentiment and specific aspects, thus limiting the performance of fine-grained affective analysis. Moreover, current work often lacks robust mechanisms for evaluating explanation quality and has not systematically explored whether high-quality explanations can directly enhance downstream sentiment polarity classification.

In contrast to these efforts, EMAA focuses specifically on the explanability in EMAA tasks. We propose a unified training framework that explicitly generates natural language explanations for each aspect and empirically validates their utility in improving sentiment polarity prediction. Our approach fills a critical gap in aspect-based sentiment explanation and introduces a more detailed and reasoning-oriented explanation mechanism into the field of multimodal affective analysis.

3 Framework

To enable explainable multimodal affective analysis, we propose a unified training framework EMAA that jointly enhances both sentiment polarity prediction and natural language explanation generation. This framework is designed to achieve two core objectives:

- generate a natural language explanation for each target aspect;
- leverage the explanation to assist aspect-based sentiment classification, thereby improving the model's robustness and interpretability.

3.1 Task Definition

Given a multimodal input sample $m_i = (S_i, I_i, T_i)$, where:

- S_i is a textual sequence consisting of multiple words,
- I_i is the corresponding image,
- T_i is a target aspect mentioned in the text,

the model aims to generate a natural language explanation E_i that justifies why a particular sentiment polarity is assigned to aspect T_i. Based on the input modalities and the generated explanation E_i, the model then predicts the sentiment polarity label $y_i \in \{positive, neutral, negative\}$ for the given aspect.

Unlike traditional sentence-level explanation tasks, this setting requires fine-grained reasoning over individual aspects, emphasizing explanation generation as a natural language reasoning process, rather than merely producing classification labels or visualizing attention weights.

3.2 Framework Overview

To address the above task, we designed a two-stage training framework, illustrated in Fig. 2, which consists of the following key components:

- **Stage I: Self-Training Supervised Fine-tuning** Starting with a small set of samples annotated with explanations, the model leverages large language models to generate pseudo-labels for additional data. This self-training phase expands the training set and guides the model in learning diverse and high-quality sentiment explanations. The primary focus is to enhance the breadth and plausibility of generated explanations.
- **Explanation Quality Filter** As the quality of auto-generated explanations varies, we introduce a filter model to assess and select high-quality explanations. This component plays a crucial role in constructing reliable preference data and ensuring the integrity of the training corpus.

- **Stage II: Direct Preference Optimization (DPO)** Building on the explanation capabilities obtained from stage I, this phase fine-tunes the model using high-quality vs. low-quality contrast preference pairs explanations. Through direct preference alignment, the model learns to favor better explanations in terms of fluency, consistency, and logical structure.

By integrating self-supervised learning with preference alignment, the proposed framework not only increases the volume and diversity of explanation data but also explicitly models preference quality. As a result, the generated explanations are semantically coherent and contribute to improved prediction of sentiment at the aspect level.

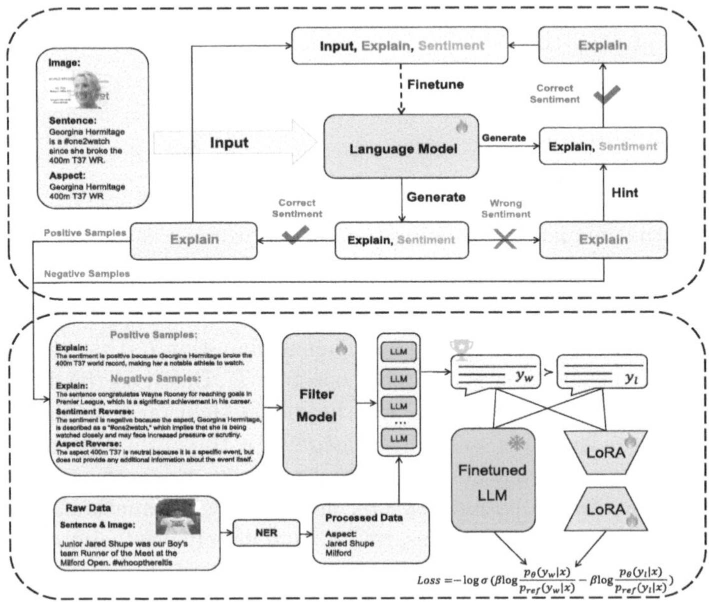

Fig. 2. Overview of the training process for EMAA.

4 Methodology

This section provides a detailed description of the core components in our proposed EMAA framework, including three main modules: self-training supervised fine-tuning, an explanation quality filter, and direct preference optimization.

4.1 Self-training Supervised Fine-tuning

In real-world datasets, most multimodal samples are annotated only with sentiment polarity labels but lack corresponding natural language explanations, limiting the scope of supervised training. To address the scarcity of high-quality explanation data, we adapt the STaR [18] framework and propose a self-training method that uses a small number of manually annotated explanations as prompts to guide large models in generating more high-quality explanations. A filtering mechanism is then applied to construct a pseudo-labeled training dataset. The overall process is shown in Algorithm 1.

Algorithm 1. Training Process of Self-Training Supervised Fine-Tuning

Input: Large-scale language model M_0, initial dataset $D = \{(m_i, y_i)\}_{i=1}^{D}$ (containing multimodal samples m_i and sentiment polarities y_i), and a small set of prompt with sentiment explanations $P = \{(m_p^i, e_p^i, y_p^i)\}_{i=1}^{P}$ (where $P \ll D$).
Output: Fine-tuned model M
Explanation Generation: Use the current model M_0 to generate sentiment explanations $\hat{e}_i$ and predicted sentiment polarities $\hat{y}_i$ for each multimodal sample m_i in dataset D.
$(\hat{e}_i, \hat{y}_i) \leftarrow M_0(m_i)$, for all $i \in [1, D]$
Reversed Generation: For samples with incorrect sentiment polarity predictions, provide the correct sentiment label as a hint and let the model generate corresponding sentiment explanations.
$(\hat{e}_{\text{rat},i}, \hat{y}_{\text{rat},i}) \leftarrow M_0(\text{add\_hint}(m_i, y_i))$, for all $i \in [1, D]$ and $\hat{y}_i \neq y_i$
Filtering: Only retain the generated sentiment explanations that correspond to the correct sentiment polarity.
$D_0 \leftarrow \{(m_i, \hat{e}_i, y_i) \mid i \in [1, D] \wedge \hat{y}_i = y_i\}$
$D_{\text{rat},0} \leftarrow \{(m_i, \hat{e}_{\text{rat},i}, y_i) \mid i \in [1, D] \wedge \hat{y}_i \neq y_i \wedge \hat{y}_{\text{rat},i} = y_i\}$
Fine-Tuning: Use the filtered datasets D_0 and $D_{\text{rat},0}$ to fine-tune the original model M.
$M \leftarrow \text{train}(M, D_0 \cup D_{\text{rat},0})$
Return M

Specifically, for each multimodal sample m_i, we first use the initial model M_0 to generate a candidate explanation $\hat{e}_i$ and sentiment polarity prediction $\hat{y}_i$:

$$\hat{e}_i, \hat{y}_i = M_0(m_i) \tag{1}$$

If the model correctly predicts the sentiment polarity, the generated explanation is retained. For incorrectly predicted samples ($\hat{y}_i \neq y_i$), we provide the ground truth polarity label y_i as an additional prompt to guide the model in producing a more appropriate explanation $\hat{e}_{rat,i}$:

$$\hat{e}_{\text{rat},i} = M_0(m_i, y_i) \tag{2}$$

We then construct two subsets of training data from these results:

- Correct prediction set:

$$D_0 = \{(m_i, \hat{e}_i) \mid \hat{y}_i = y_i\} \tag{3}$$

– Reversed explanation set:

$$D_{\text{rat},0} = \{(m_i, \hat{e}_{\text{rat},i}) \mid \hat{y}_i \neq y_i\} \tag{4}$$

Finally, we fine-tune the original model M_0 on the combined pseudo-labeled dataset to obtain an improved model M:

$$M = \text{FineTune}(M_0, D_0 \cup D_{\text{rat},0}) \tag{5}$$

By providing the correct sentiment polarity as an explicit prompt, the model learns to generate aligned explanations. This strategy effectively expands the scale and diversity of training data, enabling the model to learn from failure cases and incrementally refine its generation policy, laying the foundation for the next optimization stage.

4.2 Explanation Quality Filter

As explanations generated by fine-tuned model M may vary in quality, directly using all pseudo-labeled explanations can introduce noise that reduces model stability. To address this, we propose a discriminative model to assess explanation quality and use it as a filtering mechanism to support the construction of preference data.

In addition to using contrastive samples obtained from the previous stage, we further diversify the pool of negative examples through the following rule-based strategies:

- **Reversed Generation.** We feed incorrect sentiment polarity labels as prompts to the model, forcing it to generate mismatched explanations. This simulates what a misleading explanation would look like for the same input.
- **Aspect Swapping.** For samples containing multiple aspects, we randomly shuffle the associations between explanations and aspects to create logically inconsistent explanation samples.

We employ a pre-trained multimodal model (e.g., Bridgetower [19]) as the backbone of our filter model. The input consists of the image I_i, text S_i, aspect T_i, and candidate explanation $\hat{E}_i$, and the model outputs a probability score $P(\hat{y}_i \mid I_i, S_i, T_i, \hat{E}_i)$ indicating the explanation's quality. The model is optimized using a weighted binary cross-entropy loss to balance positive and negative samples:

$$\mathcal{L} = -\sum_{i=1}^{N} [\lambda_1 \hat{y}_i \log P + \lambda_0 (1 - \hat{y}_i) \log(1 - P)] \tag{6}$$

where λ_1 and λ_0 represent the weight coefficients of positive samples and negative samples respectively.

After training, the filter model is used to score multiple candidate explanations generated by the base model, selecting the best one to form preference pairs for the next stage.

4.3 DPO Driven Optimization

While the self-training process in Sect. 4.1 helps expand the model's ability to generate explanations, it lacks an explicit definition of "what constitutes a high-quality explanation" and does not ensure consistency or preference alignment. To address this, we use Direct Preference Optimization (DPO), a strategy that allows the model to learn to prefer better explanations through comparison-based supervision.

To enhance generalization and avoid reusing the filter model's training data for preference learning, we construct a new preference dataset based on samples from the MVSA [20] dataset. We extract aspect-level multimodal samples and use multiple pre-trained multimodal large language models (e.g., Qwen2-VL [21], LLaVA1.5 [22], Phi3.5-V [23]) to generate diverse candidate explanations for each aspect.

The explanation quality filter (Sect. 4.2) is then used to score all candidate explanations and build a preference dataset D_{pref}. The highest-scoring explanation is selected as the preferred explanation, and another lower-scoring explanation is randomly chosen as the rejected explanation:

$$e_i^{\text{pref}} = \arg\max_j f_{\text{filter}}(e_{ij}) \tag{7}$$

$$e_i^{\text{rej}} = \text{Random}(E_i \setminus \{e_i^{\text{pref}}\}) \tag{8}$$

Let (x, y_w, y_l) denote a preference pair in D_{pref}, where x is the input prompt (including image, text, and aspect), y_w is the preferred explanation, and y_l is the rejected one. The DPO objective encourages the model π_θ to increase the generation probability of y_w while decreasing that of y_l, using a reference model π_{ref} (typically the fine-tuned model before DPO) to normalize reward differences:

$$\mathcal{L}(\theta) = -\log\sigma\left(\beta\log\frac{\pi_\theta(y_w \mid x)}{\pi_{\text{ref}}(y_w \mid x)} - \beta\log\frac{\pi_\theta(y_l \mid x)}{\pi_{\text{ref}}(y_l \mid x)}\right) \tag{9}$$

Here, $\sigma(\cdot)$ denotes the sigmoid function, and β is a temperature hyperparameter that controls the strength of preference alignment. The core idea is to maximize the model's advantage on preferred examples while regularizing deviation from the reference model via an implicit KL-divergence formulation.

During training, we keep the reference model π_{ref} fixed and optimize only the target model π_θ. Through extensive preference-pair training, the model learns explanation-generation strategies that better align with human preferences, improving the naturalness, consistency, and logical soundness of the outputs.

Experimental results show that models trained with DPO outperform those without preference alignment in both semantic similarity and LLM-based evaluation metrics. Furthermore, the DPO-enhanced models exhibit stronger generalization and robustness in downstream sentiment classification tasks (see Sect. 5), demonstrating the effectiveness of incorporating preference learning into explanation generation.

5 Experiments

To comprehensively evaluate the effectiveness of the proposed explainable multimodal affective analysis method, we conduct a series of experiments covering three subtasks: aspect-based sentiment classification, explanation generation, and few-shot learning. The experiments compare our method against several strong baselines on multiple public datasets, using both automatic and human-aligned evaluation metrics for quantitative analysis.

5.1 Setup

We build our explanation-generation model upon Qwen2-VL [21], and apply LoRA and gradient checkpointing to reduce training memory overhead. During supervised fine-tuning, we set the batch size to 2, with a gradient accumulation step of 8 and a total of 2 training epochs.

The explanation quality filter is implemented based on Bridgetower [19]. We train the filter model for 6 epochs with an initial learning rate of 5×10^{-4}, using a weighted cross-entropy loss to balance positive and negative samples. Aspect extraction for the preference dataset follows the method proposed by Wang et al. [24], further fine-tuned on a social media domain named entity recognition dataset. The DPO stage is trained with the same batch size for 2 epochs. All experiments are implemented using the PyTorch framework and conducted on multiple NVIDIA Tesla V100 GPUs.

5.2 Datasets and Metrics

Filter Model Training Dataset. Table 1 presents the statistics of the dataset used to train the explanation quality filter. It contains a total of 14,807 samples, consisting of both positive and three types of negative examples. Positive samples are high-quality explanations generated by the model when the predicted sentiment polarity is correct. Negative samples are constructed through three strategies: original misclassified samples, reversed samples (generated using incorrect sentiment prompts), and aspect-swapped samples (with mismatched aspectexplanation pairs). Training the filter model on this dataset enables it to effectively distinguish between high- and low-quality explanations, laying the groundwork for constructing the explanation preference dataset used in DPO.

Table 1. Statistics of the Filter Model Training Dataset

	Positive samples	Negative samples	Reversed	Aspect swapped	Total
Average Length	178.05	182.12	155.4	151.51	166.1
Average Number of Entities	1.41	1.34	1.42	2.17	1.47
Number of Samples	3908	2833	6574	1492	14807

Explanation Preference Dataset. The explanation preference dataset is constructed based on the MVSA [20] dataset, which is a multimodal affective analysis dataset in the social media domain, originally annotated at the sentence level. To adapt it for our aspect-based task, we first apply an aspect extraction model to identify aspect terms from the text. Then, for each sample, we use multiple pre-trained large models to generate candidate explanations. These candidates are scored using the filter model, and the highest-scoring explanation is selected as the preferred sample, while a lower-scoring one is randomly selected as the rejected sample.

Table 2. Statistics of the Sentiment Explanation Preference Dataset

	MVSA-multiple	MVSA-single	Total
Original Dataset Size	19600	4869	24469
After Entity Extraction	12007	2364	14371
After Data Filtering	7950	1547	9497

To ensure the quality of the preference data, we filter out samples in which the best explanation has a score below 0.6 or the score difference between the preferred and rejected explanation is less than 0.1. After filtering, a total of 9,497 preference pairs are retained. The statistics of this dataset are shown in Table 2.

Explanation Evaluation Test Set. The explanation test set is built from 2,271 original test samples from the widely used affective analysis benchmarks Twitter-2015 and Twitter-2017. For each sample, we first use a large language model to generate a preliminary explanation as a pseudo-label. Human annotators then verify, revise, and filter the outputs to ensure quality and consistency. After this refinement process, a total of 1,023 high-quality explanation samples are retained. The statistics of this test set are presented in Table 3.

Table 3. Statistics of the Sentiment Explanation Test Dataset

	Quantity	Average Aspects	Average Length
Test Set	1023	1.81	150.35

Evaluation Metrics. In the aspect-based sentiment classification task, the model is required to predict the sentiment polarity of a target aspect based on the input textimage pair and the generated explanation. We adopt Accuracy and Macro-F1 Score as evaluation metrics to measure the model's overall classification performance across different sentiment categories.

For the explanation generation task, the model must produce a natural language explanation for each aspect, justifying the predicted sentiment polarity. Since the outputs are free-form text, traditional classification metrics are not applicable. We therefore evaluate the generated explanations along two dimensions: semantic consistency and language quality.

First, we use the SentenceTransformer model all-mpnet-base-v2 to compute the cosine similarity between generated explanations and human-written references, which serves as our semantic similarity score. This metric reflects how closely the model's explanation aligns with human understanding.

Second, we introduce a third-party large language model to score each explanation across several dimensions–including completeness, coherence, and logical consistency–on a scale from 0 to 10. This score is designed to approximate a human user's subjective judgment of explanation quality.

5.3 Aspect-Based Sentiment Classification Results

On the Twitter-2015 and Twitter-2017 datasets, our method significantly outperforms five state-of-the-art multimodal baseline models: Llava1.5 [22], Qwen-VL [25], Qwen2-VL [21], MiniCPM-V [26], and Phi3.5-V [23]. When enhanced with the explanations generated by our model, all baseline models exhibit notable improvements in classification accuracy and F1 score, indicating that high-quality explanations help the model better identify the sentiment polarity of each aspect.

Moreover, explanations generated by our fine-tuned model achieve superior downstream performance compared to those generated by the baselines themselves, further validating the effectiveness of our explanation-enhanced training strategy.

Table 4 presents the comparative results of different models on the Twitter-2015 and Twitter-2017 datasets.

In a few-shot setting, our method also demonstrates strong generalization ability. Compared to the zero-shot setup, all models show improvements in both accuracy and F1 score, with a marked reduction in output errors. Notably, the performance gains are even more significant when our generated explanations are included, highlighting the value of high-quality explanations in low-resource scenarios. Detailed results are provided in Table 5.

5.4 Explanation Generation Results

On the explanation test set, our method achieves the best performance across both evaluation metrics: a semantic similarity score of 74.86 and a language model-based quality score of 7.89, both substantially higher than those of baseline models. For instance, Phi3.5-V–the strongest baseline–achieves a similarity score of 74.76 and a quality score of 7.05.

These results confirm that our two-stage training framework significantly improves the model's ability to generate explanations that are not only seman-

Table 4. Results of Different Models on Twitter2015 and Twitter2017 Datasets

Method	Twitter-2015			Twitter-2017		
	Acc	F1	Errors	Acc	F1	Errors
Llava1.5-7B [22]	55.06	43.62	0	55.19	48.26	0
Qwen-VL-7B [25]	48.70	49.49	7.04	47.89	52.29	15.88
Qwen2-VL-7B [21]	64.90	57.36	0.10	55.59	54.67	0.49
MiniCPM-V-2.6-8B [26]	54.48	56.00	2.03	56.08	54.28	1.05
Phi3.5-V-4.2B [23]	49.66	50.91	0	56.00	53.35	0
Llava1.5 [22] + $\text{explain}_{\text{Llava1.5}}$	58.15	56.12	0	54.78	53.42	0
Qwen-VL [25] + $\text{explain}_{\text{Qwen-VL}}$	51.69	36.50	16.88	42.95	35.32	16.77
Qwen2-VL [21] + $\text{explain}_{\text{Qwen2-VL}}$	52.85	53.51	8.68	**59.72**	57.29	7.29
MiniCPM-V [26] + $\text{explain}_{\text{MiniCPM-V}}$	60.08	59.08	0.96	59.16	58.83	0.32
Phi3.5-V [23] + $\text{explain}_{\text{Phi3.5-V}}$	55.16	54.72	0	59.00	58.85	0.24
Llava1.5 [22] + $\text{explain}_{\text{Ours}}$	63.45	58.32	0	56.72	54.56	0
Qwen-VL [25] + $\text{explain}_{\text{Ours}}$	63.36	39.49	0.68	53.08	39.43	1.86
Qwen2-VL [21] + $\text{explain}_{\text{Ours}}$	63.93	55.36	0	57.29	56.36	0
MiniCPM-V [26] + $\text{explain}_{\text{Ours}}$	61.33	**59.62**	3.57	58.32	59.23	2.92
Phi3.5-V [23] + $\text{explain}_{\text{Ours}}$	**64.51**	51.28	0	59.67	**59.72**	0

Table 5. Results of Few-Shot Learning for Different Models on Twitter2015 and Twitter2017 Datasets

Method	Twitter-2015			Twitter-2017		
	Acc	F1	Errors	Acc	F1	Errors
Llava1.5-7B [22]	49.57	45.76	0	53.73	50.72	0
Qwen-VL-7B [25]	53.52	46.58	0.87	57.70	56.47	3.48
Qwen2-VL-7B [21]	66.11	59.75	0	60.21	60.35	0
MiniCPM-V-2.6-8B [26]	58.09	63.18	0.10	60.70	61.32	0.16
Phi3.5-V-4.2B [23]	59.31	58.95	0.10	60.70	60.37	0
Llava1.5 [22] + $\text{explain}_{\text{Llava1.5}}$	55.74	53.57	11.38	53.57	56.73	12.56
Qwen-VL [25] + $\text{explain}_{\text{Qwen-VL}}$	57.09	53.00	0.68	55.43	54.23	1.62
Qwen2-VL [21] + $\text{explain}_{\text{Qwen2-VL}}$	56.70	58.77	3.47	57.62	59.47	3.40
MiniCPM-V [26] + $\text{explain}_{\text{MiniCPM-V}}$	55.26	56.53	0.68	54.46	54.18	0.81
Phi3.5-V [23] + $\text{explain}_{\text{Phi3.5-V}}$	56.70	56.25	0	58.35	57.99	0
Llava1.5 [22] + $\text{explain}_{\text{Ours}}$	64.51	55.23	4.44	56.97	57.10	4.29
Qwen-VL [25] + $\text{explain}_{\text{Ours}}$	66.25	**59.39**	0.29	61.26	56.63	0.24
Qwen2-VL [21] + $\text{explain}_{\text{Ours}}$	66.92	58.21	0	**62.24**	59.72	0
MiniCPM-V [26] + $\text{explain}_{\text{Ours}}$	66.06	58.26	0.48	61.91	58.21	0.16
Phi3.5-V [23] + $\text{explain}_{\text{Ours}}$	**67.21**	57.35	0	61.75	**60.31**	0

Table 6. Performance of Sentiment Explanations Generated by Different Models in Semantic Similarity and Large Model Scoring on the Sentiment Explanation Test Set

Model-Generated Explanation	Semantic Similarity	LLM Quality Score
Llava1.5-7B [22]	71.04	6.34
Qwen-VL-7B [25]	71.62	4.23
Qwen2-VL-7B [21]	70.49	6.75
MiniCPM-V-2.6-8B [26]	73.94	6.64
Phi3.5-V-4.2B [23]	74.76	7.05
Ours Explain	**74.86**	**7.89**

tically aligned with human references but also superior in coherence, logical reasoning, and completeness. Among the baseline models, Phi3.5-V demonstrates relatively strong reasoning ability, though it still lags behind our method. See Table 6 for detailed results.

5.5 Ablation

To assess the contribution of each training component, we conduct an ablation study by removing one module at a time: Direct Preference Optimization (wo-DPO), the Explanation Filter (wo-Filter Model), and Self-Training Fine-tuning (wo-SFT).

The results show that the complete training pipeline yields the best performance in both semantic similarity and language model-based scores. Without DPO, the model struggles to align its outputs with preferred explanations, leading to degraded quality. Removing the filter model, and instead using only positivenegative pairs from earlier stages, limits the diversity and quality of training signals, thus reducing explanation performance. Additionally, skipping the self-training stage and training DPO from scratch leads to poorer results, indicating that the first-stage fine-tuning provides a crucial initialization and convergence foundation for high-quality explanation learning. See Table 7 for the full ablation results.

Table 7. Results of Ablation Experiments on the Sentiment Explanation Test Set

Method	Semantic Similarity	LLM Quality Score
Full Training (Ours)	**74.86**	**7.89**
Supervised Fine-tuning Only (wo-DPO)	70.94	6.86
Without Filter Model (wo-Filter Model)	74.18	6.92
Direct DPO (wo-SFT)	74.39	7.16

6 Conclusion

This paper presents a unified framework for explainable multimodal affective analysis (EMAA), which goes beyond sentiment classification by generating natural language explanations that reflect the reasoning behind model predictions. To achieve this, we design a two-stage training pipeline that combines self-training with supervised fine-tuning and direct preference optimization guided by an explanation quality filter.

We also construct a large-scale preference dataset and introduce a dual-perspective evaluation protocol, combining semantic similarity and LLM-based scoring to assess explanation quality. Experiments on multiple benchmarks show that our method outperforms strong multimodal baselines in both sentiment prediction and explanation generation. Ablation and few-shot experiments further validate the effectiveness and robustness of each module.

Overall, our work advances multimodal affective analysis across modeling, evaluation, and data construction, paving the way toward more interpretable sentiment understanding systems.

In future work, we plan to explore interactive feedback, adaptive preference modeling, and the construction of larger-scale, multi-label, open-domain EMAA datasets. We are also interested in cross-domain and cross-lingual generalization, as well as analyzing hidden states and attention circuits to better understand how explanations improve sentiment recognition.

Acknowledgments. This study was supported by the Headquarters Science and Technology Project of the State Grid Corporation of China (52100125002K-143-ZN).

Disclosure of Interests. The authors have no competing interests to declare that are relevant to the content of this article.

References

1. Moon, S., Neves, L., Carvalho, V.: Multimodal named entity recognition for short social media posts. arXiv preprint arXiv:1802.07862 (2018)
2. Lu, D., Neves, L., Carvalho, V., Zhang, N., Ji, H.: Visual attention model for name tagging in multimodal social media. In: Proceedings of the 56th Annual Meeting of the Association for Computational Linguistics (Volume 1: Long Papers), pp. 1990–1999 (2018)
3. Zhang, Q., Fu, J., Liu, X., Huang, X.: Adaptive co-attention network for named entity recognition in tweets. In: Proceedings of the AAAI Conference on Artificial Intelligence, vol. 32 (2018)
4. Nan, X., Mao, W., Chen, G.: Multi-interactive memory network for aspect based multimodal sentiment analysis. In: Proceedings of the AAAI Conference on Artificial Intelligence, vol. 33, pp. 371–378 (2019)
5. Jianfei, Yu., Jiang, J., Xia, R.: Entity-sensitive attention and fusion network for entity-level multimodal sentiment classification. IEEE/ACM Trans. Audio Speech Lang. Process. **28**, 429–439 (2019)

6. Khan, Z., Fu, Y.: Exploiting bert for multimodal target sentiment classification through input space translation. In: Proceedings of the 29th ACM International Conference on Multimedia, pp. 3034–3042 (2021)
7. Yang, H., Zhao, Y., Qin, B.: Face-sensitive image-to-emotional-text cross-modal translation for multimodal aspect-based sentiment analysis. In: Proceedings of the 2022 Conference on Empirical Methods in Natural Language Processing, pp. 3324–3335 (2022)
8. Wang, X., Tian, J., Gui, M., Li, Z., Ye, J., Yan, M., Xiao, Y.: Promptmner: prompt-based entity-related visual clue extraction and integration for multimodal named entity recognition. In: International Conference on Database Systems for Advanced Applications, pp. 297–305. Springer (2022)
9. Hu, X., Chen, J., Liu, A., Meng, S., Wen, L., Yu, P.S.: Prompt me up: Unleashing the power of alignments for multimodal entity and relation extraction. In: Proceedings of the 31st ACM International Conference on Multimedia, pp. 5185–5194 (2023)
10. Li, J., et al.: Prompting chatgpt in mner: enhanced multimodal named entity recognition with auxiliary refined knowledge. arXiv preprint arXiv:2305.12212 (2023)
11. Ouyang, L., et al.: Training language models to follow instructions with human feedback. Adv. Neural. Inf. Process. Syst. **35**, 27730–27744 (2022)
12. Wang, Y., et al.: Super-naturalinstructions: generalization via declarative instructions on 1600+ nlp tasks. arXiv preprint arXiv:2204.07705 (2022)
13. Lian, Z., et al.: Explainable multimodal emotion recognition. arXiv preprint arXiv:2306.15401 (2023)
14. Lian, Z., Sun, H., Sun, L., Yi, J., Liu, B., Tao, J.: Affectgpt: dataset and framework for explainable multimodal emotion recognition. arXiv preprint arXiv:2407.07653 (2024)
15. Hu, G., Zhu, Z., Hershcovich, D., Hu, L., Seifi, H., Xie, J.: Unimeec: towards unified multimodal emotion recognition and emotion cause. arXiv preprint arXiv:2404.00403 (2024)
16. Li, J., et al.: Think out loud: Emotion deducing explanation in dialogues. arXiv preprint arXiv:2406.04758 (2024)
17. Zheng, W., Xie, Q., Wang, Z., Yu, J., Xia, R.: Towards explainable multimodal depression recognition for clinical interviews. arXiv preprint arXiv:2501.16106 (2025)
18. Zelikman, E., Yuhuai, W., Jesse, M., Goodman, N.: Star: bootstrapping reasoning with reasoning. Adv. Neural. Inf. Process. Syst. **35**, 15476–15488 (2022)
19. Xiao, X., Chenfei, W., Rosenman, S., Lal, V., Che, W., Duan, N.: Bridgetower: building bridges between encoders in vision-language representation learning. In: Proceedings of the AAAI Conference on Artificial Intelligence, vol. 37, pp. 10637–10647 (2023)
20. Niu, T., Zhu, S., Pang, L., El Saddik, A.: Sentiment analysis on multi-view social data. In: MultiMedia Modeling: 22nd International Conference, MMM 2016, Miami, FL, USA, January 4-6, 2016, Proceedings, Part II 22, pp. 15–27. Springer (2016)
21. Wang, P., et al.: Qwen2-vl: enhancing vision-language model's perception of the world at any resolution. arXiv preprint arXiv:2409.12191 (2024)
22. Liu, H., Li, C., Li, Y., Lee, Y.J.: Improved baselines with visual instruction tuning. In: Proceedings of the IEEE/CVF Conference on Computer Vision and Pattern Recognition, pp. 26296–26306 (2024)
23. Abdin, M., et al.: Phi-3 technical report: a highly capable language model locally on your phone. arXiv preprint arXiv:2404.14219 (2024)

24. Wang, X., et al.: Improving named entity recognition by external context retrieving and cooperative learning. arXiv preprint arXiv:2105.03654 (2021)
25. Bai, J., et al.: Qwen-vl: a frontier large vision-language model with versatile abilities. arXiv preprint arXiv:2308.12966, vol. 1, no. 2, p. 3 (2023)
26. Yao, Y., et al.: Minicpm-v: a gpt-4v level mllm on your phone. arXiv preprint arXiv:2408.01800 (2024)

Emotional Stylization Based on Diffusion Models

Jingyuan Yang[1], Yiwang Zhong[2(✉)], Jianling Jin[3], and Zeyu Li[4]

[1] College of Computer Science and Software Engineering (CSSE), Shenzhen University, 3688 Nanhai Avenue, Shenzhen 518060, China

[2] School of Computing and Data Science (CDS), The University of Hong Kong, Pokfulam 999077, Hong Kong, China

u3665879@connect.hku.hk

[3] Shenzhen Institute for Advanced Study, University of Electronic Science and Technology of China, Shenzhen 518110, China

[4] College of Electronics and Information Engineering(CEIE), Shenzhen University, 3688 Nanhai Avenue, Shenzhen 518060, China

Abstract. In recent years, deep learning based image generation has progressed beyond traditional pixel-level reconstruction toward semantically controllable content synthesis. In emotional stylization, diffusion models, with their progressive denoising mechanism and high-fidelity generation capability, have introduced new possibilities for emotion-aware image stylization. However, emotion, as a high-level semantic concept, exhibits subjectivity and ambiguity when mapped to visual stylistic attributes such as color tone and texture patterns. Consequently, existing methods face challenges in achieving precise emotional expressiveness and style controllability. To address these issues, this paper proposes an emotional stylization framework based on Stable Diffusion, integrating the ControlNet architecture with a Low-Rank Adaptation (LoRA) fine-tuning strategy. Specifically, the UNet module within the diffusion model is directionally optimized using the ArtEmis style-emotion dataset to learn the correspondence between emotional semantics and artistic styles through color dynamics and texture features. Experimental results demonstrate that the proposed method effectively enhances emotional expressiveness, style controllability, and semantic consistency, outperforming existing approaches in emotional stylization.

Keywords: Emotional Stylization · Diffusion Model · ControlNet · LoRA

1 Introduction

1.1 Background

In recent years, deep learning has enabled significant progress in image generation. Following the introduction of Generative Adversarial Networks (GAN) [1] and influential variants such as StyleGAN [2] and BigGAN [3], image synthesis models have achieved rapid improvements and have been applied in creative domains including digital art, visual media effects, and virtual content creation. Nonetheless, GAN-based approaches

H. Liu et al. (Eds.): CEI 2025, CCIS 2881, pp. 194–212, 2026.
https://doi.org/10.1007/978-981-95-9493-1_13

are known to exhibit challenges such as mode collapse and sensitivity to training instability, which can restrict output diversity and affect generation reliability, particularly in high-resolution synthesis settings.

Diffusion-based methods [4], represented by DDPM [5], Latent Diffusion Models (LDM) [6], and implementations of Stable Diffusion, have emerged as promising alternatives due to their progressive denoising formulation, comparatively stable training behavior, and strong capacity for modeling complex image distributions. These methods have shown competitive performance in generating visually detailed and high-resolution images, motivating their exploration for style-driven and perceptually sensitive generation tasks.

In the context of emotional stylization, both visual style transfer and emotion-aware image editing are active and evolving research directions. Prior studies suggest that shifts in color tone, texture patterns, illumination, and contrast can influence affective perception, though accurately mapping latent emotional intent to explicit visual attributes remains intrinsically ambiguous and subjective. Many existing approaches operate on global or coarse-grained style representations (e.g., single latent style vector or imprecise text guidance), which can make localized control over image properties—such as region-level texture, spatial contrast distribution, color balance, and structural boundaries—difficult to regulate independently. Additionally, editing operations that are not structure-aware may risk degrading semantic coherence or disrupting fine-grained layout fidelity, an issue also observed in diffusion pipelines lacking dedicated conditional preservation mechanisms.

To address these challenges more reliably, we propose an emotional stylization framework built on Stable Diffusion, integrating ControlNet [7] to support layout-conditioned generation with spatial structure priors, and adopting LoRA [9]-based fine-tuning with an emotion-labeled subset derived from the ArtEmis dataset [8] to increase sensitivity to fine-grained emotional style patterns in the UNet backbone. By combining conditional structure preservation and emotion-profiled low-rank adaptation, the framework aims to support perceptually relevant emotional style transfer while retaining local layout constraints.

In summary, the main contributions of our work are:

(i) We present additional empirical observations on emotional stylization by analyzing how visual attributes (including color distribution, texture tendency, and illumination characteristics) can correlate with perceptual emotional style signals, while discussing limitations in semantic coherence and structure maintenance seen in prior global-style or non-conditioned pipelines.
(ii) We implement a framework combining progressive denoising, spatial structure conditioning, and emotional low-rank adaptation to support more disentangled control and adaptation toward perceptually relevant emotional visual styles.
(iii) We provide both quantitative and qualitative results showing that this pipeline can support emotion-consistent style tendencies under layout conditions, with competitive reliability compared to common one-stage global-style or text-coarse guidance pipelines. While not exhaustively benchmarking all recent models, initial comparisons motivate the framework's feasibility for artistic and interactive visual stylization applications.

2 Related Work

2.1 Visual Affective Computing

Visual affective computing, as an interdisciplinary field between computer vision and affective computing, aims to establish a computable mapping between visual features and human emotional experiences. Its core goal is to analyze how visual elements such as color, texture, and composition in images or videos influence human emotional states, enabling emotion-guided content generation and editing.

In recent years, the focus of visual affective computing has gradually shifted from emotion recognition to generation and editing. Researchers have explored decoupling emotional semantics into actionable visual features for fine-grained emotion control. Notably, the release of large-scale datasets such as ArtEmis, containing 81,000 artistic images with emotional annotations, and EmoSet, which includes six emotion attributes such as brightness, color, and scene, has significantly advanced emotion-visual mapping research and semantic-embedding-based emotion generation models.

From a technical perspective, multimodal fusion has become a key approach to overcoming the ambiguity of emotional expression. EmoGen innovatively combines CLIP's multimodal alignment with diffusion models, constructing an emotional semantic tree to map abstract emotions to concrete visual parameters. Its emotion attention mechanism dynamically adjusts the intensity of emotional expression in different regions, improving accuracy. Furthermore, conditional control frameworks like ControlNet enable emotion editing while maintaining structural consistency, with edge-guided generation effectively avoiding common semantic distortions.

Despite significant progress, the field still faces challenges such as the subjectivity of emotion annotations and difficulties in modeling cross-cultural differences. Future directions may focus on neuroscience-inspired evaluation frameworks and causal disentanglement of emotional features. These advancements not only foster innovation in artistic creation and digital therapy but also provide theoretical support for developing more human-centered human-computer interaction systems.

2.2 Diffusion Models

In the early stage of image generation, Generative Adversarial Networks (GANs) and Variational Autoencoders (VAEs) [10] were widely used, each with advantages and limitations. GANs can generate high-quality images through adversarial training between the generator and discriminator but often suffer from mode collapse and unstable training. VAEs provide training stability via probabilistic modeling in the latent space, but generated images tend to lack fine details.

To overcome these limitations, Sohl-Dickstein et al. proposed the diffusion model theory based on non-equilibrium thermodynamics, demonstrating for the first time that images can be generated using a forward diffusion process and a reverse denoising process, laying a solid theoretical foundation for subsequent diffusion models. Ho et al. introduced Denoising Diffusion Probabilistic Models (DDPMs), improving image quality and clarity through Markov chain assumptions and reparameterization. Zhang et al. further incorporated conditional control mechanisms, allowing external guidance such as text to steer the generation process, expanding diffusion models toward intelligent and diverse applications [11–14].

The rise of diffusion models has also significantly impacted style transfer. Early style transfer methods relied on convolutional neural networks, extracting content and style features (e.g., Gram matrices proposed by Gatys et al.) [15], but they lacked fine detail fidelity and flexibility. With diffusion models achieving impressive results in image generation, researchers began applying them to style transfer. Zhang et al. [16] proposed an inversion-based approach that reconstructs images in latent space and utilizes intermediate diffusion representations to achieve more natural style transfer while preserving content structure. To further enhance control and diversity, Jeong et al. [17] introduced a training-free style transfer method using the latent semantic representation of diffusion models, enabling style transfer without additional training. Additionally, Deng et al. [18], Hertz et al. [19], and Chung et al. [17] employed Transformer architectures, shared attention modules, and style injection strategies during training to improve style transfer accuracy and stability.

Moreover, cross-modal conditional methods, such as text-guided style transfer [20, 21], have expanded application scenarios, demonstrating that diffusion models can ensure high-quality outputs while supporting diverse and intelligent image editing. Inspired by these studies, this work fine-tunes a pre-trained Stable Diffusion model using LoRA, aiming to explore the intrinsic relationship between image style and emotional expression, and apply it to emotion-prompt-guided style transfer tasks.

2.3 LoRA Models

LoRA (Low-Rank Adaptation) is a parameter-efficient fine-tuning method based on low-rank matrix decomposition, designed to address the computational and storage bottlenecks of full fine-tuning large pre-trained models. Its core idea is to freeze the original model weights and introduce low-rank update matrices to learn task-specific representations. This approach significantly reduces the number of trainable parameters and memory requirements while largely preserving model performance. Comparisons on multiple datasets show that LoRA maintains or even surpasses the performance of conventional fine-tuning methods, demonstrating superior scalability and adaptability. These advantages have made LoRA a prominent approach in parameter-efficient fine-tuning and widely adopted across various tasks.

Originally, LoRA achieved remarkable success in natural language processing. Compared with full fine-tuning, it requires updating only a small subset of parameters for efficient transfer learning. For instance, applying LoRA to large language models like GPT-3 reduces the number of trainable parameters to 1/10,000 of the original, with minimal impact on inference latency. Subsequent studies [22–24] further improved LoRA's parameter efficiency and generalization ability.

In this work, we leverage LoRA to efficiently fine-tune a pre-trained Stable Diffusion model on a dataset of specific emotional styles, introducing low-rank updates in the UNet architecture to learn fine-grained emotional style features while keeping original weights frozen, which significantly reduces training costs and improves performance on tasks such as style control, emotion guidance, and structural reconstruction, with easy integration into existing architectures like ControlNet and T2I-Adapter.

3 Method

3.1 Data Preprocessing

We constructed an emotion-annotated artwork dataset using ArtEmis annotations derived from the WikiArt image collection. To support a more focused analysis of the intrinsic relationship between visual style and emotion, face-centric images and images dominated by objects that could induce semantic interference were excluded using automated face detection, supplemented with manual screening and review. CLIP was adopted to extract image semantic embeddings, capturing high-level semantics such as scene, composition, and perceptual style cues. Within each emotion category, K-means clustering was applied to these embeddings to uncover intra-class semantic groupings. This provides a data-driven basis for more targeted emotional feature learning, model fine-tuning, and controlled emotion-aware style transfer.

Dataset Classification and Filtering

This study leverages the ArtEmis dataset built on WikiArt, which includes 80,031 unique artworks by 1,119 artists, spanning 27 artistic styles (e.g., Abstract, Baroque, Cubism, Impressionism) and 45 genres (e.g., cityscape, landscape, still life, portrait). Each artwork contains dominant emotional labels supported by at least five annotators, along with brief text explanations for emotional responses. Emotional annotations are organized into eight primary emotion categories—negative (Anger, Disgust, Fear, Sadness) and positive (Amusement, Awe, Contentment, Excitement)—and an additional category "Something else" for unlisted affective perceptions.

For emotion classification, the most frequently assigned emotion label is taken as the dominant category for each image. if multiple labels have the same frequency, the image is assigned to all corresponding categories. Since many artworks contain human figures whose facial expressions and body gestures strongly influence emotional perception, face detection was applied to remove most images containing people. However, due to the abstract nature of art, some figures may not be reliably detected, and certain objects (e.g., flames, birds) can also strongly influence annotators' emotions, potentially interfering with the style-emotion relationship analysis.

Since our goal is to study the relationship between image style and emotion rather than object-driven emotional effects, retaining images dominated by specific objects could mislead the model. To reduce non-style influences, we applied automated filtering and manual review to remove such images. After multiple rounds of screening, approximately 20,000 images were retained for subsequent model training, ensuring the dataset accurately reflects the intrinsic association between style and emotion.

Fine-Grained CLIP-Based Clustering with K-means

The CLIP [26] model is a vision–language contrastive representation framework that learns aligned high-dimensional embeddings for images and their textual descriptions in a shared latent space. CLIP consists of an image encoder and a text encoder, trained to maximize similarity for matched image-text pairs while reducing it for non-matched pairs. We measure embedding alignment using cosine similarity:

$$\cos(v_i, v_t) = \frac{v_i \cdot v_t}{|v_i| \cdot |v_t|} \tag{3.1}$$

In the formula, v_i and v_t represent the feature vectors of the image and text respectively. This contrastive formulation allows CLIP to capture perceptual semantics, including scene, composition patterns, and affect-correlated visual signals, making it suitable for intra-class emotion-aware subdivision.

K-means [27] is a classic unsupervised clustering algorithm whose goal is to divide the dataset into k clusters to minimize the distance between data points in each cluster and the cluster center while making the clusters far away from each other. Specifically, given a dataset and a preset number of clusters k, the objective function optimized by the algorithm is:

$$\min_{\mu_1,\mu_2,\ldots,\mu_k} \sum_{i=1}^{k} \sum_{x \in C_i} \|x - \mu_i\|^2 \tag{3.2}$$

And μ_k represents the center (mean vector) of the k-th cluster, and C_k is the set of all data points in the k-th cluster.

First, randomly initialize and select k initial centroids. Then perform cluster assignment, calculate the Euclidean distance between each data point and all cluster centers, assign the data point to the nearest cluster, and re-calculate the centroid of the cluster.

$$\mu_i = \frac{1}{|C_i|} \sum_{x \in C_i} x_i C_i = \{x : \|x - \mu_i\|^2 \leq \|x - \mu_j\|^2, \forall j \neq i\} \tag{3.3}$$

Then repeat the cluster assignment and center update process until the centroid change is below a preset threshold or the maximum number of iterations is reached. This optimization process can effectively divide samples in the high-dimensional feature space into several semantically consistent categories, but the clustering effect is highly dependent on the selection of the number of clusters and the setting of initial centroids.

In this study, we first encode images using the CLIP model, mapping them into a unified high-dimensional semantic space to obtain embeddings that capture both low-level visual content and high-level semantics. For each emotion category, we then perform K-means clustering on these embeddings to divide images into several sub-clusters. Before clustering, L2 normalization is applied so that cosine similarity can be used for cluster assignment, which better reflects semantic similarity in the normalized high-dimensional space than directly using Euclidean distance. During iterations, each data point is assigned to the cluster with the highest cosine similarity, and centroids are updated until convergence (Fig. 1).

In our experiments, four positive emotions are clustered into ten sub-clusters in total. The choice of $k = 10$ is based on empirical observations: a smaller k tends to merge semantically different styles within the same emotion category, while a much larger k leads to over-fragmented clusters and unstable sub-cluster assignment. Setting $k = 10$ provides a reasonable trade-off between cluster compactness and style diversity, and yields interpretable emotion-related sub-clusters for subsequent model adaptation.

This method reveals the fine-grained semantic structure within each emotional category, grouping images with similar semantics into the same sub-clusters. It helps analyze intra-category visual differences and enables more accurate learning and transfer of emotional features. For example, in the "Contentment" category, images with similar content, such as mountains or port scenes, are clustered together. By computing cosine similarity between an input image and cluster centers, the closest sub-cluster can be efficiently identified, supporting precise category matching and model fine-tuning (Fig. 2).

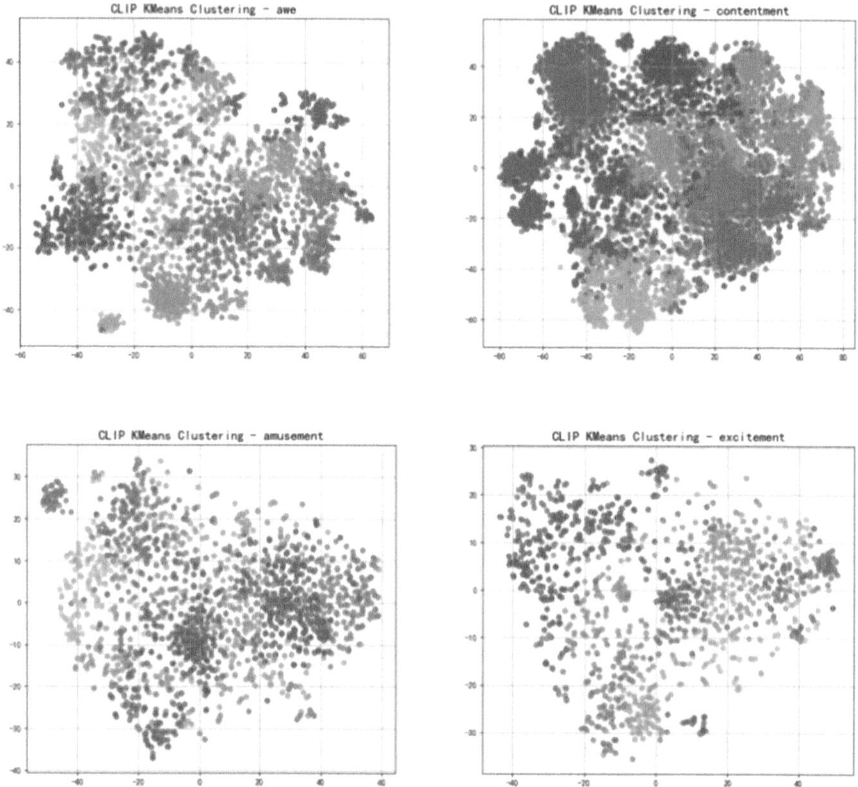

Fig. 1. Positive emotion clustering results

3.2 ControlNet

Large text-to-image generation models, such as Stable Diffusion, demonstrate impressive visual quality and versatility. However, their reliance on short text prompts often limits users' ability to precisely control image details and structural information. This limitation becomes particularly evident when handling fine-grained conditional inputs, such as edge maps, segmentation masks, human poses, or depth maps. Under these conditions, conventional models cannot achieve the desired level of prompt precision or fine-grained control, which restricts their practical use in tasks requiring detailed structure or exact content alignment.

Zhang et al. introduced ControlNet as a conditional diffusion control architecture that preserves pre-trained knowledge while injecting structural priors through a parallel learned control branch. ControlNet clones the backbone network into locked weights and trainable weights. The locked copy remains fixed to maintain model priors from large-scale pre-training. The trainable copy learns only conditional integration behavior, thereby preventing dominant backbone features from being unintentionally altered while enabling conditional signals to contribute additively. This design prevents harmful noise

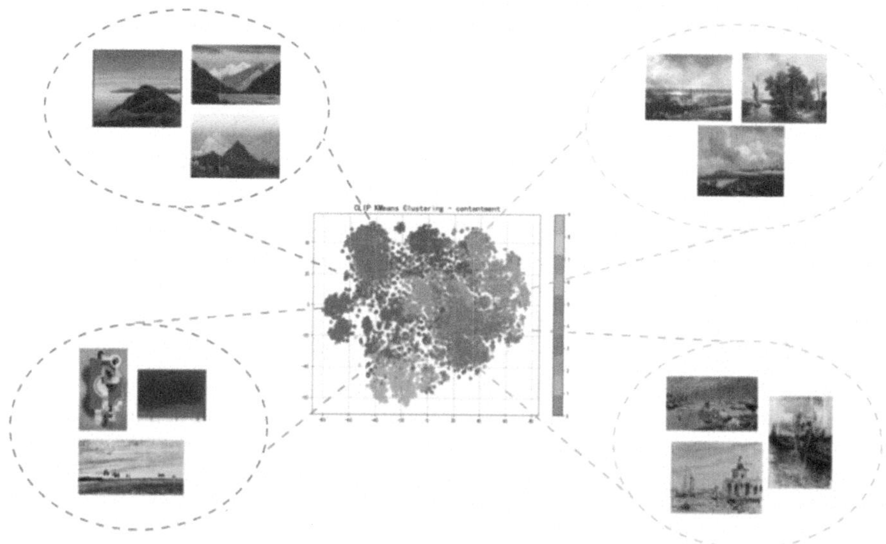

Fig. 2. Contentment clustering examples

from affecting the deep features of the large diffusion backbone while enabling precise, fine-grained control over the generated images.

ControlNet also introduces a zero-convolution layer, initialized with near-zero weights, allowing conditional guidance to begin with minimal perturbation on deep features, and progressively amplify its impact during training. Formally, let the original diffusion noise prediction be $\epsilon(\mathrm{y}, \mathrm{x_t}, \mathrm{t}, \mathrm{y})$, where $\mathrm{x_t}$ is the current noisy image, t is the time step, and y is other conditional information such as text prompts. On this basis, ControlNet adds a conditional feature $\Delta \mathrm{f_c}(\mathrm{x_t}, \mathrm{t}, \mathrm{c})$ extracted by the control network, where c represents additional control conditions (such as edges, segmentation, or key point maps), making the entire noise prediction process:

$$\epsilon(y, \mathrm{x_t}, t, y, c) = \epsilon_0(\mathrm{x_t}, t, y) + \int \Delta c(\mathrm{x_t}, t, c) \tag{3.4}$$

The introduction of the zero convolution layer ensures that the control branch has minimal impact on the entire generation process in the initial stage. As training proceeds, its contribution is gradually amplified, thereby realizing a smooth transition from global pre-trained knowledge to local precise control.

From a mathematical perspective, diffusion model training involves two main processes: the forward process, which gradually adds noise to data, and the reverse process, which restores the original image from noise. The model's objective is to accurately predict the added noise at each step, typically measured by mean squared error, so that the reverse process can reconstruct the original image.

$$\mathrm{L_{simple}} = \mathbb{E}_{\mathrm{x_t},\mathrm{t}} \|\epsilon - \epsilon_0(\mathrm{x_t}, t)\|^2 \tag{3.5}$$

After introducing ControlNet, the loss function is also extended to a conditional version (Formula 3.8). When calculating the prediction error, the control condition c mentioned above is introduced as the input of the model.

$$L = \mathbb{E}_{x_t,t,y,c} \|\epsilon - \epsilon_0(x_t, t, y, c)\|^2 \tag{3.6}$$

The mean square error is still used to measure the difference between the predicted and real noise, but here it is calculated on noise predictions that include additional control information. This design allows the model not only to learn image recovery from noise across different time steps but also to leverage control conditions for more accurate noise prediction, effectively constraining image details and structures while preserving content.

Building on this, the study uses Canny, Softedge, Lineart, Depth Map, and Segmentation as conditional inputs to ControlNet, paired with their official pre-trained models, providing multi-dimensional structural constraints for the diffusion model. To assess the impact of different control conditions, systematic experiments are conducted across multiple emotional categories and semantic scenes, evaluating the model's performance in content consistency and computational overhead. Effect diagrams are presented below (Fig. 3).

Fig. 3. Comparison of effects of various input conditions

Experimental results indicate that depth maps preserve global spatial hierarchy but are sensitive to noise, particularly for distant content. Segmentation maps strongly separate semantic regions but require high inference-time memory and compute overhead, making large-batch inference challenging.For edge-based conditional forms (Canny, Softedge, Lineart), experiments show similar baseline structural constraints, while Canny signals provide more complete contours, better edge continuity, and higher texture-relevant detail retention.

Considering editing performance, detail retention, and computational cost, this study selects Canny maps as the main ControlNet condition, offering stable and reliable structural guidance for emotional style transfer.

3.3 LoRA-Based Fine-Tuning

As introduced in the related work on the LoRA algorithm in Sect. 2, LoRA is mainly proposed to address the high-cost parameter adaptation problem of pre-trained deep learning models. Traditional fine-tuning approaches need to update the full network parameters, which incurs heavy GPU memory and computation overhead. To mitigate this, LoRA freezes the primary parameters of the pre-trained backbone and injects trainable low-rank matrix updates as an additive weight increment ΔW for each layer. This allows lightweight directional adaptation without disturbing the original knowledge stored in W_0. The training principle is shown in Fig. 4.

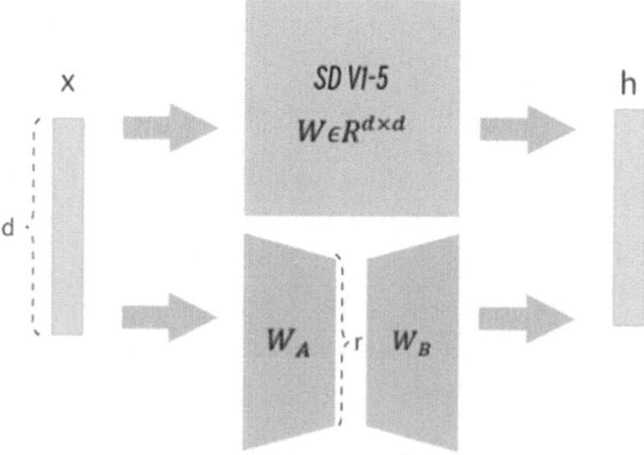

Fig. 4. LoRA training

Specifically, for a given layer with a main weight matrix W_0, directly updating these $d \times k$ parameters is expensive and may interfere with the pre-training prior. LoRA approximates task-specific style offsets by decomposing ΔW into a product of two smaller trainable matrices, so that it can be efficiently optimized while W_0 stays unchanged. The formulation and variables are shown below:

$$\mathrm{W}^* = \mathrm{W}_0 + \alpha \Delta W, \mathrm{W}_0 \in \mathbb{R}^{\mathrm{d} \times \mathrm{k}} \tag{3.7}$$

$$\Delta W = BA, B \in \mathbb{R}^{\mathrm{d} \times \mathrm{r}}, A \in \mathbb{R}^{\mathrm{r} \times \mathrm{k}} \tag{3.8}$$

$$\mathrm{W}^* = \mathrm{W}_0 + \alpha BA \tag{3.9}$$

This design captures task-relevant style information via $\Delta W = BA$, reducing trainable parameters from the $\mathrm{d} \times \mathrm{k}$ scale to $(\mathrm{d} + \mathrm{k}) \times \mathrm{r}$. The hyperparameter r affects the representational capacity for emotional style attributes such as color and texture, while α balances the fusion strength to avoid early instability. Since only ΔW is optimized, image spatial structure and core semantics are not overwritten (Fig. 5).

The artwork dataset is first grouped into eight emotion categories using CLIP embeddings, then subdivided into semantically consistent sub-clusters for fine-grained routing. Up to 100 images per cluster are selected, and WD-generated labels are standardized via automation and manual correction. Independent LoRA increments are learned for each cluster within the Stable Diffusion v1.5 framework, forming emotion-exclusive, cluster-exclusive plug-and-play weight adaptations, which act as lightweight editors during inference. This supports heterogeneous artwork scenes to obtain stable modulation of emotional style under emotion prompts with low structural mutation.

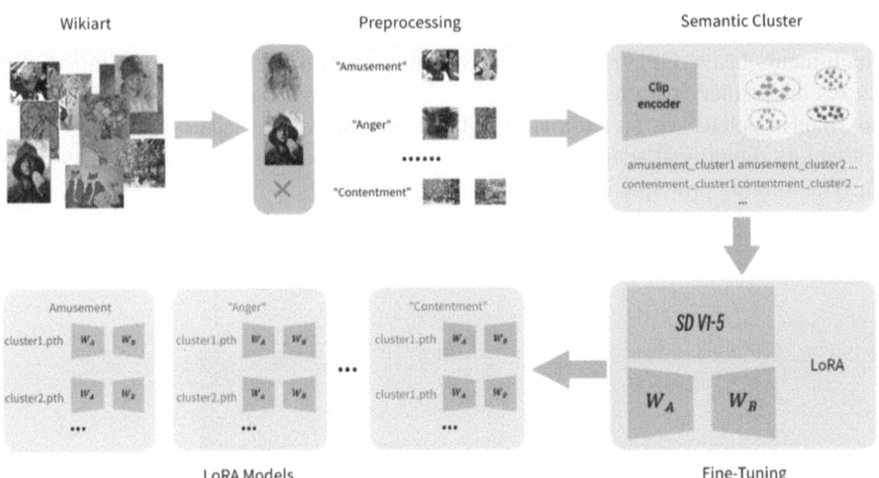

Fig. 5. Data preprocessing and LoRA training pipeline

Experimental observations confirm that this pipeline enhances routing reliability and emotional-style stability across diverse semantic scenes and complex artwork content, verifying its adaptability and effectiveness for emotion-controlled image style enhancement tasks.

3.4 Stable Diffusion-Based Image Emotion Stylization

This study selects Stable Diffusion v1.5 (SD v1.5) as the foundation to build an emotion-aware image style editing system. Although SD v1.5 offers strong generative capability and supports prompt-driven guidance, it is not inherently optimized for emotional style modulation, especially across highly diverse artistic content. To address this, the system accepts an input image and a concise emotional prompt to generate an output that reflects the target emotional style while preserving structure (Fig. 6).

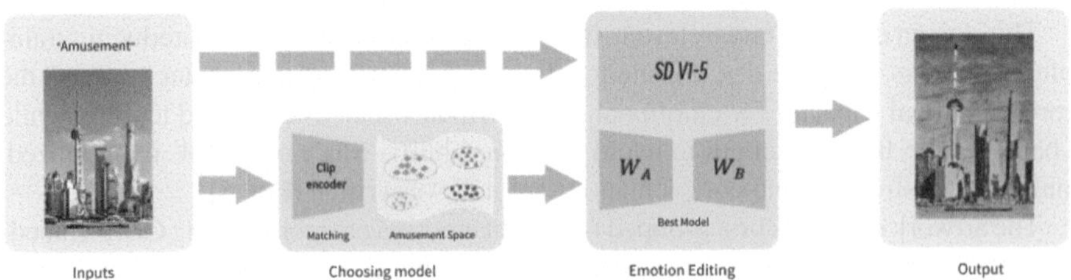

Fig. 6. Inference Process

During inference, the CLIP visual encoder turns the input image into a high-dimensional feature vector, which acts as a routing index into the clustered emotion space from Sect. 3.1. By measuring distances to cluster centers, the system selects the closest emotion cluster and its LoRA sub-model. This process is strictly for model selection, not for interpreting or altering the image's core semantic identity. The selected LoRA weights are loaded and combined with SD model to form a customized latent-space style editor, and conditional prompts guide iterative style modulation with minimal impact on structure.

Under the joint effect of SD and the routed LoRA module, the system performs perceptually natural emotion-tendency style editing while retaining dominant content semantics. Experimental verification indicates improved adaptability and inference stability for emotion-conditioned style transfer, supporting the overall feasibility and consistency of the pipeline and the fixed-seed routing strategy, without asserting universal optimality.

4 Results

4.1 Editing Effect

In diffusion-based emotional image generation, empirical experiments indicate that initial noise maps and random seeds influence local texture, lighting, and global style, which may introduce variance in emotional-style consistency.

To improve stability, this study applies a multi-seed sampling and evaluation protocol within each of the eight predefined emotion categories. Instead of defining the seed empirically, multiple random seeds are tested to generate a pool of candidate outputs for every emotion cluster. These candidates are then evaluated holistically, considering how naturally they reflect the target emotion prompt, how coherent and visually harmonious the resulting style appears, and whether the original structural semantics are preserved without quality degradation. The seed that achieves the most balanced emotional alignment and visual quality is selected and fixed for subsequent generation, ensuring more stable and consistent emotion-driven style editing (Fig. 7).

It can be observed from the figure that for each emotion present both distinct emotional visual traits and stable appearance quality. For example, Amusement images tend toward high saturation, vivid colors, and relaxed impressions. Awe emphasizes bright, open spatial compositions to convey visual scale and impact. And Fear adopts low brightness and high contrast dark tones to express tension without copying literal objects or layouts from any reference image.

Overall, the generated images exhibit natural emotional expressiveness, strong style coherence, and stable content structure, confirming the method's reliability for emotional style editing tasks.

4.2 Comparision

This study aims to realize the editing of image style and expressiveness based on emotion control. Its core goal is not only to change the style features of images but also to enhance the naturalness and consistency of emotional expression. Given that the implementation mechanism of this method has certain similarities with traditional style transfer methods, this section selects three representative image style transfer models

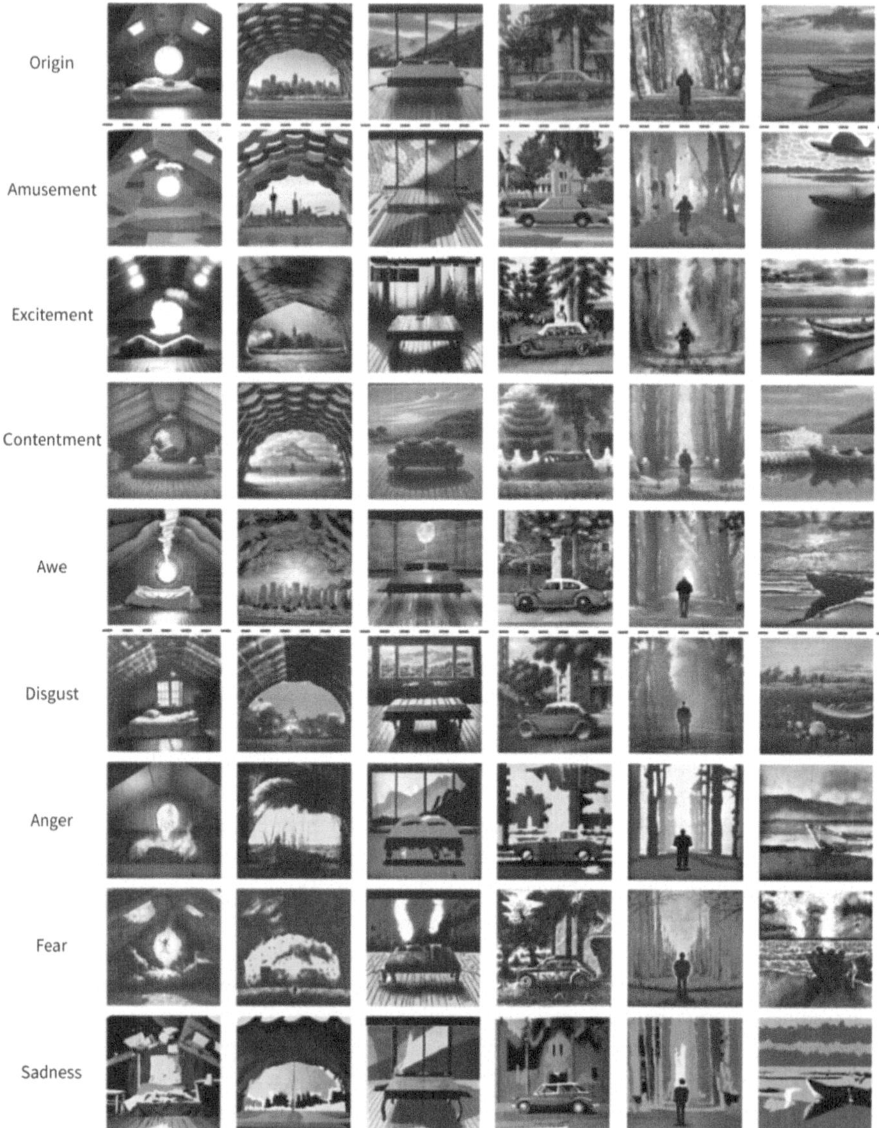

Fig. 7. Emotional stylization results based on our study

StyledID [28], StyleShot [29], and AdaIN [28] as comparative baselines, and compares their performance from both qualitative and quantitative aspects.

Qualitative Comparison

Considering that traditional style transfer methods rely on a style image while this method uses target emotion labels as conditional prompts, we manually select a representative style image from each emotion category for comparison in multi-emotion style editing tasks. Figure 8 shows the generation effect comparison between this method and three traditional models.

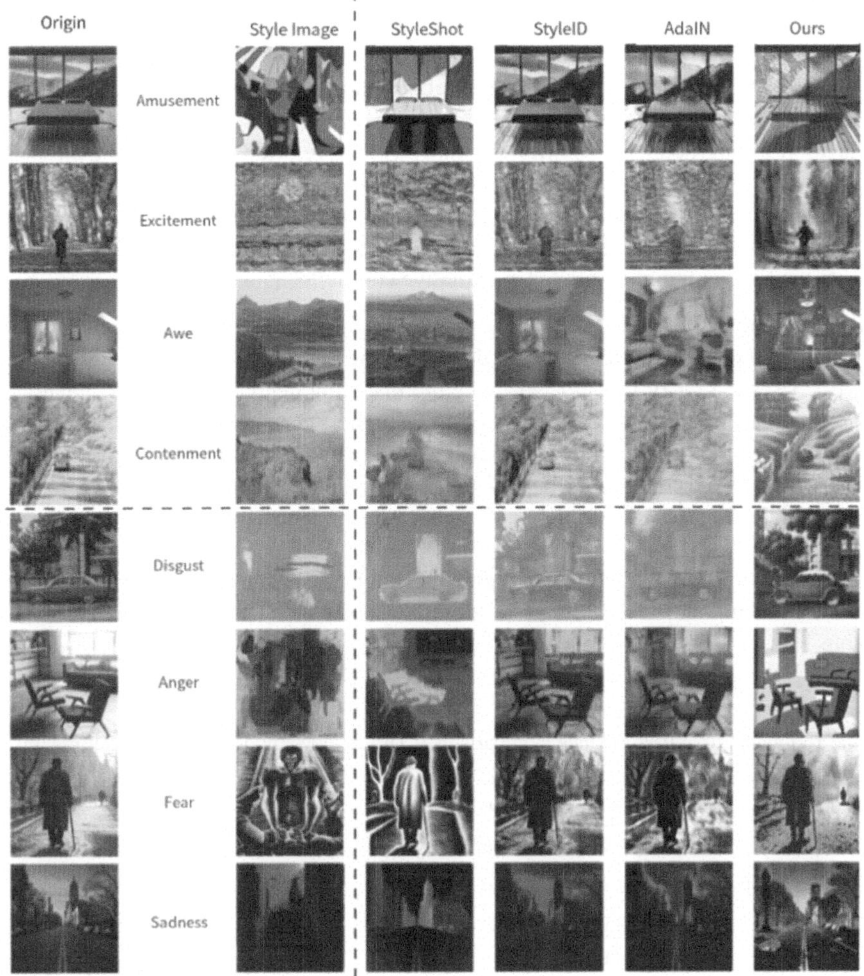

Fig. 8. Comparison of generation effects with three style transfer methods

From the results, traditional methods often transfer textures and colors directly from the style image, which can cause unbalanced proportions and abrupt styles without emotional guidance. For example, AdaIN shows rigid color coverage and unnatural texture mixing. StyleID improves local style expression but struggles to maintain overall content. And StyleShot's semantic module is ineffective with default descriptions, limiting expressive results.

In contrast, the proposed method integrates both image content semantics and multi-dimensional style representations for the target emotion, enabling conditional style adjustment based on emotion. This preserves the original content structure while incorporating style elements consistent with the target emotion, improving visual coherence and emotional accuracy. The generated images appear more natural and visually appealing, balancing diversity and consistency effectively.

Quantitative Comparison
Different from traditional style transfer pipelines, the emotion-guided stylization in this work does not depend exclusively on reference style images, and instead conditions stylization through concise emotion prompts. Therefore, the style similarity measurement methods commonly used in traditional style transfer tasks (such as Gram matrix, style loss, etc.) are not applicable to the evaluation needs of this experiment. To more comprehensively evaluate the actual performance of each method in this task, this study selects the following indicators for quantitative comparison:

PSNR: Measures the pixel-level similarity between the generated image and the original image. A higher value indicates better detail retention.
CLIP-I: Uses the CLIP model to evaluate the matching degree between the generated image and the emotion/semantic description. A higher score indicates that the semantic information of the generated image is more consistent with the original image.
Emo-A: Counts the consistency between the emotional label conveyed by the generated image and the target emotional label. A higher value indicates more accurate emotional expression.
Emo-S: Examines the coherence and unity of emotional expression in various parts of the image. A higher value indicates a more consistent overall emotional performance (Table 1).

Table 1. Quantitative Performance Comparison of Different Methods in Emotion Editing Tasks

Method	PSNR↑	CLIP-I↑	Emo-A↑	Emo-S↑
StyleID [28]	12.382	**0.774**	26.00%	0.116
StyleShot [29]	8.133	0.585	34.25%	0.179
AdaIN [28]	11.331	0.698	27.50%	0.104
Ours	**12.335**	0.663	**34.38%**	**0.182**

From the table, the PSNR results indicate that this method shows slightly higher detail retention than StyleID, and maintains clearer textural fidelity compared to StyleShot and AdaIN. Although the CLIP-I similarity is lower than StyleID, the score still suggests reasonable semantic alignment, while StyleID may capture high embedding similarity without explicitly accounting for affective coherence, which can make its similarity score less indicative for emotion-conditioned stylization. The Emo-A and Emo-S metrics show that this method demonstrates stronger alignment with the target emotion prompt and more globally coherent emotional style tendencies among the compared pipelines.

In summary, while traditional methods have advantages in certain visual aspects, their reliance on a single style image and structural limitations hinder fine and consistent emotion transfer. In contrast, the proposed method effectively integrates emotional semantics with visual style, preserves content structure, and achieves superior image expressiveness and emotional accuracy, showing strong application potential and research value.

4.3 Ablation Experiments

To verify the effectiveness of the data processing workflow, ablation experiments were conducted to assess the impact of each stage on generation quality, including emotion classification, face removal and manual screening, and fine-grained clustering. For each stage, a corresponding LoRA model was trained and evaluated:

Stage 1: Classify the WikiArt dataset into eight emotion categories and train 8 emotion-driven LoRA models.
Stage 2: Based on Stage 1, remove face images and perform manual screening, then train 8 optimized LoRA models.
Stage 3: Based on Stage 2, perform fine-grained clustering within each emotion category, resulting in 80 LoRA models with high-consistency styles.

In the above three stages, the same test set is used for image generation, and the generation results are quantitatively evaluated and qualitatively analyzed from multiple dimensions (such as CLIP-I, LPIPS, Emo-A, etc.). The generation results are shown in Fig. 9.

Fig. 9. Ablation study of the three stages

The figure shows that staged data processing progressively improves emotional style expression. In the first stage, generated images differ little due to mismatches between emotion labels and overall style, making emotional expression vague. After face removal and manual screening in the second stage, style boundaries become clearer, with noticeable differences in color and texture. In the final stage, fine-grained clustering further enhances emotional distinguishability, clarifying the link between style features and emotions and significantly strengthening the model's ability to convey emotional styles (Table 2).

Table 2. Quantitative Comparison of Model Performance Across Three Stages of Data Processing

Stage	PSNR↑	CLIP-I↑	Emo-A↑	Emo-S↑
1	12.27	**0.699**	21.75%	0.0669
2	12.311	0.657	26.50%	0.108
3	**12.45**	0.663	**34.38%**	**0.1819**

Emo-A and Emo-S show steady increases from 21.75% to 34.38% and 0.0669 to 0.1819, indicating stronger affect-related feature aggregation and more consistent perceptual style coherence across image regions. PSNR shows only minor variation, as it measures fidelity to the input image's original structure and semantics, which are not directly targeted for modulation in this study. Since the proposed stylization pipeline conditions style primarily through perceptual attributes such as color tone, light patterns, and texture tendencies rather than semantic identity, the overall layout and key semantics remain largely preserved, leading to limited impact on PSNR while enabling measurable shifts in affect-aligned style consistency across stages.

5 Discussion and Conclusion

This study introduces an emotional stylization framework built on Stable Diffusion and LoRA, incorporating dataset preprocessing, sub-clustering in the CLIP embedding space, and LoRA fine-tuning aligned with emotional categories. During inference, input images are first analyzed for emotion-related cues, after which LoRA weights with close semantic affinity are selected and integrated into the base diffusion model to enable emotion-conditioned stylization. Experimental results indicate that the framework can maintain core image content while reflecting emotional attributes through variations in color, texture, and style, offering a feasible and practical approach compared to traditional style transfer methods.

While the current results are encouraging, several limitations remain. The effectiveness of content preservation depends on the interaction between ControlNet conditions and prompt guidance, and determining an optimal balance is still an open challenge. Parameter exploration in this study is relatively constrained by available computational resources, suggesting potential for future improvement via broader or automated hyperparameter optimization. Additionally, some emotional styles exhibit similarity in their visual expression, particularly among categories with shared valence, which may be influenced by the granularity of annotations and dataset composition.

Future work could focus on refined data selection, more detailed labeling of emotional nuance, and enhanced representations of emotion-aware style features, with the goal of expanding stylistic diversity and increasing fidelity of emotional expression. These directions may help further improve the expressiveness and robustness of diffusion-based emotional stylization.

Acknowledgements. This work was supported in parts by NSFC (62302312) and Guangdong Science and Technology Program (2023A1515011440).

References

1. Goodfellow, I.J., Pouget-Abadie, J., Mirza, M., et al.: Generative adversarial nets. Adv. Neural Inf. Process. Syst. **27** (2014)
2. Karras, T., Laine, S., Aila, T.: A style-based generator architecture for generative adversarial networks. In: Proceedings of the IEEE/CVF Conference on Computer Vision and Pattern Recognition, pp. 4401–4410 (2019)
3. Brock, A., Donahue, J., Simonyan, K.: Large scale GAN training for high fidelity natural image synthesis. arXiv preprint arXiv:1809.11096 (2018)
4. Sohl-Dickstein, J., Weiss, E., Maheswaranathan, N., et al.: Deep unsupervised learning using nonequilibrium thermodynamics. In: International Conference on Machine Learning, pp. 2256–2265. PMLR (2015)
5. Ho, J., Jain, A., Abbeel, P.: Denoising diffusion probabilistic models. Adv. Neural. Inf. Process. Syst. **33**, 6840–6851 (2020)
6. Rombach, R., Blattmann, A., Lorenz, D., et al.: High-resolution image synthesis with latent diffusion models. In: Proceedings of the IEEE/CVF Conference on Computer Vision and Pattern Recognition, pp. 10684–10695 (2022)
7. Zhang, L., Rao, A., Agrawala, M.: Adding conditional control to text-to-image diffusion models. In: Proceedings of the IEEE/CVF International Conference on Computer Vision, pp. 3836–3847 (2023)
8. Achlioptas, P., Ovsjanikov, M., Haydarov, K., et al.: ArtEmis: affective language for visual art. In: Proceedings of the IEEE/CVF Conference on Computer Vision and Pattern Recognition, pp. 11569–11579 (2021)
9. Hu, E.J., Shen, Y., Wallis, P., et al.: Lora: Low-rank adaptation of large language models. ICLR **1**(2), 3 (2022)
10. Kingma, D.P., Welling, M.: Auto-encoding variational bayes [EB/OL], 20 December 2013
11. Mou, C., Wang, X., Xie, L., et al.: T2i-adapter: learning adapters to dig out more controllable ability for text-to-image diffusion models. In: Proceedings of the AAAI Conference on Artificial Intelligence **38**(5), 4296–4304 (2024)
12. Bar-Tal, O., Yariv, L., Lipman, Y., et al.: MultiDiffusion: fusing diffusion paths for controlled image generation (2023)
13. Huang, L., Chen, D., Liu, Y., et al.: Composer: creative and controllable image synthesis with composable conditions. arXiv preprint arXiv:2302.09778 (2023)
14. Wang, X., Kontkanen, J., Curless, B., et al.: Generative powers of ten. In: Proceedings of the IEEE/CVF Conference on Computer Vision and Pattern Recognition, pp. 7173–7182 (2024)
15. Gatys, L.A., Ecker, A.S., Bethge, M.: A neural algorithm of artistic style. arXiv preprint arXiv:1508.06576 (2015)
16. Zhang, Y., Huang, N., Tang, F., et al.: Inversion-based style transfer with diffusion models. In: Proceedings of the IEEE/CVF Conference on Computer Vision and Pattern Recognition, pp. 10146–10156 (2023)
17. Chung, J., Hyun, S., Heo, J.P.: Style injection in diffusion: a training-free approach for adapting large-scale diffusion models for style transfer. In: Proceedings of the IEEE/CVF Conference on Computer Vision and Pattern Recognition, pp. 8795–8805 (2024)
18. Deng, Y., Tang, F., Dong, W., et al.: StyTr2: image style transfer with transformers. In: Proceedings of the IEEE/CVF Conference on Computer Vision and Pattern Recognition, pp. 11326–11336 (2022)
19. Hertz, A., Voynov, A., Fruchter, S., et al.: Style aligned image generation via shared attention. In: Proceedings of the IEEE/CVF Conference on Computer Vision and Pattern Recognition, pp. 4775–4785 (2024)

20. Loeschcke, S., Belongie, S., Benaim, S.: Text-driven stylization of video objects. In: Karlinsky, L., Michaeli, T., Nishino, K. (eds.) Computer Vision – ECCV 2022 Workshops. ECCV 2022. Lecture Notes in Computer Science, vol. 13804, pp. 594–609. Springer, Cham (2023). https://doi.org/10.1007/978-3-031-25069-9_38:
21. Kwon, G., Ye, J.C.: CLIPstyler: image style transfer with a single text condition. In: Proceedings of the IEEE/CVF Conference on Computer Vision and Pattern Recognition, pp. 18062–18071 (2022)
22. Si, C., Wang, X., Yang, X., et al.: FloRA: low-rank core space for n-dimension, p. 10. arXiv preprint arXiv:2405.14739 (2024)
23. Chang, D., Li, Y.: DLoRA-TrOCR: mixed text mode optical character recognition based on transformer. arXiv preprint arXiv:2404.12734 (2024)
24. Lin, Y., Ma, X., Chu, X., et al.: LoRA dropout as a sparsity regularizer for overfitting control. arXiv preprint arXiv:2404.09610 (2024)
25. Mikels, J.A., Fredrickson, B.L., Larkin, G.R., et al.: Emotional category data on images from the international affective picture system. Behav. Res. Methods **37**, 626–630 (2005)
26. Radford, A., Kim, J.W., Hallacy, C., et al.: Learning transferable visual models from natural language supervision. In: International Conference on Machine Learning, pp. 8748–8763. PmLR (2021)
27. Arthur, D., Vassilvitskii, S.: k-means++: The Advantages of Careful Seeding. Stanford (2006)
28. Huang, X., Belongie, S.: Arbitrary style transfer in real-time with adaptive instance normalization. In: Proceedings of the IEEE International Conference on Computer Vision, pp. 1501–1510 (2017)
29. Gao, J., Sun, Y., Liu, Y., et al.: StyleShot: a snapshot on any style. IEEE Trans. Pattern Anal. Mach. Intell. (2025)
30. Yang, J., Feng, J., Luo, W., et al.: EmoEdit: evoking emotions through image manipulation. arXiv preprint arXiv:2405.12661 (2024)

Discrete Wavelet Transform Mix Augmentation Based Contrastive Learning for Skeletal Micro-gesture Recognition

Yiming Zhang, Sirui Zhao(✉), Hongkai Sui, Tong Xu, and Enhong Chen(✉)

University of Science and Technology of China, Hefei, Anhui, China
siruit@ustc.edu.cn

Abstract. As subtle manifestations of human affect and cognitive processes, micro-gestures (MGs) hold critical potential for advancing emotion-aware human-computer interaction systems. However, progress in MG recognition remains critically impeded by the absence of well-annotated, balanced datasets that faithfully preserve the transient non-verbal cues. To address this challenge, we propose a novel Discrete Wavelet Transform Mix (DWTMiX) Augmentation based Contrastive Learning framework for skeletal micro-gesture recognition. Specifically, to precisely model the multiscale feature of MGs, the discrete wavelet transform is introduced to decompose the original MG signals into high-frequency and low-frequency components. Afterwards, we propose a cross-sample high-frequency shuffling and recombination technique, which constructs challenging contrastive sample pairs through high-frequency feature exchange and low-frequency base fusion. Finally, this enhancement strategy is incorporated into a contrastive learning framework, tailored for skeleton-based MG recognition. Comprehensive evaluations on three datasets, iMiGUE, SMG and MA-52 demonstrate the superior performance of our proposed method.

Keywords: Micro gesture · Human-machine interaction · Contrastive learning · Wavelet transform

1 Introduction

Body gestures serve as crucial indicators of human communication for conveying intentions and affective states [26], with accurately understanding human body gestures is a prerequisite for advanced natural human-computer interaction (HCI) systems. As a distinctive category of body gestures, Micro-gestures (MGs), such as scratching the head or rubbing hands, are spontaneous, subtle movements that reflect emotional states [24]. As shown in Fig. 1, unlike regular body gestures, MGs are involuntary and harder to control, making them more reliable for conveying hidden emotions, especially when individuals try to mask

H. Liu et al. (Eds.): CEI 2025, CCIS 2881, pp. 213–226, 2026.
https://doi.org/10.1007/978-981-95-9493-1_14

their feelings [4]. However, analyzing MGs is more challenging due to their low intensity, high variability, and complex contextual factors, posing a significant obstacle for MG recognition in the field of Human-Computer Interaction.

Currently, while significant advances have been achieved in MG recognition, supervised-learning based methods [13,17,18] remain constrained by three critical data bottlenecks: limited dataset scale, inconsistent annotation quality, and insufficient gesture variability. Meanwhile, with the advent of unsupervised learning, numerous skeleton-based action recognition studies [1,12,15] have explored effective contrastive strategies to learn discriminative action features from limited unlabeled data, achieving promising recognition performance. Encouraged by this, there are now a few studies [9,28] that investigate the impact of contrastive learning on MG recognition. However, these studies often overlook the unique characteristics of MGs, such as their short duration and localized occurrence. For instance, MGs typically last under 3 s, which is much shorter than the duration of regular gestures [4].

Additionally, to alleviate the insufficiency of labeled data samples, conventional contrastive learning techniques generate contrastive pairs through data augmentation. However, simply extending standard augmentations leads to diminishing returns. To tackle this issue, SkeleMix [7] utilizes skeleton topology to create hard contrastive pairs by mixing skeleton sequences, thereby enhancing performance in action recognition tasks. Nevertheless, there is still a lack of similar data augmentation methods specifically tailored for micro-gestures (MGs).

(a) Waving hand.

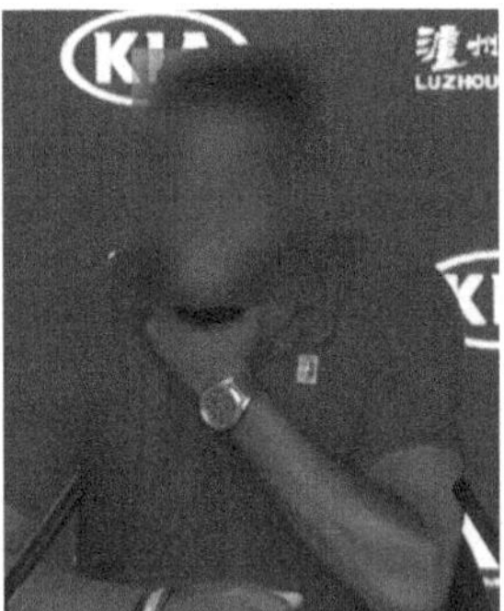

(b) Scratching neck.

Fig. 1. The examples of gestures and micro-gestures from two datasets: (a) regular gesture, waving-hands from UTKinect-Action3D dataset [33]; (b) micro-gesture, scratching-neck from iMiGUE dataset [24]. The gesture ‘waving hands’ exhibits greater magnitude and longer duration, conveying a clear social significance of greeting, while MG scratching-neck’ involves smaller magnitude and shorter duration, reflecting the inner emotional state (tension) of the character

Considering the subtle and rapid nature of micro-gestures (MGs), and motivated by the successful application of SkeleMix in skeleton-based action recognition, We propose DWTMiX, a novel strategy for enhancing hard contrastive pairs of MG skeleton data via discrete wavelet transform (DWT), which manipulates skeleton data in the time-frequency domain to enable the model to learn more representations from short-term features. Specifically, we treat skeleton data from MG clips as one-dimensional temporal signals and decompose them using DWT. To optimize the use of these decomposed signals for constructing new samples, we introduce a cross-sample high-frequency shuffling and recombination technique. Concretely, we utlize random weight gains to the high-frequency components and then recombine the high-frequency components of the same batch with the low-frequency components of other samples in a shuffled manner, thereby generating a diverse set of hard contrastive pairs.

Along with this line, we propose a contrastive learning framework for unsupervised skeleton-based MG recognition based on DWTMiX, termed DWTMiX-CLR, which integrates local similarity and global features in skeleton sequences. Finally, we evaluate our proposed DWTMiXCLR on three MG or micro-action datasets, including iMiGUE [24], SMG [4], and MA-52 [11]. The main contributions of our work are summarized as follows:

- We introduce the discrete wavelet transform to decompose the MG signal into high-frequency and low-frequency components, which provides a new perspective for analyzing MGs in the time-frequency domain.
- We propose a cross-sample high-frequency shuffling and recombination technique DWTMiX and a customized contrastive learning framework DWTMiX-CLR, specifically designed for self-supervised skeleton-based MG recognition tasks.
- Through comprehensive comparative analysis and ablation experiments, we demonstrate the superiority of our proposed DWTMiXCLR in micro-gesture recognition, and the effectiveness of the proposed DWTMiX augmentation strategy.

2 Related Works

2.1 Micro-gesture Recognition

At the Micro-Gesture Analysis and Hidden Emotion Understanding (MiGA) Challenge, early work focused on skeleton-based recognition networks. Li [18] proposed a 3D-CNN-based MG recognition network to process skeletal data, while Huang [17] presented a deep framework that incorporated an ensemble hypergraph convolution transformer. For online MG recognition in long videos, Guo [13] introduced a framework combining graph convolution and multi-scale transformer encoders. Additionally, Shah [29] designed a graph encoding convolutional network with self-attention layers to learn spatial-temporal context representations of skeleton points.

Recent research has advanced along several directions. Multi-modal fusion has proven effective for MG recognition: Gu et al. [10] proposed MM-Gesture, which integrates skeletal joints, limb movements, RGB videos, optical flow, depth maps, and Taylor-series video representations, achieving top performance on the iMiGUE dataset. For online MG detection, Liu et al. [22] combined spatial-temporal attention with hand-crafted data augmentation to improve classification and precise temporal localization of micro-gestures. Similarly, Liu et al. [23] introduced learnable query points for online MG recognition, enabling simultaneous gesture detection and classification in long videos.

Unsupervised and self-supervised approaches are gaining attention due to limited labeled data. Shah et al. [30] proposed a prior-guided self-supervised framework that mitigates the harmful effects of naive data augmentation in skeleton-based MG recognition. Li et al. [20] introduced prototypical calibration to refine ambiguous micro-action samples through contrastive learning and hierarchical prototype representation. Gao et al. [8] explored identity-free micro-gesture understanding to support emotional reasoning, highlighting the role of MGs in affective computing. In addition, Xu et al. [34] combined topology-aware skeletal representations with semantic label embeddings for fine-grained MG recognition and emotion understanding.

Furthermore, integrating contextual and multimodal information has emerged as a promising trend. Li et al. [21] proposed a visual-text contrastive learning framework to leverage text embeddings for context-aware MG recognition, improving both classification accuracy and emotion understanding. Overall, recent work indicates that combining multi-modal data, temporal attention, prototype-guided calibration, and self-supervised learning substantially enhances the recognition of subtle micro-gestures in both offline and online settings.

2.2 Contrastive Learning

As a discriminative approach, contrastive earning aims to learn useful representations by contrasting positive pairs (similar samples) against negative pairs (dissimilar samples). Different augmentation strategies can generate contrastive pairs, and contrastive loss is proposed for the measurement of similarities. For example, the Moco series [14] [6] used momentum to update encoder parameters and built a queue to store negative pairs. SimCLR [5] was proposed as a simple contrastive learning framework and emphasized the importance of augmentation strategies and the size of the training batch. SwAV [3] was proposed as a computationally efficient contrastive learning framework that could simultaneously group data while ensuring consistency between the cluster assignments produced for different enhancements of the same sample.

3 Methodology

3.1 Overview of DWTMiXCLR

In this section, we will formally introduce our proposed DWTMiXCLR, a novel contrastive learning framework based on Discrete Wavelet Transform Mix

(DWTMiX) augmentation for skeleton micro-gesture recognition. The overall framework of DWTMiXCLR is intuitively illustrated in Fig. 2, which mainly consists of global learning, local learning, and the DWTMiX augmentation module. Concretely, our framework follow a similar paradigm of MoCov2 [6] for global representation learning of skeleton clips. However, we extend this paradigm by introducing a novel local representation learning module and the DWTMiX augmentation strategy, which significantly enhance the model's ability to capture both global and fine-grained features in skeleton data, setting our work apart from existing methods.

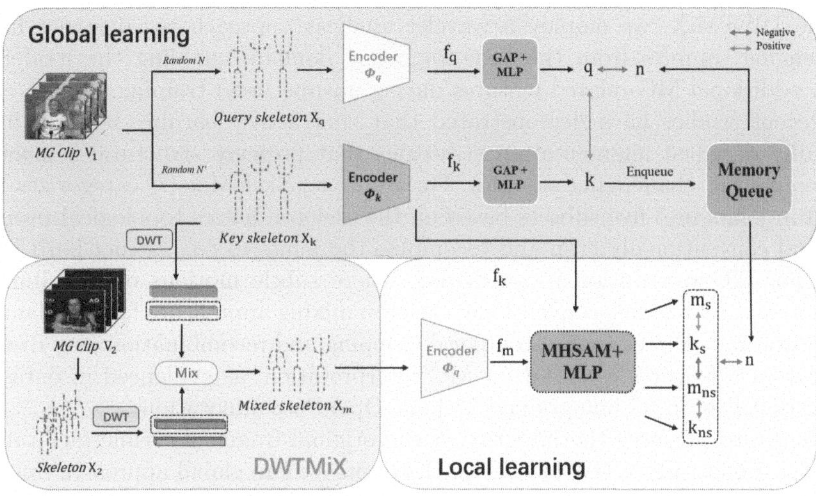

Fig. 2. The overview of DWTMiXCLR, which consists of global learning, local learning, and the DWTMiX augmentation module

3.2 Global Learning Based on MoCov2

As shown in Fig. 2, our framework adopts the pipeline of MoCov2 for the global representation learning of skeleton clips. In a systematic manner, the input skeleton sequence X is transformed into two distinct sequences X_k and X_q, through random augmentation, including shear and temporal crop as described in [19]. Subsequently, two encoders are employed to map the augmented sequences into embeddings f_k and f_q. While the query encoder updates its parameters via backpropagation, the key encoder updates through a momentum update mechanism: $\theta_k \leftarrow m\theta_k + (1 - m)\theta_q$, where m denotes the momentum coefficient. The embeddings f_k and f_q are then processed through global average pooling and a aingle-layer MLP to generate positive pairs k and q. For negative pairs, we utilize a memory queue $N_K = \{n_0, n_1, ..., n_{K-1}\}$ to store the positive key embeddings for each mini-batch.

The basic InfoNCE loss function [27] is used for global contrast learning:

$$L_{info} = -log(\frac{exp(q \cdot k/\tau)}{\sum_{i=0}^{K} exp(q \cdot n_i/\tau) + exp(q \cdot k/\tau)}), \tag{1}$$

where $\cdot$ refers to the dot product that computes the similarity between two embeddings q and k. n_i denotes the negative sample obtained from the memory queue. τ refers to the temperature hyperparameter that controls the learning speed.

3.3 DWTMiX Augmentation

In the DWTMiX, we employ a wavelet analysis approach to construct more challenging samples from the time-frequency domain, enabling the model to learn additional MG-related features during unsupervised training.

Recent studies have demonstrated that contrastive learning benefits from carefully designed augmentation strategies that preserve structural semantics while creating challenging samples. For example, SkeleMix [7] categorizes the skeleton joints into five subsets based on the skeleton data's topological properties and conventionally crop and recombine the joints to reconstruct hard samples. For MG recognition in particular, where subtle motions occupy limited spatiotemporal regions, conventional skeleton mixing approaches face fundamental limitations. Direct spatial-temporal cropping and recombination may distort critical local features essential for MG interpretation, as evidenced in datasets like iMiGUE with its fine-grained 25-joint OpenPose annotations.

Hence, to preserve the integrity of the original fragments while facilitating CutMix, we introduce DWTMiX, which adopts a more global approach. Specifically, for the original skeleton data X with dimensions $N \times C \times T \times V \times M$, where N is the batch size, C is the number of channels, T is the length of the time series, V is the number of joints, and M is the number of subjects (typically 1 in MG datasets), we merge channels, joints, and subjects, treating X as a group of one-dimensional time signals $N \times CVM \times T$. Subsequently, we decompose the skeleton data into high-frequency and low-frequency components based on the time channels using discrete wavelet transform. Employing the Haar orthogonal basis, we utilize one-dimensional convolution to achieve a fast wavelet transform, resulting in the low-frequency component X_{low} and the high-frequency component:

$$X_{high} = X * h_{high}, \tag{2}$$

$$X_{low} = X * h_{low}, \tag{3}$$

where $h_{low} = [\frac{1}{\sqrt{2}}, \frac{1}{\sqrt{2}}]$ and $h_{high} = [\frac{1}{\sqrt{2}}, -\frac{1}{\sqrt{2}}]$. The low-frequency component X_{low} focuses more on the global motion trends, while the high-frequency component X_{high} emphasizes local motion details. Leveraging the characteristics of MGs, we introduce random gains ranging from 0 to 0.8 on the high-frequency component to construct challenging samples with prominent high-frequency features. Since wavelet transformation is reversible, we recombine the high-frequency and low-frequency components of different samples within the same batch and generate new challenging samples through wavelet reconstruction.

3.4 Local Contrastive Learning

In the local contrastive learning module, we utilize a multi-head attention module to generate masked pairs from skeletons, which was first proposed in SkeAttenCLR [16], enabling the learning of salient features while suppressing irrelevant ones. A local contrastive learning branch here is built to expand the number of negative pairs and especially allow the network to learn to focus on parts with key action semantics. SkeAttenCLR applies SkeleMix to generate new negative pairs, while we replace it with DWTMiX. After DWTMiX augmentation, a new sequence X_m is generated and will be embedded by the encoder query to get the local comparative feature f_m. Then, the multi-head self-attention mask module (MHSAM) [32] is designed to embed the encoder output at the feature level and generate a soft mask for contrastive pair construction. Specifically, a pair of soft masks M_s and M_{ns} are generated by:

$$M_s = Sigmoid(\lambda \cdot proj(x_{attn})), \tag{4}$$

$$M_{ns} = I - M_s, \tag{5}$$

where x_{attn} refers to the output attention matrix from MHSAM, and λ is a hyperparameter that adjusts the tolerance of neutral features.

After obtaining the masks, we use them to separate the feature-level embedding extracted by the encoder into salient and non-salient features. Inputs f_m and f_k are transformed in both salient and non-salient ways to obtain m_s, m_{ns}, k_s and k_{ns} by dot producting with M_s and M_{ns} (Fig. 3).

In common with global contrastive learning, we adopt InfoNCE as the loss function of local contrastive learning:

$$L_s = -log(\frac{e^{m_s \cdot k_s / \tau}}{\sum_{i=0}^{K} e^{m_s \cdot n_i / \tau} + e^{m_s \cdot k_s / \tau} + e^{m_s \cdot m_{ns} / \tau}}), \tag{6}$$

$$L_{ns} = -log(\frac{e^{m_{ns} \cdot k_{ns} / \tau}}{\sum_{i=0}^{K} e^{m_{ns} \cdot n_i / \tau} + e^{m_{ns} \cdot k_{ns} / \tau} + e^{m_s \cdot m_{ns} / \tau}}). \tag{7}$$

The overall loss function is calculated by weighted summing the three contrastive losses in Formula 1, 6 and 7.

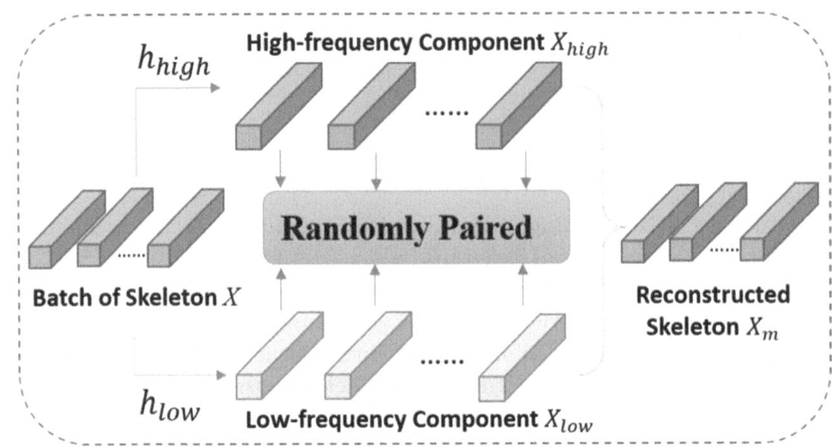

Fig. 3. An outline of our DWTMiX augmentation

4 Experiment

4.1 Experimental Datasets

To comprehensively validate the effectiveness of our proposed DWTMiXCLR, we conduct experiments on three MG or micro-action datasets: iMiGUE [24], SMG [4], two benchmark datasets for the MiGA Workshop and Challenge to explore using body gestures for hidden emotional state analysis, MA-52 [11], a newly established micro-action dataset. Particularly, in MA-52, micro-actions are categorized into 52 distinct fine-grained categories, and are collected as RGB videos. We detect and extract the skeleton points of the human body from these original videos using OpenPose [2].

4.2 Evaluation Metrics and Protocol

We adopt the KNN cluster to monitor self-supervised accuracy during unsupervised contrastive training. The model with the highest KNN score is selected for subsequent evaluation. We follow the linear evaluation protocol, which is widely adopted in existing work. The backbone parameters obtained during the unsupervised training stage are frozen, and a single linear layer is added after the backbone for supervised fine-tuning. The model is evaluated using Top-1 and Top-5 accuracy. For fair comparison, we only report results from a single joint stream.

4.3 Experimental Settings

To maintain the consistency of the input scale, we crop all skeleton clips in the temporal dimension to a fixed length of 90 frames. Clips longer than 90 frames are truncated, while those shorter than 90 frames are padded with zeros. During unsupervised representation learning, we use the SGD optimizer with an initial learning rate of 0.01, a momentum of 0.9, and a weight decay of 0.0001, and to train the model for 300 epochs. The learning rate is reduced to one-tenth of the original value at the 250th epoch. During linear fine-tuning, we use the SGD optimizer with a basic learning rate of 0.3 and a 10-epoch warm-up. The model is trained for 100 epochs, and the learning rate is reduced to one-tenth of the original value at the 60th epoch. All other parameters not explicitly mentioned here are set according to SkeAttnCLR [16]. The experiments are conducted on a single NVIDIA GeForce RTX 3090 GPU using PyTorch.

4.4 Experimental Results

Results on iIMiGUE Dataset. We compare our proposed methods with previously published methods, including P&C [31], U-S-VAE Z [24], A-EDGCN [28], CDCLR [9] and SkeAttnCLR [16]. The results are presented in Table 1. Compared with the current SOTA method [9] in MG recognition, our method achieves an improvement of 8.72% in Top-1 accuracy and 5.67% in Top-5 accuracy on the iMiGUE dataset. The experimental results demonstrate the effectiveness of our contrastive learning framework for MG recognition.

Results on SMG Dataset. For the reason that there are few existing self-supervised methods tested on the SMG dataset, we only evaluate DWTMiXCLR on SMG and compare its performance with the baselines outlined in [4]. We compare the linear evaluation results of DWTMiX with the supervised learning results utilizing identical backbones, as shown in Table 2. In particular, DWT-MiX demonstrates a slight discrepancy compared to supervised learning on ST-GCN, while exhibiting a substantial performance gap of 20% on MS-G3D. This may be related to the fact that MS-G3D is less suitable as a framework in contrastive learning, often leading to overfitting, a phenomenon also described in [28].

Results on MA-52 Dataset. As shown in Table 3, our method yields performance comparable to that of the supervised ST-GCN in terms of Top-5 accuracy, and outperforms that of the supervised ST-GCN in terms of Top-1 accuracy. The supervised ST-GCN method attains a Top-1 accuracy of 42.50%, whereas our proposed DWTMiXCLR method improves upon this result, reaching 44.00%, marking an increase of 1.5%. The higher Top-1 accuracy compared with the supervised method suggests that DWTMiXCLR enhances the discriminative power of learned representations in unsupervised pretraining, making it better suited for the following MG classification.

4.5 Results Analysis

Different Gains on the High-Frequency Component. We explore the impact of various gains on the high-frequency component through experiments

Table 1. Comparison results with unsupervised SOTA methods on iMiGUE dataset

Method	Top-1 Accuracy%	Top-5 Accuracy%
P&C [31]	31.67	64.93
U-S-VAE Z [24]	32.43	64.30
A-EDGCN [28]	37.5	N/A
CDCLR [9]	39.38	76.40
SkeAttnCLR [16]	<u>45.62</u>	**83.82**
DoCLR [8]	41.94	81.6
DWTMiXCLR(Our method))	**47.72**	<u>83.03</u>

Table 2. Results on SMG dataset

Method	Top-1 %	Top-5 %
Supervised learning(ST-GCN) [35]	41.48	86.07
Supervised learning(MS-G3D) [4]	**61.75**	<u>91.48</u>
DWTMiX(ST-GCN)(Our method)	<u>55.41</u>	**92.62**

to optimize the hyperparameters. The results are detailed in Fig. 4, demonstrating that the setting '$\alpha = 0.8$' achieves the best performance. Notably, the Top-1 accuracy remains relatively stable across the range of α, while the Top-5 accuracy exhibits more pronounced fluctuations. This observation supports our hypothesis regarding the importance of MG features captured in the high-frequency component of DWTMiX.

Comparison of Different Backbones. To demonstrate the versatility of our approach, we evaluate DWTMiX using different backbone architectures and report their performance in Table 4. In addition to ST-GCN [35], we include MS-G3D [25] and GRU, as they are commonly used as backbones in various existing methods, such as P&C [31], U-S-VAE Z [24], A-EDGCN [28], and CDCLR [9]. Our method demonstrates competitive performance, closely approaching CDCLR when using the GRU backbone while outperforming it across all other metrics. Notably, MS-G3D, which excels in supervised learning on iMiGUE, exhibits suboptimal performance within our framework, suggesting that its complexity may make it prone to overfitting on iMiGUE. A-EDGCN [28], a simplified

Table 3. Results on MA-52

Method	Top-1%	Top-5%
Supervised learning(ST-GCN) [35]	42.50	**78.84**
DWTMiXCLR(Our method)	**44.00**	78.61

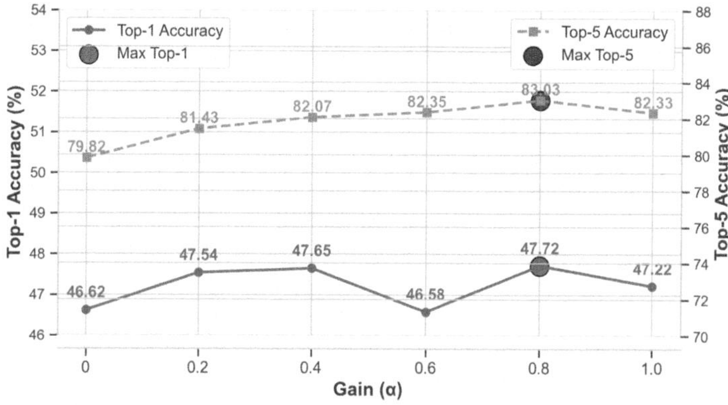

Fig. 4. Experimental results with different gains on the high-frequency component

version of MS-G3D, exhibits improved performance, supporting this hypothesis (Table 5).

Table 4. Experimental results with different backbones

Backbone	Top-1 %	Top-5 %
ST-GCN	**47.72**	**83.03**
MS-G3D	45.92	81.83
GRU	39.24	75.84

Table 5. Ablation study of DWTMiX and other augmentation methods

Method	Top-1%	Top-5%
Baseline augmentation [16]	44.17	80.93
SkeleMix [7]	45.62	**83.82**
DWTMiX(Our method)	**47.72**	83.03

4.6 Ablation Study

We conduct an ablation study to evaluate the performance of our DWTMiX augmentation compared to the original baseline augmentation (shear and temporal crop) and SkeleMix on the iMiGUE dataset. Our results demonstrate that the proposed DWTMiX augmentation outperforms both the baseline and SkeleMix, highlighting the effectiveness of our tailored augmentation approach. Specifically, DWTMiX achieves a 3.47% improvement over the baseline augmentation and a 2.03% improvement over SkeleMix. Notably, regardless of the chosen parameter α, our method consistently outperforms SkeleMix by approximately 1%, suggesting that random seed variations have minimal impact on the superior performance of our approach.

5 Conclusion

In this paper, we proposed DWTMiXCLR, a novel contrastive learning framework based on Discrete Wavelet Transform Mix (DWTMiX) augmentation for skeleton-based MG recognition. We incorporated the discrete wavelet transform to decompose the MG signal into high-frequency and low-frequency components, offering a novel approach to analyzing MGs in the time-frequency domain. By reshuffling the skeleton samples in the time-frequency domain, DWTMiX enhances the representation of MG skeleton clips and provides abundant hard contrastive pairs in MG recognition. The Experimental evaluations conducted on the iMiGUE, SMG and MA-52 datasets demonstrated significant performance improvements over SOTA methods.

Acknowledgments. This work was supported in part by the grants from National Natural Science Foundation of China (No. 62406264, No. 61727809).

References

1. Abdelfattah, M., Hassan, M., Alahi, A.: Maskclr: attention-guided contrastive learning for robust action representation learning. In: Proceedings of the IEEE/CVF Conference on Computer Vision and Pattern Recognition, pp. 18678–18687 (2024)
2. Cao, Z., Hidalgo, G., Simon, T., Wei, S.E., Sheikh, Y.: Openpose: realtime multi-person 2d pose estimation using part affinity fields. IEEE Trans. Pattern Anal. Mach. Intell. **43**, 172–186 (2018)
3. Caron, M., Misra, I., Mairal, J., Goyal, P., Bojanowski, P., Joulin, A.: Unsupervised learning of visual features by contrasting cluster assignments. Le Centre pour la Communication Scientifique Directe - HAL - Grenoble Ecole de Management, Le Centre pour la Communication Scientifique Directe - HAL - Grenoble Ecole de Management, December 2020
4. Chen, H., Shi, H., Liu, X., Li, X., Zhao, G.: Smg: a micro-gesture dataset towards spontaneous body gestures for emotional stress state analysis. Int. J. Comput. Vision **131**, 1346–1366 (2023)
5. Chen, T., Kornblith, S., Norouzi, M., Hinton, G.E.: A simple framework for contrastive learning of visual representations. ArXiv **abs/2002.05709** (2020)
6. Chen, X., Fan, H., Girshick, R.B., He, K.: Improved baselines with momentum contrastive learning. ArXiv **abs/2003.04297** (2020)
7. Chen, Z., Liu, H., Guo, T., Chen, Z., Song, P., Tang, H.: Contrastive learning from spatio-temporal mixed skeleton sequences for self-supervised skeleton-based action recognition. ArXiv **abs/2207.03065** (2022)

8. Gao, R., Liu, X., Xing, B., Yu, Z., Schuller, B.W., Kälviäinen, H.: Identity-free artificial emotional intelligence via micro-gesture understanding. arXiv preprint arXiv:2405.13206 (2024)
9. Gao, R., Liu, X., Yang, J., Yue, H.: Cdclr: clip-driven contrastive learning for skeleton-based action recognition. In: 2022 IEEE International Conference on Visual Communications and Image Processing (VCIP), pp. 1–5 (2022)
10. Gu, J., Wang, X., Li, W., Wei, Y., Wu, J., Guo, Y.: Mm-gesture: towards precise micro-gesture recognition through multimodal fusion (2025), https://arxiv.org/abs/2507.08344
11. Guo, D., Li, K., Hu, B., Zhang, Y., Wang, M.: Benchmarking micro-action recognition: Dataset, methods, and applications. IEEE Transactions on Circuits and Systems for Video Technology, pp. 1–1 (2024). https://doi.org/10.1109/TCSVT.2024.3358415
12. Guo, T., Liu, H., Chen, Z., Liu, M., Wang, T., Ding, R.: Contrastive learning from extremely augmented skeleton sequences for self-supervised action recognition. In: AAAI Conference on Artificial Intelligence (2021)
13. Guo, X., Peng, W., Huang, H., Xia, Z.: Micro-gesture online recognition with graph-convolution and multiscale transformers for long sequence (2023)
14. He, K., Fan, H., Wu, Y., Xie, S., Girshick, R.: Momentum contrast for unsupervised visual representation learning. In: 2020 IEEE/CVF Conference on Computer Vision and Pattern Recognition (CVPR), June 2020. https://doi.org/10.1109/cvpr42600.2020.00975, http://dx.doi.org/10.1109/cvpr42600.2020.00975
15. Hu, J., Hou, Y., Guo, Z., Gao, J.: Global and local contrastive learning for self-supervised skeleton-based action recognition. IEEE Trans. Circuits Syst. Video Technol. **34**(11), 10578–10589 (2024). https://doi.org/10.1109/TCSVT.2024.3410301
16. Hua, Y., et al.: Part aware contrastive learning for self-supervised action recognition. In: Proceedings of the Thirty-Second International Joint Conference on Artificial Intelligence. IJCAI 2023 (2023). https://doi.org/10.24963/ijcai.2023/95, https://doi.org/10.24963/ijcai.2023/95
17. Huang, H., Guo, X., Peng, W., Xia, Z.: Micro-gesture classification based on ensemble hypergraph-convolution transformer. Micro-gesture Anal. Hidden Emotion Understand. **2023**, 9 (2023)
18. Li, K., Guo, D., Chen, G., Peng, X., Wang, M.: Joint skeletal and semantic embedding loss for micro-gesture classification. arXiv preprint arXiv:2307.10624 (2023)
19. Li, L., Wang, M., Ni, B., Wang, H., Yang, J., Zhang, W.: 3d human action representation learning via cross-view consistency pursuit. 2021 IEEE/CVF Conference on Computer Vision and Pattern Recognition (CVPR), pp. 4739–4748 (2021)
20. Li, X., Guo, Y., Chen, Z.: Prototypical calibrating ambiguous samples for micro-action recognition (2024), https://arxiv.org/abs/2412.14719
21. Li, X., Xing, J., Liu, P.: Enhancing micro gesture recognition for emotion understanding via context-aware visual-text contrastive learning (2024), https://arxiv.org/abs/2405.01885
22. Liu, P., Li, X., Wang, Y., Wei, J., She, Q., Guo, Y.: Online micro-gesture recognition using data augmentation and spatial-temporal attention (2025), https://arxiv.org/abs/2507.09512
23. Liu, P., et al.: Micro-gesture online recognition using learnable query points (2024), https://arxiv.org/abs/2407.04490

24. Liu, X., Shi, H., Chen, H., Yu, Z., Li, X., Zhao, G.: imigue: an identity-free video dataset for micro-gesture understanding and emotion analysis. 2021 IEEE/CVF Conference on Computer Vision and Pattern Recognition (CVPR), pp. 10626–10637 (2021)
25. Liu, Z., Zhang, H., Chen, Z., Wang, Z., Ouyang, W.: Disentangling and unifying graph convolutions for skeleton-based action recognition. 2020 IEEE/CVF Conference on Computer Vision and Pattern Recognition (CVPR), pp. 140–149 (2020)
26. Noroozi, F., Corneanu, C.A., Kamińska, D., Sapinski, T., Escalera, S., Anbarjafari, G.: Survey on emotional body gesture recognition. IEEE Trans. Affect. Comput. **12**, 505–523 (2018)
27. van den Oord, A., Li, Y., Vinyals, O.: Representation learning with contrastive predictive coding. ArXiv **abs/1807.03748** (2018)
28. Shah, A., Chen, H., Shi, H., Zhao, G.: Efficient dense-graph convolutional network with inductive prior augmentations for unsupervised micro-gesture recognition. In: 2022 26th International Conference on Pattern Recognition (ICPR), pp. 2686–2692 (2022)
29. Shah, A., Chen, H., Zhao, G.: Representation learning for topology-adaptive micro-gesture recognition and analysis. In: IJCAI-MIGA Workshop & Challenge on Micro-gesture Analysis for Hidden Emotion Understanding (MiGA), 21 July 2023 Macao, China. Redaktion Sun SITE (2023)
30. Shah, R., Chen, L., Zhao, Q.: Naive data augmentation might be toxic: data-prior guided self-supervised representation learning for micro-gesture recognition (2024), https://oulurepo.oulu.fi/handle/10024/51981
31. Su, K., Liu, X., Shlizerman, E.: Predict & cluster: unsupervised skeleton based action recognition. In: 2020 IEEE/CVF Conference on Computer Vision and Pattern Recognition (CVPR), pp. 9628–9637 (2019)
32. Vaswani, A., et al.: Attention is all you need. In: NIPS (2017)
33. Xia, L., Chen, C.C., Aggarwal, J.K.: View invariant human action recognition using histograms of 3d joints. In: 2012 IEEE Computer Society Conference on Computer Vision and Pattern Recognition Workshops, pp. 20–27. IEEE (2012)
34. Xu, H., Cheng, L., Wang, Y., Tang, S., Zhong, J.: Towards fine-grained emotion understanding via skeleton-based micro-gesture recognition (2025), https://arxiv.org/abs/2506.12848
35. Yan, S., Xiong, Y., Lin, D.: Spatial temporal graph convolutional networks for skeleton-based action recognition. In: AAAI Conference on Artificial Intelligence (2018)

A Hybrid Neural Code for Operant Control Decomposing Firing Rate and Precise Spike Timing Contributions to Neural Synchrony

Tianyu Zheng[1,4], Tao Feng[1,4], Yuqi Yang[1,5], and Shaomin Zhang[1,2,3,4](✉)

[1] Key Laboratory of Biomedical Engineering of Ministry of Education, Qiushi Academy for Advanced Studies, Zhejiang University, Hangzhou, China
shaomin@zju.edu.cn

[2] State Key Laboratory of Brain-Machine Intelligence, Zhejiang University, Hangzhou, China

[3] The MOE Frontier Science Center for Brain Science and Brain-Machine Integration, Zhejiang University, Hangzhou, China

[4] Department of Biomedical Engineering, Zhejiang University, Hangzhou, China

[5] Computer Science and Technology, Zhejiang University, Hangzhou, China

Abstract. The debate concerning whether neural information is primarily transmitted via firing rate or precise spike timing remains central to neuroscience. Here, we tried to address this fundamental ambiguity in the primary motor cortex (MI) using a novel Brain-Machine Interface (BMI) task where rats were trained to voluntarily modulate neuronal population synchrony for reward. This operant conditioning paradigm allowed for the quantitative decomposition of the neural control signal into its coarse- and fine-timescale components. Behavioral analysis confirmed robust and stable control, marked by a synchronized elevation in population firing rate within the 300 ms pre-reward window. Temporal perturbation testing demonstrated that the coarse-timescale rate modulation alone provides a robust, near-threshold signal, confirming the capacity of firing rate for reliable information transmission. Crucially, we quantified the Rate-Independent Coincidence Spiking Pair count (RI-NCSP) —a metric designed to filter out chance coincidences driven by elevated firing rates—revealing a statistically significant Excess Synchrony that emerged exclusively during successful trials. Our finding proves that the precise spike timing contributes information independently of the firing rate increase. Finally, we utilized a multi-class Support Vector Machine (SVM) to assess feature utility. Decoding accuracy achieved with the combined feature of both components was significantly superior to that of either component alone. These results imply a Multiscale Hybrid Code architecture for neural coding, where the coarse rate component provides robustness and the precise timing component offers critical informational refinement. This framework is essential for the future design of BMI systems that leverage multiscale feature fusion for optimizing performance and efficiency.

Keywords: Brain-Machine Interface (BMI) · Rate Coding · Temporal Coding

H. Liu et al. (Eds.): CEI 2025, CCIS 2881, pp. 227–240, 2026.
https://doi.org/10.1007/978-981-95-9493-1_15

1 Introduction

Action potentials (APs) serve as the fundamental currency for information transfer and computation within the central nervous system. A long-standing and central question in neuroscience is how these transient electrical signals efficiently encode and transmit the vast amount of information required for complex perception and behavior. Historically, the mechanisms of neural coding have centered on a fundamental dichotomy between two classical models: Rate Coding and Precise Temporal Coding [1]. Rate coding posits that information is conveyed by the average firing frequency of neurons over relatively long time windows, offering a robust and intuitive signal representation. Conversely, temporal coding suggests that information is encoded in the precise timing of individual spikes or the exact synchronization relationships between neurons, a mechanism capable of providing high-fidelity information transfer with potential energy efficiency.

The contemporary view, however, acknowledges that the optimal coding strategy is highly dependent on the specific biological context, computational requirements, and the complexity of the information being processed. For instance, theories of efficient coding indicate that neural circuits prioritize removing predictable or redundant temporal information to achieve optimal prediction and storage [2]. Consequently, the focus of the debate has shifted from determining which code is universally superior to understanding how these two mechanisms interact, coexist, and are strategically recruited when the brain is actively engaged in learned, complex behavioral tasks.

The high-dimensional nature of complex motor and cognitive tasks necessitates information representation beyond the capacity of single neurons, giving rise to the concept of the Population Code [3]. In this framework, the information capacity is shaped by the diversity of neural activity, spatio-temporal response profiles, and critically, the cross-neural correlations within the ensemble. Neuronal Synchrony [4], a key form of correlation, is hypothesized to function as a versatile code that helps define functional relationships and provides the flexibility required for rapid neural representations.

Despite its presumed importance, a key mechanistic ambiguity in the study of synchrony persists: is the synchronous activity observed across a neuronal population merely a passive by-product of a generalized, coarse-timescale increase in the ensemble's firing rate (i.e., pseudo-synchrony caused by rate coding), or does it reflect an actively generated, precise temporal association that carries non-redundant information independent of the rate increase? Resolving this ambiguity is crucial, as the answer dictates whether Brain-Machine Interfaces (BMIs) must decode only the firing frequency or also integrate precise spike timing.

To address this fundamental question in a rigorous, active behavioral context, we employed a novel BMI task based on operant conditioning [5, 6]. This paradigm requires rats to voluntarily modulate the collective synchronous activity of a targeted cortical neuronal ensemble (e.g., in the motor cortex) to achieve a required number of coincidental spiking pairs (NCSP) for reward acquisition. This closed-loop setup provides a powerful platform for quantitatively decomposing the informational contributions of different coding features within a learned, goal-directed behavior.

Our central hypothesis is that successful and stable control of the novel BMI task relies on a Multiscale Hybrid Code architecture. In this architecture, coarse-timescale firing rate modulation provides the fundamental robust and reliable signal drive, while precise action potential temporal synchrony offers a high-fidelity information refinement mechanism, acting as a temporal gate. This hybrid strategy represents an efficient solution for the brain to balance the robustness inherent to rate coding with the high informational capacity offered by temporal coding.

To test this hypothesis, we systematically trained over-trained rats on the novel BMI task and quantitatively decomposed the neural control signal. We found that the success signal is indeed a hybrid, bimodal representation. Through a perturbation analysis (Fig. 4), we demonstrated that the coarse-timescale rate increase is enough to provide a robust, near-threshold control signal. Crucially, to distinguish true temporal coordination from random overlaps caused by high activity, we quantified the RI-NCSP by subtracting the expected chance coincidences from the actual count (Fig. 5A). This analysis provided evidence that a statistically significant Excess Synchrony exists, which carries independent temporal information. Finally, using a multi-class Support Vector Machine (SVM) on multiscale features, we proved that the Hybrid Feature, combining the 300 ms rate information with 15 ms synchrony information, yields a maximal decoding accuracy significantly superior to either single feature alone (Fig. 6). These results provide conclusive empirical evidence for the Multiscale Hybrid Code and establish a necessary framework for the design of next-generation Brain-Machine Interface systems that utilize multiscale feature fusion for optimal performance.

2 Method

2.1 Surgery and Electrophysiology

All surgical and experimental procedures were conducted in accordance with the Guide for the Care and Use of Laboratory Animals (China Ministry of Health) and were approved by the Animal Care Committee of Zhejiang University, China.

The study utilized ten male Sprague-Dawley (SD) rats ($N = 10$ rats) for behavioral training and chronic electrophysiological recording. All procedures were approved by the institutional animal care and use committee. Prior to training, the animals underwent sterile surgery for the chronic implantation of multi-channel microelectrode arrays into the target cortical region (Primary Motor Cortex, M1). Electrophysiological signals were acquired using an established recording system (Blackrock, USA), and action potentials were isolated and sorted offline using standard techniques to obtain the spike trains of single or multi-unit activity used in the control paradigm and subsequent analyses.

2.2 Behavioral Task

The experiment employed a novel BMI task paradigm based on instrumental conditioning (Fig. 1A) [7]. The objective was to mediate the rats to actively generate a required pattern of neuronal synchrony within a pre-selected ensemble of recorded cortical neurons. The reward (e.g., water or juice pellet) was delivered in a closed-loop manner, contingent upon the instantaneous neural synchrony exceeding a predefined threshold for a specific duration. The synchrony metric used for real-time decoding was the number of coincidental spiking pairs (NCSP) of the trigger and target neurons. The task involved a baseline block used for threshold determination and a subsequent task block where operant control was attempted (Fig. 1A, lower panel).

2.3 Behavioral Quantification

Task proficiency was assessed by quantifying the successful modulation of neural activity. Performance during the over-trained stage was analyzed by comparing the success rate and the number of hits per minute achieved during the task block against the corresponding metrics during the baseline period. Statistical significance was determined using the Wilcoxon signed-rank test. For all subsequent neural encoding analyses, data were restricted to successful trials recorded during the identified stable performance plateau phase of each session (Fig. 1B).

2.4 Hits-Per-Min (HPM)

The hits per minute (HPM) quantifies performance in controlling temporal neuroprosthetics. To account for potential variations in baseline performance across sessions, we computed the HPM gain, which normalizes each session by subtracting the baseline HPM estimated from the task.

2.5 Perturbation Analysis for Rate Robustness

To isolate the informational contribution of the coarse rate structure, a perturbation experiment (Jitter condition) was conducted offline (Fig. 4B). The precise temporal structure of the neuronal activity was destroyed by temporally jittering the spike times by 15 ms [8], effectively preserving the overall spike count (coarse rate) within the 300 ms window while eliminating fine synchrony. The success rate under this Jitter condition (Jitter) was then recalculated offline and statistically compared against the original success rate (Raw) and the chance level using the Wilcoxon signed-rank test.

2.6 Rate-Independent Precise Synchrony

To confirm the existence of a precise temporal code independent of the firing rate increase, we calculated the Rate-Independent NCSP (RI-NCSP) (Fig. 5A). The Expected NCSP, which represents synchrony due only to chance coincidence driven by elevated firing rates, was modeled using the Poisson process null hypothesis based on the measured average firing rates of the neuronal pairs [9]. The RI-NCSP was then defined as the Actual NCSP minus the Expected NCSP. A significant positive RI-NCSP within the 300 ms success window was used as evidence of functional, rate-independent temporal correlation.

2.7 Cross-Correlation Histogram (CCH)

The precise structure of the temporal relationship between the trigger and target neurons was visualized and quantified using the Cross-Correlation Histogram (CCH) [10, 11] (Fig. 5B, 5C). CCHs were computed for neuronal pairs during the 350 ms pre-success window by histogramming the time differences between the spikes of the two neurons. The presence of a narrow peak in the CCH was tested for statistical significance to confirm precise short-timescale synchrony [12].

2.8 Decoding Performance Analysis

A decoding analysis was performed using a multi-class Support Vector Machine (SVM) to quantify the predictive efficacy of different coding schemes. **Feature Definition:** Three distinct feature sets were defined for the SVM input: (1) Rate Feature: The average firing rate of the two neurons within the 300 ms pre-success window.(2) Temporal Feature: The number of coincident spikes (NCSP) within a narrow 15 ms bin between the two neurons in the same 300 ms window.(3) Hybrid Feature: A combined feature vector integrating both the Rate Feature and the Temporal Feature.

The SVM was trained and tested using cross-validation techniques. Decoding performance was evaluated using Prediction Accuracy (mean and standard deviation) for each of the three feature sets. The primary goal was to statistically demonstrate that the accuracy achieved by the Hybrid Feature was significantly superior to the accuracy achieved by either the Rate Feature or the Temporal Feature alone.

3 Results

3.1 Behavioral Acquisition and Stability of NCSP Control

To investigate the multiscale encoding strategy underlying active neural control, we trained 10 Sprague-Dawley (SD) rats on the population synchrony-based Neuroprosthetic Control of Synchronous Population (NCSP) task (Fig. 1A, upper panel). The task required the rats to actively modulate the spiking activity of a pre-selected cortical ensemble to reach a target synchrony threshold for reward acquisition (Fig. 1A, lower panel).

Following over-training, all subjects rapidly achieved high levels of stable performance within single recording sessions. The learning curve from a representative rat demonstrated a rapid acquisition phase followed by performance stabilizing into a high-level plateau after a number of trials (Fig. 1B).

We quantified the performance across all over-trained sessions. The success rate (SR) during the closed-loop task block was significantly higher than the baseline control period (Wilcoxon signed-rank test, $N = 10$, $p = 0.002$; Fig. 1C). Furthermore, the operational efficacy, quantified as the number of Hits per minute, was also significantly elevated compared to baseline activity (Wilcoxon signed-rank test, $N = 10$, $p = 0.002$; Fig. 1D). These results confirm that over-trained animals achieved robust, voluntary control over the required neuronal population pattern.

Based on this observed stable performance, all subsequent analyses of neural activity were restricted to trials within the identified plateau phase of each session to ensure the data analyzed corresponded to successful and stable NCSP control.

The high and stable behavioral performance achieved in the over-trained stage allowed us to qualitatively examine the underlying neural activity patterns mediating successful control of the novel BMI task. Examination of single-trial raster plots and instantaneous firing rates revealed two distinct activity phenotypes used by the rats to achieve the required Coincidence Spiking Pair count (NCSP target) (Fig. 2).

In the first representative successful trial (Fig. 2A), the required synchrony was achieved through a highly temporally precise clustering of action potentials. The raster

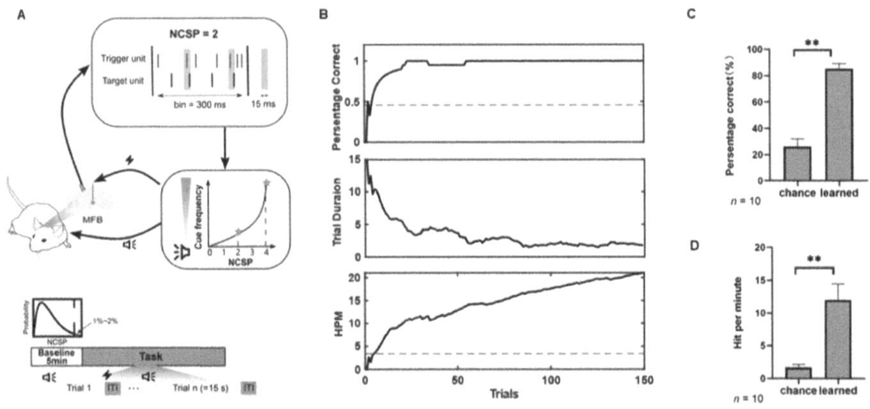

Fig. 1. Schematic of the BMI task and single session performance. (A) Upper panel: closed-loop BMI paradigm in which rats obtain rewards by modulating neural activity to reach the NCSP target. Lower panel: each session consists of a baseline block and a task block, with the baseline period used to determine the NCSP threshold. (B) Learning curve from a representative rat within a single day, showing performance reaching a plateau after a number of trials. (C) In the over-trained stage, success rates were significantly higher than baseline (N = 10, Wilcoxon test, $p = 0.002$). (D) Hit per minute were also significantly higher than baseline (N = 10, Wilcoxon test, $p = 0.002$).

plot (upper panel) shows spikes occurring in tight, short-timescale synchrony. Concurrently, the instantaneous firing rate (lower panel, smoothed with a Gaussian kernel) remained relatively modest over the 300 ms success window. This pattern suggests a control strategy heavily emphasizing precise spike timing.

Conversely, a second representative successful trial demonstrated a distinct pattern of neural activity (Fig. 2B). In this case, the NCSP target was met mainly through a strong, transient elevation in the instantaneous firing rate. The instantaneous firing rate (lower panel) shows a robust increase lasting approximately 150 ms within the 300 ms success window. This high-rate activation suggests a coarse-timescale, rate-based strategy, where the target synchrony was achieved predominantly through the increased probability of chance coincidence driven by a high firing frequency burst.

These qualitatively distinct single-trial patterns demonstrate that the learned novel BMI task control utilizes at least two underlying neural phenotypes: one relying heavily on precise spike synchrony, and the other relying on a transient increase in coarse-timescale firing rate. These observations necessitate a subsequent quantitative decomposition of the informational contributions of rate and timing to overall BMI control, which is addressed in the following sections.

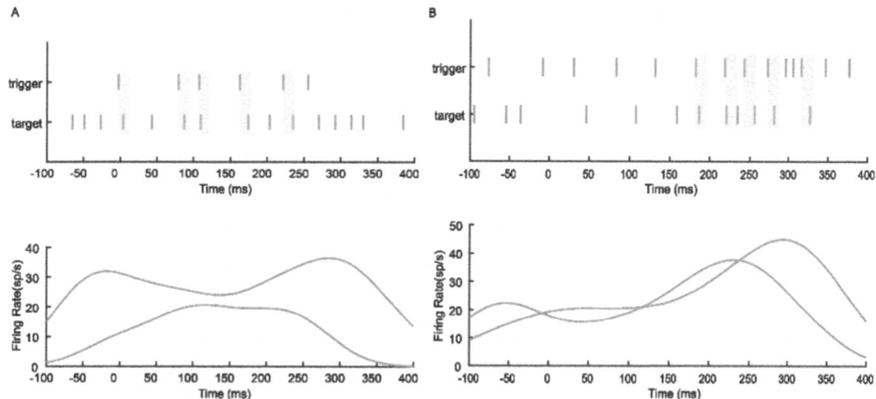

Fig. 2. Two Single trial sample. Two representative neural patterns during successful trials. (A) Upper panel: raster plot; lower panel: instantaneous firing rate smoothed with a Gaussian kernel. The 0–300 ms window marks the success period, during which the two neurons reached NCSP = 5 through precise spike synchrony. (B) Same as (A), but in this trial the NCSP = 5 was achieved through a transient increase in instantaneous firing rate rather than precise synchrony.

3.2 Coarse-Timescale Firing Rate Provides Robust BMI Control

To quantitatively assess the role of coarse-timescale firing rate modulation (as qualitatively suggested in Fig. 2), we first examined the population activity dynamics time-locked to the moment of reward delivery. The Peri-event Time Histogram (PETH) from a representative rat showed a clear and pronounced emergence of neuronal activity (Fig. 3, left panel). When averaged across all ten over-trained rats, the Z-scored firing rates confirmed a highly synchronized increase in population activity that robustly emerged in the 300 ms window preceding the reward onset (Fig. 3, right panel).

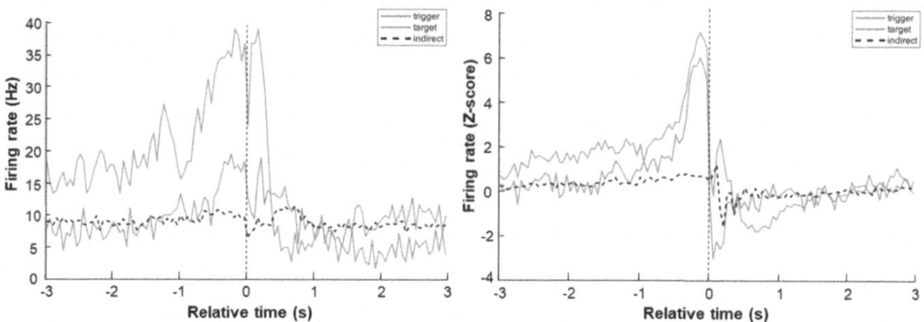

Fig. 3. Peri-event time histogram of neural activity aligned to reward delivery. Left panel: firing rate from a representative rat. Right panel: Z-scored firing rates averaged across ten rats. A clear increase in population activity emerges in the 300 ms preceding reward.

We statistically confirmed this observation by comparing the activity in this critical window against the baseline period. The average firing rates of the neuronal pairs during the 300 ms pre-reward window were significantly higher than their respective baseline rates (Fig. 4A). This robust elevation in population excitability provides the underlying signal for the novel BMI control.

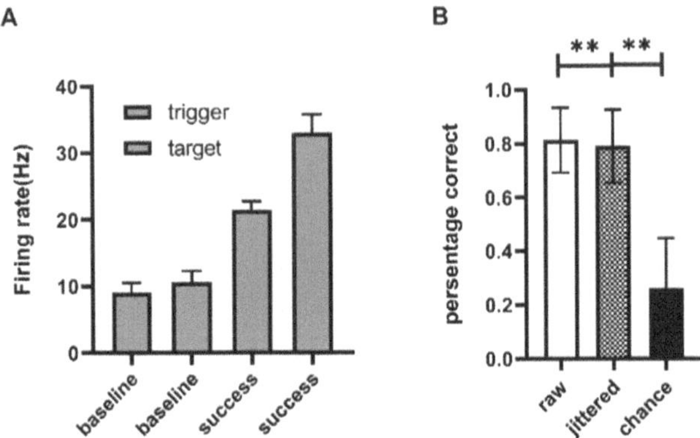

Fig. 4. Task success is associated with neuronal firing rates. (A) The average firing rates of two neurons during the 300 ms preceding reward were higher than their respective baseline rates. (B) Success rates under different conditions: Raw, original task performance; Jitter, offline recalculation of task performance after temporally jittering neuronal activity by 15 ms during the task; Chance, expected success rate from the baseline period. Success rates after jittering remained significantly above chance (n = 10, Wilcoxon test, p = 0.0039).

We next sought to determine the informational contribution of this coarse-timescale structure to the overall task performance by disrupting the fine temporal structure. We performed a perturbation analysis where we offline recalculated the task performance after temporally jittering neuronal activity by 15 ms (Jitter condition). This manipulation was designed to destroy precise spike synchrony while preserving the coarse firing rate structure within the 300 ms window.

The resulting performance under the Jitter condition showed a decrease compared to the Raw, original task performance. However, the success rates after temporal jittering remained significantly above the Chance level (Wilcoxon test, N = 10, p = 0.0039; Fig. 4B). This result demonstrates that the coarse-timescale increase in firing rate alone provides a robust, near-threshold signal sufficient for successful BMI control.

3.3 Precise Temporal Encoding Reveals Rate-Independent Synchrony

The perturbation analysis (Fig. 4B) demonstrated that the coarse-timescale rate structure provided robust, though sub-optimal, BMI control. We next investigated whether the successful operation of the novel BMI task was also supported by precise temporal relationships between the trigger and target neurons, independent of the background firing rate increase [13].

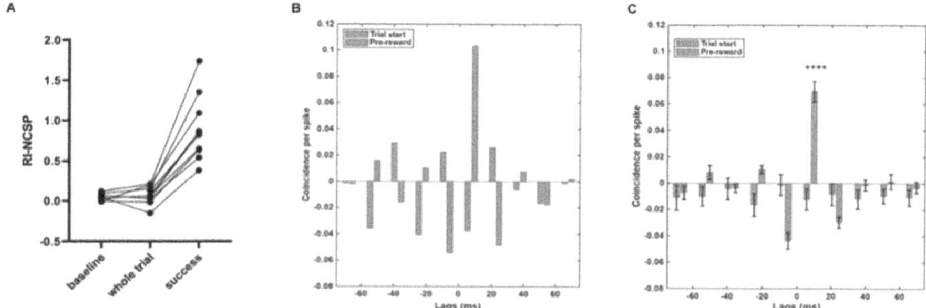

Fig. 5. Task success is also related to the temporal relationships between neurons. (A) Rate-independent NCSP under three conditions, calculated as RI-NCSP = actual NCSP − expected NCSP from two neurons firing independently according to a Poisson distribution. RI-NCSP is present during the success window but near zero during baseline and across the entire task. (B) Cross-correlation histogram from a representative rat showing a significant temporal relationship between the trigger and target neurons, with the trigger neuron leading the target before reward. (C) Same as in (B), averaged across ten rats ($p = 0.0001$).

To quantify this rate-independent synchrony, we calculated the RI-NCSP by subtracting the Expected NCSP from the Actual NCSP count. The Expected NCSP was derived from the Poisson null hypothesis, which assumes the two neurons fire independently according to their measured firing rates (Fig. 5A). The RI-NCSP was near zero during the baseline period and across the entire duration of the task. Crucially, a significant positive RI-NCSP emerged exclusively during the success window (Pre-Reward 300 ms), confirming the presence of Excess Synchrony that cannot be explained by the elevation in firing rate alone (Fig. 5A). This finding provides direct evidence that a functional, precise temporal code contributes independently to the BMI control signal.

We further investigated the structure of this temporal relationship using the Cross-Correlation Histogram (CCH) of the neuronal pairs. The CCH from a representative rat showed a clear peak, indicating a strong temporal relationship where the trigger neuron consistently led the target neuron prior to the reward delivery (Fig. 5B). When averaged across all ten over-trained rats, the population CCH confirmed this directional temporal relationship (Fig. 5C). The presence of a narrow and highly significant peak in the average CCH (p equals 0.0001) confirms the utilization of a precise, short-timescale timing mechanism in the novel BMI task [14].

3.4 Multiscale Feature Fusion Maximizes Decoding Efficacy

Sections 3.3 and 3.4 demonstrated that successful BMI control utilizes two complementary neural features: the coarse-timescale firing rate and the precise temporal synchrony [15]. To quantify the informational synergy between these two dimensions, we assessed the prediction performance of a multi-class Support Vector Machine (SVM) using three distinct feature sets (Fig. 6).

The feature sets were defined as follows: the Rate Feature utilized the average firing rate of the two neurons within the 300 ms success window (coarse timescale); the Temporal Feature utilized the number of coincident spikes within a 15 ms window (precise timescale); and the Hybrid Feature combined both the Rate and Temporal vectors as input.

The classifier achieved a mean prediction accuracy of 48.57% ± 17.59% using the Rate Feature alone (Fig. 6, left panel). The Temporal Feature alone performed worse, yielding an accuracy of 37.86% ± 12.50% (Fig. 6, middle panel). In stark contrast, the Hybrid Feature, which combined both the coarse rate and precise temporal information, achieved a significantly higher prediction accuracy of 72.14% ± 16.37% (Fig. 6, right panel).

This superior performance of the combined features was consistent across all ten subjects (Table 1). The Hybrid Feature consistently yielded the highest decoding accuracy for every individual subject when compared to the corresponding Rate Feature and Temporal Feature alone (Table 1).

These decoding results provide conclusive evidence that the novel BMI task is encoded by a Multiscale Hybrid Code. The integration of coarse-timescale rate modulation with precise temporal synchrony demonstrates a synergistic informational advantage, leading to maximal decoding accuracy and confirming the necessity of multiscale feature fusion for optimal BMI control.

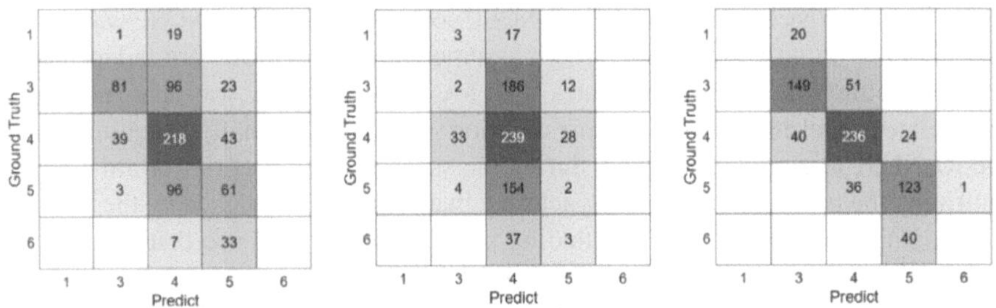

Fig. 6. Confusion matrices for NCSP prediction using a multi-class SVM with different feature sets. The left panel: the rate feature, defined as the average firing rate of two neurons within a 300 ms window. The middle panel: the temporal feature, defined as the number of coincident spikes within 15 ms between the two neurons in the same window, with prediction accuracies of 48.57% ± 17.59% and 37.86% ± 12.50%. The right panel: the hybrid feature, combining both rate and temporal features, with a prediction accuracy of 72.14% ± 16.37%. Prediction performance is higher for the hybrid feature than for either feature alone.

Table 1. Prediction accuracy of the multi-class SVM across subjects

Subject	Rate Feature	Temporal Feature	Hybrid Feature
1	30.45% ± 14.23%	33.64% ± 15.07%	48.18% ± 12.55%
2	34.25% ± 6.59%	24.75% ± 5.31%	45.25% ± 6.06%
3	38.45% ± 9.64%	32.93% ± 7.63%	56.38% ± 10.45%
4	32.00% ± 8.01%	30.00% ± 10.76%	44.25% ± 10.67%
5	48.57% ± 17.59%	37.86% ± 12.50%	72.14% ± 16.37%
6	31.87% ± 15.95%	31.87% ± 15.43%	35.00% ± 11.89%

(*continued*)

Table 1. *(continued)*

Subject	Rate Feature	Temporal Feature	Hybrid Feature
7	33.25% ± 8.16%	30.25% ± 10.82%	69.00% ± 10.71%
8	48.06% ± 9.24%	41.39% ± 10.11%	63.33% ± 6.60%
9	31.43% ± 19.44%	14.29% ± 9.27%	33.57% ± 14.86%
10	29.38% ± 8.63%	28.12% ± 10.04%	40.31% ± 12.25%

4 Discussion and Scientific Implications

4.1 Resolution of the Neural Coding Controversy: The Multiscale Hybrid Strategy

The core scientific ambiguity addressed in this study is whether successful neural control is encoded solely by the robust, long-timescale firing rate (Rate Coding) or by high-fidelity, short-timescale spike timing (Precise Temporal Coding). Our results, derived from the novel BMI task paradigm, definitively resolve this controversy by providing empirical evidence for a Multiscale Hybrid Code architecture.

We demonstrated a clear hierarchical and complementary contribution of two distinct neural features: the coarse-timescale rate modulation and the precise temporal synchrony. Specifically, the perturbation experiment (Fig. 4B) confirmed that the sustained firing rate increase in the 300 ms window alone is enough to provide a robust, near-threshold control signal, as evidenced by performance remaining significantly above the chance level. Conversely, the decoding analysis (Fig. 6 and Table 1) proved that integrating this rate feature with the precise temporal feature yields a maximal decoding accuracy (up to 72.14%), which is significantly superior to either feature alone. This synergistic informational advantage confirms that the neural circuit utilizes both dimensions in a complementary manner to maximize control efficiency and reliability.

4.2 Mechanistic Interpretation: The Two-Stage Coding Model in Operant Conditioning

Our findings support a "Two-Stage Coding Model" rooted in the dynamic properties of cortical microcircuits, where the first stage sets the necessary biophysical context for the second.

The first stage establishes the **Coarse-Timescale Drive** (Rate). The pronounced increase in population firing rate (Fig. 3) likely drives the pyramidal neurons into a "High-Conductance State".[16–19]. In this state, the intense synaptic bombardment drastically reduces the effective membrane time constant, often shrinking it from ~ 20ms to ~ 2-5ms. This biophysical shift effectively forces the neuron to switch its operational mode from a slow temporal integrator to a fast "coincidence detector," rendering it sensitive to precise spike timing rather than just average rate. Thus, the high firing rate is not merely a control signal but a permissive condition that sharpens the network's temporal resolution.

The second stage involves **Precise Temporal Gating** mediated by cortical circuitry[20]. The high-rate excitatory drive from Stage 1 is sufficient to recruit high-threshold Parvalbumin-positive (PV +) interneurons[21]. These fast-spiking interneurons, which exhibit synchrony that is strongly firing-rate dependent, provide strong Feedforward Inhibition (FFI) to the pyramidal neurons. The delay between the excitatory input and the subsequent FFI creates a narrow "window of opportunity" (typically 1-4ms) during which postsynaptic neurons can integrate spikes[22]. This active inhibition acts as a temporal gate, filtering out asynchronous inputs and ensuring that only precisely synchronized spike packets (the Excess Synchrony observed in Fig. 5A) can drive downstream targets. Consequently, the "Two-Stage" nature of the code reflects a physiological hierarchy: the metabolic cost of high firing rates (Stage 1) is invested to recruit the inhibitory machinery (Stage 2) that enforces high-fidelity communication.

4.3 Implications for Next-Generation Brain-Machine Interfaces (BMIs)

The demonstrated superiority of the Hybrid Feature (Fig. 6) has profound implications for the engineering design of future invasive BMI systems. Conventional BMI decoding often relies on slow-timescale features, such as spike counts or low-frequency LFP power. Our results provide empirical proof that such single-scale approaches are inherently suboptimal.

To maximize information transfer rate and system robustness, future BMI algorithms must adopt a **multiscale feature fusion** framework[23]. The distinct performance contribution of the 15 ms synchrony feature highlights that temporal information is not merely an epiphenomenon but a vital component that should be actively integrated during online decoding.

Furthermore, the structure of this hybrid code is particularly advantageous for energy-efficient computing. Models optimized for processing spike-timing events, such as Spiking Neural Networks (SNNs), are biologically inspired and consume significantly less power than traditional Artificial Neural Networks. By integrating our multiscale features into SNN-based decoding models (Multiscale Feature Fusion SNNs)[24], it is possible to achieve high accuracy and high computational efficiency simultaneously, paving the way for the development and commercialization of compact, implantable, and long-term clinical BMI devices.

4.4 Limitations and Future Directions

While this study robustly demonstrated the structure and function of the multiscale hybrid code, a key limitation lies in the lack of direct causal manipulation of the precise temporal component. Although our perturbation (jittering) experiment demonstrated the informativeness of the rate component, future work must employ techniques such as targeted optogenetics or precise electrical micro-stimulation to selectively **induce or disrupt** the narrow CCH peak within the 300 ms window. A dosage-dependent change in BMI performance resulting from this manipulation would unequivocally establish the causal role of precise timing.

Additionally, future analysis should investigate the underlying network dynamics, particularly the relationship between the observed precise synchrony and broader network oscillations (e.g., gamma rhythms)[25]. Establishing whether the rate-independent synchrony is phase-locked to specific oscillatory states would provide further insight into how this temporal code facilitates the integration of information across different frequencies and brain regions[26].

Acknowledgments. This work is funded by: the STI 2030-Major Projects (No.2022ZD0208600), Key R&D Program for Zhejiang (No. 2021C03003, 2022R52033, 2022C03029, 2023C03081, 2023C03026, 2024C03002).

References

1. Kiselev, M.: Rate coding vs. temporal coding - is optimum between? In: Proceedings of the 2016 International Joint Conference on Neural Networks (IJCNN), pp. 1355–1359 (2016). https://doi.org/10.1109/IJCNN.2016.7727355
2. Price, B.H., Gavornik, J.P.: Efficient temporal coding in the early visual system: existing evidence and future directions. Front. Comput. Neurosci. **16** (2022). https://doi.org/10.3389/fncom.2022.929348
3. Panzeri, S., Macke, J.H., Gross, J., Kayser, C.: Neural population coding: combining insights from microscopic and mass signals. Trends Cogn. Sci. **19**, 162–172 (2015). https://doi.org/10.1016/j.tics.2015.01.002
4. Panzeri, S., Moroni, M., Safaai, H., Harvey, C.D.: The structures and functions of correlations in neural population codes. Nat. Rev. Neurosci. **23**, 551–567 (2022). https://doi.org/10.1038/s41583-022-00606-4
5. Fetz, E.E.: Operant conditioning of cortical unit activity. Science **163**, 955–958 (1969). https://doi.org/10.1126/science.163.3870.955
6. Ning, Y., Zhang, S., Guan, H., Xu, K., Zheng, X.: Volitional modulation of temporal spiking patterns uncovers the ability of temporal coding in abstract skills learning. In: Proceedings of the 2019 9th International IEEEEMBS Conference on Neural Engineering, NER (2019). 10/gh4wr8
7. Ning, Y., Zheng, T., Wan, G., Han, J., Liu, T., Zhang, S.: Neural implementation of precise temporal patterns in motor cortex (2022). https://www.biorxiv.org/content/10.1101/2022.04.27.489682v1, https://doi.org/10.1101/2022.04.27.489682
8. Amarasingham, A., Harrison, M.T., Hatsopoulos, N.G., Geman, S.: Conditional modeling and the jitter method of spike resampling. J. Neurophysiol. **107**, 517–531 (2012). https://doi.org/10.1152/jn.00633.2011
9. Grün, S.: Data-driven significance estimation for precise spike correlation. J. Neurophysiol. **101**, 1126–1140 (2009). https://doi.org/10.1152/jn.00093.2008
10. Narayanan, N.S., Laubach, M.: Methods for studying functional interactions among neuronal populations. In: Hyder, F. (eds.) Dynamic Brain Imaging. METHODS IN MOLECULAR BIOLOGY™, vol. 489, pp. 135–165. Humana Press (2009). https://doi.org/10.1007/978-1-59745-543-5_7
11. Bengtsson, F., Geborek, P., Jörntell, H.: Cross-correlations between pairs of neurons in cerebellar cortex *in vivo*. Neural Netw. **47**, 88–94 (2013). https://doi.org/10.1016/j.neunet.2012.11.016
12. Wiegner, A.W., Wierzbicka, M.M.: A method for assessing significance of peaks in cross-correlation histograms. J. Neurosci. Methods **22**, 125–131 (1987). https://doi.org/10.1016/0165-0270(87)90006-9

13. Cutts, C.S., Eglen, S.J.: Detecting pairwise correlations in spike trains: an objective comparison of methods and application to the study of retinal waves. J. Neurosci. **34**, 14288–14303 (2014). https://doi.org/10.1523/JNEUROSCI.2767-14.2014
14. Uhlhaas, P., Pipa, G., Lima, B., Melloni, L., Neuenschwander, S., Nikolić, D., Singer, W.: Neural synchrony in cortical networks: history, concept and current status. Front. Integr. Neurosci. **3** (2009). https://doi.org/10.3389/neuro.07.017.2009
15. Hasegawa, H.: Population rate codes carried by mean, fluctuation and synchrony of neuronal firings. Phys. Stat. Mech. Its Appl. **388**, 499–513 (2009). https://doi.org/10.1016/j.physa.2008.10.033
16. Fetz, E.E.: Volitional control of neural activity: implications for brain–computer interfaces. J. Physiol. **579**, 571–579 (2007). https://doi.org/10.1113/jphysiol.2006.127142
17. Prescott, S.A., Ratté, S., De Koninck, Y., Sejnowski, T.J.: Nonlinear interaction between shunting and adaptation controls a switch between integration and coincidence detection in pyramidal neurons. J. Neurosci. Off. J. Soc. Neurosci. **26**, 9084–9097 (2006). https://doi.org/10.1523/JNEUROSCI.1388-06.2006
18. Stoll, A., Maier, A., Krauss, P., Gerum, R., Schilling, A.: Coincidence detection and integration behavior in spiking neural networks. Cogn. Neurodyn. **18**, 1753–1765 (2024). https://doi.org/10.1007/s11571-023-10038-0
19. Broicher, T., Malerba, P., Dorval, A.D., Borisyuk, A., Fernandez, F.R., White, J.A.: Spike phase locking in CA1 pyramidal neurons depends on background conductance and firing rate. J. Neurosci. **32**, 14374–14388 (2012). https://doi.org/10.1523/JNEUROSCI.0842-12.2012
20. Hu, H., Agmon, A.: Properties of precise firing synchrony between synaptically coupled cortical interneurons depend on their mode of coupling. J. Neurophysiol. **114**, 624–637 (2015). https://doi.org/10.1152/jn.00304.2015
21. D'Souza, R.D., Meier, A.M., Bista, P., Wang, Q., Burkhalter, A.: Recruitment of inhibition and excitation across mouse visual cortex depends on the hierarchy of interconnecting areas. eLife **5**, e19332 (2016). https://doi.org/10.7554/eLife.19332
22. Puzerey, P.A., Galán, R.F.: On how correlations between excitatory and inhibitory synaptic inputs maximize the information rate of neuronal firing. Front. Comput. Neurosci. **8** (2014). https://doi.org/10.3389/fncom.2014.00059
23. Baroni, F., Fulcher, B.D.: Synchrony, oscillations, and phase relationships in collective neuronal activity: a highly comparative overview of methods. PLOS Comput. Biol. **21**, e1013597 (2025). https://doi.org/10.1371/journal.pcbi.1013597
24. Song, Y., Han, L., Zhang, T., Xu, B.: Multiscale fusion enhanced spiking neural network for invasive BCI neural signal decoding. Front. Neurosci. **19**, 1551656 (2025). https://doi.org/10.3389/fnins.2025.1551656
25. Perrenoud, Q., de O. Fonseca, A.H., Airhart, A., Bonanno, J., Mao, R., Cardin, J.A.: Flexible perceptual encoding by discrete gamma events. Nature, 1–8 (2025). https://doi.org/10.1038/s41586-025-09604-9
26. Ainsworth, M., Lee, S., Cunningham, M.O., Traub, R.D., Kopell, N.J., Whittington, M.A.: Rates and rhythms: a synergistic view of frequency and temporal coding in neuronal networks. Neuron **75**, 572–583 (2012). https://doi.org/10.1016/j.neuron.2012.08.004

EEG-Based Depression Recognition: A Federated Domain Generalization Approach with Dynamic Weight Aggregation

Lang He[1,2,3(✉)], Yan Liu[1], and Yongzhen Zhu[1]

[1] School of Computer Science and Technology, Xi'an University of Posts and Telecommunications, 618 Chang'an West Steet, Chang'an District, Xi'an 710121, Shaanxi, China
langhe@xupt.edu.cn

[2] Shaanxi Key Laboratory of Network Data Analysis and Intelligent Processing, Xi'an University of Posts and Telecommunications, 618 Chang'an West Steet, Chang'an District, Xi'an 710121, Shaanxi, China

[3] Xi'an Key Laboratory of Big Data and Intelligent Computing, Xi'an University of Posts and Telecommunications, 618 Chang'an West Steet, Chang'an District, Xi'an 710121, Shaanxi, China

Abstract. Depression is a major global mental health disorder, and the electroencephalogram (EEG) signals have emerged as a promising non-invasive biomarker for its objective assessment. However, the clinical deployment of EEG-based depression detection is hindered by strict privacy regulations, heterogeneous data distributions across institutions, and the impossibility of centralized data integration, resulting in severe data silos and limited model generalizability. To overcome the above-mentioned limitation, we propose a federated domain generalization (FedDG) framework for privacy-preserving EEG-based depression recognition. The framework introduces a fairness-aware global objective that minimizes client-level empirical risk while constraining the variance of generalization gaps across sever domains, thereby promoting consistent cross-domain performance. Furthermore, we develop a generalization adjustment (GA) aggregation strategy that dynamically modulates client weights. The proposed method was evaluated on three publicly EEG depression datasets: MODMA, EDRA, and HUSM, and achieved accuracy rates of 57.76%, 54.14%, and 56.77%, respectively. Experimental results demonstrate that the proposed FedDG framework substantially enhances robustness and generalization to unseen domains while preserving data privacy, offering a viable pathway toward clinically scalable and institution-independent EEG-based depression detection.

Keywords: Depression · EEG · Domain Generalization · Federated Learning (FL)

1 Introduction

According to the latest global disease burden data released by the world health organization (WHO), approximately one billion people are currently affected by

H. Liu et al. (Eds.): CEI 2025, CCIS 2881, pp. 241–257, 2026.
https://doi.org/10.1007/978-981-95-9493-1_16

various forms of mental disorders, with depression alone impacting 280 million individuals. Projections indicate that by 2030, depression will become the mental disorder imposing the heaviest disease burden worldwide [1,2]. China's mental health epidemiological survey further indicates that the number of depression patients in the country has exceeded 95 million, with approximately 30 million people experiencing varying degrees of depressive symptoms annually. Notably, students constitute nearly 50% of all patients, with minors accounting for approximately 30%. The prevalence of depression among adolescents has risen to 15%–20%, approaching adult levels, indicating a significant escalation in mental health risks among young populations [3]. Major depressive disorder (MDD) ranks among the most prevalent and highly disabling mental illnesses. Its primary clinical features include persistent depressive mood, marked anhedonia, and varying degrees of impairment in cognitive and behavioral functioning [4]. The impact of this disorder varies greatly at the individual level: mild cases typically manifest as reduced quality of life and limited work efficiency, while severe cases may involve profound psychological distress and even suicidal behaviors [5,6]. Concurrently, depression exhibits a pronounced trend toward younger onset, making adolescents and young adults a high-risk group requiring special attention. Given depression's chronic course, high recurrence rate, and substantial disability burden, its cumulative impact on individuals, families, and societal systems has become increasingly severe.

Depression arises from complex interactions among biological susceptibility, psychological traits, lifestyle habits, and social environment, with factors such as vitamin B12 and folate deficiencies, genetic predisposition, personality traits (e.g., sensitivity, self-blame, anxiety), unhealthy lifestyles (e.g., poor sleep, unbalanced diet, lack of exercise), weak social support, prolonged loneliness, and inappropriate medication use significantly increasing risk or worsening symptoms [7,8]. Despite its high prevalence, depression remains difficult to diagnose early due to subtle initial symptoms, limited clinical recognition of emotional and cognitive changes, and inadequate access to treatment-leading to severe consequences such as academic disruption and over 700,000 annual global deaths, while less than 10% of patients in resource-limited regions receive effective treatment [9]. With AI-driven medical systems expanding, healthcare institutions increasingly rely on multi-source data to improve diagnostic accuracy; however, strict privacy regulations such as GDPR and PIPL restrict data sharing, forming "data silos." To address this, Google introduced FL in 2016, enabling collaborative model training without exchanging raw data [10–18]. FL allows institutions to update models locally and share only parameters for global aggregation, achieving centralized performance while maintaining data locality and privacy, thus breaking data silos and promoting cross-institutional collaboration in diagnostics and prediction [19,20]. Therefore, this study investigates FL-based EEG depression recognition methods.

In FL-based EEG depression recognition, three core challenges arise. First, strict medical data privacy regulations, such as GDPR and personal information protection laws-prevent inter-institutional data sharing, resulting in limited, fragmented datasets and "data silos" that hinder global model generalization. Second, EEG data from different institutions exhibit substantial domain differences due to variations in acquisition devices, electrode configurations, and patient populations, producing Non-IID characteristics that impair cross-domain generalization. Third, traditional FL methods (e.g., FedAvg [21]) rely on fixed aggregation weights, neglecting each client's contribution to generalization; clients with low-quality or idiosyncratic data can slow convergence and degrade global model performance. To address these issues, this study proposes the following corresponding solutions: (1) the FedDG framework [22] ensures "data available but invisible," allowing clients to retain local data while participating in collaborative training via encrypted parameter transmission. (2) a global objective function with dual-objective optimization is designed: minimizing the average empirical risk across clients to guarantee baseline performance, and incorporating a generalization gap variance regularization term [23] to constrain cross-client performance differences, enhancing fairness and consistency. (3) a GA-based dynamic aggregation algorithm is employed: during local training, each client computes its generalization gap, and during global aggregation, weights are adjusted dynamically based on this gap-clients with smaller gaps receive higher weights, others lower. A linear step-size decay further ensures rapid early convergence and stable later updates. Together, these strategies enable the global model to better align with cross-domain generalization requirements, improving recognition performance on unseen domains.

The key contributions of our study can be concluded as follows:

(1) FedDG framework for privacy-preserving EEG-based depression recognition is proposed. It enables collaborative model training across institutions without sharing raw EEG data, ensuring strong privacy protection.
(2) GA aggregation strategy is proposed. It adaptively adjusts client weights based on generalization gaps, ensuring balanced optimization. This enhances model stability and improves cross-domain generalization.

2 Related Works

This section briefly outlines depression recognition techniques. To comprehensively understand existing research findings, we delve into the technical application of federated domain generalization in EEG signal recognition.

With the rapid development of AI, machine learning relying on large datasets has become mainstream, yet single-source data often lacks sufficient quantity and quality for effective training. Data sharing across institutions is difficult, and rising privacy concerns, especially in healthcare-further restrict centralized data collection. Google's FL framework addresses these issues by enabling collaborative training without exposing raw data. Unlike traditional distributed methods [24–27], which emphasize communication efficiency, FL targets privacy-preserving large-scale distributed learning. FedAvg improves communication efficiency by coordinating updates between clients and servers, but heterogeneous data and device capabilities can cause unbalanced contributions and degrade global model performance. To mitigate this, FedProx [28] adds a proximal term to stabilize local training under Non-IID conditions, reducing communication costs without harming accuracy [29]. SCAFFOLD introduces control variates to correct client drift and reduce communication overhead [30], while FedNova accelerates convergence and improves performance under heterogeneous settings [31].

Google's TensorFlow Federated framework (2019) addresses distributed computation and privacy challenges and has been applied to tasks such as next-word and emoji prediction on mobile devices. The Federated AI Technology Enabler (FATE), developed by WeBank, is the first industrial-grade open-source FL framework, supporting horizontal FL, vertical FL, and federated transfer learning [32], enabling secure cross-institutional data collaboration in fields such as finance. FL has also been applied across various domains: Fauzi et al. used it for stress detection via multimodal smartwatch data [33]; Lee et al. designed a privacy-preserving platform for cross-institutional patient similarity learning [34]; Liu et al. applied tensor decomposition to extract meaningful representations from large-scale electronic health records in FL settings [35]. Additionally, Huang and Brisimi et al. [36,37] demonstrated that FL can effectively train predictive models, such as cardiac-patient mortality prediction, using distributed hospital data. Xu et al. proposed a privacy-preserving FL framework. This framework fuses multi-source mobile health data from multiple perspectives, enabling collaborative model training without sharing patient data [38]. Li et al. proposed an asynchronous federated optimization algorithm to extract meaningful information from data collected from Weibo users' posts (including nicknames, follower counts, following counts, and post content) to build a depression detection model for identifying depression among Weibo users [39]. Results demonstrated superior performance over other benchmark algorithms on Non-IID datasets [40], while simultaneously enhancing training efficiency and convergence speed while safeguarding user privacy. Liu et al. proposed a clinical decision support framework employing federated deep learning (FDL) to identify individuals experiencing depression and provide intervention recommendations for clinicians [41]. These studies demonstrate that federated learning not only protects patient privacy but also enables cross-institutional collaboration. By eliminating the need for centralized data sharing, it provides an effective solution for depression detection and treatment. Patient data remains securely stored at each institution, preventing sensitive information leakage, while collaborative training through model update exchange allows institutions to share knowledge without compromising privacy.

3 Our Method

In this part, we initiate by presenting an illustration of our framework, which can be found in Sect. 3.1. Subsequently, we elaborate the proposed architecture in Sect. 3.2, 3.3, and 3.4.

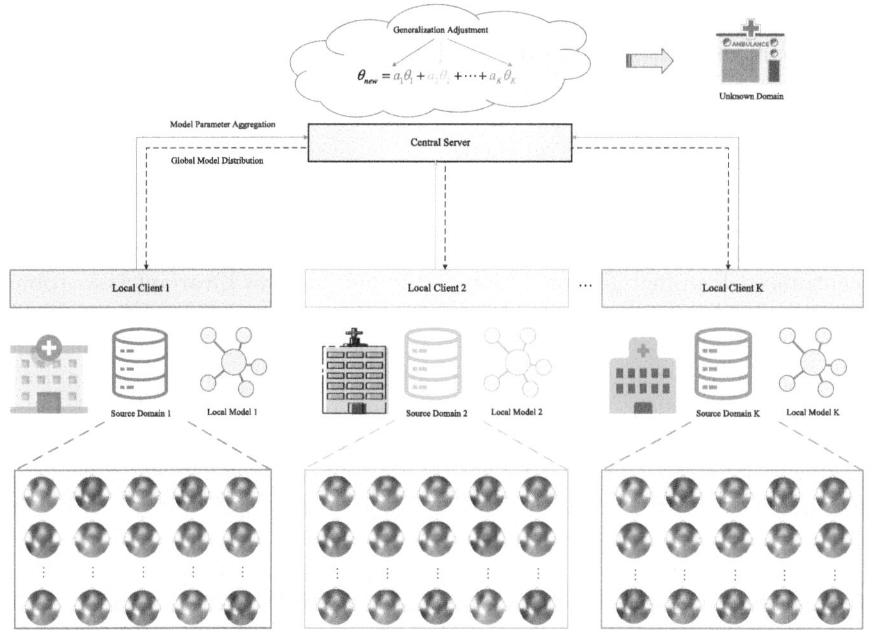

Fig. 1. Pipeline of our proposed architecture

3.1 Architecture Overview

Existing depression detection relies on centralized multi-center training, but data-sharing restrictions limit its practicality. Although FL protects privacy, heterogeneous data often degrades global performance and causes optimization unfairness. To address privacy, cross-domain generalization, and fairness simultaneously, we propose a federated domain generalization framework combining a GA strategy with an improved global objective. GA uses the performance gap between local and global models to dynamically adjust client weights, mitigating the bias of fixed FedAvg weighting. A dual-objective function-minimizing average empirical risk and constraining generalization-gap variance-ensures both performance and cross-client consistency. Together, GA dynamic weighting and dual-objective optimization enhance cross-institutional generalization and fairness under privacy constraints.

FL has been limited in privacy-preserving cross-institutional depression detection due to severe client heterogeneity, as EEG data vary across hospitals in geography, equipment, sampling, and individual differences. Such Non-IID distributions hinder global model generalization, while traditional fixed-weight aggregation allows clients with limited or low-quality data to overly influence the global model. Moreover, conventional FL focuses on empirical risk and overlooks cross-domain generalization. To address these issues, this chapter enhances global generalization by reducing the gap between each client's performance and its locally optimal model. As shown in Fig. 1, the proposed method dynamically adjusts client aggregation weights to better handle Non-IID data and improve cross-domain robustness. By optimizing an objective function that integrates a fairness regularization term, the approach iteratively updates client weights to minimize the generalization gap, thereby improving the global model's consistency and adaptability across all clients.

3.2 Global Model Learning

In centralized learning, generalization techniques such as invariant risk, robust optimization, and fairness rely on multi-domain data within a single batch, which is infeasible in federated domain generalization due to client data isolation. To overcome this, we propose a global objective function that improves fairness and cross-client generalization without aggregating raw data. It minimizes the average risk across clients while adding a fairness regularization term to reduce risk variance, mitigating performance bias and enhancing robustness. This enables effective generalization across diverse and unseen domains in federated settings. Under federated domain generalization, let the set of all domains be $D = D_1, D_2, ..., D_i$, where each D_i is an independent distribution. In practice, only sampled domains $\hat{D} = \hat{D}_1, \hat{D}_2, ..., \hat{D}_M$ are accessed, with M clients participating. Each domain $\hat{D}_i$ contains sample pairs (x, y), where x is the input and y the label. A loss function $\mathcal{L}$ measures the difference between the model prediction $f(x;\sigma)$ (parameterized by σ) and y. For a domain $D_i \in D$, its expected risk is defined as:

$$\mathcal{E}_{D_i}(\sigma) = \mathbb{E}_{(x,y)\in D_i}[\mathcal{L}(f(x;\sigma), y)] \tag{1}$$

The expected risk represents the model's average loss over all samples in a domain. Since complete domain data is unavailable in practice, it is estimated using sampled data. Suppose N_i samples are drawn from domain $\hat{D}_i$, denoted as $\hat{D}_i = \{x_j^i, y_j^i\}_{j=1}^{N_i}$; the empirical risk is then defined as:

$$\widehat{\mathcal{E}}_{\hat{D}_i}(\sigma) = \frac{1}{N_i}\sum\nolimits_{j=1}^{N_i} \mathcal{L}\left(f(x_j^i;\sigma), y_j^i\right) \tag{2}$$

Empirical risk approximates the model's performance in a domain using limited sampled data. The main goal of federated domain generalization is to minimize the overall loss across all domains. Since only the sampled domains $\hat{D}$ are accessible in practice, the optimization objective is approximated using the empirical risk:

$$\min_{\sigma}\mathcal{E}_{\mathcal{D}}(\sigma) \approx \sum_{i=1}^{M} p_i\widehat{\mathcal{E}}_{\hat{D}_i}(\sigma) = \sum_{i=1}^{M} p_i \sum_{j=1}^{N_i} \mathcal{L}\left(f(x_j^i;\sigma), y_j^i\right) \tag{3}$$

Among them, the weight $p_i = \frac{N_i}{\sum_{i=1}^{M} N_i}$ is dynamically adjusted according to the sample size of each domain, ensuring that domains with a larger sample size contribute more to the total loss.

Theoretically, the flatness of each domain can be quantified by the performance difference between the global model and the local model on that domain, defined specifically as:

$$G_{\hat{D}_i}(\sigma) = G_{\hat{D}_i}\left(\sum_j a_j \sigma_j^*\right) = \widehat{\mathcal{E}}_{\hat{D}_i}\left(\sum_j a_j \sigma_j^*\right) - \widehat{\mathcal{E}}_{\hat{D}_i}(\sigma_i^*) \tag{4}$$

Among them, σ_i^* denotes the locally optimal model parameters obtained by the client through training on local data $\hat{D}_i$, and $\sigma = \sum_j a_j \sigma_j^*$ is the model parameter after global aggregation. The generalization gap $G_{\hat{D}_i}(\sigma)$ reflects the performance loss of the global model on domain $\hat{D}_i$, i.e., the difference in empirical risk between the global model and the locally optimal model, which can effectively characterize the generalization ability of the model on this domain.

Based on the above theory and inspired by variance regularization [42] in robust optimization, this study proposes a new global optimization objective. It enforces the flatness of the global model across all domains by constraining the variance of each client's generalization gap, formulated as follows:

$$\begin{aligned} \min_{a_1,\ldots,a_M,\sigma} \quad & \hat{\mathcal{E}}_{\hat{D}}(\sigma) = \sum_{i=1}^{M} a_i \hat{\mathcal{E}}_{\hat{D}_i}(\sigma) + \beta \mathrm{Var}\left(\{G_{\hat{D}_i}(\sigma)\}_{i=1}^{M}\right) \\ \text{s.t.} \quad & \sum_{i=1}^{M} a_i = 1, \quad \sigma = \sum_{i=1}^{M} a_i \sigma_i, \quad \text{and } \forall i,\ a_i \geq 0. \end{aligned} \tag{5}$$

Here, $a = (a_1, a_2, \cdots, a_M)$ is a learnable client weight vector used to dynamically adjust each client's contribution to the global model. The hyperparameter $\beta \in [0, \infty]$ balances global empirical risk minimization and fairness of domain generalization gaps: when $\beta = 0$, the objective reduces to classic FedAvg, minimizing weighted empirical risk; when $\beta \to \infty$, the optimization enforces equal generalization gaps across clients, maximizing flatness and enhancing the model's robustness and generalization.

3.3 Dynamic Parameter Aggregation

In FL, fixed aggregation weights can reduce global model fairness and degrade performance for clients with heterogeneous data. To address this, a GA-based algorithm is employed to dynamically optimize client weights, balancing contributions and enhancing both generalization and fairness. Using evolutionary strategies from genetic algorithms, each client's performance change before and after aggregation is calculated: clients with increased loss are assigned higher weights to accelerate convergence, while those with reduced loss receive lower weights, guiding the global model toward equitable cross-client performance. In practice, a and σ_i cannot be optimized simultaneously in FL, as aggregation weights a_i are linked to the corresponding generalization gaps $G_{\hat{D}_i}(\sigma)$. Adjusting a_i effectively influences the variance of generalization gaps. Thus, optimization is divided into two stages: (1) local training, where model parameters σ_i are optimized via gradient descent; (2) aggregation, where a_i is optimized using GA to minimize the variance of generalization gaps, yielding a global model with improved generalization.

During training, there exists an interactive relationship between the aggregation weight a_i and the generalization gap $G_{\hat{D}_i}(\sigma)$. Specifically, for a given domain k, the relationship between the global parameter σ and the local model parameter σ_k can be expressed as:

$$\sigma = \sigma_k + \Delta\sigma \tag{6}$$

Among them, $\Delta\sigma = (1-a_k)\sigma_k + \sum_{i\neq k} a_i\sigma_i$ represents a perturbation applied to σ_k. For $\hat{\mathcal{E}}_{\hat{D}_i}(\sigma)$, if $a_k$is increased, the proportion of $\{a_i\}_{i\neq k}$ will decrease accordingly, thereby reducing the magnitude of the perturbation $\Delta\sigma$. In this case, the global model σ will be closer to the local optimal value σ_k, which will make the loss of $\hat{\mathcal{E}}_{\hat{D}_k}(\sigma)$ on domain $\hat{D}_k$ gradually decrease. In the next round of training, the new global model σ) will be used as the initial weight for all clients, which will improve the proximity between σ_k and $\Delta\sigma$, and thus gradually reduce the mean value of the generalization gap.

Suppose there are M clients participating in training under the FL framework, and the corresponding training dataset is $\hat{D} = \{\hat{D}_1, \hat{D}_2, \ldots, \hat{D}_M\}$, where each $\hat{D}_i$ represents a training domain. Let the total number of communication rounds be R, the number of local training steps per round be E, and assume the local training algorithm is $\mathcal{A}lg(\sigma_i^r, \hat{D}_i, E)$. Before the start of each round of local training, an additional evaluation of the global model σ^r is required to calculate its generalization gap, and the specific calculation method is as follows:

$$G_{\hat{D}_i}(\sigma^r) = \hat{\mathcal{E}}_{\hat{D}_i}(\sigma^r) - \hat{\mathcal{E}}_{\hat{D}_i}(\sigma_i^{r-1}),\ i = 1, 2, \ldots, M \tag{7}$$

Then, the local training phase $\mathcal{A}lg(\sigma^r, \hat{D}_i, E)$ is initiated. After the training is completed, $G_{\hat{D}_i}(\sigma^r)$ and the updated local model parameter $\sigma_i^{r\prime}$ are sent to the server. A strategy for updating aggregation weights a_i based on the contribution of each client is designed on the server side. Specifically, given the generalization gaps $\{G_{\hat{D}_i}(\sigma^r)\}_{i=1}^M$ of all domains and the weights a^{r-1} from the previous round, the new weight a^r is calculated using the following formulas:

$$a_i^{r\prime} = \frac{(G_{\hat{D}_i}(\sigma^r) - \mu) * d^r}{\max_j(G_{\hat{D}_j}(\sigma^r) - \mu)} + a_i^{r-1} \tag{8}$$

$$a_i^r = \frac{a_i^{r\prime}}{\sum_{i=1}^M a_i^{r\prime}} \tag{9}$$

Here, $\mu = \frac{1}{M}\sum_{i=1}^M G_{\hat{D}_i}(\sigma^r)$, $d^r = (1 - r/R) * d$, and the hyperparameter $d \in (0, 1)$ controls the magnitude of each weight adjustment, serving as a substitute for β in Eq. 5. To stabilize training, a linear decay strategy is applied: using a fixed step size may cause weight instability later, while the gradual reduction of the generalization gap can slow early convergence. After each adjustment, $a_i^{r\prime}$

is clipped to [0,1], and the sum of all weights is normalized to 1. The global model σ^{r+1} is then aggregated using the updated weights a^r and broadcast to all clients as initialization for the next round.

3.4 Cross-Domain Generalization

This study minimizes generalization gaps across clients by optimizing the global model's objective function, achieving more balanced performance across all clients. Client weights are dynamically adjusted based on their generalization ability, and parameter aggregation is performed to enhance the global model's generalization. Once the global model σ^R is obtained, it is directly applied to an unseen target domain D_t for depression recognition without additional training, relying solely on the model's generalization capability. The recognition function is expressed as:

$$\hat{y} = f_{\sigma^R}(x),\ x \sim D_t \tag{10}$$

where $f_{\sigma^R}(\cdot)$ represents the recognition process based on the global model σ^R, and $\hat{y}$ is the depression state predicted by the model.

4 Experiments

4.1 Datasets

The proposed framework was evaluated on three public EEG datasets related to depression, selecting a subset of spatially representative electrodes with Cz as the reference to ensure comparability and limit computational cost.

The MODMA dataset includes 24 patients with severe depression (13 males; mean age 30.5 ± 10.7 years) and 29 healthy controls (20 males; mean age 31.6 ± 9.3 years). EEG was recorded using a 128-channel HydroCel Geodesic Sensor Net at 250 Hz for 5 min of eyes-closed resting-state under standardized conditions. The EDRA dataset comprises 26 depressed participants (16 males; mean age 21.9 ± 1.99 years) and 24 healthy controls (19 males; mean age 21.3 ± 1.34 years). EEG was acquired with a 64-electrode cap (62 channels retained plus 1 VEOG) in an electromagnetically shielded environment during eyes-closed resting-state, after participants completed the PROMIS depression scale and other questionnaires. The HUSM dataset contains 34 patients with major depressive disorder (17 males, 17 females; mean age 40.3 ± 12.9) and 30 healthy controls (21 males, 9 females; mean age 38.3 ± 15.6). EEG recordings used 19-channel caps at 256 Hz during 5-minute closed and open-eye sessions; only closed-eye resting-state data were used. Patients underwent a two-week medication washout, and the study followed international diagnostic criteria with ethical approval.

4.2 Experimental Setup

This section evaluates the effectiveness of the proposed method through experiments. Optimal experimental parameters were determined via multiple trials, the impact of different parameter aggregation methods was compared, and the contribution of the GA strategy to model generalization was assessed. Experiments were conducted on the MODMA, EDRA, and HUSM datasets, with one domain sequentially chosen as the target and the remaining two as source domains. Within each source domain, 90% of the data was randomly used for training and 10% for validation, following [43]. The local model was trained with a batch size of 64 and a learning rate of 0.001, over 5 local epochs per round. A total of 40 communication rounds were performed between clients and server, with a GA step size of 0.05.

4.3 Parameter Selection

Within the federated domain generalization framework, parameter selection is critical for training efficiency and cross-domain performance. This study evaluates key parameters, including the number of local training iterations, GA step size, and decay strategies. Local training iterations of 1, 3, 5, 7, and 10 were tested to assess their effect on convergence, recognition accuracy, and generalization, with results shown in Table 1. Performing 5 iterations per client per round yielded the highest average accuracy across the three datasets (55.65%), balancing convergence, feature learning, and overfitting, and was adopted for all subsequent experiments. For the GA algorithm, step sizes of 0.001, 0.005, 0.1, and 0.2 were evaluated with a linear decay strategy to gradually reduce update magnitude over communication rounds, preventing instability as generalization gaps narrow. As shown in Table 2, using an initial step size of 0.005 with decay achieves the highest average accuracy (56.22%) versus 53.81% without decay, while very small step sizes (0.001) limit convergence and larger steps (0.1–0.2) are stable but suboptimal. The decay strategy facilitates rapid early convergence and fine-tuned late-stage optimization, enhancing both training stability and cross-domain generalization, and is applied in all subsequent experiments.

Table 1. The impact of local training epochs on performance on MODMA, EDRA and HUSM databases

Iteration Count	MODMA(%)	EDRA(%)	HUSM(%)	Average(%)
1	52.00	51.64	51.72	51.79
3	51.99	54.70	50.77	52.49
5	57.76	54.14	56.77	**56.22**
7	52.00	52.26	54.25	52.82
10	60.58	49.80	54.15	54.84

Table 2. The impact of fixed step size and decay strategies on the GA Algorithm on MODMA, EDRA and HUSM databases

step size		MODMA(%)	EDRA(%)	HUSM(%)	Average(%)
0.001	w/o D	52.17	50.78	53.59	52.18
	w D	52.00	50.00	55.80	**52.60**
0.005	w/o D	56.05	52.58	52.79	53.81
	w D	57.76	54.14	56.77	**56.22**
0.1	w/o D	51.96	56.91	52.38	54.35
	w D	53.91	53.89	52.75	**55.05**
0.2	w/o D	52.25	52.71	53.89	52.95
	w D	56.56	54.72	49.49	**53.59**

4.4 Performances of GA

To evaluate the effectiveness of the GA algorithm, several classic FL methods addressing client heterogeneity were selected, including FedAvg, FedProx, Scaffold, and FedSAM. FedProx introduces a proximity term to mitigate differences in client data distributions, Scaffold reduces client update bias via control variables, and FedSAM enhances local model flatness to improve generalization. The GA algorithm was integrated with each method across the three datasets, and performance comparisons before and after GA integration are presented in Table 3.

Table 3. The impact of GA algorithm on overall performance on MODMA, EDRA and HUSM databases

Method		MODMA(%)	EDRA(%)	HUSM(%)	Average(%)
FedAvg	w/o GA	58.91	51.07	56.94	55.64
	w GA	57.76	54.14	56.77	**56.22**
FedProx	w/o GA	55.88	48.94	55.62	53.48
	w GA	57.29	51.12	54.68	**54.36**
Scaffold	w/o GA	52.00	52.17	49.90	51.36
	w GA	52.14	52.51	50.33	**51.66**
FedSAM	w/o GA	52.00	48.94	51.89	50.94
	w GA	52.08	51.06	53.46	**52.20**

Table 3 indicates that "w/o GA" denotes results without the GA algorithm, while "w GA" denotes results with GA integration. Across all FL methods, incorporating GA consistently improves domain generalization. Specifically, FedAvg's average accuracy increased from 55.64% to 56.22%, FedProx from 53.48% to 54.36%, Scaffold from 51.36% to 51.66%, and FedSAM from 50.94% to 52.20%.

FedSAM+GA achieved the largest improvement (1.26%), while Scaffold+GA showed the smallest (0.3%). GA also enhanced cross-client consistency, reducing overreliance on any single client. Overall, FedAvg+GA attained the best performance, demonstrating that GA dynamically adjusts client weights, narrows generalization gaps, and optimizes aggregation to improve cross-domain generalization over fixed-weight methods.

Compare with the State of the Art Methods. The method performance under the joint domain generalization framework, this study selected three classical deep learning approaches ResNet, SE_ResNet, and MLP local models for comparison. The primary objective was to evaluate the performance of local models within this framework by comparing their average accuracy. The experimental results are presented in Table. 4.

Table 4. The impact of FedDG local models on performance on MODMA, EDRA and HUSM databases

Method	MODMA(%)	EDRA(%)	HUSM(%)	Average(%)
ResNet	56.27	52.74	54.69	54.57
SE_ResNet	52.16	55.28	53.25	53.56
MLP	52.36	56.48	54.83	54.56
Ours	57.76	54.14	56.77	**56.22**

Table. 4 demonstrates that theproposed method achieves higher average accuracy than three classical deep learning approaches: ResNet, SE_ResNet, and MLP. ResNet achieves an average accuracy of 54.57%, SE_ResNet attains 53.56%, and MLP reaches 54.56%, while the proposed method achieves an average accuracy of 56.22%. These results validate the superiority of the proposed method in cross domain tasks. By dynamically adjusting client weights and optimizing the feature aggregation process, it better adapts to different data distributions, thereby enhancing the model's generalization performance.

Performance Analysis Across Different Subjects. To evaluate the proposed method's effectiveness in cross-subject depression recognition, cross-subject generalization experiments were conducted on three datasets. Each dataset was divided into multiple subject domains, with each subject forming an independent domain, following the partitioning approach in [43]. Domains were created sequentially based on filenames, maintaining balanced numbers of depressed patients and healthy controls, while any remaining subjects were excluded. The resulting domain partitioning for all three datasets is summarized in Table 5.

Experiments on the MODMA, EDRA, and HUSM datasets used 12-fold cross-validation, with each individual forming a domain (MODMA 1–12, EDRA

Table 5. The domain partitioning results for the MODMA, EDRA, and HUSM Datasets

Dataset	Number of MDD and HC per domain(MDD, HC)	Number of domains
MODMA (24 MDD, 29 HC)	(2,2)	12
EDRA (26 MDD, 24 HC)	(2,2)	12
HUSM (34 MDD, 30 HC)	(2,2)	15

1–12). In each fold, one domain was the target and the remaining 11 were sources, and recognition accuracy was computed for the target. The process was repeated for all domains, and the final accuracy was averaged across folds. As shown in Table 6 and Fig. 2, the proposed method achieved average accuracies of 55.75% (MODMA), 54.02% (EDRA), and 53.49% (HUSM), demonstrating stable cross-subject performance and effective mitigation of inter-individual variation, enhancing generalization.

Table 6. The performance of cross-subject on MODMA, EDRA, and HUSM Datasets

MODMA		EDRA		HUSM	
Target	Accuracy(%)	Target	Accuracy(%)	Target	Accuracy(%)
MODMA 1	53.67	EDRA 1	58.47	HUSM 1	56.35
MODMA 2	60.04	EDRA 2	52.84	HUSM 2	52.14
MODMA 3	50.94	EDRA 3	54.39	HUSM 3	53.67
MODMA 4	54.31	EDRA 4	53.28	HUSM 4	59.43
MODMA 5	52.89	EDRA 5	55.76	HUSM 5	51.99
MODMA 6	53.67	EDRA 6	52.31	HUSM 6	54.73
MODMA 7	54.96	EDRA 7	50.24	HUSM 7	52.65
MODMA 8	57.46	EDRA 8	53.79	HUSM 8	51.89
MODMA 9	56.48	EDRA 9	54.03	HUSM 9	61.29
MODMA 10	59.34	EDRA 10	53.48	HUSM 10	53.06
MODMA 11	53.47	EDRA 11	54.62	HUSM 11	52.27
MODMA 12	61.76	EDRA 12	54.99	HUSM 12	53.91
				HUSM 13	51.58
				HUSM 14	50.21
				HUSM 15	55.84
Average	55.75	Average	54.02	Average	53.49

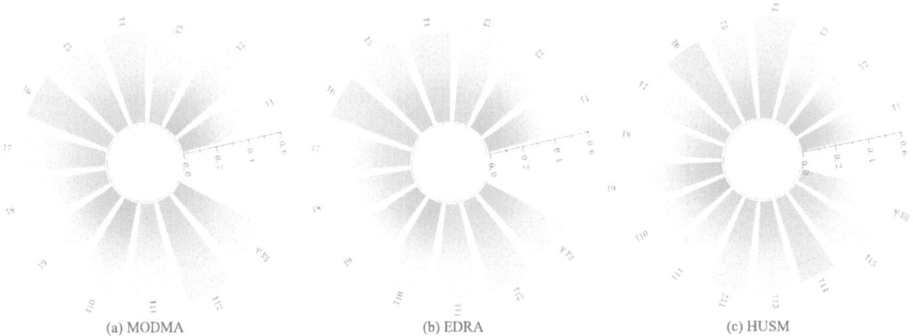

Fig. 2. The performance of cross-subject on MODMA, EDRA, and HUSM Datasets

5 Conclusions

This study proposes FedGA, an EEG-based federated learning framework for depression recognition that enables multi-institutional collaboration without data sharing, ensuring privacy protection and improved cross-domain performance. A global objective function is introduced to enhance generalization by minimizing the generalization gap across clients, and a genetic algorithm dynamically adjusts client weights accordingly. FedGA achieves 57.76%, 54.14%, and 56.77% accuracy on the MODMA, EDRA, and HUSM datasets, surpassing traditional FL methods. Results show that FedGA substantially improves global model generalization to unseen domains.

Acknowledgment. This work is supported by National Natural Science Foundation of China (grant 62376215), the Open Fund of National Engineering Laboratory for Big Data System Computing Technology (Grant No. SZU-BDSC-OF2024-16), the Key Research and Development Project of Shaanxi Province (2024GX-YBXM-137), and the Key Research and Development Project of Xianyang (L2024-ZDYF-ZDYF-SF-0067).

References

1. Chase, T.N.: Apathy in neuropsychiatric disease: diagnosis, pathophysiology, and treatment. Neurotox. Res. **19**(2), 266–278 (2011)
2. He, L., Li, Z., Tiwari, P., et al.: Depressformer: leveraging video swin transformer and fine-grained local features for depression scale estimation. Biomed. Signal Process. Control **96**, 106490 (2024)
3. Chen, X., Li, F., Zuo, H., et al.: Trends in prevalent cases and disability-adjusted life-years of depressive disorders worldwide: findings from the global burden of disease study from 1990 to 2021. Depress. Anxiety **2025**(1), 5553491 (2025)
4. He, L., Zhu, Y.: STC-ND: leveraging spatiotemporal characteristics with NeXtVLAD for depression detection from few-channel EEG signals. In: CSIG Conference on Emotional Intelligence, Springer Nature Singapore, Singapore, pp. 219–236 (2024)

5. Hawton, K., i Comabella, C.C., Haw, C., et al.: Risk factors for suicide in individuals with depression: a systematic review. J. Affect. Disord. **147**(1-3), 17–28 (2013)
6. Toh, W.L., Thomas, N., Rossell, S.L.: Auditory verbal hallucinations in bipolar disorder (BD) and major depressive disorder (MDD): a systematic review. J. Affect. Disord. **184**, 18–28 (2015)
7. Kılıçaslan, A.K., Yıldız, S., Kurt, O., et al.: Personality characteristics, anxiety sensitivity, anxiety, and depression levels on patients diagnosed with psychogenic pruritus. Alpha Psychiatry **23**(5), 243 (2022)
8. He, L., Niu, M., Tiwari, P., et al.: Deep learning for depression recognition with audiovisual cues: a review. Inf. Fusion **80**, 56–86 (2022)
9. Cd, M.: Projections of global mortality and burden of disease from 2002 to 2030. PLoS Med. **3**, 2011–2030 (2006)
10. Konečný, J., McMahan, H.B., Ramage, D., et al.: Federated optimization: Distributed machine learning for on-device intelligence. arXiv preprint arXiv:1610.02527 (2016)
11. He, L., Yang, W., Zhao, J., et al.: FedDAAM: federated domain adversarial learning with attention mechanism for privacy preserving multimodal depression assessment. IEEE Trans. Circ. Syst. Video Technol. (2025)
12. He, L., Chen, K., Zhao, J., et al.: LMVD: a large-scale multimodal vlog dataset for depression detection in the wild. Inf. Fusion 103632 (2025)
13. He, L., Zhao, J., Zhang, J., et al.: LMTformer: facial depression recognition with lightweight multi-scale transformer from videos. Appl. Intell. **55**(3), 195 (2025)
14. He, L., Cao, C.: Automated depression analysis using convolutional neural networks from speech. J. Biomed. Inform. **83**, 103–111 (2018)
15. He, L., Jiang, D., Sahli, H.: Automatic depression analysis using dynamic facial appearance descriptor and dirichlet process fisher encoding. IEEE Trans. Multimedia **21**(6), 1476–1486 (2018)
16. He, L., Guo, C., Tiwari, P., et al.: Intelligent system for depression scale estimation with facial expressions and case study in industrial intelligence. Int. J. Intell. Syst. **37**(12), 10140–10156 (2022)
17. He, L., Guo, C., Tiwari, P., et al.: DepNet: an automated industrial intelligent system using deep learning for video-based depression analysis. Int. J. Intell. Syst. **37**(7), 3815–3835 (2022)
18. He, L., Tiwari, P., Lv, C., et al.: Reducing noisy annotations for depression estimation from facial images. Neural Netw. **153**, 120–129 (2022)
19. Pathak, R., Wainwright, M.J.: FedSplit: an algorithmic framework for fast federated optimization. Adv. Neural. Inf. Process. Syst. **33**, 7057–7066 (2020)
20. He, L., Li, Z., Tiwari, P., et al.: LSCAformer: long and short-term cross-attention-aware transformer for depression recognition from video sequences. Biomed. Signal Process. Control **98**, 106767 (2024)
21. McMahan, B., Moore, E., Ramage, D., et al.: Communication-efficient learning of deep networks from decentralized data. In: Artificial Intelligence and Statistics, PMLR, pp. 1273–1282 (2017)
22. Zhang, R., Xu, Q., Yao, J., et al.: Federated domain generalization with generalization adjustment. In: Proceedings of the IEEE/CVF Conference on Computer Vision and Pattern Recognition, pp. 3954–3963 (2023)
23. Oyedotun, O.K., Papadopoulos, K., Aouada, D.: A new perspective for understanding generalization gap of deep neural networks trained with large batch sizes. Appl. Intell. **53**(12), 15621–15637 (2023)

24. Smith, V., Forte, S., Ma, C., et al.: CoCoA: a general framework for communication-efficient distributed optimization. J. Mach. Learn. Res. **18**(230), 1–49 (2018)
25. Sahu, A.K., Jakovetic, D., Bajovic, D., et al.: Communication-efficient distributed strongly convex stochastic optimization: Non-asymptotic rates. arXiv preprint arXiv:1809.02920 (2018)
26. Lian, X., Zhang, C., Zhang, H., et al.: Can decentralized algorithms outperform centralized algorithms? a case study for decentralized parallel stochastic gradient descent. In: Advances in Neural Information Processing Systems, vol. 30 (2017)
27. He, L., Chan, J.C.W., Wang, Z.: Automatic depression recognition using CNN with attention mechanism from videos. Neurocomputing **422**, 165–175 (2021)
28. Cui, J., Li, Y., Zhang, Q., et al.: A federated learning framework using fedprox algorithm for privacy-preserving palmprint recognition. In: Chinese Conference on Biometric Recognition. Springer Nature Singapore, Singapore, pp. 187–196 (2024)
29. Li, T., Sahu, A.K., Zaheer, M., et al.: Federated optimization in heterogeneous networks. Proc. Mach. Learn. Syst. **2**, 429–450 (2020)
30. Karimireddy, S.P., Kale, S., Mohri, M., et al.: Scaffold: stochastic controlled averaging for federated learning. In: International Conference on Machine Learning, PMLR, pp. 5132–5143 (2020)
31. Wang, J., Liu, Q., Liang, H., et al.: Tackling the objective inconsistency problem in heterogeneous federated optimization. Adv. Neural. Inf. Process. Syst. **33**, 7611–7623 (2020)
32. Liu, Y., Fan, T., Chen, T., et al.: Fate: an industrial grade platform for collaborative learning with data protection. J. Mach. Learn. Res. **22**(226), 1–6 (2021)
33. Fauzi, M.A., Yang, B., Blobel, B.: Comparative analysis between individual, centralized, and federated learning for smartwatch based stress detection. J. Personalized Med. **12**(10), 1584 (2022)
34. Lee, J., Sun, J., Wang, F., et al.: Privacy-preserving patient similarity learning in a federated environment: development and analysis. JMIR Med. Inform. **6**(2), e7744 (2018)
35. Liu, D., Dligach, D., Miller, T.: Two-stage federated phenotyping and patient representation learning. In: Proceedings of the Conference, Association for Computational Linguistics. Meeting, vol. 2019, p. 283 (2019)
36. Huang, L., Shea, A.L., Qian, H., et al.: Patient clustering improves efficiency of federated machine learning to predict mortality and hospital stay time using distributed electronic medical records[J]. J. Biomed. Inform. **99**, 103291 (2019)
37. Brisimi, T.S., Chen, R., Mela, T., et al.: Federated learning of predictive models from federated electronic health records. Int. J. Med. Informatics **112**, 59–67 (2018)
38. Xu, X., Peng, H., Bhuiyan, M.Z.A., et al.: Privacy-preserving federated depression detection from multisource mobile health data. IEEE Trans. Industr. Inf. **18**(7), 4788–4797 (2021)
39. Li, J., Jiang, M., Qin, Y., et al.: Intelligent depression detection with asynchronous federated optimization. Complex Intell. Syst. **9**(1), 115–131 (2023)
40. Yang, Q., Liu, Y., Chen, T., et al.: Federated machine learning: concept and applications. ACM Trans. Intell. Syst. Technol. (TIST) **10**(2), 1–19 (2019)
41. Liu, Y.: Depression clinical detection model based on social media: a federated deep learning approach. J. Supercomput. **80**(6) (2024)

42. Krueger, D., Caballero, E., Jacobsen, J.H., et al.: Out-of-distribution generalization via risk extrapolation (rex). In: International Conference on Machine Learning, PMLR, pp. 5815–5826 (2021)
43. Xu, Q., Zhang, R., Zhang, Y., et al.: A fourier-based framework for domain generalization. In: Proceedings of the IEEE/CVF Conference on Computer Vision and Pattern Recognition, pp. 14383–14392 (2021)

Gaze-OSV: Gaze Target Detection with Object Saliency and Vector Modeling

Zichu Zhang[1], Yuchen Zhao[2], and Zhiyong Wang[1](✉)

[1] Harbin Institute of Technology, Shenzhen, China
wangzhiyong@hit.edu.cn
[2] ADD Tech. Ltd., Shanghai, China

Abstract. Gaze serves as a pivotal element in non-verbal communication, effectively reflecting human visual attention. In this paper, we introduce object saliency as a critical prior for predicting gaze targets. Most existing methods predominantly rely on extracting global scene features, thereby neglecting the semantic distinction between background and foreground objects. However, compared to the unstructured background, human gaze is inherently biased towards specific, salient objects. To address this, we propose a novel Gaze Target Detection with Object Saliency and Vector Modeling framework (Gaze-OSV), which incorporates a human-object context module. Unlike prior works, Gaze-OSV features a Residual Object Saliency Injection mechanism that utilizes a trainable object detector to explicitly highlight potential targets. Furthermore, it implicitly models the human-object visual interaction by combining these enhanced features with a learnable Gaze Vector Token. Extensive experiments on two standard benchmarks, GazeFollow and VideoAttentionTarget, demonstrate the effectiveness and superior performance of Gaze-OSV.

Keywords: Gaze Target Detection · Object Saliency · Visual Attention

1 Introduction

Gaze behavior serves as a pivotal signal in human non-verbal communication, offering a direct window into an individual's visual attention and cognitive state [7,10]. In the field of computer vision, gaze target detection–the task of locating where a person is looking within a scene–has attracted significant research interest due to its wide applicability. Accurately estimating gaze is essential for understanding human intentions [1], analyzing social interactions [8], and facilitating human-robot interaction [27]. A recent survey by Ghosh et al. [11] highlights that unlike gaze estimation in controlled laboratory settings, gaze target detection in the wild requires a comprehensive understanding of the geometric and semantic relationship between the person and the scene content.

H. Liu et al. (Eds.): CEI 2025, CCIS 2881, pp. 258–270, 2026.
https://doi.org/10.1007/978-981-95-9493-1_17

Early approaches to this problem largely relied on geometric cues derived from head pose estimation. With the advent of deep learning, the two-stream architecture established by Recasens et al. [19] became the dominant paradigm. In this framework, one branch extracts features from the head crop to infer orientation, while another processes the entire scene image to identify salient regions [5,16]. Subsequent works have extended this pipeline by incorporating additional modalities such as monocular depth maps [2,9] or temporal information in videos [6]. More recently, Transformer-based architectures have been introduced to model long-range dependencies, utilizing self-attention mechanisms to refine the localization of heads and targets [20,25].

Despite these advancements, a fundamental limitation persists in most existing methodologies: they predominantly rely on extracting **global scene features** (holistic scene encoding) to regress the gaze heatmap [24]. Treating the scene as a uniform grid often leads to the inclusion of unstructured background noise, neglecting the semantic layout of the environment. However, psychological studies and recent object-aware approaches suggest that human gaze is inherently **object-biased**–we tend to fixate on specific, salient objects rather than empty spaces or background textures [21]. By ignoring the explicit distinction between foreground objects and the background, conventional global-feature methods often struggle in cluttered scenes where the visual link between the observer and the target object is ambiguous.

To address this limitation, we propose a novel Gaze Target Detection with Object Saliency and Vector Modeling framework (Gaze-OSV), which explicitly incorporates object saliency as a prior to guide the gaze target detection process. Instead of relying solely on holistic scene features, our approach synergizes a trainable object detector with a large-scale vision transformer. Specifically, we generate an explicit object saliency map to modulate the scene features via a residual connection, effectively highlighting interactive regions while suppressing background noise. Furthermore, we introduce a learnable gaze vector token within the decoder to explicitly model the geometric gaze direction, which guides the model to pinpoint the target with high precision.

The main contributions of this paper are summarized as follows:

- We identify the limitations of global feature-based gaze target detection and introduce object saliency as a critical prior to enhance scene understanding.
- We propose Gaze-OSV, a novel framework that features a Residual Object Saliency Injection mechanism to fuse explicit object cues with semantic features, and a Gaze Vector Token to model geometric gaze direction.
- We perform extensive experiments on two standard benchmarks, GazeFollow [19] and VideoAttentionTarget [6]. The results demonstrate the effectiveness and superior performance of our approach.

2 Related Work

2.1 Gaze Target Detection

Gaze target detection aims to localize the point where a person is looking within a scene. While early methods focused on constrained laboratory settings [15], the seminal work by Recasens et al. [19] extended this task to unconstrained "in-the-wild" scenarios by proposing a deep two-stream architecture. Following this paradigm, researchers have explored various strategies to enhance feature representation. For instance, Lian et al. [16] introduced multi-scale attention fields to capture gaze cues at different resolutions.

Beyond basic appearance features, recent approaches have sought to incorporate richer geometric and contextual cues. Zhao et al. [28] formulated the problem as learning to draw sight lines in 3D space, explicitly modeling the geometric projection of gaze. Similarly, Chen et al. [4] proposed a unified framework that jointly models head pose, eye position, and scene context, demonstrating that fusing multiple cues significantly boosts robustness in complex environments.

With the advent of Vision Transformers, the focus has shifted towards capturing long-range dependencies and fine-grained details. Tu et al. [25] utilized a Transformer-based encoder-decoder structure to simultaneously detect heads and regress gaze targets. More recently, Miao et al. [17] argued that global heatmaps might lose local details and proposed a patch-level distribution prediction method to achieve more precise localization. Ryan et al. [20] further pushed the boundary by leveraging large-scale learned encoders (DINOv2) to extract robust semantic features without extensive fine-tuning.

2.2 Object-Aware and Interaction-Based Gaze Analysis

A significant paradigm shift in recent years involves moving from pixel-level regression to understanding the semantic interactions between the observer and scene objects. Tonini et al. [24] proposed an object-aware framework that explicitly detects all potential target objects to model their relationship with the head. Wang et al. [26] introduced GaTector, a unified framework designed to predict the specific object category being stared at, which was later improved by Jin et al. [14] to eliminate dependencies on head priors.

To better model the complex dependencies between humans and objects, Hu et al. [13] proposed a Visual-Spatial Graph (VSG) and a graph attention network to infer the interaction probabilities between the target person and scene elements, generating an interactive attention map. Yang et al. [27] further explored body-part interactions as cues for gaze inference.

Unlike previous graph-based or bounding-box-based methods that require complex interaction reasoning [13,24], our approach explicitly leverages object saliency as a direct visual prior. We argue that saliency offers a more continuous and natural representation of visual attention, effectively guiding the model to focus on salient foreground objects without the need for explicit graph construction.

3 Methodology

3.1 Overview

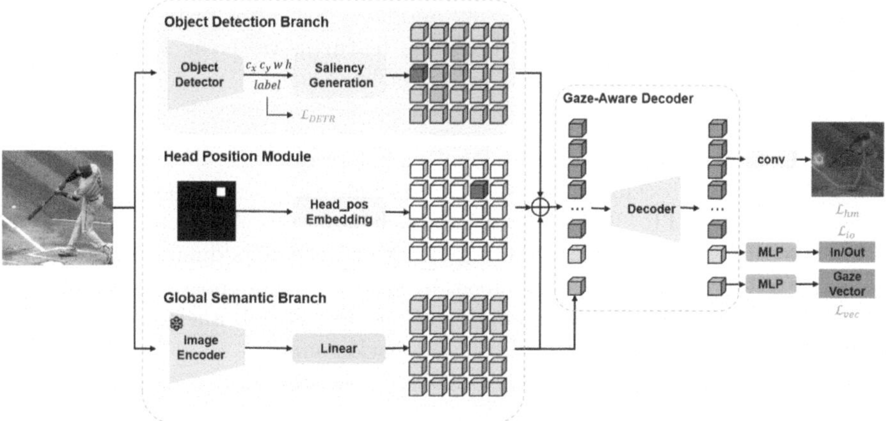

Fig. 1. The architecture of **Gaze-OSV**. Unlike single-stream approaches, we synergize a semantic encoder with a trainable object detector. The framework features a Residual Object Saliency Injection module to highlight interactive regions and a Gaze Vector Token to explicitly guide the decoding of the gaze target

The primary objective of Gaze-OSV is to map a scene image $\mathbf{I} \in \mathbb{R}^{3\times H\times W}$ and a head bounding box $\mathbf{b}_h$ to a precise gaze probability heatmap $\mathbf{H} \in \mathbb{R}^{H_{out}\times W_{out}}$. As depicted in Fig. 1, we depart from the standard single-encoder paradigm by introducing a context-object synergistic architecture. The pipeline unfolds in three stages: (1) **Dual-Stream Feature Encoding**, where global semantic contexts and discrete object cues are extracted in parallel to overcome the limitations of holistic representations; (2) **Saliency-Guided Feature Fusion**, which injects explicit object priors into the visual features via a residual modulation mechanism; (3) **Vector-Aware Decoding**, where a specialized Gaze Vector Token interacts with the enhanced features to pinpoint the target via a Transformer decoder.

3.2 Visual Feature Extraction

To accurately estimate gaze in complex environments, the model requires both a high-level understanding of the scene layout and a fine-grained perception of interactive objects. We address this by designing a dual-branch extractor.

Global Semantic Branch. Instead of relying on standard supervised backbones, we leverage the powerful representation capabilities of foundational models. We select **DINOv2** [18] as our semantic encoder due to its robustness in capturing dense visual descriptors. The input image $\mathbf{I}$ is resized to 448×448 and fed into the frozen DINOv2 encoder. This yields a dense feature map $\mathbf{F}_{vis} \in \mathbb{R}^{H \times W \times D}$ (where $H = W = 32$ and $D = 256$ after projection). Unlike Gaze-LLE [20] which relies solely on these features, we treat $\mathbf{F}_{vis}$ as a base representation to be further refined by object-level cues.

Object Localization Branch. Global encoders often produce blurred activations for small or occluded objects. To mitigate this, we introduce a parallel branch utilizing DETR [3]. This branch explicitly reasons about object instances within the same image $\mathbf{I}$. By predicting latent object embeddings and bounding boxes, DETR provides precise localization signals. This explicit object reasoning complements the implicit semantics of the DINOv2 branch, ensuring that potential gaze targets are distinct from the background.

Head Position Module. Since the input image may contain multiple people, specifying the target observer is crucial. We encode the spatial location of the target person by generating a binary mask from the head bounding box $\mathbf{b}_h$. This mask is downsampled to align with the spatial dimensions of $\mathbf{F}_{vis}$ and projected into a position embedding. We then inject this spatial condition into the visual features via element-wise addition, effectively explicitly directing the model's attention to the "gazer" within the scene.

3.3 Object Saliency Mining and Injection

While the Object Detection Branch provides discrete object predictions, these need to be integrated into the continuous feature space of the Scene Encoder to guide gaze target detection effectively.

Saliency Map Generation. We process the outputs from the DETR branch to construct a continuous Object Saliency Map $\mathbf{M}_{obj} \in \mathbb{R}^{H \times W}$. The detector yields a set of object queries, from which we extract class logits and bounding boxes. We filter these predictions based on a confidence threshold τ (empirically set to 0.8). For each valid object detection with confidence score s_i and bounding box b_i, we populate the corresponding spatial region in $\mathbf{M}_{obj}$ with s_i. This map explicitly highlights regions containing interactive objects, bridging the gap between discrete detections and dense visual features.

Residual Feature Modulation. To fuse the object priors into the visual stream without disrupting the pre-trained feature space, we propose a residual modulation mechanism applied directly on the spatial feature maps. The visual features $\mathbf{F}_{vis}$ are modulated by the object saliency map $\mathbf{M}_{obj}$ as follows:

$$\mathbf{F}'_{vis} = \mathbf{F}_{vis} + \mathbf{F}_{vis} \odot (\mathbf{M}_{obj} - \tau) \quad (1)$$

where $\odot$ denotes element-wise multiplication with broadcasting along the channel dimension. This operation effectively enhances features in salient object regions while suppressing background noise (where $\mathbf{M}_{obj} < \tau$), serving as a hard attention mechanism guided by object detection.

3.4 Gaze-Aware Decoder

To effectively decode the gaze target, we introduce a specialized decoder that leverages explicit gaze direction cues.

Gaze Vector Token. Unlike previous methods that rely solely on implicit scene context, we introduce a specialized Gaze Vector Token to guide the prediction of the gaze direction. Specifically, we perform global average pooling on the head-enhanced feature map $\mathbf{F}_{vis}$ to obtain a global context vector. This vector is then projected via a Multi-Layer Perceptron (MLP) to generate the gaze vector token $\mathbf{t}_{vec} \in \mathbb{R}^d$. This token summarizes the geometric gaze cues derived from the head pose and scene context.

Decoding and Prediction. We flatten the spatial feature map $\mathbf{F}'_{vis}$ into a sequence of tokens. The gaze vector token $\mathbf{t}_{gaze}$ is then added to this visual sequence, along with a learnable task token $\mathbf{t}_{in/out}$:

$$\mathbf{Seq}_{in} = [\mathbf{t}_{in/out}, \mathbf{t}_{gaze}, \text{Flatten}(\mathbf{F}'_{vis})] \quad (2)$$

The sequence $\mathbf{Seq}_{in}$ is processed by a Transformer decoder with self-attention layers. The gaze vector token $\mathbf{t}_{gaze}$ interacts with scene tokens to highlight regions along the gaze path. Finally, the visual tokens are reshaped back to $H' \times W' \times D'$ and upsampled via a deconvolutional head to regress the final probability heatmap $\mathbf{H}$. The $\mathbf{t}_{gaze}$ token output is also used to regress an explicit gaze direction vector for auxiliary supervision.

3.5 Loss Function

Our model is trained end-to-end using a multi-task objective function:

$$\mathcal{L}_{total} = \lambda_{hm}\mathcal{L}_{hm} + \lambda_{vec}\mathcal{L}_{vec} + \lambda_{io}\mathcal{L}_{io} + \lambda_{detr}\mathcal{L}_{detr} \quad (3)$$

where $\mathcal{L}_{hm}$ is the Binary Cross-Entropy (BCE) loss for the heatmap; $\mathcal{L}_{vec}$ is the Mean Squared Error (MSE) loss for the gaze vector; $\mathcal{L}_{io}$ is the BCE loss for the in/out classification; and $\mathcal{L}_{detr}$ represents the auxiliary detection losses (bounding box and classification) from the DETR branch to ensure high-quality object priors. We empirically set the weights as $\lambda_{hm} = 2.0$, $\lambda_{vec} = 2.0$, $\lambda_{io} = 1.0$, and $\lambda_{detr} = 1.0$.

4 Experiments

4.1 Datasets and Evaluation Metrics

Datasets. We conduct comprehensive evaluations on two widely recognized benchmarks in the field of gaze estimation.

- **GazeFollow** [19]: This large-scale dataset is a cornerstone for static gaze analysis, aggregating diverse images from multiple sources such as COCO and ImageNet. It comprises approximately 122,000 images featuring over 130,000 individuals. A distinguishing feature of its test set (4,782 instances) is the inclusion of multi-observer annotations (10 annotations per head), which provides a robust ground truth distribution for handling gaze ambiguity.
- **VideoAttentionTarget** [6]: To assess performance in dynamic and complex social scenarios, we utilize this video-based benchmark derived from 1,331 clips. It provides frame-level annotations for 164,541 heads. Consistent with established protocols [6,20], we adopt a sampling strategy that selects one frame every five frames during training to mitigate temporal redundancy while maintaining data diversity.

Evaluation Metrics. Our evaluation methodology aligns with standard practices [6,19]. We report:

- **AUC**: Evaluates the overlap between the predicted heatmap and the ground truth fixation distribution.
- **Avg. Dist.**: The mean Euclidean distance between the predicted gaze point and the ground truth location.
- **Min. Dist.**: Used specifically for the GazeFollow test set, measuring the distance to the closest annotation among multiple human annotators.
- **AP**: Employed for the VideoAttentionTarget dataset to measure the classification performance of in-frame versus out-of-frame gaze targets.

4.2 Implementation Details

Model Configuration. Our framework is implemented using PyTorch. For the visual encoder, we employ the DINOv2 (ViT-Base/14) [18] backbone initialized with pre-trained weights. To leverage its robust semantic representations without catastrophic forgetting, we freeze the DINOv2 parameters during training. The input images are resized to a resolution of 448×448. For the object saliency branch, we utilize a DETR architecture (with ResNet-50) [3]. Unlike the visual encoder, the DETR branch is not frozen. Instead, it is trained directly on the target dataset to learn object localization cues specifically tailored to the gaze following task.

Fig. 2. Qualitative results of Gaze-OSV on test set. The top row shows the input images, and the bottom row displays the predicted gaze heatmaps. Our model accurately localizes gaze targets across various scenarios

Training Protocol. We utilize the AdamW optimizer with a batch size of 16. The initial learning rate is set to 1×10^{-3}, managed by a Cosine Annealing scheduler. The model is trained for 15 epochs on the GazeFollow dataset. For the VideoAttentionTarget dataset, we fine-tune the model initialized from GazeFollow weights. The loss weights in Eq. (3) are empirically set as $\lambda_{hm} = 2.0$ for heatmap regression, $\lambda_{vec} = 2.0$ for gaze vector regression, $\lambda_{io} = 1.0$ for in/out classification, and $\lambda_{detr} = 1.0$ for the auxiliary detection loss. All experiments are performed on a single NVIDIA RTX 3090 GPU.

4.3 Experimental Results

Table 1. Quantitative comparison on the **GazeFollow** test set. The best results are highlighted in **bold**, and the second best are underlined

Method	Backbone	AUC ↑	Avg. Dist. ↓	Min. Dist. ↓
Recasens et al. [19]	AlexNet	0.878	0.190	0.113
Chong et al. [5]	ResNet-50	0.896	0.187	0.112
Lian et al. [16]	ResNet-50	0.906	0.145	0.081
Tu et al. [25]	ResNet-50	0.928	0.122	0.065
Gupta et al. [12]	EfficientNet	0.943	0.114	0.056
Miao et al. [17]	ResNet-50	0.934	0.123	0.065
Tafasca et al. [22]	ResNet-50	0.939	0.122	0.062
Tafasca et al. [23]	ViT-B	<u>0.944</u>	0.113	0.057
Gaze-LLE [20]	DINOv2-B	**0.954**	<u>0.108</u>	<u>0.050</u>
Ours	DINOv2-B	**0.954**	**0.105**	**0.047**

Comparison on GazeFollow. Table 1 presents the quantitative comparison with existing methods on the GazeFollow test set. Our method achieves competitive performance compared to recent approaches. Specifically, it surpasses multi-modal methods like Gupta et al. [12] and shows comparable results to recent Transformer-based models. This indicates that by explicitly incorporating object saliency, our model can effectively mitigate background noise and improve localization accuracy (Avg. Dist. and Min. Dist.) in complex scenes. We visualize the predicted gaze heatmaps on sample images from target dataset in Fig. 2. The top row displays the input scenes, while the bottom row shows the predicted heatmaps overlaid on the images. The green bounding boxes indicate the head positions of the target persons.

Comparison on VideoAttentionTarget. We further evaluate our model on the VideoAttentionTarget dataset to assess its robustness in dynamic scenes. As shown in Table 2, our method demonstrates favorable performance in identifying in-frame targets (AUC and Dist.) and detecting out-of-frame gaze (AP). While it may not surpass the current best model in all metrics, the results validate the effectiveness of the proposed gaze vector token in capturing geometric likelihoods.

Table 2. Quantitative comparison on the **VideoAttentionTarget** test set. The best results are highlighted in **bold**, and the second best are underlined

Method	Backbone	AUC ↑	Dist. ↓	AP ↑
Chong et al. [6]	ResNet-50	0.860	0.134	0.853
Hu et al. [13]	ResNet-50	0.880	0.118	0.881
Tonini et al. [24]	ResNet-50	0.862	0.125	0.742
Gupta et al. [12]	EfficientNet	0.914	0.110	0.879
Miao et al. [17]	ResNet-50	0.917	<u>0.109</u>	**0.908**
Tafasca et al. [22]	ResNet-50	0.914	<u>0.109</u>	0.834
Tafasca et al. [23]	ViT-B	–	**0.107**	0.891
Gaze-LLE [20]	DINOv2-B	**0.934**	0.111	0.889
Ours	DINOv2-B	<u>0.933</u>	<u>0.109</u>	<u>0.892</u>

4.4 Ablation Study

To validate the contribution of each proposed component, we conduct a comprehensive ablation study on the GazeFollow dataset. We use the standard Gaze-LLE [20] architecture (with DINOv2-Base) as our strong baseline. Specifically, we evaluate the following configurations:

- **Model A (Baseline)**: The base model without the Object Saliency Injection and the Gaze Vector Token. This represents the scenario where both components are ablated.
- **Model B (w/ Object Saliency)**: The model equipped with the DETR-based Object Saliency Injection but without the Gaze Vector Token. This validates the impact of explicit object priors.
- **Model C (Full Method)**: Our complete framework incorporating both Object Saliency and the Gaze Vector Token.

Table 3. Ablation study on the GazeFollow dataset. We progressively add the Object Saliency module and the Gaze Vector Token to the baseline. The best performance is shown in **bold**

Model	Object Saliency	Vector Token	AUC ↑	Avg. Dist. ↓	Min. Dist. ↓
A	×	×	**0.954**	0.108	0.050
B	✓	×	**0.954**	0.107	0.048
C	✓	✓	**0.954**	**0.105**	**0.047**

Effectiveness of Object Saliency Injection. We first analyze the impact of incorporating the explicit object prior. Comparing Model B with the Baseline (Model A), we observe that while the AUC remains stable at 0.954, the distance metrics show a clear improvement. Specifically, the Avg. Dist. decreases from 0.108 to 0.107, and the Min. Dist. drops from 0.050 to 0.048. This indicates that although the baseline DINOv2 encoder is already capable of capturing the general gaze direction (hence the high AUC), the DETR-derived saliency map provides crucial spatial cues that help the model pinpoint the exact target location more precisely within the salient regions, effectively filtering out background noise in cluttered scenes.

Effectiveness of Gaze Vector Token. We further investigate the role of the explicit Gaze Vector Token. As shown in Table 3, adding this component (Model C) yields the best overall performance. Compared to Model B, the Avg. Dist. is further reduced to 0.105, and the Min. Dist. reaches 0.047. The Gaze Vector Token explicitly models the geometric relationship between the head pose and the scene, serving as a learnable query that fine-tunes the localization. The consistent improvement in distance metrics suggests that this geometric guidance complements the semantic object priors, enabling the decoder to resolve spatial ambiguities that appearance features alone cannot address.

5 Discussion and Conclusion

5.1 Limitations

While our proposed framework achieves state-of-the-art performance, there are several limitations worth noting. First, our reliance on the object saliency map is primarily spatial rather than semantic. The current module treats all detected objects as potential targets based on their detection confidence scores, without explicitly reasoning about the semantic compatibility between the person and the object. Although the DINOv2 backbone captures implicit semantics, the injected prior remains a relatively simple objectness indicator. Second, the performance of the saliency branch is inherently upper-bounded by the capability of the underlying object detector (DETR). In scenarios with extremely small objects or severe occlusion where the detector fails, the guidance provided by the saliency map becomes negligible or even noisy. Future work could explore integrating multimodal semantics (e.g., using language descriptions of the scene) to filter salient objects more intelligently.

5.2 Conclusion

In this paper, we presented Gaze-OSV, a novel gaze target detection framework that integrates large-scale foundational visual features with explicit object priors. We identified that standard global scene encoders often struggle to distinguish targets in cluttered environments. To address this, we proposed a Residual Object Saliency Injection mechanism that modulates visual features with explicit object localization cues derived from a DETR branch. Furthermore, we introduced a learnable Gaze Vector Token to explicitly model the geometric gaze direction. Extensive experiments on standard benchmarks demonstrate that our method achieves promising results and proves the validity of combining semantic scene understanding with explicit geometric and object-level constraints.

References

1. Admoni, H., Scassellati, B.: Social eye gaze in human-robot interaction: a review. J. Hum.-Robot Interact. **6**(1), 25–63 (2017)
2. Bao, J., Liu, B., Yu, J.: Escnet: gaze target detection with the understanding of 3d scenes. In: Proceedings of the IEEE/CVF Conference on Computer Vision and Pattern Recognition, pp. 14126–14135 (2022)
3. Carion, N., Massa, F., Synnaeve, G., Usunier, N., Kirillov, A., Zagoruyko, S.: End-to-end object detection with transformers. In: European Conference on Computer Vision, pp. 213–229. Springer (2020)
4. Chen, W., Xu, H., Zhu, C., Liu, X., Lu, Y., Zheng, C., Kong, J.: Gaze estimation via the joint modeling of multiple cues. IEEE Trans. Circuits Syst. Video Technol. **32**(3), 1390–1402 (2021)
5. Chong, E., Ruiz, N., Wang, Y., Zhang, Y., Rozga, A., Rehg, J.M.: Connecting gaze, scene, and attention: Generalized attention estimation via joint modeling of gaze and scene saliency. In: Proceedings of the European Conference on Computer Vision (ECCV), pp. 383–398 (2018)

6. Chong, E., Wang, Y., Ruiz, N., Rehg, J.M.: Detecting attended visual targets in video. In: Proceedings of the IEEE/CVF Conference on Computer Vision and Pattern Recognition, pp. 5396–5406 (2020)
7. Emery, N.J.: The eyes have it: the neuroethology, function and evolution of social gaze. Neurosci. Biobehav. Rev. **24**(6), 581–604 (2000)
8. Fan, L., Wang, W., Huang, S., Tang, X., Zhu, S.C.: Understanding human gaze communication by spatio-temporal graph reasoning. In: Proceedings of the IEEE/CVF International Conference on Computer Vision, pp. 5724–5733 (2019)
9. Fang, Y., et al.: Dual attention guided gaze target detection in the wild. In: Proceedings of the IEEE/CVF Conference on Computer Vision and Pattern Recognition, pp. 11390–11399 (2021)
10. Frischen, A., Bayliss, A.P., Tipper, S.P.: Gaze cueing of attention: visual attention, social cognition, and individual differences. Psychol. Bull. **133**(4), 694 (2007)
11. Ghosh, S., Dhall, A., Hayat, M., Knibbe, J., Ji, Q.: Automatic gaze analysis: a survey of deep learning based approaches. IEEE Trans. Pattern Anal. Mach. Intell. **46**(1), 61–84 (2023)
12. Gupta, A., Tafasca, S., Odobez, J.M.: A modular multimodal architecture for gaze target prediction: application to privacy-sensitive settings. In: Proceedings of the IEEE/CVF Conference on Computer Vision and Pattern Recognition, pp. 5041–5050 (2022)
13. Hu, Z., et al.: Gaze target estimation inspired by interactive attention. IEEE Trans. Circuits Syst. Video Technol. **32**(12), 8524–8536 (2022)
14. Jin, Y., Guo, G., Wang, B.: Gatector+: a unified head-free framework for gaze object and gaze following prediction. arXiv preprint arXiv:2510.25301 (2025)
15. Kellnhofer, P., Recasens, A., Stent, S., Matusik, W., Torralba, A.: Gaze360: physically unconstrained gaze estimation in the wild. In: Proceedings of the IEEE/CVF International Conference on Computer Vision, pp. 6912–6921 (2019)
16. Lian, D., Yu, Z., Gao, S.: Believe it or not, we know what you are looking at! In: Asian Conference on Computer Vision, pp. 35–50. Springer (2018)
17. Miao, Q., Hoai, M., Samaras, D.: Patch-level gaze distribution prediction for gaze following. In: Proceedings of the IEEE/CVF Winter Conference on Applications of Computer Vision, pp. 880–889 (2023)
18. Oquab, M., et al.: Dinov2: learning robust visual features without supervision. arXiv preprint arXiv:2304.07193 (2023)
19. Recasens, A., Khosla, A., Vondrick, C., Torralba, A.: Where are they looking? In: Advances in Neural Information Processing Systems, vol. 28 (2015)
20. Ryan, F., Bati, A., Lee, S., Bolya, D., Hoffman, J., Rehg, J.M.: Gaze-lle: gaze target estimation via large-scale learned encoders. In: Proceedings of the Computer Vision and Pattern Recognition Conference, pp. 28874–28884 (2025)
21. Tafasca, S., Gupta, A., Bros, V., Odobez, J.M.: Toward semantic gaze target detection. Adv. Neural. Inf. Process. Syst. **37**, 121422–121448 (2024)
22. Tafasca, S., Gupta, A., Odobez, J.M.: Childplay: a new benchmark for understanding children's gaze behaviour. In: Proceedings of the IEEE/CVF International Conference on Computer Vision, pp. 20935–20946 (2023)
23. Tafasca, S., Gupta, A., Odobez, J.M.: Sharingan: a transformer architecture for multi-person gaze following. In: Proceedings of the IEEE/CVF Conference on Computer Vision and Pattern Recognition, pp. 2008–2017 (2024)
24. Tonini, F., Dall'Asen, N., Beyan, C., Ricci, E.: Object-aware gaze target detection. In: Proceedings of the IEEE/CVF International Conference on Computer Vision, pp. 21860–21869 (2023)

25. Tu, D., Min, X., Duan, H., Guo, G., Zhai, G., Shen, W.: End-to-end human-gaze-target detection with transformers. In: 2022 IEEE/CVF Conference on Computer Vision and Pattern Recognition (CVPR), pp. 2192–2200. IEEE (2022)
26. Wang, B., Hu, T., Li, B., Chen, X., Zhang, Z.: Gatector: a unified framework for gaze object prediction. In: Proceedings of the IEEE/CVF Conference on Computer Vision and Pattern Recognition, pp. 19588–19597 (2022)
27. Yang, Y., Yin, Y., Lu, F.: Gaze target detection by merging human attention and activity cues. In: Proceedings of the AAAI Conference on Artificial Intelligence, vol. 38, pp. 6585–6593 (2024)
28. Zhao, H., Lu, M., Yao, A., Chen, Y., Zhang, L.: Learning to draw sight lines. Int. J. Comput. Vision **128**(5), 1076–1100 (2020)

PA-HOI: Pose-Aware Human–Object Interaction Modeling for Abnormal Behavior Detection in Children

Wei Zheng[1], Yuchen Zhao[2], and Zhiyong Wang[1](✉)

[1] Harbin Institute of Technology, Shenzhen, China
wangzhiyong@hit.edu.cn
[2] ADD Tech. Ltd., Shanghai, China

Abstract. Human–object interaction (HOI) understanding in pediatric wards is essential for monitoring abnormal behaviors and preventing fall-related accidents. Unlike generic HOI scenarios, clinical safety monitoring requires fine-grained reasoning over human pose to identify subtle but high-risk actions such as leaning outside the bed or climbing over the rails. Existing transformer-based HOI detectors primarily rely on bounding-box and appearance cues, making them insufficient for modeling detailed body configurations. We propose a pose-aware HOI (**PA-HOI**) detection framework that implicitly embeds skeleton structure into the interaction reasoning process. The core contribution is a pose-aware graph-attention module that introduces a global pose context node and performs structured message passing across interaction proposals, enabling the model to capture discriminative limb orientations and body–object spatial dependencies. We evaluate our method on a private pediatric-ward dataset containing nine abnormal behaviors and ten environmental entities. The proposed approach achieves a mean Average Precision of **85.78%**, substantially outperforming other contemporary HOI frameworks. These results demonstrate the effectiveness of integrating skeleton-aware structural information for reliable clinical safety monitoring.

1 Introduction

Human behavior is a direct manifestation of cognitive activity and intention, and visual understanding of behavior plays a fundamental role in intelligent systems. In real-world scenarios, human actions are rarely isolated; instead, they are often expressed through interactions with surrounding objects or other people. Understanding human behavior therefore requires not only recognizing body motion itself, but also reasoning about the semantic relationships between a person and the environment. Compared with isolated action recognition, human–object interaction (HOI) detection offers a more comprehensive formulation by explicitly modeling interactions in the form of ⟨human, object, action⟩ triplets, which enables structured semantic understanding of complex scenes [1,2].

H. Liu et al. (Eds.): CEI 2025, CCIS 2881, pp. 271–285, 2026.
https://doi.org/10.1007/978-981-95-9493-1_18

Early studies established benchmarks and evaluation protocols such as V-COCO [1] and HICO-DET [2], which laid the foundation for subsequent model development. Since then, HOI detection has attracted increasing attention due to its importance for applications including surveillance, assistive robotics, video understanding, and human–computer interaction. Recent advances in deep learning have enabled steady progress in this field [3–9]. However, despite these achievements, accurate HOI recognition in abnormal scenarios remains challenging, particularly when the target actions are subtle and highly dependent on body configuration.

This challenge becomes especially pronounced in clinical environments such as pediatric wards. Children often exhibit unpredictable and potentially dangerous behaviors such as leaning over bed rails, standing on the edge of the bed, or climbing out without assistance. Conventional action recognition systems, which focus primarily on motion patterns or appearance, are insufficient for modeling such fine-grained behaviors. They fail to capture critical spatial relations between body parts and surrounding objects, which are essential for distinguishing hazardous actions from visually similar safe ones. In contrast, HOI detection naturally integrates human pose, object identity, and spatial configuration, making it a more suitable framework for clinical safety monitoring.

Nevertheless, existing HOI methods still suffer from three key limitations. First, most detectors rely heavily on bounding-box representations, which include large amounts of background and fail to localize anatomically relevant regions such as hands, arms, and legs [10,11]. Second, although pose information has been introduced in several works, it is typically used as auxiliary input without explicitly modeling the structural relationships among joints [12,13]. As a result, the spatial topology of the human skeleton is underutilized. Third, interaction reasoning is often performed at the proposal level, where pose-related information is loosely coupled with appearance or spatial features, making it difficult to capture coordinated body configurations.

To address these challenges, we propose **PA-HOI**, a pose-aware human–object interaction detection framework tailored for abnormal behavior understanding in pediatric wards. Our key insight is that unsafe actions are not merely defined by coarse bounding-box relationships, but by precise skeletal configurations and their proximity to surrounding objects. We therefore introduce a pose-aware graph-attention module that explicitly models anatomical structure, geometric relations, and confidence-aware connectivity among body parts and objects. By embedding pose information into a structured reasoning graph, the proposed model can capture subtle but crucial interaction patterns that previous methods often overlook.

We evaluate PA-HOI on a private dataset collected from a real pediatric ward environment, covering nine abnormal behaviors and ten types of common ward objects. Experimental results demonstrate that our method consistently outperforms strong HOI baselines while maintaining inference efficiency. These findings confirm that skeleton-aware reasoning provides a reliable and effective solution for clinical safety monitoring.

Contributions. Our main contributions are summarized as follows:

- We introduce a pose-aware HOI framework for abnormal behavior detection in pediatric wards, bridging the gap between pose estimation and interaction reasoning.
- We design a structured pose graph with confidence-gated adjacency to explicitly model anatomical topology and pose–object relations.
- We build and evaluate the proposed approach on a real-world clinical dataset and demonstrate consistent improvement over state-of-the-art HOI detectors.

2 Related Work

2.1 Human–Object Interaction Detection

HOI detection aims to jointly localize humans and objects while recognizing their semantic interactions. Early benchmarks such as V-COCO [1] and HICO-DET [2] established standard evaluation protocols and promoted large-scale research on HOI understanding.

Existing HOI methods can be broadly categorized into one-stage and two-stage approaches. One-stage methods predict interaction triplets directly from image features via unified architectures, focusing on interaction points or union regions to capture human–object relations [3–6]. More recently, Transformer-based models significantly improved global reasoning by introducing cross-attention between object queries and image features, such as HOI-Transformer [7], QPIC [8], HOTR [9], Disentangled Transformer [14], GEN-VLKT [15], Relational Context Learning [16], and MSTR [17]. Although these models demonstrate strong representation capacity, they require retraining detection pipelines and often struggle when training data is limited.

Two-stage methods first perform object detection and then explicitly infer interactions over detected human–object pairs. This design benefits from mature detectors and enables flexible integration of additional cues such as pose, semantic priors, and instance relations. Classical works including iCAN [18] and Chao et al. [19] introduced instance-centric attention and multi-stream architectures to capture interaction patterns. Subsequent methods enhanced semantic generalization and object-invariant reasoning [10,20]. However, most two-stage approaches rely on shallow feature concatenation, which limits their ability to capture deeper structural dependencies.

2.2 Graph-Based HOI Modeling

Graph-based reasoning explicitly represents humans, objects, and their relations as nodes and edges, and performs interaction understanding via message passing.

Qi et al. [21] first formulated HOI recognition as a structured inference problem by building a graph parsing network over human and object nodes. Their method showed that explicit graph structures can capture contextual and functional relations beyond what is available from bounding boxes alone. He et al. [22]

further exploited scene graphs for HOI detection, integrating object relations and human–object dependencies into a unified relational graph, and demonstrated improved robustness under occlusion and visual ambiguity.

More recently, STIP [23] explored structure-aware Transformer reasoning over interaction proposals, injecting graph-like relational bias into a Transformer-based HOI detector. While these graph-based methods successfully model object-centric and instance-level relations, they pay limited attention to the anatomically structured nature of human pose. In abnormal scenarios, however, subtle limb configurations often define hazard patterns, highlighting the need for explicit pose-aware graph reasoning as pursued in this work.

2.3 Pose-Aware HOI Detection

Human pose provides highly discriminative cues by highlighting action-relevant body regions instead of relying solely on full bounding boxes. PMFNet [11] proposed a multi-level pose-aware feature network with body-part attention to capture fine-grained interactions. ViPLO [13] introduced a pose-conditioned self-loop graph on top of vision transformers to refine human representations. Other works leveraged action co-occurrence priors [12] or transferable interactiveness knowledge [24] to better exploit pose and semantic constraints for interaction modeling.

Despite these advances, most pose-aware methods either treat keypoints as auxiliary inputs or apply loosely structured graph models. The intrinsic kinematic hierarchy of the human body is rarely encoded in a principled way, and noisy keypoints may degrade performance when pose confidence is low. In contrast, our approach builds an explicit confidence-gated pose graph with geometric priors, allowing anatomically meaningful message passing between parts, joints, and objects.

2.4 Temporal HOI Detection in Videos

While image-based HOI detection focuses on single frames, many real-world interactions unfold over time. Temporal HOI methods incorporate motion dynamics and cross-frame dependencies to better distinguish visually similar actions and to understand interaction evolution.

Xi et al. [25] proposed ACoLP, an open-set video HOI detection framework that models videos as action-centric chains of gaze prompts, improving generalization to unseen interactions. Wang et al. [26] introduced an interaction-centric spatio-temporal context reasoning framework for multi-person video HOI recognition, combining context fusion with temporal modeling. Li et al. [27] designed a heterogeneous graph neural network that explicitly distinguishes active (human) and passive (object) roles in videos, while Sun et al. [28] formulated spatio-temporal HOI detection by jointly reasoning over trajectories, pose, motion, and semantic context.

These methods demonstrate that temporal modeling is crucial for complex video understanding but typically requires large-scale annotated videos and

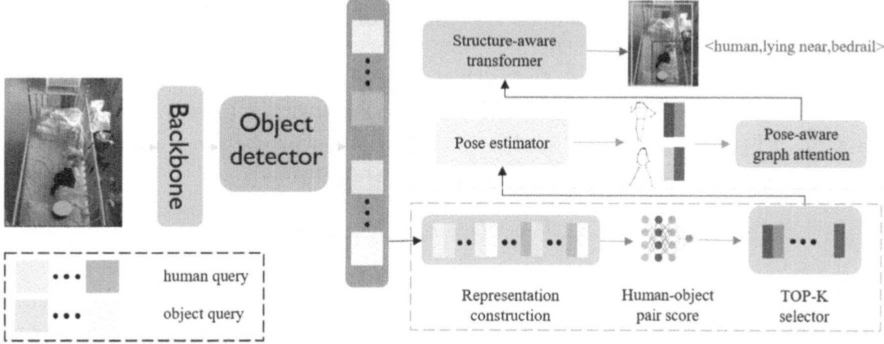

Fig. 1. Overview of the proposed PA-HOI framework. The model first detects human and object instances via a DETR-based backbone. Pose-aware geometric features are extracted from human keypoints and integrated into interaction proposals. A pose-aware graph-attention module further enhances relational reasoning before the interaction decoder predicts final action labels.

substantial computational resources. In this work, we focus on accurate frame-level HOI reasoning in pediatric wards while keeping the proposed pose-aware graph design compatible with future temporal extensions.

3 Method

In this section, we introduce PA-HOI, a pose-aware human–object interaction detection framework designed for abnormal behavior monitoring in pediatric wards. The overall architecture is shown in Fig. 1. PA-HOI enhances the STIP framework by incorporating skeleton-guided geometric features and a pose-aware graph-attention mechanism.

3.1 Overview

Given an input image, we first employ a DETR-based detector to obtain human and object bounding boxes. Human keypoints are extracted using ViTPose, which serve as the foundation for pose-aware geometric reasoning. Interaction proposals are constructed following STIP, after which we enrich each proposal with a set of pose-derived features, including pose-to-object vectors, part-level overlap cues, and global spatial descriptors. Finally, a pose-aware graph-attention module performs structured relational reasoning before the interaction decoder predicts the final action labels.

3.2 Interaction Proposal Generation

Given an input image, we use a DETR-based detector to obtain a set of human and object instances. Each detected instance i is represented by a bounding box

b_i, a class distribution, and a decoder embedding $f_i \in \mathbb{R}^d$. Human instances are selected as those classified as the *person* category, while all remaining foreground detections are treated as potential object candidates.

For every human–object pair (h, o), we construct an interaction proposal. Following STIP, a lightweight multilayer perceptron predicts an interactionness score for each pair, and the top K proposals are retained:

$$\mathcal{P} = \{(h_k, o_k)\}_{k=1}^{K}.$$

DETR-Based Proposal Feature. For each retained proposal (h, o), we construct an initial proposal feature vector by combining appearance, geometry, semantic, and union-region cues:

$$F_{\text{det}}(h, o) = f_h \parallel f_o \parallel \phi_{\text{spatial}}(b_h, b_o) \parallel \phi_{\text{sem}}(o).$$

- Appearance features: the human and object instance embeddings (f_h, f_o) extracted from the DETR decoder.
- Spatial layout: a geometric descriptor derived from the normalized bounding boxes (b_h, b_o), including relative offsets, distance, angle, overlap area, union area, and normalized box sizes, projected by a learned linear layer:

$$\phi_{\text{spatial}}(b_h, b_o) = \text{MLP}_{\text{spatial}}(g(b_h, b_o)).$$

- Object semantics: the semantic embedding of the object, computed by projecting the class-probability vector using a label embedding matrix:

$$\phi_{\text{sem}}(o) = p_o^{\top} E_{\text{obj}},$$

  where p_o is the softmax output of the object classifier.

The resulting initial proposal feature $F_{\text{det}}(h, o)$ forms the base interaction representation. This representation is subsequently enriched with pose-aware geometric features in Sect. 3.3 and further refined through structured pose-graph reasoning in Sect. 3.4.

3.3 Pose-Aware Feature Construction

While the DETR-based proposal feature $F_{\text{det}}(h, o)$ captures appearance, spatial layout, and semantic cues, it lacks fine-grained body-structure information that is crucial for distinguishing abnormal behaviors. To address this, PA-HOI incorporates pose-aware geometric features extracted from ViTPose keypoints. These features explicitly encode how human limbs are configured relative to the object, forming an enhanced representation:

$$F_{\text{pose}}(h, o) = \phi_{\text{vec}}(\{p_i, c_o\}) \parallel \phi_{\text{IOB}}(\{\text{IOB}_i\}),$$

where p_i denotes the i-th keypoint of the human and c_o is the object center. The two components are described below.

Pose-to-Object Geometric Vectors. For each detected human, ViTPose provides 17 keypoints $\{p_i \in \mathbb{R}^2\}_{i=1}^{17}$. Given the object center c_o, we compute a geometric vector for every keypoint:

$$v_i = p_i - c_o,$$

representing the direction and relative displacement of each body part with respect to the object. These vectors encode characteristic limb orientations (e.g., leaning outward, bending toward the rails, or reaching toward the bedside) that strongly correlate with dangerous actions. All vectors are concatenated and projected through a linear layer:

$$\phi_{\text{vec}} = \text{MLP}_{\text{vec}}\big(\text{Concat}(v_1, \ldots, v_{17})\big).$$

Skeleton-Aware Overlap Descriptors. To capture extremely fine-grained physical interactions between specific body parts and objects, PA-HOI constructs a local region box around each human keypoint. For a keypoint p_i, we derive a compact keypoint-centered region B_i^{kp} using p_i as the center and its adjacent skeleton joints as the corners. This produces a set of 17 local regions that reflect the spatial extent of each anatomical joint.

For every region, we compute its normalized overlap with the object box B_o:

$$\text{IOB}_i = \frac{\text{Area}\Big(B_i^{\text{kp}} \cap B_o\Big)}{\text{Area}(B_h)},$$

where B_h is the human bounding box. These skeleton-aware overlap values capture subtle limb–object contacts (e.g., a hand touching the bedrail, a foot pressing on the bed edge) that strongly correlate with hazardous behaviors.

The resulting 17-dimensional vector is projected through a learnable MLP:

$$\phi_{\text{IOB}} = \text{MLP}_{\text{IOB}}\big(\text{Concat}(\text{IOB}_1, \ldots, \text{IOB}_{17})\big).$$

The final pose-aware representation is obtained by concatenating $F_{\text{pose}}(h, o)$ with the DETR-based proposal feature $F_{\text{det}}(h, o)$. This enriched feature encodes appearance, spatial layout, object semantics, and detailed human pose structure, and is further processed by the structured pose-graph reasoning module described in Sect. 3.4.

3.4 Pose-Aware Graph Reasoning

Although the pose-aware features in Sect. 3.3 enrich individual proposals, many abnormal behaviors emerge from coordinated body configurations that cannot be modeled by simple vector concatenation. To explicitly capture human structural dependencies and their geometric relation to the target object, PA-HOI introduces a compact pose-aware graph reasoning module, as illustrated in Fig. 2. For each human–object pair (h, o), we construct a 25-node graph composed of a

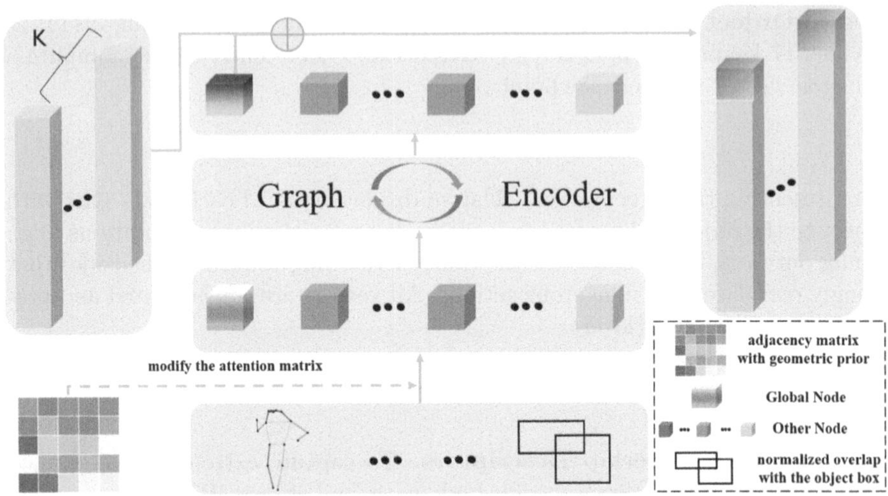

Fig. 2. Overview of the proposed pose-aware graph reasoning module. The graph integrates anatomical priors, geometric relations, and adjacency matrix with geometric prior to produce a global pose token for each human–object pair.

global node, six anatomical part nodes, seventeen keypoint nodes, and one object node. The keypoint nodes encode raw coordinates and pose-to-object displacement vectors; part nodes aggregate features from grouped keypoints; and the object node encodes its box parameters (c_x, c_y, w, h). The initial node embeddings are stacked into $X \in \mathbb{R}^{25\times d}$.

To incorporate human structural priors, we construct an adjacency matrix with geometric prior that reflects both anatomical connectivity and human–object relations. Skeleton edges follow the COCO kinematic tree; part–keypoint relations connect each part node to its constituent joints; keypoint–object relations are weighted by inverse spatial distance,

$$w_i^{kp\text{-}obj} = 1 - \frac{\|p_i - c_o\|}{\max_j \|p_j - c_o\|},$$

which encourages stronger interactions for joints closer to the object; and part–object relations use the IoU between part boxes and the object box to encode local physical proximity. These relations form the base adjacency A.

To further suppress unreliable pose estimates, each node receives a confidence score derived from keypoint detection confidence, part-average confidence, or object classification confidence. These are assembled into a pairwise confidence matrix $C = cc^{\top}$. A learnable edge-type weight matrix W modulates the structural adjacency, yielding the confidence-gated normalized adjacency:

$$\hat{A}_{ij} = \frac{A_{ij}\, C_{ij}\, W_{ij}}{\sum_j A_{ij}\, C_{ij}\, W_{ij} + \varepsilon}.$$

Given X and $\hat{A}$, the graph encoder updates all node embeddings,

$$H = \mathrm{GNN}(X, \hat{A}),$$

and the output of the global node H_0 serves as the compact pose-aware token. Finally, this token is concatenated with the proposal representation from Sect. 3.3 to form the enhanced feature used by the interaction decoder:

$$F_{\text{final}}(h, o) = F_{\text{det}}(h, o) \parallel F_{\text{pose}}(h, o) \parallel H_0.$$

3.5 Interaction Decoder

The fused interaction feature, which already integrates detector appearance information, pose-aware geometric cues, and the global pose token from the graph reasoning module, is mapped into a query embedding through a lightweight projection layer. These query embeddings are then refined by a single-layer Transformer decoder that performs cross-attention over the DETR encoder memory, allowing each interaction candidate to incorporate scene-level contextual cues. To prevent the decoder from attending to irrelevant regions in the busy clinical environment, we apply a spatial layout mask that restricts attention to the union region of the human and object boxes. The refined query representation is finally fed into a classification head to produce logits over the abnormal behavior categories:

$$y_k = \mathrm{MLP}_{\text{act}}(\tilde{q}_k).$$

This decoding process enhances the pose-aware interaction representation with global context while preserving the fine-grained structural cues essential for accurate recognition of subtle and hazardous behaviors.

3.6 Training Objective

PA-HOI is trained end-to-end following the DETR bipartite matching framework and the HOI loss formulation of STIP. The model jointly optimizes object detection, interaction proposal prediction, and action classification. The detection branch uses the standard DETR loss, which combines cross-entropy for category classification with L1 and GIoU losses for bounding-box regression. For each sampled human–object proposal, an interactionness score is supervised using binary cross-entropy to distinguish valid interactions from negatives. The final interaction queries produced by the decoder are optimized using a multi-label binary cross-entropy loss over the predefined abnormal action set. The overall objective is a weighted sum of the three components:

$$\mathcal{L} = \mathcal{L}_{\text{det}} + \lambda_{\text{prop}}\mathcal{L}_{\text{prop}} + \lambda_{\text{act}}\mathcal{L}_{\text{act}}.$$

All pose-aware components, including the geometric features and the structured pose graph, are trained implicitly through gradients propagated from the HOI classification loss, requiring no additional supervision and ensuring full end-to-end optimization.

4 Experiments

4.1 Dataset

We collected daily ward videos from Shenzhen Children's Hospital and, with the assistance of medical staff, screened, edited, and annotated fall-prone behaviors. A total of 41 four-minute videos were retained after clinical review. All procedures were approved by the Institutional Review Board (Application No. 202403002) and conducted in accordance with the Helsinki Declaration. No personal information of the subjects is disclosed.

Frames are sampled at 2 fps and filtered to remove blur and ambiguous cases. Each frame is annotated with human boxes, object boxes, and one of nine abnormal actions (e.g., leaning on the rail, climbing over the rail, standing on the bed edge). Ten types of ward-related objects such as bed, caregiver, nurse, and auxiliary beds are also labeled. Approval for all ethical and experimental procedures was granted by the Institutional Review Board of the Children's Hospital of Shenzhen (Application No. 202403002) and performed in line with the Helsinki Declaration. Strict privacy protection protocols were implemented, ensuring no personal information is disclosed.

To avoid temporal leakage, the dataset is split by video into training, and testing sets. Unlike V-COCO and HICO-DET, our dataset contains single-role safety interactions (human–object only) without additional semantic roles. Therefore, we follow the evaluation protocol of STIP but report mAP over the nine abnormal actions, without $\mathrm{AP}_{role1}/\mathrm{AP}_{role2}$, which are specific to the multi-role annotation scheme of V-COCO.

4.2 Implementation Details

PA-HOI is implemented in PyTorch and trained end-to-end on four NVIDIA RTX 3090 GPUs. We use the AdamW optimizer with an initial learning rate of 1×10^{-4} for the DETR backbone and 1×10^{-3} for the HOI branches. The batch size is set to 16, and all models are trained for 100 epochs with a cosine learning-rate schedule. During inference, we keep the top-K interaction proposals per image and evaluate all methods using mAP on the test set. All ablation baselines and comparisons are trained under identical settings for fair evaluation.

4.3 Main Results

We compare PA-HOI with three representative HOI detectors commonly adopted in human–object interaction research: STIP [23], LogicHOI [29], and ConCue [30]. All models are trained under identical settings described in Sect. 4.2. The mean Average Precision (mAP) over the nine abnormal actions is reported in Table 1.

PA-HOI achieves an mAP of **85.78%**, outperforming all baseline methods. The improvement is especially notable for actions requiring fine-grained pose understanding–such as leaning outside the bed, standing on the bed edge, and

Table 1. Comparison with existing HOI detectors on the pediatric ward dataset.

Method	mAP (%)
ConCue [30]	78.42
LogicHOI [29]	82.70
STIP [23]	85.09
PA-HOI (ours)	**85.78**

Table 2. Ablation study of key components in PA-HOI.

Configuration	mAP (%)
Baseline	85.09
+ Pose-to-object vectors	85.22
+ Skeleton-aware IOB descriptors	85.38
+ Both geometric pose features	85.50
+ Pose-aware graph reasoning only	85.41
+ Pose features + Graph reasoning (ours)	**85.78**

climbing over the rails–where appearance- or box-level cues alone are not sufficient. These results demonstrate the effectiveness of incorporating skeleton-aware geometric features and structured pose reasoning for reliable clinical safety monitoring.

4.4 Ablation Study

To evaluate the contribution of each component in PA-HOI, we progressively add pose-aware geometric features and the structured graph reasoning module. All models are trained under identical settings described in Sect. 4.2. The results are summarized in Table 2.

Geometric pose cues provide consistent improvements over the baseline detector: pose-to-object vectors encode limb orientation relative to the object, while skeleton-aware IOB descriptors capture fine-grained part–object proximity. Combining both leads to a strong proposal-level representation (85.50% mAP).

Introducing the pose-aware graph reasoning module alone improves the baseline to 85.41%, indicating that structured human anatomy and confidence-aware geometric relations can benefit HOI detection even without explicit pose features. Finally, combining both geometric pose cues and the graph module yields the best performance of 85.78%, demonstrating the complementary nature of detailed pose geometry and structured relational reasoning in recognizing subtle and abnormal behaviors.

Table 3. Comparison of adjacency matrix variants within the pose-aware graph reasoning module. "Multiplicative" and "Additive" are applied on top of the geometric-prior adjacency, while "Identity" replaces it with a unit diagonal matrix.

Adjacency variant	mAP (%)
Learnable (multiplicative)	**85.78**
Learnable (additive)	85.26
Identity adjacency (no structural prior)	84.42

4.5 Analysis of Adjacency Matrix Variants

To further investigate the role of the adjacency formulation in the proposed pose-aware graph reasoning module, we compare three variants of the adjacency matrix design: (i) a learnable multiplicative form, (ii) a learnable additive form, and (iii) an identity adjacency without any structural or geometric prior. All variants use the same pose-aware features (IOA + 256-d pose vectors + 128-d IOB descriptors) and differ only in how the final adjacency is constructed. Results are presented in Table 3.

In the *learnable multiplicative* variant, a learnable matrix W is applied elementwise to the geometric-prior adjacency A, i.e., $A' = A \odot W$, before confidence gating and normalization. This formulation achieves the best performance, suggesting that scaling the prior edges allows the model to adapt relation strengths while preserving the anatomical topology. The *additive* variant instead uses a residual correction $A' = A + \Delta A$ and yields slightly lower mAP, likely because directly perturbing the prior structure introduces noise into the kinematic relations. When the adjacency is replaced by the identity matrix, only self-connections remain and all structural and geometric priors are removed, leading to a pronounced drop to 84.42%. These results highlight that both a meaningful structural prior and an appropriate learnable modulation are crucial for effective pose-aware graph reasoning.

5 Conclusion

In this paper, we presented PA-HOI, a pose-aware human–object interaction detection framework tailored for safety monitoring in pediatric wards. Building on a STIP-style transformer detector, PA-HOI augments interaction proposals with skeleton-guided geometric cues, including pose-to-object displacement vectors and skeleton-aware overlap descriptors, and further refines them through a compact pose-aware graph reasoning module. The proposed graph encoder leverages an adjacency matrix with geometric prior and learnable modulation to propagate information over global, part, keypoint, and object nodes, yielding a pose-aware global token that is fused into the interaction representation.

Extensive experiments on a clinically collected pediatric-ward dataset show that PA-HOI achieves 85.78% mAP, outperforming STIP and recent HOI detectors such as LogicHOI and ConCue under identical settings. Ablation studies confirm that both the pose-aware geometric features and the structured graph reasoning contribute consistently to performance, while analysis of adjacency variants highlights the importance of combining anatomical priors with learnable edge weighting.

In future work, we plan to extend PA-HOI to temporally-aware HOI detection in continuous video streams, incorporate multi-role interactions involving caregivers and medical staff, and investigate deployment-oriented optimizations for real-time clinical monitoring systems in broader hospital environments.

References

1. Gupta, S., Malik, J.: Visual semantic role labeling. arXiv preprint arXiv:1505.04474 (2015)
2. Chao, Y.-W., Wang, Z., He, Y., Wang, J., Deng, J.: HICO: a benchmark for recognizing human-object interactions in images. In: Proceedings of the IEEE International Conference on Computer Vision, pp. 1017–1025 (2015)
3. Kim, B., Choi, T., Kang, J., Kim, H.J.: UnionDet: union-level detector towards real-time human-object interaction detection. In: European Conference on Computer Vision, pp. 498–514. Springer, Heidelberg (2020)
4. Liao, Y., Liu, S., Wang, F., Chen, Y., Qian, C., Feng, J.: PPDM: parallel point detection and matching for real-time human-object interaction detection. In: Proceedings of the IEEE/CVF Conference on Computer Vision and Pattern Recognition, pp. 482–490 (2020)
5. Wang, T., Yang, T., Danelljan, M., Khan, F.S., Zhang, X., Sun, J.: Learning human-object interaction detection using interaction points. In: Proceedings of the IEEE/CVF Conference on Computer Vision and Pattern Recognition, pp. 4116–4125 (2020)
6. Zhong, X., Qu, X., Ding, C., Tao, D.: Glance and gaze: inferring action-aware points for one-stage human-object interaction detection. In: Proceedings of the IEEE/CVF Conference on Computer Vision and Pattern Recognition, pp. 13234–13243 (2021)
7. Zou, C., et al.: End-to-end human object interaction detection with HOI transformer. In: Proceedings of the IEEE/CVF Conference on Computer Vision and Pattern Recognition, pp. 11825–11834 (2021)
8. Tamura, M., Ohashi, H., Yoshinaga, T.: QPIC: query-based pairwise human-object interaction detection with image-wide contextual information. In: Proceedings of the IEEE/CVF Conference on Computer Vision and Pattern Recognition, pp. 10410–10419 (2021)
9. Kim, B., Lee, J., Kang, J., Kim, E.-S., Kim, H.J.: HOTR: end-to-end human-object interaction detection with transformers. In: Proceedings of the IEEE/CVF Conference on Computer Vision and Pattern Recognition, pp. 74–83 (2021)
10. Liu, X., Li, Y.-L., Lu, C.: Highlighting object category immunity for the generalization of human-object interaction detection. In: Proceedings of the AAAI Conference on Artificial Intelligence, vol. 36, pp. 1819–1827 (2022)
11. Wan, B., Zhou, D., Liu, Y., Li, R., He, X.: Pose-aware multi-level feature network for human object interaction detection. In: Proceedings of the IEEE/CVF International Conference on Computer Vision, pp. 9469–9478 (2019)

12. Kim, D.-J., Sun, X., Choi, J., Lin, S., Kweon, I.S.: Detecting human-object interactions with action co-occurrence priors. In: European Conference on Computer Vision, pp. 718–736. Springer, Heidelberg (2020)
13. Park, J., Park, J.-W., Lee, J.-S.: ViPLO: vision transformer based pose-conditioned self-loop graph for human-object interaction detection. In: Proceedings of the IEEE/CVF Conference on Computer Vision and Pattern Recognition, pp. 17152–17162 (2023)
14. Zhou, D.: Human-object interaction detection via disentangled transformer. In: Proceedings of the IEEE/CVF Conference on Computer Vision and Pattern Recognition, pp. 19568–19577 (2022)
15. Liao, Y., Zhang, A., Lu, M., Wang, Y., Li, X., Liu, S.: GEN-VLKT: simplify association and enhance interaction understanding for hoi detection. In: Proceedings of the IEEE/CVF Conference on Computer Vision and Pattern Recognition, pp. 20123–20132 (2022)
16. Kim, S., Jung, D., Cho, M.: Relational context learning for human-object interaction detection. In: Proceedings of the IEEE/CVF Conference on Computer Vision and Pattern Recognition, pp. 2925–2934 (2023)
17. Kim, B., Mun, J., On, K.-W., Shin, M., Lee, J., Kim, E.-S.: MSTR: multi-scale transformer for end-to-end human-object interaction detection. In: Proceedings of the IEEE/CVF Conference on Computer Vision and Pattern Recognition, pp. 19578–19587 (2022)
18. Gao, C., Zou, Y., Huang, J.-B.: iCAN: instance-centric attention network for human-object interaction detection. arXiv preprint arXiv:1808.10437 (2018)
19. Chao, Y.-W., Liu, Y., Liu, X., Zeng, H., Deng, J.: Learning to detect human-object interactions. In: 2018 IEEE Winter Conference on Applications of Computer Vision (WACV), pp. 381–389. IEEE (2018)
20. Bansal, A., Rambhatla, S.S., Shrivastava, A., Chellappa, R.: Detecting human-object interactions via functional generalization. In: Proceedings of the AAAI Conference on Artificial Intelligence, vol. 34, pp. 10460–10469 (2020)
21. Qi, S., Wang, W., Jia, B., Shen, J., Zhu, S.-C.: Learning human-object interactions by graph parsing neural networks. In: Proceedings of the European Conference on Computer Vision (ECCV), pp. 401–417 (2018)
22. He, T., Gao, L., Song, J., Li, Y.-F.: Exploiting scene graphs for human-object interaction detection. In: Proceedings of the IEEE/CVF International Conference on Computer Vision, pp. 15984–15993 (2021)
23. Zhang, Y., Pan, Y., Yao, T., Huang, R., Mei, T., Chen, C.-W.: Exploring structure-aware transformer over interaction proposals for human-object interaction detection. In: Proceedings of the IEEE/CVF Conference on Computer Vision and Pattern Recognition, pp. 19548–19557 (2022)
24. Li, Y.-L., et al.: Transferable interactiveness knowledge for human-object interaction detection, in: Proceedings of the IEEE/CVF Conference on Computer Vision and Pattern Recognition, pp. 3585–3594 (2019)
25. Xi, N., Meng, J., Yuan, J.: Open set video hoi detection from action-centric chain-of-look prompting. In: Proceedings of the IEEE/CVF International Conference on Computer Vision, pp. 3079–3089 (2023)
26. Wang, Y., Xi, N., Meng, J., Yuan, J.: Interaction-centric spatio-temporal context reasoning for: multi-person video HOI recognition. In: European Conference on Computer Vision, pp. 419–435. Springer (2024)
27. Li, Q., Yan, J., Zhang, J., Li, Y., Zheng, Z.: Learning human-object interactions in videos by heterogeneous graph neural networks. In: 2024 IEEE 17th International Conference on Signal Processing (ICSP), pp. 459–464. IEEE (2024)

28. Sun, X., He, Y., Ren, T., Wu, G.: Spatial-temporal human-object interaction detection. arXiv preprint arXiv:2508.17270 (2025)
29. Li, L., Wei, J., Wang, W., Yang, Y.: Neural-logic human-object interaction detection. Adv. Neural. Inf. Process. Syst. **36**, 21158–21171 (2023)
30. Zhan, Y.-W., Liu, F., Luo, X., Xu, X.-S., Nie, L., Kankanhalli, M.: Enhancing HOI detection with contextual cues from large vision-language models. In: Proceedings of the 33rd ACM International Conference on Multimedia, pp. 8557–8566 (2025)

A Study of Sleep Monitoring for Emotional Health via the Smart Pillow

Qi Fang[1], Qianwen Tan[2], Ziqian Bai[1,2(✉)], Peicen Zhao[1,2], and Diandian Sun[1,2]

[1] Southern University of Science and Technology, Shenzhen, China
12332652@mail.sustech.edu.cn

[2] Southern University of Science and Technology, Shenzhen, China
12332673@mail.sustech.edu.cn, baizq@sustech.edu.cn

Abstract. The pillow, being a common item in the daily sleep environment, is naturally integrated into people's surroundings, making it an ideal tool for sleep posture monitoring while requiring minimal effort. Sleep posture significantly impacts overall sleep quality, which in turn affects emotional well-being. However, current wearable monitoring devices and interactive pillows often draw users' attention, potentially disrupting their sleep and emotional state. This research aims to validate the following hypotheses: (1) Are people willing to learn about their sleeping positions and emotional health data using an interactive pillow? (2) How can sensors be seamlessly integrated into the interactive pillow to monitor sleep posture without disturbing the user? (3) What are the users' preferences and feedback regarding both tangible and intangible systems? Therefore, we have developed a non-intrusive system that includes an interactive pillow and a mobile application. The interactive pillow features a 4×6 Velostat pressure-sensitive array that utilizes piezoresistive properties to detect pressure changes. It can capture posture data without disturbing the user, while the mobile app provides real-time analysis and personalized recommendations. This system also offers insights into behavior changes related to sleep posture through non-intrusive, subtle interactions, which would contribute to better sleep quality and overall emotional health. It is found that the interactive pillow system can effectively enhance sleep quality and emotional well-being by offering personalized, data-driven insights and recommendations.

Keywords: Sleeping Posture Monitoring · Subtle Interaction · Tangible Interaction · Emotional Health Intervention

1 Introduction

Sleep quality is a fundamental determinant of human health and overall well-being [1]. Extensive epidemiological research has shown that impaired sleep is

Q. Fang and Q. Tan—Co-first authors contributed equally to this work.

H. Liu et al. (Eds.): CEI 2025, CCIS 2881, pp. 286–300, 2026.
https://doi.org/10.1007/978-981-95-9493-1_19

strongly linked to a broad spectrum of adverse health outcomes, including elevated risk of cardiovascular morbidity [2], obesity and metabolic dysregulation [3], diabetes [4], and mental health disorders such as depression and anxiety [5]. Beyond these clinical consequences, insufficient or fragmented sleep disrupts core cognitive processes–such as attention, executive functioning, and decision-making–and deteriorates psychomotor performance, thereby increasing the likelihood of traffic accidents, occupational injuries, and safety-critical failures [6].

Within the rapidly advancing field of emotional intelligence and affective computing, sleep quality has gained heightened relevance due to its bidirectional interactions with emotional regulation, stress responsiveness, and affective stability [7]. Emotional dysregulation arising from poor sleep can compromise the reliability of affect sensing models and diminish the robustness of human–AI interaction. Conversely, intelligent systems capable of monitoring, interpreting, and supporting healthy sleep–emotion dynamics offer promising opportunities for advancing affect-aware health technologies. However, existing posture-monitoring solutions rely heavily on wearable sensors or camera-based systems, both of which can compromise comfort, privacy, or ecological validity. These limitations are especially problematic in emotionally sensitive contexts, where intrusive sensing may inadvertently disturb sleep, alter affective states, or undermine emotional health interventions.

To address these challenges, we explore whether a pillow can serve as a non-intrusive, emotionally neutral platform for posture monitoring and behavioral guidance. Naturally integrated into the sleep environment, a pillow offers an ideal medium for unobtrusive sensing and affect-aware interaction. We will verify the following hypotheses through user research and experiments:

1. Will people use an interactive pillow to learn about their sleeping positions and emotional health data? Understanding user preferences is essential for technology adoption.
2. How can sensors be integrated into the pillow to monitor sleep posture without disturbing the user? The system must operate silently and unobtrusively.
3. What are users' preferences and feedback on both tangible and intangible aspects of the system? This is crucial for long-term engagement.

In this study, we developed a non-intrusive system that includes an interactive pillow equipped with a 4×6 Velostat pressure-sensitive array and a mobile application. The Velostat array detects pressure changes using piezoresistive properties, capturing posture data without disturbing the user. The app provides real-time analysis and personalized recommendations. By integrating tangible and intangible interfaces, our system aims to maintain emotional comfort while offering feedback and behavioral guidance. This work introduces two key innovations:

1. A subtle sensing system using a Velostat-based 4×6 pressure matrix that operates silently and unobtrusively, unlike wearable or camera-based solutions that alter sleep environments or user behavior.

2. A cross-modal emotional health intervention combining a tangible interface (the pillow) for passive data capture and an intangible interface (the app) for personalized recommendations and subtle behavioral guidance, preserving emotional comfort and enabling feedback.

2 Related Work

2.1 Sleep Posture Monitoring Technologies

In existing research, the detection of sleeping postures has become quite mature, and there are many existing techniques for detecting sleeping postures in sleep environments. They can be roughly classified into the following types:

1. `Wearable devices`: Mainstream wearable technologies, such as IMUs [8], chest straps, and neck accelerometers, capture posture and physiological signals using accelerometers [9], gyroscopes [10,11], and heart rate or breathing sensors [12,13]. However, these devices have notable limitations: 1) They can cause discomfort when worn, and long-term use may lead to skin irritation or sleep disturbances; 2) Their battery life is limited, requiring frequent recharging.
2. `Non-contact devices`: To address the issue of wearable sensors monitoring sleeping postures, many studies have delved deeply into non-contact sleep monitoring methods, such as visual recognition based on optical cameras [14], thermal imaging [15], depth cameras [16,17], radar [18], among others. However, some of them still encounter certain problems: 1) Camera-based methods may fail in low light or when obstructed, and they may also bring about certain privacy and security issues; 2) Methods such as thermal imaging and radar are too costly and require exposure, making it difficult to integrate them well into the bedding system.

However, in non-contact sleep monitoring devices, the method based on pressure sensors [19,20] can be better integrated with bedding on the bed compared to other methods, forming intelligent bedding products. Therefore, this study also adopts the combination of pressure sensors and pillows for design exploration to explore the feasibility and effectiveness of pressure sensor-based pillows in monitoring sleep postures.

2.2 Pressure Sensors in Sleep Posture Monitoring

In existing research on sleep position monitoring using pressure sensors, mattresses are commonly chosen for sensor integration [19–21]. However, this approach often requires extensive sensor arrays, leading to high costs and complex wiring. Additionally, not all areas of the mattress are fully utilized, resulting in wasted space and inefficient sensor layouts [21]. In contrast, integrating pressure sensors into pillows offers several advantages: 1) Pillows are smaller and more regular in shape, allowing for a more concise and efficient sensor layout; 2) The contact area between the pillow and the head/neck is concentrated, enabling more precise capture of pressure changes related to sleep postures; 3) Pillows are an essential part of the sleep environment and are naturally accepted by users, making them ideal for non-intrusive monitoring.

Given these benefits, this study integrates sensors into the pillow. This design minimally disrupts user sleep habits and aligns with non-intrusive interaction principles. By combining real-time posture monitoring with mobile applications, it also provides personalized emotional health support.

2.3 Pillows in Sleep Posture Monitoring

With the deepening of research, more and more scholars are also turning their attention to the field of pillow integrated sensors. Many studies have adopted smart pillows with built-in sensors for temperature [22], pressure, light [23], vibration, etc. to monitor sleeping postures. However, despite these contributions, some temperature and light sensors may be affected in terms of accuracy and acquisition when the ambient temperature changes significantly or the light intensity varies greatly. Our research focuses on the development of a non-intrusive, interactive pillow that integrates a 4×6 Velostat pressure-sensitive array. Velostat, a flexible and cost-effective material, offers high sensitivity and reliability in detecting pressure changes. Moreover, our system goes beyond mere data collection by incorporating a mobile application that offers real-time analysis and personalized recommendations. This integration of subtle interaction technology allows users to receive actionable insights without disrupting their sleep. By focusing on user comfort, data accuracy, and personalized feedback, our interactive pillow aims to provide a seamless and effective solution for sleep posture monitoring and emotional health intervention.

3 User Study: The Necessity of Sleeping Posture Data Monitoring

3.1 Questionnaires

Unlike traditional methods that use wearable devices or mattresses, our study uses pillows to detect and monitor sleep posture. This approach avoids sleep disturbances caused by wearables and minimises interference from other bedding. Specifically, we use a low pillow to measure pressure on the shoulders and neck, thereby enhancing posture detection. Our survey explores people's interest in sleep posture data and investigates correlations between demographics, health conditions and sleep quality. This will help us to identify specific user groups for targeted research and provide personalised sleep posture recommendations.

Survey Question Settings. Health Problem Statistics and Categories: Seven common diseases possibly related to sleep health (hypertension, diabetes, bronchitis, etc.) and seven health issues that may affect sleep quality (such as shoulder and neck discomfort, joint pain, etc.) were categorized. Referencing the International Classification of Diseases-10 (ICD-10), the common diseases identified in this study were classified into diabetes, cardiovascular, respiratory system, musculoskeletal, sensory, and other diseases, totaling six categories.

1. **Mental Health Assessment**: The Patient Health Questionnaire-4 (PHQ-4) [24] was used to assess participants' mental health symptoms over the past two weeks. This tool is a concise and reliable measure for identifying depression and anxiety.
2. **Sleep Quality Assessment**: The Pittsburgh Sleep Quality Index (PSQI) [25] was employed to evaluate participants' sleep quality over the past month. Additionally, using a Likert five-point scale, participants were surveyed on their interest in understanding sleep posture information, including posture type, duration, impact on sleep quality, personalized sleep advice based on health conditions, and professional sleep recommendations.

Survey Results. The questionnaire was completed by 71 respondents. Ages ranged from 18 years or younger (4.23%, n = 3) to over 30 years old (4.23%, n = 4), with the majority aged 18–25 years (77.46%, n = 55). The gender distribution was 19.72% male, 76.06% female, and 4.23% preferring not to say. Among respondents, 83.1% (n = 59) reported long-term sedentary work. The top three health issues affecting sleep quality were shoulder and neck discomfort (n = 32), lumbar and back discomfort (n = 22), and frequent headaches (n = 17). Results of PHQ-4 and PSQI Survey (Fig. 2) showed: 7.04% severe, 39.44% mild, 29.58% normal mood, and 23.94% moderate depression and anxiety. The PSQI data indicated that 75.55% of participants had satisfactory sleep, with 60.56% rating it as "Fairly good" and 15.49% as "Very good." The remaining 24.21% rated their sleep as "Fairly bad" (19.72%) or "Very bad" (4.23%). Figure 1 shows a negative correlation between physical discomforts (lumbar, shoulder, and leg pain) and sleep quality, with shoulder and neck discomfort having a significant impact on sleep quality and onset.

Table 1. The Pearson Correlation between physical discomforts and ease of falling asleep, sleep quality and PSQI result.

	Difficulty faling asleep (Sleep quality(High score means bad)	Sleep quality (High score means bad)	PSQI Result
Lumbar and back discomfort	0.168	0.204	0.266*
Shoulder and neck discomfort	0.342**	0.299*	−0.404**
Leg discomfort	0.165	0.200	−0.262**

$*p < 0.05 **p < 0.01$

Table 1 shows correlation coefficients for factors influencing sleep, such as posture, duration, quality, and recommendations. Significant positive correlations were found, which are crucial for designing sleep monitoring systems. Notably, the strong correlation between "Sleeping posture" and "Posture duration" (r = 0.654, p <0.01) underscores the importance of monitoring posture durations. The correlation between "Posture-quality relationship" and "Customized posture recommendations" (r = 0.633, p <0.01) highlights the value of personalized sleep guidance. Additionally, the high correlation between "Professional recommendations" and "Posture-quality relationship" (r = 0.702, p < 0.01) indicates that expert advice aligns closely with factors affecting sleep quality. Integrating such insights can enhance sleep hygiene through monitoring systems.

Table 2. The correlation coefficients for factors influencing sleep, including sleeping posture, duration of posture, quality and sleeping recommendations.

	Mean	Standard Deviation	Sleeping posture	The duration of sleeping postures	The relationship between posture and quality	Personalized sleeping posture recommendations	Professional sleeping posture recommendations
Sleeping posture	3.661	0.822	1				
The duration of sleeping postures	3.881	0.790	0.654**	1			
The relationship between posture and quality	4.254	0.863	0.585**	0.551**	1		
Personalized sleeping posture recommendations	4.051	0.797	0.527**	0.558**	0.633**	1	
Professional sleeping posture recommendations	4.051	0.775	0.487**	0.573**	0.702**	0.693**	1

$^{*}p < 0.05$ $^{**}p < 0.01$

4 Hardware Design

4.1 Material Selection

Velostat, a polyethylene-carbon composite material, was chosen for the sensing matrix due to its pressure-sensitive properties. In its resting state, the sparse distribution of graphite particles within the polymer matrix results in high resistance. When pressure is applied, these particles realign, increasing conductivity and reducing resistance. This change in resistance allows for indirect measurement of pressure. Velostat is also flexible, cost-effective, and chemically stable [26].

4.2 Classification of Postures

The paper defines nine sleeping postures using a 3×3 grid format: central supine, left lateral supine, right lateral supine, central left lateral, left lateral left lateral, right lateral left lateral, central right lateral, left lateral right lateral, and right lateral right lateral. This method enhances sleep posture recognition by considering both pressure concentration areas and variations in pressure patterns caused by different postures, aligning more closely with real-life scenarios than existing methods [27].

4.3 Principle of Sensor Matrix

The sensor array is constructed using 304 stainless steel wires (0.1 mm diameter) as conductors and controlled by an Arduino Uno. Resistance values of each sensor unit are read via multiplexing scanning, row by row and column by column. In the circuit setup, row electrodes connect to the Arduino's analog input pins for voltage reading, while column electrodes link to digital output pins for level control. A driving voltage (Vg) is sequentially applied to each column. To prevent interference, one column is activated at a time by setting its electrode to a low level (0V), while others remain in a high impedance state. Row electrodes then scan and read the voltage on each row, reflecting the resistance at the intersection point. This method reduces the required pin count from twice the number of modules to the sum of rows and columns.

4.4 Design of the Interactive Pillow and Sensor Layout

4 * 6 Velostat Pressure Sensitive Sensor Array. Based on the questionnaire results, in the final design solution, a rectangular low pillow with dimensions of 55 cm × 35 cm was selected. The density of pressure-sensitive sensor units on the pillow was deliberately reduced, and the monitoring range was extended to include the edge areas of the pillow to enhance overall monitoring effectiveness. It was decided that the center-to-center distance between adjacent pressure-sensitive sensor units would be set horizontally at 10 cm and vertically at 8 cm.

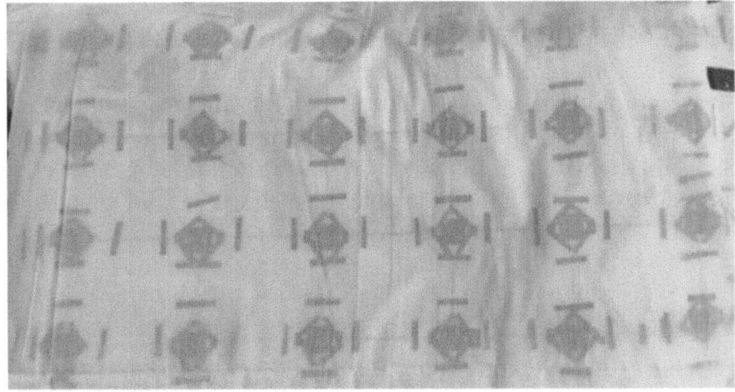

Fig. 1. Preliminary Hardware Prototype Diagram

This layout comprises 24 independent new Velostat pressure-sensitive sensor units, each with dimensions of 20 mm $\times$ 20 mm, arranged together in a 4×6 matrix structure (Fig. 1).

5 Software Design

The software component of the pillow-based sleep posture detection and monitoring system developed in this study is primarily designed with the following criteria:

5.1 Interface Design Element

To align the software UI with the study's theme, the following design guidelines are applied: 1) The UI should be simple, displaying only key information from the pillow sensor in a peripheral display to minimize cognitive load and allow quick processing without disrupting primary tasks; 2) Feedback mechanisms should be subtle, avoiding mandatory or intrusive prompts, to help users notice posture issues or suggestions without interrupting their activities; 3) The color scheme includes primary (deep blue), secondary, and background (deep black) colors, inspired by the night sky to create a comfortable atmosphere conducive to sleep [29]. This scheme guides user interactions and enhances the overall experience; 4) Icons and other elements will be selected from open-source libraries, adhering to the established color scheme principles.

5.2 Software Functions

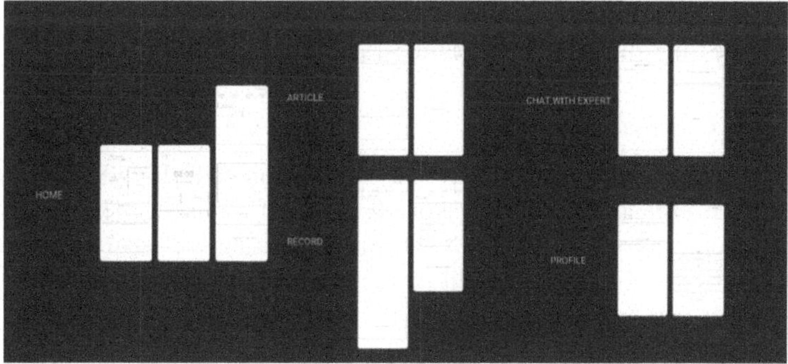

Fig. 2. Preliminary Prototype of the Software

The preliminary prototype of the software of this research comprises five main components (Fig. 2):

1. `Homepage`: The functionalities of the homepage include: 1) Setting wake-up and sleep times to enable the system to start recording data during the user's sleep period; 2) Viewing the latest data analysis, which provides insights into the user's sleeping posture data from their most recent sleep session, including the types of sleeping positions, the duration spent in each position, and personalized sleep recommendations.
2. `Article Reading`: The functionalities of the article page include: 1) Accessing the latest and most comprehensive articles and resources related to sleep, allowing users to learn and acquire relevant sleep knowledge; 2) Viewing and reading the specific content of each article in detail.
3. `Data Records`: The functionalities of the records page include: 1) The ability to select and view daily, weekly, monthly, or yearly records of data; 2) Detailed examination of data, which encompasses the percentage of time spent in each sleep posture during sleep, the duration of each posture, as well as the times of falling asleep and waking up.
4. `Expert Advice`: The functionalities of the Connect with Experts page include: 1) The option to select from various experts in the field; 2) Engaging in one-on-one, detailed consultations with the selected expert for personalized sleep advice and recommendations.
5. `Personal Information`: The functionalities of the Profile page include: 1) Basic account operations, such as accessing the help manual, logging out of the account, adjusting settings, and configuring personal information; 2) Customizing personal information, which includes setting a nickname, selecting a gender, uploading a profile picture, entering age, occupation, medical conditions, and sleep habits.

6 User Test

The purpose of this test is to: 1) Determine if it can detect and differentiate between nine different sleep postures; 2) Assess if it can conduct long-term sleep posture monitoring and identify various stages of sleep postures.

6.1 Sensor Calibration

Before conducting this pilot experiment, we calibrated the sensors employed in this research endeavor, with the specific goal of exploring the possibility of obtaining a preliminary evaluation of an individual's sleep posture via the pillow. To achieve this, we conducted a calibration experiment for testing (Fig. 3). The experimental design is outlined as follows:

1. `Calibration Experiment Materials`: A $2\,\text{mm} \times 2\,\text{mm}$ square sample randomly cut from the experimental material, Velostat; 304 stainless steel wire with a diameter of 0.1 mm, serving as the conductor; An Arduino Uno, functioning as the controller.
2. `Calibration Experiment Task`: Conduct pressure tests on the sample sequentially using standard weights of different capacities, and record the corresponding resistance values displayed.

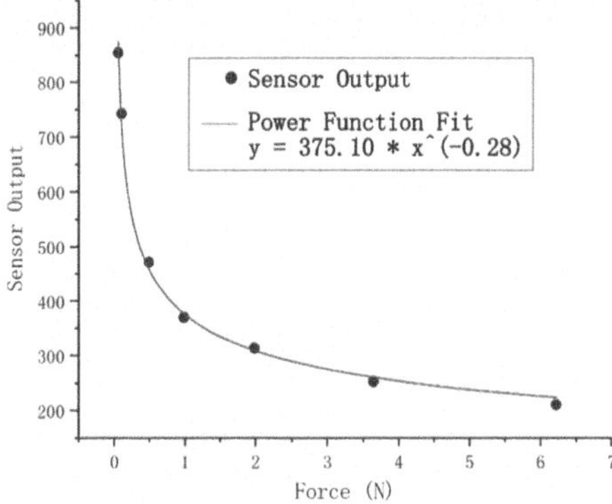

Fig. 3. Power Function Fit Curve between Sensor Output and Applied Pressure.

6.2 Experiment 1: Nine Types of Sleeping Positions Classification

The first experiment aims to investigate whether the prototype can detect nine different sleep postures. In this part of the experiment, participants (N = 9) are required to lie on the test prototype in nine different sleep postures:

1. Supine position with the head at the center of the pillow (referred to as M-M in subsequent articles).
2. Left log position with the head at the center of the pillow (referred to as M-L in subsequent articles).
3. Right log position with the head at the center of the pillow (referred to as M-R in subsequent articles).
4. Supine position with the head on the left side of the pillow (referred to as L-M in subsequent articles).
5. Left log position with the head on the left side of the pillow (referred to as L-L in subsequent articles).
6. Right log position with the head on the left side of the pillow (referred to as L-R in subsequent articles).
7. Supine position with the head on the right side of the pillow (referred to as R-M in subsequent articles).
8. Left log position with the head on the right side of the pillow (referred to as R-L in subsequent articles).
9. Right log position with the head on the right side of the pillow (referred to as R-R in subsequent articles).

The above task requires participants to lift their necks to change sleeping positions, and changes should only be made once the data has stabilized. This experiment took place at the Chuangyuan Laboratory of Southern University of Science and Technology, using the preliminary prototype as shown in Fig. 1 of this study.

For each sleeping position, three tests were conducted (Fig. 4), and the sensor values were averaged and rounded to two decimal places. However, due to

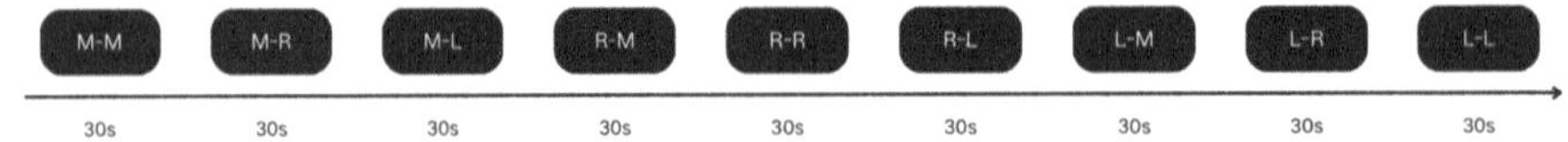

Fig. 4. Illustration of the Sleep Posture Sequence for the Testing Task.

equipment malfunction, only two tests were completed for the R-M posture, while three valid tests were obtained for the other eight positions. The sensor output was calculated by subtracting the baseline average from the maximum reading of 1023. Data points corresponding to masses less than 15g and z-axis coordinates below 379.65 were excluded to minimize noise.

Result. We compared the data from Experiment One with the actual postures through 3D modeling to observe whether there were relatively obvious characteristic patterns presented under nine different sleeping positions. By comparing the sleeping postures of real people during the test process, the pressure value of the edge sensor unit is regarded as noise, which may be affected by the test prototype tape and eventually be discarded.

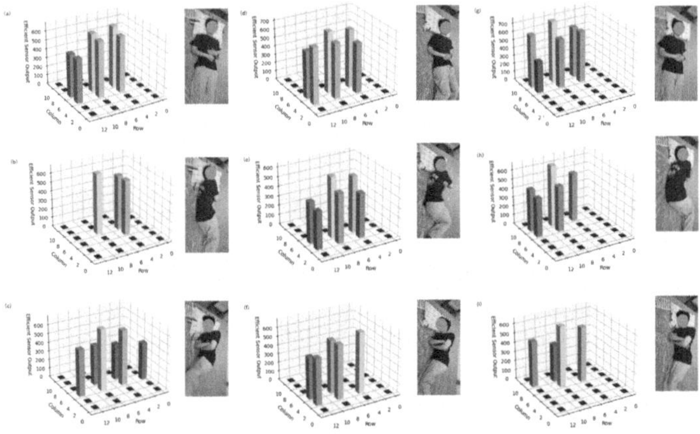

Fig. 5. The data of nine sleeping positions were compared with those of real people.

The results obtained from this task are shown in Fig. 5. It can be seen from the results that: 1) When lying on the back, the pressure on the neck is less than that on the head, and the pressure changes of the six sensors are significant when lying on the back; 2) When lying on one's side, the pressure on the face is less than that on the back of the head; 3) When placed at different positions on the pillow, the sensors of different columns will experience pressure changes. The above test results enable us to utilize this observed pattern to identify users' sleeping postures.

6.3 Experiment 2: Monitoring of Sleeping Posture Changes

The second experiment aims to investigate whether the prototype can distinguish between different and identical sleep postures when participants continuously change their sleeping positions. In this part of the experiment, participants are required to sequentially switch between the M-M, M-R, and M-M sleep postures. Each posture should be maintained for 30 s before transitioning to the next. This experiment took place at the Xinyuan Laboratory of Southern University of Science and Technology, using the preliminary prototype (Fig. 1).

We fitted the experimental data to a curve that established the correlation between the output voltage of the sensor and the applied pressure. This relationship helps to obtain the required assessment of sleep positions. This curve accurately reflects the corresponding changes in the sensor output voltage with pressure, enabling us to analyze and evaluate the user's sleeping posture based on this consistent pattern (Fig. 6 a)).

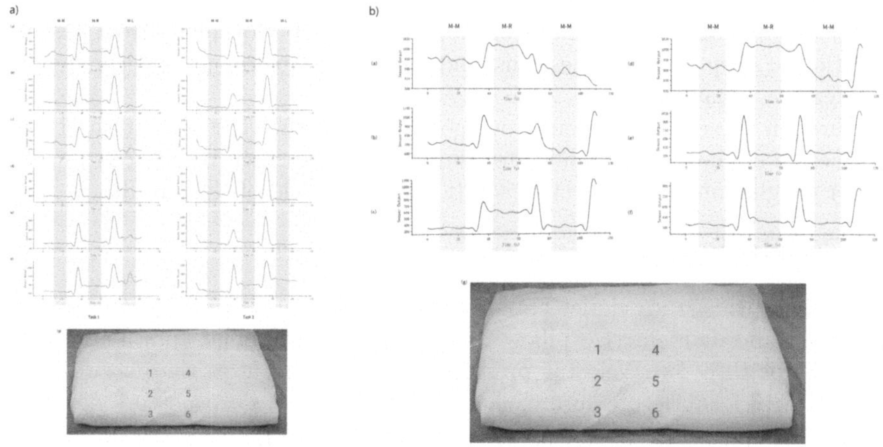

Fig. 6. a) 6 Sensor Units Sensor Output in 3 Sleeping Positions. b) Sensor Output Repeatedly Tested by 6 Sensor Units in 3 Sleeping Positions.

We also selected the M-M, M-R, and M-L processes from the experiment and analyzed the voltage-time correlation graphs for sensors 1–6 during these processes (Fig. 6 b)).

From the results, we can observe: 1) When transitioning between different sleep postures, the sensors in contact with the head exhibit distinct numerical changes; 2) When adopting the same sleep posture, the sensors in contact with the head display approximately similar readings. These two significant outcomes demonstrate that the output voltage of the relevant sensors undergoes regular variations in response to dynamic changes in sleep posture, enabling us to continuously monitor users' sleep postures over an extended period based on this identifiable pattern.

7 Limitation and Future Work

This study validated the pressure-sensitive pillow's ability to identify different sleeping postures through preliminary and dynamic testing, and presented the accompanying app prototype. It established a foundational subtle interaction sleep health system covering detection, identification, feedback, and suggestions. However, limitations remain: 1) The pillow's continuous accuracy in posture recognition hasn't been verified through long-term testing; 2) Real-world sleep environment testing is lacking, limiting the assessment of user satisfaction with the implicit interaction system; 3) The current design may face issues like displacement or creasing during use, affecting performance.

This also clarifies the direction for our future research improvements: 1) Investigate sensor distribution and quantity on various pillow shapes, especially optimizing layouts for S-shaped pillows with neck support to enhance posture recognition accuracy; 2) Develop personalized sleep recognition algorithms by creating a comprehensive database of pressure distribution data from diverse individuals, accounting for varied sleep habits. Conduct long-term user testing in real sleep environments to fully assess the system's performance, from posture detection to sleep health suggestions, and understand its impact on sleep quality and hygiene behaviors.

Through these improvements, our goal is to enhance the stability and user satisfaction of the system, while ensuring that our research results can provide deeper insights and more effective solutions for the field of sleep health.

8 Conclusion

Conclusively, this study designs a non-invasive sleep monitoring system, including an advanced interactive pillow and a companion mobile app. The pillow, embedded with a 4×6 Velostat pressure sensor matrix, uses the piezoresistive effect to detect subtle pressure changes for unobtrusive sleep posture data collection; the app enables real-time analysis and delivers personalized recommendations. Most existing studies focus on technical performance, ignoring monitoring systems' interactive impacts on sleep environments and user behaviors. This system's core contribution is its "hardware perception + APP analysis" design: it converts monitoring data into actionable sleep health interventions, realizing the shift from "passive monitoring" to "active health management" and maximizing data value. Future research will conduct long-term real-world user tests to explore how integrating implicit interaction systems into sleep environments affects sleep health and hygiene behaviors.

References

1. Alecci, L., Abdalazim, N., Alchieri, L., Gashi, S., Santini, S.: On the mismatch between measured and perceived sleep quality. In: Adjunct Proceedings of the 2022 ACM International Joint Conference on Pervasive and Ubiquitous Computing and the 2022 ACM International Symposium on Wearable Computers, pp. 148–152. Association for Computing Machinery, New York, NY, USA (2023). https://doi.org/10.1145/3544793.3563412

2. Cappuccio, F.P., Cooper, D., D'Elia, L., Strazzullo, P., Miller, M.A.: Sleep duration predicts cardiovascular outcomes: a systematic review and meta-analysis of prospective studies. Eur. Heart J. **32**(12), 1484–1492 (2011). https://doi.org/10.1093/eurheartj/ehr007
3. Spiegel, K., Leproult, R., Van Cauter, E.: Impact of sleep debt on metabolic and endocrine function. Lancet **354**(9188), 1435–1439 (1999). https://doi.org/10.1016/S0140-6736(99)01376-8
4. Knutson, K.L.: Impact of sleep and sleep loss on glucose homeostasis and appetite regulation. Sleep Med. Clin. **2**(2), 187–197 (2007). https://doi.org/10.1016/j.jsmc.2007.03.004
5. Baglioni, C., Battagliese, G., Feige, B., Spiegelhalder, K., Nissen, C., Voderholzer, U., Lombardo, C., Riemann, D.: Insomnia as a predictor of depression: a meta-analytic evaluation of longitudinal epidemiological studies. J. Affect. Disord. **135**(1–3), 10–19 (2011). https://doi.org/10.1016/j.jad.2011.01.011
6. Killgore, W.D.: Effects of sleep deprivation on cognition. Prog. Brain Res. **185**, 105–129 (2010). https://doi.org/10.1016/B978-0-444-53702-7.00007-5
7. Goldstein, A.N., Walker, M.P.: The role of sleep in emotional brain function. Annu. Rev. Clin. Psychol. **10**, 679–708 (2014). https://doi.org/10.1146/annurev-clinpsy-032813-153716
8. Eyobu, O. S., Kim, Y. W., Cha, D., Han, D. S.: A real-time sleeping position recognition system using IMU sensor motion data. In: 2018 IEEE International Conference on Consumer Electronics (ICCE), Las Vegas, NV, USA, pp. 1–2 (2018). https://doi.org/10.1109/ICCE.2018.8326209
9. Xu, K., et al.: A wearable body condition sensor system with wireless feedback alarm functions. Adv. Mater. **33**(18), e2008701 (2021). https://doi.org/10.1002/adma.202008701
10. Doheny, E. P., Lowery, M. M., Russell, A., Ryan, S.: Estimation of respiration rate and sleeping position using a wearable accelerometer. In: Annual International Conference on IEEE Engineering in Medicine and Biology Society, pp. 4668–4671 (2020). https://doi.org/10.1109/EMBC44109.2020.9176573
11. Abdulsadig, R. S., Singh, S., Patel, Z., Rodriguez-Villegas, E.: Sleep posture detection using an accelerometer placed on the neck. In: 44th Annual International Conference of the IEEE Engineering in Medicine & Biology Society (EMBC), Glasgow, Scotland, United Kingdom, pp. 2430–2433 (2022). https://doi.org/10.1109/EMBC48229.2022.9871300
12. Jafari Tadi, M., Lehtonen, E., Saraste, A., et al.: Gyrocardiography: a new non-invasive monitoring method for the assessment of cardiac mechanics and the estimation of hemodynamic variables. Sci Rep. **7**, 6823 (2017). https://doi.org/10.1038/s41598-017-07248-y
13. Morra, S., et al.: Ballistocardiography and seismocardiography detection of hemodynamic changes during simulated obstructive apnea. Physiol. Meas. **41**(6), 065007 (2020). https://doi.org/10.1088/1361-6579/ab924b
14. Zhang, Y., Xiao, A., Zheng, T., Xiao, H., Huang, R.: The relationship between sleeping position and sleep quality: a flexible sensor-based study. Sensors (Basel) **22**(16), 6220 (2022). https://doi.org/10.3390/s22166220
15. Jakkaew, P., Onoye, T.: Non-contact respiration monitoring and body movements detection for sleep using thermal imaging. Sensors (Basel) **20**(21), 6307 (2020). https://doi.org/10.3390/s20216307
16. Tam, A.Y., et al.: Depth-camera-based under-blanket sleep posture classification using anatomical landmark-guided deep learning model. Int. J. Environ. Res. Pub. Health **19**(20), 13491 (2022). https://doi.org/10.3390/ijerph192013491

17. Ren, A., Dong, B., Lv, X., Zhu, T., Hu, F., Yang, X.: A non-contact sleep posture sensing strategy considering three dimensional human body models. In: 2016 2nd IEEE International Conference on Computer and Communications (ICCC), Chengdu, China, pp. 414–417 (2016). https://doi.org/10.1109/CompComm.2016.7924734
18. Lai, D.K.-H., et al.: Vision Transformers (ViT) for blanket-penetrating sleep posture recognition using a triple ultra-wideband (UWB) radar system. Sensors **23**(5), 2475 (2023). https://doi.org/10.3390/s23052475
19. Kau, L.-J., Wang, M.-Y., Zhou, H.: Pressure-sensor-based sleep status and quality evaluation system. IEEE Sens. J. **23**(9), 9739–9754 (2023). https://doi.org/10.1109/JSEN.2023.3262747
20. Hu, Q., Tang, X., Tang, W.: A real-time patient-specific sleeping posture recognition system using pressure sensitive conductive sheet and transfer learning. IEEE Sens. J. **21**(5), 6869–6879 (2021). https://doi.org/10.1109/JSEN.2020.3043416
21. Liu, Z., Li, G., Wang, C., Cascioli, V., McCarthy, P.W.: Unobtrusive sleep posture detection using a smart bed mattress with optimally distributed triaxial accelerometer array and parallel convolutional spatiotemporal network. Sensors (Basel) **25**(12), 3609 (2025). https://doi.org/10.3390/s25123609
22. Jun, W.-H., Hong, Y.-S.: Detection of sleep posture via humidity fluctuation analysis in a sensor-embedded pillow. Bioengineering **12**, 480 (2025). https://doi.org/10.3390/bioengineering12050480
23. Veiga, A., Garcia, L., Parra, L., Lloret, J., Augele, V.: An IoT-based smart pillow for sleep quality monitoring in AAL environments. In: 2018 Third International Conference on Fog and Mobile Edge Computing (FMEC), Barcelona, Spain, pp. 175–180 (2018). https://doi.org/10.1109/FMEC.2018.8364061
24. Löwe, B., et al.: A 4-item measure of depression and anxiety: validation and standardization of the patient health questionnaire-4 (PHQ-4) in the general population. J. Affect. Disord. **122**(1–2), 86–95 (2010). https://doi.org/10.1016/j.jad.2009.06.019
25. Buysse, D.J., Reynolds, C.F., III., Monk, T.H., Berman, S.R., Kupfer, D.J.: The Pittsburgh sleep quality index: a new instrument for psychiatric practice and research. Psychiatry Res. **28**(2), 193–213 (1989). https://doi.org/10.1016/0165-1781(89)90047-4
26. Giovanelli, D., Farella, E.: Force sensing resistor and evaluation of technology for wearable body pressure sensing. J. Sensors **2016**, 9391850:1–9391850:13 (2016). https://doi.org/10.1155/2016/9391850
27. Wang, H., et al.: SleepSense: smart pillow with pressure-sensitive FBG-embedded silicone buttons. IEEE Sens. J. **23**, 19324–19331 (2023). https://doi.org/10.1109/JSEN.2023.3295114
28. Dzedzickis, A., et al.: Polyethylene-carbon composite (Velostat®) based tactile sensor. Polymers **12**, e3000 (2020). https://doi.org/10.3390/polym12122905
29. Lan, X.: Research on sleep APP design based on visual communication analysis. Mod. Econ. Manage. Forum (2022). https://doi.org/10.32629/memf.v3i6.1060

SA-RADE: Scattering-Augmented Multimodal Personality Prediction with a Lightweight Residual-Adapter Ensemble

Haodong Li, Yiwei Gong, Qiwei Wu, Na Liu(✉), and Qirong Mao

School of Computer Science and Communication Engineering, Jiangsu University, Zhenjiang 212013, China
na.liu@ujs.edu.cn

Abstract. This paper addresses the HEXACO personality trait regression task in Asynchronous Video Interviews (AVI) for Track 1 of the ACM Multimedia AVI Grand Challenge 2025, and proposes a lightweight yet robust scattering-augmented multimodal prediction framework termed SA-RADE. We first employ SigLIP2, emotion2vec+, and SFR-Embedding-Mistral to extract visual semantic, affective acoustic, and textual semantic representations, respectively, followed by question-level temporal pooling. We then introduce the Wavelet Scattering Transform (WST) as a complementary visual stream, computing high-frequency facial texture statistics–mean, standard deviation, and salient energy–over five semantic facial regions to capture micro-expressions and subtle deformations that are informative for personality inference. To effectively fuse heterogeneous cues, we design a Residual-Adapter Deep Ensemble (RADE) regressor, which improves training stability and generalization by averaging multiple MLP sub-models and learning complementary cross-modal residuals via a gated adapter branch. Experiments on the official AVI-2025 dataset show that SA-RADE delivers stable performance across four HEXACO traits, achieving a markedly lower average MSE than baseline methods and yielding strong overall results, thereby demonstrating the effectiveness of scattering-based texture cues and lightweight ensemble learning for AVI personality computing.

Keywords: Asynchronous Video Interviews · Multimodal Regression · Wavelet Scattering Transform · Personality Recognition

1 Introduction

Personality computing has become an important research topic in affective computing, humancomputer interaction, and intelligent assessment systems, owing to the growing need for scalable, objective, and automated evaluation tools in recruitment, education, and digital psychology. Traditional personality assessment relies heavily on standardized questionnaires (e.g., NEO-PI-R, BFI-2,

H. Liu et al. (Eds.): CEI 2025, CCIS 2881, pp. 301–312, 2026.
https://doi.org/10.1007/978-981-95-9493-1_20

HEXACO-PI-R) and structured interviews, but these methods suffer from self-report biases, susceptibility to social desirability, and limited ecological validity [1–3]. With the rapid development of deep learning and large-scale multimodal benchmarks, automatic personality prediction from video, audio, and text has emerged as a compelling alternative capable of capturing implicit behavioral signals that reveal stable psychological traits [4–6].

Asynchronous Video Interviews (AVIs) provide a naturalistic medium for eliciting trait-relevant behaviors, and recent challenges, such as the AVI Grand Challenge 2025 [7,8], have further accelerated research progress by offering well-curated multimodal datasets and standardized evaluation protocols. In particular, Track 1 of the challenge focuses on regressing four HEXACO personality dimensions (HonestyHumility, Extraversion, Agreeableness, Conscientiousness) based on subject responses to psychologist-designed prompts, emphasizing the extraction of subtle behavioral cues such as micro-expressions, prosodic patterns, and semantic reasoning.

Existing multimodal personality prediction models typically follow a feature-engineering paradigm: pre-trained encoders generate modality-specific embeddings, followed by shallow fusion strategies or monolithic regression heads [5,9,10]. However, these approaches face several limitations. (1) Insufficient modeling of high-frequency facial micro-dynamics. Recent studies show that trait-relevant expressions often manifest as short-lived texture variations or regional muscle activations that are poorly captured by global visual backbones [4,11]. (2) Under-exploitation of cross-modal complementarity. Personality emerges from integrated behavioral patterns across appearance, speech, and language; yet naive concatenation or uniform weighting fails to capture the heterogeneous contributions of each modality [6,12]. (3) Lack of lightweight but robust regressors. Deep fusion transformers or large MLPs often overfit small-scale personality datasets, while single-head regressors exhibit instability across traits and interview questions.

To address these challenges, this paper proposes SA-RADE, a Scattering-Augmented Residual-Adapter Deep Ensemble framework designed for lightweight and stable multimodal personality prediction. Our contributions are threefold:

- We incorporate Wavelet Scattering Transform (WST) as an additional visual pathway to model high-frequency facial texture variations. By computing scattering coefficients over semantic facial regions and aggregating them through statistical pooling, the model captures fine-grained, psychologically relevant micro-expressions that standard visual encoders tend to overlook.
- We propose a novel ensemble regressor that combines multiple lightweight MLP sub-models with a gated residual adapter. This design enhances robustness, reduces training variance, and effectively learns cross-modal corrective signals, providing strong generalization under limited data conditions typical of personality regression tasks.
- We develop a unified multimodal pipeline that employs SigLIP2 for visual semantics, Emotion2Vec+ for affective acoustics, and SFR-Embedding-

Mistral for linguistic reasoning, complemented by question-level temporal pooling to align AVI responses. This integration produces compact and discriminative representations that support stable personality regression across all HEXACO traits.

2 Related Work

2.1 Multimodal Personality Computing

Multimodal personality computing has progressed rapidly with the availability of large-scale datasets and advances in deep representation learning. Early benchmarks such as First Impressions demonstrated that personality traits can be predicted from brief multimodal video clips by leveraging facial expressions, gestures, vocal prosody, and linguistic markers [13]. Subsequent surveys highlight the complementary value of these modalities and the importance of modeling subtle behavioral cues that reflect stable psychological traits [14].

Recently, the AVI Grand Challenge 2025 introduced a more structured and psychologically grounded benchmark for HEXACO regression in Asynchronous Video Interviews (AVIs), providing standardized prompts, multimodal recordings, and high-quality human ratings [7]. This setting is more naturalistic and behaviorally rich than traditional lab-controlled datasets, offering unique opportunities for automatic trait inference. Several works have begun exploring this domain, showing that state-of-the-art encoders for vision, audio, and text, such as Vision Transformers [15], Emotion2Vec-style speech models [16], and LLM-based semantic embeddings [5].

However, existing AVI systems primarily rely on semantic-level encoders and often overlook high-frequency facial micro-dynamics, despite psychological findings showing that subtle facial deformations (e.g., micro-smiles, muscle tension) contribute significantly to personality impressions [17]. Moreover, multimodal fusion methods frequently adopt either naive concatenation or heavy cross-modal transformers, leading to inefficiencies or overfitting on the limited training samples typical of AVI datasets. These limitations motivate the need for feature representations that capture fine-grained visual cues and fusion strategies that maintain stability under small-data conditions.

2.2 Scattering-Based Facial Representation

Wavelet Scattering Transform (WST) provides a principled framework for capturing high-frequency texture patterns in images, offering stability to small deformations and invariance to translations [18]. It has been successfully applied in diverse areas where fine-grained structural information is essential, including material recognition and affective facial analysis [19,20]. Although such high-frequency descriptors are well aligned with psychological theories of micro-expression analysis, scattering-based representations remain underexplored in

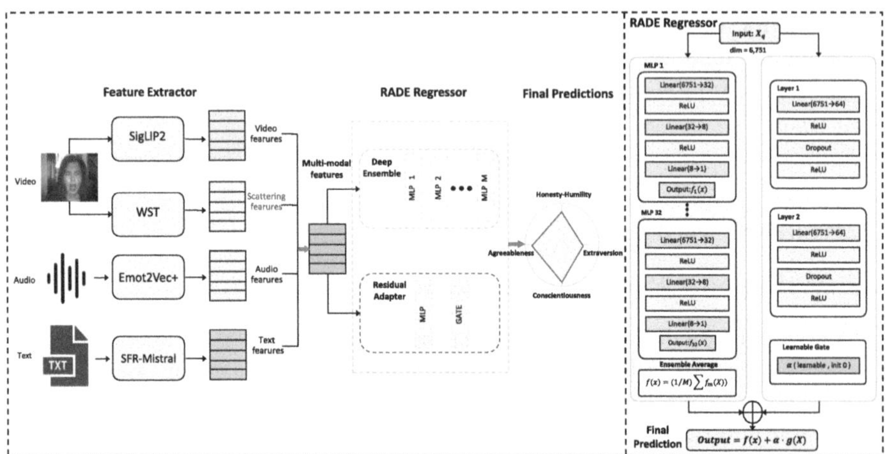

Fig. 1. Overall architecture of the proposed SA-RADE framework.

personality computing, where subtle facial textures may encode trait-relevant behavioral tendencies [21–23].

In parallel, lightweight fusion and ensemble learning approaches have shown promise for multimodal inference. Shared MLP-based regressors used in recent AVI studies effectively balance expressiveness and robustness [5], while ensemble strategies help reduce variance and improve model stability in both performance prediction and multimodal trait analysis [13]. However, prior work has not combined ensemble methods with modality-aware residual adaptation, which can correct inter-modal inconsistencies and enhance generalization across heterogeneous AVI responses.

Our work builds upon and extends these research threads by integrating region-wise scattering features with a Residual-Adapter Deep Ensemble, offering a lightweight, stable, and psychologically grounded solution for multimodal personality regression in AVIs.

3 Method

Figure 1 illustrates the overall architecture of our approach. Given asynchronous interview videos, we first extract question-level multimodal representations from three standard modalities (visual, acoustic, and transcript) and an additional scattering-based facial texture modality. The resulting features are concatenated into a unified vector per question and fed into our Residual-Adapter Deep Ensemble (RADE) regressor, which combines a deep ensemble backbone with a gated residual adapter to model subtle cross-modal interactions for personality prediction.

3.1 Multimodal Feature Extraction

To represent cross-modal personality-related cues in asynchronous video interviews, we extract three types of features—visual, acoustic, and transcript-based—for each subject across the six questions $q \in \{1, \ldots, 6\}$. These features are temporally aggregated at the question level, yielding a structured multimodal input for downstream regression modeling.

For each question video, we uniformly sample frames from the original stream at a fixed interval (one frame every 30 frames), obtaining a frame sequence $\{V_q^{(t)}\}_{t=1}^{T_q^v}$. Each sampled frame is fed into the SigLIP2 vision encoder to produce a 1152-dimensional frame-level embedding $f_{\text{SigLIP2}}(V_q^{(t)}) \in \mathbb{R}^{1152}$. To derive a question-level global representation, we apply temporal max pooling along the time dimension:

$$\mathbf{v}_q(k) = \max_{1 \le t \le T_q^v} f_{\text{SigLIP2}}(V_q^{(t)})(k), \quad k = 1, \ldots, 1152, \tag{1}$$

which yields the question-level visual feature vector $\mathbf{v}_q \in \mathbb{R}^{1152}$.

For each segmented question audio clip, we extract an audio frame sequence $\{A_q^{(t)}\}_{t=1}^{T_q^a}$ and use the emotion2vecplus-seed model to obtain emotion-related frame-level embeddings $f_{\text{emo2vec+}}(A_q^{(t)}) \in \mathbb{R}^{768}$. To obtain a unified question-level audio feature, we apply temporal max pooling over the time dimension:

$$\mathbf{a}_q(k) = \max_{1 \le t \le T_q^a} f_{\text{emo2vec+}}(A_q^{(t)})(k), \quad k = 1, \ldots, 768, \tag{2}$$

yielding the question-level acoustic vector $\mathbf{a}_q \in \mathbb{R}^{768}$.

For each question video, we first perform automatic speech recognition using a Whisper-medium model to obtain the transcript s_q, and then encode it with the SFR-Embedding-Mistral model to produce a 4096-dimensional semantic embedding. We take the representation of the last token in the final hidden layer as the question-level text vector:

$$\mathbf{t}_q = f_{\text{SFR-Mistral}}(s_q) \in \mathbb{R}^{4096}. \tag{3}$$

In addition to the above three modalities, we further incorporate facial texture features based on wavelet scattering as a complementary visual description; the extraction procedure is detailed in Sec. 3.2.

3.2 Compact Facial Scattering Representation

Figure 2 provides an overview of our facial scattering feature extraction pipeline. To encode stable and informative local structure, we apply the Wavelet Scattering Transform (WST) to each spatial region of the input image. The facial image in each frame is partitioned into five semantic regions. Each region provides a localized signal $f_r(x)$ from which we extract scattering-based frequency features.

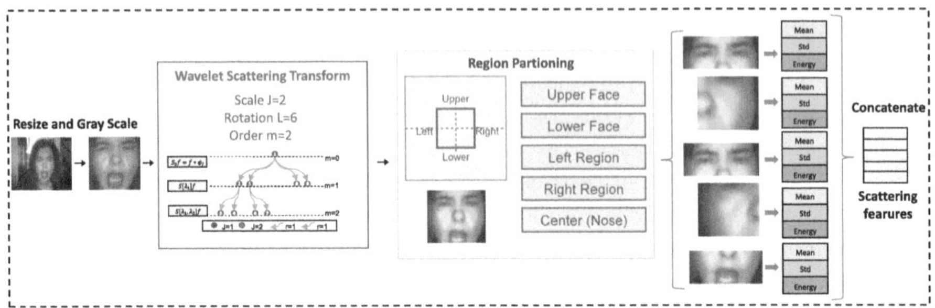

Fig. 2. Detailed procedure of extracting wavelet scattering (SC) facial texture features.

Given a region signal $f_r(x)$, the first-order WST extracts translation-invariant and deformation-stable descriptors. Specifically, the wavelet coefficients are computed as:

$$W_J f = \left\{ f * \phi_J, f * \psi_{2^j \gamma}(x) \right\}_{j<J} \quad (4)$$

where $\psi_{2^j \gamma}$ denotes a set of directional wavelets at scale 2^j and orientation γ, and ϕ_J is a low-pass filter.

To ensure stability and energy preservation, the modulus operation is applied before filtering:

$$S_J[2^j \gamma] f = \left| f * \psi_{2^j \gamma}(x) \right| * \phi_J \quad (5)$$

For deeper invariance and high-frequency information recovery, higher-order paths are formed by cascading wavelet and modulus operations:

$$S[\lambda_1, \lambda_2, \cdots, \lambda_m] f = ||\cdots|f * \psi_{\lambda_1}| * \psi_{\lambda_2} \cdots| * \psi_{\lambda_m}| * \phi_J \quad (6)$$

where $\lambda_m = 2^{j_m} \gamma_m$ and m is the path length. Each scattering layer outputs a low-frequency scattering coefficient $S_J[\lambda] f$ and a modulus-transformed signal $U_\lambda f$, enabling propagation to the next layer.

To build a compact and interpretable descriptor for each region, we compute three statistical measures from the first-order scattering response map: **Mean** μ_r: overall scattering intensity, reflecting average activation in the region; **Standard deviation** σ_r: degree of texture variability, indicative of local structural diversity; **Salient energy** E_r: the mean of the top 20% response magnitudes, highlighting the most active substructures. The final regional scattering feature is composed of these three statistics:

$$F(x_0) = [\mu_r, \sigma_r, E_r]_{r=1}^{5} \quad (7)$$

where x_0 denotes a single input image (or video frame), and r indexes the five semantic facial regions. Concatenating the three statistics across all regions produces a compact descriptor of dimension $5 \times 3C$, with C being the number of first-order scattering channels. Specifically, we compute region-wise wavelet scattering responses and pool their energy statistics into this vector, yielding an interpretable and low-dimensional frequency-domain characterization of fine-grained facial textures for multimodal personality regression.

3.3 Residual-Adapter Deep Ensemble

Given the question-level multimodal feature vector $\mathbf{x}_q \in \mathbb{R}^d$ (concatenated audio, video, text, and SC features), we propose a Residual-Adapter Deep Ensemble (RADE) for personality regression. RADE combines the stability of deep ensembles with an additional residual adapter branch, providing extra representational power to capture subtle cross-modal interactions.

Deep Ensemble Backbone. We instantiate M independently initialized MLP regressors $\{f_m\}_{m=1}^{M}$ with the same architecture. Each regressor maps the flattened input to a scalar trait score:

$$f_m(\mathbf{x}_q) = W_m^{(3)}\,\sigma\Big(W_m^{(2)}\,\sigma\Big(W_m^{(1)}\mathbf{x}_q\Big)\Big), \tag{8}$$

where $\sigma(\cdot)$ is the ReLU activation. In practice, each MLP consists of three linear layers with hidden widths 32 and 8. The ensemble prediction is obtained by averaging:

$$f(\mathbf{x}_q) = \frac{1}{M}\sum_{m=1}^{M} f_m(\mathbf{x}_q). \tag{9}$$

Residual Adapter Branch. To further enrich the predictive function, we attach a lightweight residual adapter $g(\mathbf{x}_q)$ implemented as a shallow MLP with configurable hidden width and depth:

$$g(\mathbf{x}_q) = \mathrm{MLP}_{\mathrm{adp}}(\mathbf{x}_q). \tag{10}$$

The final prediction integrates the adapter output through a learnable scalar gate α:

$$\hat{y}_q = f(\mathbf{x}_q) + \alpha\, g(\mathbf{x}_q). \tag{11}$$

We initialize $\alpha = 0$, so RADE starts from the ensemble solution and progressively learns residual refinements during optimization. This gated residual formulation allows the adapter to focus on complementary cues that are not fully captured by the backbone, thereby improving regression accuracy without introducing unstable shifts.

3.4 Training and Optimization Strategy

We train our residual-adapter deep ensemble in a supervised regression manner on the question-level multimodal vectors, with trait labels linearly normalized to $[0, 1]$. The model is optimized using Adam to minimize mean squared error, $\mathcal{L} = \frac{1}{N}\sum_q(\hat{y}_q - \tilde{y}_q)^2$. To keep the residual correction conservative, the gating parameter α is initialized to zero and trained with a smaller learning rate than the backbone and adapter. Validation loss is monitored for learning-rate decay and early stopping, and the checkpoint with the lowest validation loss is selected for final testing, where predictions are rescaled back to $[1, 5]$.

4 Experiment

4.1 Dataset

We use the official dataset of the ACM Multimedia AVI Challenge 2025. The data were collected via an asynchronous video interview (AVI) platform designed under Trait Activation Theory (TAT). Participants applied to a fictitious management traineeship position and completed a structured AVI consisting of six questions answered independently. During each response, the platform recorded continuous video and audio streams and provided corresponding speech transcripts, yielding synchronized visual, acoustic, and textual modalities. Subjects were instructed to respond to each question within 1–2 min. The six questions follow a fixed order: the first two are generic interview questions, while the last four are personality-oriented past-behavior questions created by psychologists based on the HEXACO model. Specifically, Q3–Q6 target Honesty–Humility, Extraversion, Agreeableness, and Conscientiousness, respectively, whereas Q1–Q2 have no associated personality labels. Therefore, Track 1 is formulated as a per-question regression task: each personality-answer video (Q3–Q6) is mapped to a single continuous trait score in the range of $[1, 5]$. Trait annotations were provided by five independent raters using behavioral rating scales, and the final label for each personality question is obtained by averaging their scores.

The dataset contains interview recordings from 644 subjects (307 men, 309 women, and 28 non-binary), with ages ranging from 20 to 60 years. Following the official protocol, the data are split by subjects into a training set, a validation set, and a test set with 450, 64, and 130 subjects, respectively. Joint sampling is adopted to ensure that gender, age, and work-experience distributions are similar across the three splits.

4.2 Experiments Settings

For each sample, we load the offline extracted multimodal features (`.npy`) of a specified interview question, including audio, video, text, and scattering features, which are matched by the `id_question` prefix and concatenated along the feature dimension as the final input. The feature dimensions of the four modalities are 768 (audio), 1152 (video), 4096 (text), and 735 (scattering), resulting in a 6751-dimensional input vector. The target labels are continuous scores in the range of 1–5 provided by the dataset, and are linearly normalized to $[0, 1]$ before training for stable optimization.

We adopt the Residual Adapter Deep Ensemble (RADE) model. The backbone is a deep ensemble of 32 independent three-layer MLPs (6751→32→8→1), and the ensemble prediction is obtained by averaging the outputs of all sub-networks. On top of the backbone, we add a lightweight two-layer residual adapter (6751→64→1) to learn complementary residual signals, combined with the backbone through a learnable gating coefficient initialized to zero, so that the model starts equivalent to the original ensemble and gradually benefits from residual enhancement. The model is trained with MSELoss and the Adam optimizer. The learning rate for the backbone and adapter is set to 1×10^{-3}, while the gate parameter uses a 0.1× smaller learning rate. We use a batch size of 32 and train for up to 200 epochs. ReduceLROnPlateau is applied for adaptive learning-rate decay, and early stopping (patience = 12) is used to mitigate overfitting. The best checkpoint is selected on the validation set and the final performance is reported on the test set using MSE as the primary metric.

Table 1. The final mean squared error results on the test dataset

Team/User Name	Honesty-Humility	Extra-version	Agree-ableness	Conscien-tiousness	Average
AVI-2025 baseline [7]	0.1915	**0.1105**	0.2287	0.1877	0.1796
ABC-Lab	**0.1436**	0.2864	0.1440	**0.0969**	0.1677
The innovators	0.1560	0.1623	0.1501	0.1114	0.1449
CAS-MAIS	0.1530	0.1490	0.1511	0.1210	0.1435
Jezoid	0.1578	0.1487	**0.1389**	0.1036	0.1372
SA-RADE (Ours)	0.1507	0.1154	0.1578	0.1165	**0.1351**

4.3 Results and Analysis

Table 1 reports the final mean squared error (MSE) on the test set across four personality traits and their average. All results in Table 1 are taken from the official leaderboard released in [7]. Overall, our SA-RADE achieves an average MSE of 0.1351, ranking second among all submissions. Compared with the AVI-2025 baseline (0.1796), SA-RADE reduces the average error by 0.0445 (about 24.8% relative improvement), demonstrating the effectiveness of combining scattering-augmented facial texture cues with a lightweight residual-adapter ensemble.

Looking into individual traits, SA-RADE performs particularly well on *Extraversion*, reaching an MSE of 0.1154, which is close to the best-performing baseline result (0.1105) and noticeably better than most competing methods. This suggests that our multimodal temporal pooling together with SC facial texture statistics captures expressive and socially salient behavioral cues that are strongly correlated with extraversion. On *Honesty-Humility* and *Agreeableness*, our results remain competitive but do not attain the lowest errors, indicating that these traits may rely more on subtle discourse-level or long-term interaction patterns that are harder to infer from question-level cues. For *Conscientiousness*, SA-RADE achieves 0.1165, comparable to other strong methods, showing stable generalization.

Overall, SA-RADE delivers a competitive average performance without introducing heavy or unstable modeling components. The gated residual adapter in RADE likely contributes to this robustness: starting from the deep ensemble backbone and progressively learning residual corrections enables the model to exploit complementary cross-modal interactions while avoiding overfitting under limited data. Meanwhile, the scattering-based facial descriptor provides an interpretable, low-dimensional frequency-domain signal that supplements standard visual embeddings and strengthens the capture of high-frequency micro-expression cues. Together, these two design choices yield consistent and stable gains over the baseline and demonstrate strong competitiveness on the benchmark.

4.4 Ablation Study

Effect of Scattering Features. Table 2 shows that removing scattering cues (**w/o SC**) increases the average MSE from 0.1351 to 0.1388. Although the drop is modest, the full model consistently performs better overall, indicating that SC provides complementary facial texture information beyond standard AVT features.

Effect of the Residual Adapter. Disabling the residual adapter (**w/o Residual Adapter**) leads to a larger degradation, raising the average MSE to 0.1411. The worst case is removing both SC and the adapter, where the error sharply increases to 0.2079. These results confirm that the gated residual adapter is a key contributor to performance, and it works best when combined with scattering-based facial cues.

Table 2. Ablation results on the test dataset (MSE).

Method	Honesty-Humility	Extra-version	Agree-ableness	Conscien-tiousness	Average
SA-RADE (full)	0.1507	0.1154	**0.1578**	**0.1165**	**0.1351**
w/o SC (AVT-RADE)	0.1621	**0.1116**	0.1626	0.1189	0.1388
w/o Residual Adapter (SC-DeepEns)	**0.1473**	0.1227	0.1685	0.1257	0.1411
w/o SC + Residual Adapter	0.1904	0.2442	0.2148	0.1822	0.2079

Table 3. Ablation on residual adapter configurations in RADE.

Variant	Hidden	Depth	Honesty-Humility	Extra-version	Agree-ableness	Conscien-tiousness	Average
Base (default)	64	2	0.1507	**0.1154**	**0.1578**	**0.1165**	**0.1351**
Tiny	16	2	0.1602	0.1176	0.1632	0.1214	0.1406
Small	16	3	0.1558	0.1578	0.1597	0.1241	0.1493
Large	64	3	**0.1484**	0.1163	0.1627	0.1219	0.1373

Effect of Residual Adapter Capacity. We further vary the residual adapter width and depth to examine its capacity effect. As shown in Table 3, the default setting (**Adapter-Base**, hidden = 64, depth = 2) yields the best average MSE (0.1351). Reducing the width to 16 (**Adapter-Tiny**) slightly degrades performance, suggesting insufficient residual capacity. Increasing depth hurts more noticeably (**Adapter-Small**, 16 × 3), especially on Extraversion, indicating overfitting under limited width. A deeper but wider adapter (**Adapter-Large**, 64×3) is competitive but still worse than the default. Overall, a compact 64×2 adapter provides the most reliable residual enhancement.

5 Conclusion

In this work, we proposed SA-RADE for HEXACO personality regression in the AVI-2025 Track 1 benchmark. Our framework integrates question-level multimodal representations from SigLIP2 visual semantics, emotion2vec+ acoustic affect, and SFR-Embedding-Mistral linguistic embeddings, and further augments them with a compact wavelet scattering (SC) facial texture stream computed over five semantic regions. To fuse these heterogeneous cues robustly under limited data, we designed a Residual-Adapter Deep Ensemble (RADE) regressor that combines the stability of deep ensembles with a gated residual adapter for complementary cross-modal corrections.

Experiments on the official AVI-2025 dataset demonstrate that SA-RADE achieves strong and stable performance across all four traits, attaining an average test MSE of 0.1351 and showing competitive generalization on the benchmark. Ablation studies verify that both scattering-based texture features and the residual adapter contribute to performance gains, and that a compact adapter configuration (hidden = 64, depth = 2) offers the best trade-off between expressiveness and robustness. In future work, we plan to explore finer-grained temporal modeling beyond max pooling and more adaptive region or frequency selection for scattering features, aiming to further enhance trait-specific sensitivity and generalization in asynchronous interview settings.

References

1. Costa, P.T., McCrae, R.R.: The revised neo personality inventory (neo-pi-r). SAGE Handbook Pers. Theor. Assess. **2**(2), 179–198 (2008)
2. Soto, C.J., John, O.P.: The next big five inventory (bfi-2): developing and assessing a hierarchical model with 15 facets to enhance bandwidth, fidelity, and predictive power. J. Pers. Soc. Psychol. **113**(1), 117 (2017)
3. Ashton, M.C., Lee, K.: Empirical, theoretical, and practical advantages of the hexaco model of personality structure. Pers. Soc. Psychol. Rev. **11**(2), 150–166 (2007)
4. Junior, J.C.J., et al.: First impressions: a survey on vision-based apparent personality trait analysis. IEEE Trans. Affect. Comput. **13**(1), 75–95 (2019)
5. Li, J., He, Y., Xu, J., Luo, T., Hu, Z., Hong, R., Wang, M.: Traits run deep: Enhancing personality assessment via psychology-guided llm representations and multimodal apparent behaviors. In: Proceedings of the 33rd ACM International Conference on Multimedia, pp. 13,901–13,908 (2025)
6. Zhao, X., Tang, Z., Zhang, S.: Deep personality trait recognition: a survey. Front. Psychol. **13**(839), 619 (2022)
7. Zhang, T., et al.: Assessing personality traits and interview performance from asynchronous video interviews. In: Proceedings of the 33rd ACM International Conference on Multimedia, pp 13,895–13,900 (2025)

8. Cui, J., et al.: Less is more? textual-only language model for avi challenge 2025. In: Proceedings of the 3rd International Workshop on Multimodal and Responsible Affective Computing, pp. 69–74 (2025)
9. Giritlioğlu, D., et al.: Multimodal analysis of personality traits on videos of self-presentation and induced behavior. J. Multimodal User Interfaces **15**(4), 337–358 (2021)
10. Ryumina, E., Karpov, A.: Impact of visual modalities in multimodal personality and affective computing. Int. Arch. Photogramm. Remote. Sens. Spat. Inf. Sci. **48**, 217–224 (2023)
11. Safavi, F., Patel, K., Vinjamuri, R.: Facial expression recognition with an efficient mix transformer for affective human-robot interaction. IEEE Trans. Affect. Comput. (2025)
12. Tang, B., et al.: Pose as a modality: a psychology-inspired network for personality recognition with a new multimodal dataset. Proc. AAAI Conf. Artif. Intell. **39**, 1538–1546 (2025)
13. Escalante, H.J., et al.: Modeling, recognizing, and explaining apparent personality from videos. IEEE Trans. Affect. Comput. **13**(2), 894–911 (2020)
14. Kalateh, S., Estrada-Jimenez, L.A., Nikghadam-Hojjati, S., Barata, J.: A systematic review on multimodal emotion recognition: building blocks, current state, applications, and challenges. IEEE Access **12**, 103,976–104,019 (2024)
15. Dosovitskiy, A.: An image is worth 16x16 words: transformers for image recognition at scale. arXiv preprint arXiv:2010.11929 (2020)
16. Ma, Z., et al.: emotion2vec: self-supervised pre-training for speech emotion representation. Find. Assoc. Comput. Linguist. ACL **2024**, 15747–15760 (2024)
17. Singh, J., Malik, P.: Unveiling hidden emotions: a review of microexpression recognition, classification, and datasets. Multimedia Tools Appl. 1–56 (2025)
18. Mallat, S.: Wavelets for a vision. Proc. IEEE **84**(4), 604–614 (1996)
19. Wiatowski, T., Tschannen, M., Stanic, A., Grohs, P., Bölcskei, H.: Discrete deep feature extraction: a theory and new architectures. In: International Conference on Machine Learning, PMLR, pp. 2149–2158 (2016)
20. Wiatowski, T., Bölcskei, H.: A mathematical theory of deep convolutional neural networks for feature extraction. IEEE Trans. Inf. Theory **64**(3), 1845–1866 (2017)
21. Liu, N., Zhang, F., Chang, L., Duan, F.: Scattering-based hybrid network for facial attribute classification. Front. Comput. Sci. **18**(3), 183,313 (2024)
22. Minskiy, D., Bober, M.: Scattering-based hybrid networks: an evaluation and design guide. In: 2021 IEEE International Conference on Image Processing (ICIP), pp. 2793–2797. IEEE (2021)
23. Minskiy, D., Bober, M.: Efficient hybrid network: inducting scattering features. In: 2022 26th International Conference on Pattern Recognition (ICPR), pp. 2300–2306. IEEE (2022)

Principles of Clinical Protocols Design for Children with Autism Spectrum Disorder

Yuchen Zhao[1], Jiarui Tang[2], Haixia Zheng[3], and Honghai Liu[3](✉)

[1] ADD Tech. Ltd., Shanghai, China
[2] Meta Platforms, Inc., Menlo Park, CA, USA
[3] Portsmouth University, Portsmouth, UK
honghai.liu@port.ac.uk

Abstract. Clinical protocols are crucial to quality health care delivery for children with autism spectrum disorder (ASD). This paper discusses the principles for designing clinical protocols including autistic assessment, diagnosis and intervention. Five principles are proposed and verified with design scenarios covering cognition, emotion, motor and societal capabilities during cognitive development. it is noticed giving priority to autistic children that features of autistic symptoms are effectively induced and also heavily correlated with impaired social capabilities. This paper paves the way for principles of clinical protocols design for developmental and cognitive issues such as ASD.

Keywords: Clinical protocols · autism spectrum disorder · early screening and intervention · human machine systems

1 Introduction

Autism spectrum disorder (ASD) is one of the most common neurodevelopmental disorders in childhood. Its main manifestations are social communication disorders, language communication disorders, and abnormal behavior and interests. It is evident that the prevalence of ASD among 8-year-old children in the United States reached 1 in 44 in 2018 and increased to 1 in 36 in 2020, making it one of the fastest-growing diseases globally [1–3]. Autistic children suffer varying degrees of functional impairments in social communication, cognition, motor skills, etc. resulting in lifelong adverse effects covering the education and care of autistic children, as well as issues in adulthood occurred by societal problems [1, 5]. It is also evident that behavioral screening and interventions can significantly improve both short-term and long-term outcomes for autistic children. Regarding to performance of behavioral assessment and intervention, protocols are crucial for standardizing care, reducing risks, and provide a framework for consistent and evidence-based treatment in various clinical settings [4, 5]. Clinical protocols are nothing but detailed, written documents that outline the plan for a clinical study or a specific medical procedure. They serve as a roadmap, describing the study's objectives, design, and methodology, while also ensuring the safety of participants and the integrity of the data collected. Game based assessment and intervention are common representation for

H. Liu et al. (Eds.): CEI 2025, CCIS 2881, pp. 313–320, 2026.
https://doi.org/10.1007/978-981-95-9493-1_21

interaction of clinical protocols to patients such as autistic children. A device facilitating such games is a teaching method commonly used as an auxiliary intervention therapy for children with autism spectrum disorder. In this paper, we introduce practical early screening, assessment and intervention tasks, or you could call them plans for autism and verify their effectiveness. Further we visualize the effectiveness of the behavioral tasks for the purpose of autistic therapy through self-developed auxiliary treatment devices and designed game-based protocols. The research objectives, design and methodology are proposed and discussed while ensuring the safety of participants and the integrity of the collected data for understanding in clinical scenarios, eventually future research on intervention and treatment plans. The primary contributions of this study are the proposed five aspects of clinical protocols design and their potential facilitated devices.

2 Key Aspects of Design Clinical Protocols for Autistic Children

The purpose of design various clinical protocols is clear of seeking better solutions to serve as a comprehensive guide for conducting a clinical investigation, ensuring the safety of participants and the integrity of the data. The key aspects include key components, standardization, evidence-based practice, regulatory compliance and difference resolving from guidelines [4, 8]. First an autistic protocol must be self-contained, typically consisting of the components such as the study's background, objectives, design, patient selection criteria, assessment or intervention task, and methods for assessing safety and efficacy. Secondly a component named standardization provides a locally agreed-upon standard to which clinicians and organizations can work and be audited with a goal to improve overall healthcare quality. Thirdly evidence-based practice is another must component of an autistic protocol that promotes evidence-based practices by providing a systematic task for specific impaired social medical scenarios. Fourthly the autistic protocol in clinical trials is a mandatory document that must be submitted to regulatory bodies like the FDA. Finally, a protocol specifies the exact steps to follow once a management decision has been made when a difference is occurred from a clinical guideline that provides general, evidence-based recommendations for managing a condition.

3 Principles of Clinical Protocols Design for Children with ASD

Designing clinical protocols for autistic children requires a tailored approach that addresses their unique neurodevelopmental profile, emphasizing adaptability, inclusivity, and evidence-based practices. A list of key principles for design clinical protocols are provided as below in research and clinical best practices.

Individualized Assessment and Flexibility. Recognize the heterogeneous nature of ASD, where symptoms and responses vary widely across individuals. Protocols must incorporate personalized assessments to identify strengths, challenges, and co-occurring conditions, ensuring interventions align with each child's specific needs. Flexibility is critical to accommodate diverse learning paces and behavioral patterns. We use structured yet adaptable tools to evaluate communication skills and sensory sensitivities, allowing protocols to evolve as the child progresses. For instance, the clinical protocol called "Search What You See" as shown in Fig. 1. A Child is asked to find the object that meets the criteria among several visible objects, then based on the child's first attempt, targeted test is conducted to determine whether the child has cognitive barriers to specific colors, shapes, and objects, next confirm whether the child has abnormal behavior and interest in a specific period or object during this process, finally in subsequent intervention courses, guide children to establish correct cognition accordingly. The process includes three levels, i.e., mixed color search, increasing difficulty, and two separate levels, i.e., same color but different shape and same shape but different color levels that reduce difficulty when the current player cannot pass.

Fig. 1. Clinical Protocol "Search What You See".

Inclusive and Mediated Learning Environments. Leverage technology and structured routines to reduce anxiety and enhance engagement. Digital tools such as interactive apps or controllable sensory devices has capability of acting as mediators to familiar children with new contexts such as clinical settings or therapeutic activities. This approach helps mitigate stress and fosters skill acquisition in a supportive framework. For example, a child is instructed to freely express themselves in a free virtual-reality environment as shown Fig. 2. And collect relevant data through hidden devices at the same time. Behavioral recognition such as a multi-task facial expression recognition network, could be developed for the child behavior analysis, e.g., [11, 15, 16]. The backbone of the network utilizes a pre-trained ResNet18 model to extract the original RGB image. The DCAPM module is employed to extract multi-scale image features, while the AFFM module enhances edge information and extracts dynamic features. Subsequently, these extracted facial features are fed into both the auxiliary branch and the target branch of the network.

Early Intervention Focused on Core Domains. Prioritize early and targeted interventions for social communication, cognitive development, and repetitive behaviors.

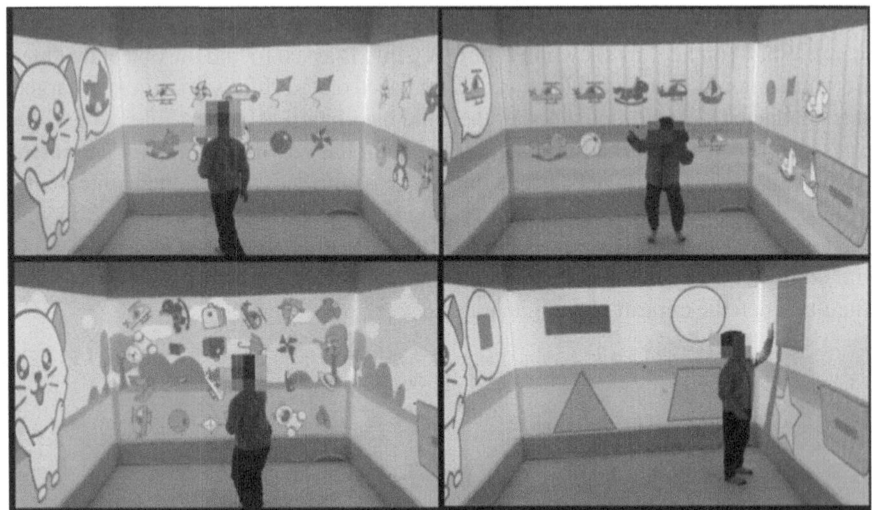

Fig. 2. Allowing children to freely express themselves in unrestricted settings.

Protocols be integrated with evidence-based methods such as behavioral therapy or social skills training, to address foundational deficits during critical developmental windows[4–7]. Early support maximizes functional independence and long-term quality of life. For example, we develop imitation-based tasks and play-based protocols to stimulate social interaction and emotional attunement, using video-recorded sessions for remote monitoring and feedback as the Clinical Protocol "Explore". As shown in Fig. 3, a subject is encouraged to explore a small world: first they can freely explore the home in the game that can be manually adjusted to be closer to their real home, starting from the child's room at the beginning, then exploring various rooms in the home, and next starting to explore the broader world outside the home. During this process, necessary guidance and intervention should be provided to help children develop correct lifestyle habits.

Collaborative Nursing in Multiple Aspects. Engage caregivers as active partners in protocol design and implementation. The symptoms and reactions of ASD vary from child to child, for those clinical protocols that follows a fixed process, when the preset three-stage guidance has reached the highest level, but the progress is still lagging behind, manual guidance needs to be introduced. For instance, we have designed a Immersive Child Behavioral Development Assessment and Intervention System (CAVE, as Fig. 2). In the scenario simulation of CAVE, children immerse themselves through the device, enter specific scenes, and learn the interactions that will occur in that scene, and learn basic social interaction methods, such as learning the operation rules of traffic lights and correct crossing methods in immersive cross street scenes, at the same time, the CAVE device will use various data sensors, primarily vision sensors, from multiple angles and types to record and analyze children's data performance. Metric functions would be developed to measure autistic behavior of the child under the clinical protocols. However, some children who try it for the first time may need some time to adapt, and

Fig. 3. Clinical Protocol "Explore".

due to the high degree of freedom of CAVE, children's behavioral will also have more variables. Therefore, special attention should be paid to process guidance and reducing negative feedback [5–9].

Rigorous Yet Relevant Design Cycles. Apply iterative design processes such as the relevance-rigor-design cycle, to ensure protocols are clinically meaningful and theoretically grounded. Regularly evaluate outcomes through feedback from stakeholders, including experts, therapists, and families, to refine interventions for usability and effectiveness. For example, we continue to have focus group discussions with ASD specialists to validate guidelines, ensuring protocols adapt to emerging research and diverse cultural contexts.

Easy to Understand, Minimization of Distress. The clinical protocols design is required to be based on standards that are easy for children to understand and accept. First to minimize text menus, text options, and other content that need to be read should be minimized as much as possible. For instance, the text "Please find the red square" should not appear as the scenario shown in Fig. 2, instead use intuitive icons, voice/sound effects, and interactive object based visual effects (such as zooming in/out/blinking of individual objects) to guide. Secondly, elements in clinical protocols that are as concise and easy to understand as possible. The elements in the game should be concise and clear, avoiding the use of overly colorful colors and unnecessary complexity. Unless necessary, it is not recommended to use real portraits or objects from the real world. The special effects in games should be based on interactive objects as much as possible, for example, when children need to pay attention to a certain item, the item should be zoomed in/out/flickered instead of having an arrow pointing to it. Thirdly, minimize negative feedback as much as possible. It is important to note that unless necessary, children should not be explicitly told that they have "made a mistake" or "failed". It is also important to reduce children's sense of frustration (especially at the beginning); When children achieve success and make progress, they should be clearly praised and motivated through visual and auditory means. In addition, it is also necessary to pay attention to limiting and controlling the degree of interaction that children can have in games, so that the vast majority of their behaviors can achieve good results. In games that encourage exploration, it is particularly important to pay attention to this point. Some game behaviors that may lead to negative results should be restricted or countermeasures should be taken in advance. Finally, less guidance If clinical protocol goes smoothly [11–14]. Usually clinical protocols will be multiple levels of guidance, starting from the lower level by default. When a child does not make progress for a prolonged period of time, the level of guidance will increase, and when it reaches its peak, nursing staff will need to intervene and provide proactive assistance. If the child's progress is smooth, the guidance should be gradually lowered until it reaches its minimum, reducing the impact of guidance on the child.

4 Devices Facilitating Clinical Protocols

What follows design of clinical protocols is to develop a device or equipment to facilitate them for clinical scenarios as shown in Fig. 4. Given the clinical requirements multiple sensors would be selected to enable interaction between the clinical protocols and patients. Generally speaking, the interactive parameters for autistic children during treatment courses include sound feedback, gaze, body posture, and interactive feedback [17]. It can record children's participation and completion indicators while conducting the course, and the system's own analysis module can intelligently generate indicators of children's stage rehabilitation effects. While children are playing, we will collect various data from them, such as reaction time, focus on objects, corresponding efficiency in responding to different guidance, and accuracy in game behavior. And after the intervention treatment is completed, output relevant data records [15–17]. Each child's data is individually archived and further analyzed. Preliminary screening, assessment and treatment can be generated through data understanding in multiple clinical protocols. Data collected from children with ASD on the devices are employed to quantify the effectiveness of clinical protocols intervention and also to improve recognition accuracy after multiple attempts, additionally, comparison of data between the experimental groups are also used to measure and quantify the performance of the systems with the designed clinical protocols [18]. Hence the devices integrating clinical protocols provide a platform for autistic assessment and intervention.

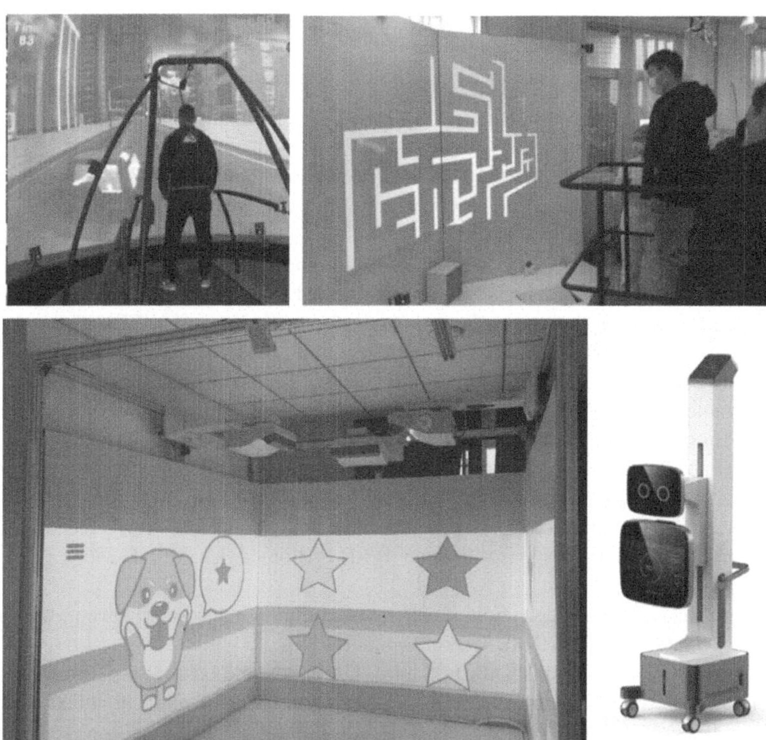

Fig. 4. Devices Facilitating Clinical Protocols for Autistic Children.

5 Conclusions

This paper discusses principles of the clinical protocols for children with autism spectrum disorder. Five principles are presented covering individualized assessment and flexibility, inclusive and mediated learning environments, early intervention focused on core domains, collaborative nursing in multiple aspects, most importantly, easy to understand and minimization of distress. Examples of devices developed in our lab are also presented to faceplate and evaluate the designed clinical protocols for autistic assessment and intervention. This paper proposes a framework for effective clinically scenarios oriented systems for autistic children.

References

1. Lord, C., Cook, E.H., Leventhal, B.L., Amaral, D.G.: Autism spectrum 737 disorders. Neuron **28**(2), 355–363 (2000)
2. Liu, J., et al.: Multimodal emotion recognition for children with autism spectrum disorder in social interaction. Int. J. Hum. Comput. Interact. **40**(8), 1921–1930 (2024)
3. Maenner, M.J., et al.: Prevalence and characteristics of autism spectrum disorder among children aged 8 years—autism and developmental disabilities monitoring network, 11 sites, United States, 2020. MMWR Surveill. Summaries **72**(2), 1–14 (2023)

4. Council, N.R., et al.: Educating Children With Autism. National Academies Press, Washington, DC (2001)
5. American Psychiatric Association: DSM-5 Task Force, Diagnostic and Statistical Manual of Mental Disorders: Dsm-5, 5th edn., p. 754. American Psychiatric Publishing, Washington, DC (2013)
6. Wadhera, T., Mahmud, M.: Brain functional network topology in autism spectrum disorder: a novel weighted hierarchical complexity metric for electroencephalogram. IEEE J. Biomed. Health Inform. **27**(4), 1718–1725 (2023)
7. Han, J., Jiang, G., Ouyang, G., Li, X.: A multimodal approach for identifying autism spectrum disorders in children. IEEE Trans. Neural Syst. Rehabil. Eng. **30**, 2003–2011 (2022)
8. Li, J., et al.: Appearance-based gaze estimation for ASD diagnosis. IEEE Trans. Cybern. **52**(7), 6504–6517 (2022)
9. Vallefuoco, E., Bravaccio, C., Gison, G., Pecchia, L., Pepino, A.: Personalized training via serious game to improve daily living skills in pediatric patients with autism spectrum disorder. IEEE J. Biomed. Health Inform. **26**(7), 3312–3322 (2022)
10. Liu, J., et al.: Social recognition of joint attention cycles in children with autism spectrum disorders. IEEE Trans. Biomed. Eng. **71**(1), 237–246 (2024)
11. Nie, W., et al.: Computational interpersonal communication model for screening autistic toddlers: a case study of response-to-name. IEEE J. Biomed. Health Inf. **28**(6), 3683–3694 (2024)
12. Perochon, S., et al.: Early detection of autism using digital behavioral phenotyping. Nature Med. **29**(10), 2489–2497 (2023). 782
13. Bovery, M., Dawson, G., Hashemi, J., Sapiro, G.: A scalable off-the- shelf framework for measuring patterns of attention in young children and its application in autism spectrum disorder. IEEE Trans. Affect. Comput. **12**(3), 722–731 (2021)
14. Hashemi, J., et al.: Computer vision analysis for quantification of autism risk behaviors. IEEE Trans. Affect. Comput. **12**(1), 215–226 (2021)
15. Wang, Z., Liu, J., He, K., Xu, Q., Xu, X., Liu, H.: Screening early children with autism spectrum disorder via response-to-name protocol. IEEE Trans. Industr. Inf. **17**(1), 587–595 (2021)
16. Liu, J., et al.: Early screening of autism in toddlers via response-to-instructions protocol. IEEE Trans. Cybern. **52**(5), 3914–3924 (2022)
17. Tang, C., et al.: Automatic identification of high-risk autism spectrum disorder: a feasibility study using video and audio data under the still-face paradigm. IEEE Trans. Neural Syst. Rehabil. Eng. **28**(11), 2401–2410 (2020)
18. Tofighi, G., Afarin, N.A., Raahemifar, K., Venetsanopoulos, A.N.: Hand pointing detection using live histogram template of forehead skin. In: Proceedings of the IEEE International Conference on Digital Signal Processing, pp. 383–388 (2014)

Author Index

H. Liu et al. (Eds.): CEI 2025, CCIS 2881, pp. 321–322, 2026.
https://doi.org/10.1007/978-981-95-9493-1

The manufacturer's authorised representative in the EU is Springer Nature Customer Service Centre GmbH, Europaplatz 3, 69115 Heidelberg, Germany. If you have any concerns regarding our products, please contact ProductSafety@springernature.com

Printed and bound by CPI Group (UK) Ltd, Croydon, CR0 4YY
07/07/2026
02160913-0008